AMERICAN SWASTIKA

AMERICAN SWASTIKA

by Charles Higham

Doubleday & Company, Inc.
Garden City, New York
1985

Library of Congress Cataloging in Publication Data

Higham, Charles.
American swastika.

Bibliography: p. 309
Includes index.
1. Fascism—United States—History—20th century.
2. National Socialism—History.   3. United States—
Politics and government—1945–   .   I. Title.
E743.5.H5   1985   320.5′33

ISBN 0-385-17874-3
Library of Congress Catalog Card Number 82–45528

First Edition

For Pamela and Philippe Mora

Acknowledgments

I am grateful to the following for their help: Kathie Nicastro, of the Diplomatic Records Branch, National Archives and Records Service; John Taylor and George Wagner, of the same institution's Modern Military Branch; Marcus Cunliffe; Robert Parks, of the Franklin D. Roosevelt Memorial Library, Hyde Park, New York; James Hall, of the FBI; the staff of the Army Intelligence and Security Command, Fort Meade, Maryland, and Thomas F. Conley, chief; George Shalou and the officers of the National Archives at Suitland, Maryland; Pierre Sauvage; Philippe and Pamela Mora; John Costello, who obtained major documents for me; the Department of the Treasury; Michel Thomas; Dr. Charles Kremer; Rabbis Marvin Hier and Abraham Cooper, of the Simon Wiesenthal Center of Holocaust Studies; David Goldman; Bernard C. Lauren; Peter Carey; Mae Brussell; Lydia Blades; Charles R. Allen, Jr; John Graham; Ralph Blumenthal; Carolle F. Carter; Martin Mendelson; Jozo Tomasevitch; Kurt Tauber; Mrs. Ladislas Farago; Jane Chesis; Paul Erdman; Joe Conason; Martin Rosenblatt; Gerald Turbow; Professor Robert Dallek; Brigadier General Albert C. Wedemeyer (retired); Brigadier General Carter W. Clarke (retired); Professor Klaus von Klemperer; Frances Mercer, who typed the manuscript; Howard Davis, who helped research it; and Adrian Zackheim, whose inspired guidance assisted me throughout.

Contents

Introduction

As I write these words, the trial of Klaus Barbie, the alleged mass murderer of Lyon in World War II, who successively worked for the Nazi SS and SD and the U.S. Army Counter-Intelligence Corps (CIC), has been set for 1985 in France. When the trial takes place, the spotlight will once again inconveniently be thrown on the subject of U.S. official collaboration with Nazis in the alleged interests of anti-Soviet action after World War II.

It was announced in the issue of *Time* magazine for December 19, 1983, that Hermann Abs, honorary chairman of the Deutsche Bank, had led a consortium that included the West German Government in purchasing at Sotheby's, in London, the twelfth-century German illuminated manuscript *The Gospels of Henry the Lion** for the equivalent of 11.7 million dollars, the highest auction price ever paid for an artwork. *Time* quoted Abs as saying, regarding his native country of Germany and in terms that may provide some bleak amusement to students of economic history, "Future generations will know the good side of our history—its more noble moments—and not just the horrible days of its recent past." One has charitably to assume that the editors and researchers of *Time* magazine neglected to comment on this statement through an oversight, rather than through deliberate negligence. However, when the Emmy-

* The subject was a favorite of Heinrich Himmler.

Award-winning French film director Pierre Sauvage wrote in protest, the magazine refused to print his letter.

Almost exactly a year before, on December 7, 1982, *Time*'s rival publication, *Newsweek*, published, also without comment, the fact that the aforesaid Hermann Abs had been appointed head of a special banking council at the Vatican, heading up an investigation into the Ambrosiano and Calvi banking scandals which had engulfed the Italian economy and in which an archbishop from Chicago, Gregory Marcinkus, had allegedly been involved. I was struck at the time by the peculiarity of the fact that the Holy See had chosen to engage for this post the former personal banker of Adolf Hitler and head of the Deutsche Bank, which played an important role in the German economic despoliation of Nazi-occupied Europe. It was interesting also to note that Abs had been on the supervisory board of I.G. Farben, the Nazi industrial trust, at a time when a substantial sum was appropriated by that company for the construction of the rubber factory of Auschwitz.

I drew the matter to the attention of Rabbis Marvin Hier and Abraham Cooper of the Wiesenthal Center of Holocaust Studies shortly after the *Newsweek* item appeared. The rabbis called a press, radio, and television conference at which the three of us expressed dismay at the appointment by the world's most powerful religious leader, Pope John Paul II, of a former financier of Hitler who had at one time employed that selfsame pontiff in one of his subsidiary companies as a slave laborer in Poland. We made clear that the matter had been brought to the attention of the Papal Nuncio and the Vatican Secretary of State, who were weighing the matter at the time the press conference took place.

It was agreed that because of their great importance, the New York *Times* and *The Wall Street Journal* would be given special consideration in the matter. Hence, the rabbis and I gave the *Times* and the *Journal* interviews ahead of other media representatives. The *Times*'s Ralph Blumenthal filed a lengthy story. It was editorially withdrawn just hours before press time and replaced by an innocuous column item. Similarly, the *Journal* prepared a lengthy story, including reports from Bonn, Berlin, and Rome, and again the story was pulled—this time in its entirety.

The result of the conference at the Wiesenthal Center was that there was some public discussion but, in effect, the matter sank without a trace. When the aforementioned rabbis thereafter made an official visit to the Vatican, they were advised that they should not discuss the Abs issue while in audience with the Pope. They were advised privately, "The matter will take care of itself." However, like most matters of its kind, it did not; in short, at the time of this writing, Herr Abs is still in office, as well as officially representing the West German Government in art purchases.

The Barbie case came to worldwide attention shortly thereafter. Allan A. Ryan, Jr., an attorney in the Department of Justice Office of Special Investigations in charge of pursuing the matter of the Barbie connection with the U.S. Army in postwar Europe, spent several months preparing a report on the case accompanied by a volume of documentary materials declassified for public inspection under the terms of the Freedom of Information Act, and issued an official apology by the United States to the French Government. However, this valuable apology and release were not without disturbing aspects. First, the report itself was incomplete; many documents on Barbie not directly related to his involvement with U.S. Military Intelligence were not released, but merely summarized, and the summaries failed to take into account a number of important matters, including the fact that the Barbie operation was a mere part of a much larger operation, the Gehlen operation, which was incorporated and sanctioned by the Pentagon, and that Barbie's operation was compromised by Soviet penetration, largely useless, utterly corrupt, and known about at high government levels as well as at the low, in-the-field level of general operations. Moreover, the British Government, invoking the terms of the Official Secrets Act, precluded from release much crucial documentation, a fact to which, much to his credit, Mr. Ryan publicly referred.

However, his decision not to issue a number of documents was, I believe, a mistake; and the moral statements that he issued in the report were undesirable. He stated in sum that it was quite in order to use a former Nazi if that personage would be of use against the Soviets in a cold war; and he indicated that Barbie was scarcely a war criminal like Himmler, a rash extension of his role as an official into the realm of larger, politico-philosophical commentary. Mr. Ryan's explanation to me was that all documents not showing Barbie's U.S. connections were excluded; but this had the effect of eliding vital information dealt with inadequately in his summary.

I contacted the one person in the United States who would seem to be capable of providing an enlightened comment on the matter. That person was Michel Thomas, a leader of the French Resistance who had suffered from Barbie's attentions and who had been selected as chief witness for the prosecution in the forthcoming trial in France. I spoke with M. Thomas by telephone at his home near New York City. He confirmed that he was shocked and dismayed by the Ryan report, since, he stated, it effectively whitewashed the crucial role in the protection and support of Barbie that had been given by the Overseas Military Government of the United States in Germany after World War II.

He felt strongly that the report, so far from being complete, was designed to protect those in high places while exposing lesser fry in the armed services who worked with Barbie in the field. He shared my concern at the statements made by Mr. Ryan in the report that it was perfectly all right to use a Nazi mass murderer as a counterintelligence agent against the Soviets, because all was fair in the Cold War. This morally questionable statement, supported by inadequate documentation and misleading assertions, in his view (as in mine) rendered the report severely inadequate. Indeed, M. Thomas asserted that he had filed an exhaustive report on Barbie at the Munich headquarters of the Counter-Intelligence Corps in 1945, which had since conveniently disappeared in order to whitewash the role of its recipients, the military executives in the Berlin High Command. Later, Mr. Ryan publicly denied the very existence of such a report.

Once again, I turned to Rabbis Hier and Cooper and to the support of the Simon Wiesenthal Center. With characteristic swiftness, the rabbis acted upon my suggestion and flew M. Thomas to Los Angeles so that he could testify anew at a press conference. Once again, all media were present, and on this occasion, as before, the New York *Times* soft-pedaled the story. When Ralph Blumenthal attempted to file a piece, he was informed that the story would instead be obtained from the wire services. Only the Washington *Post* chose to deal with the matter in any substance, followed by the Los Angeles *Times* with a somewhat milder article.

Mr. Ryan soon afterward resigned from the Office of Special Investigations to write a book on his experiences and to resume private practice as an attorney in Washington, D.C. His subsequent behavior is of interest. He sent a letter to the London *Times* in November 1983 in direct rebuttal of charges made in Tom Bowers's biography of Barbie that he had suppressed certain documents in his report on the case.

In February 1983, Delacorte Press published the precursor of this volume, *Trading with the Enemy*, which disclosed in documentation the fact that many American corporations, in collusion with certain figures of President Franklin D. Roosevelt's Cabinet, dealt directly and improperly, with Nazi Germany, via neutral countries, from Pearl Harbor until the end of World War II. I appeared on the "Today" show, discussing the matter with Jane Pauley; and the NBC radio evening news provided very full coverage. I also toured the country, where lengthy newspaper articles in major-city newspapers and talk-show appearances confirmed an enthusiastic and entirely approving response to my statements. However, the Establishment ignored *Trading with the Enemy*, despite the fact that it went through several printings. No response was heard, with one exception, from any of the leading financial and industrial bodies dealt with in the book. The one exception was the Chase Manhattan Bank. Its vice president in charge of international publicity, Mr. Kenneth Mills, was heard to say on the air following my broadcast on NBC News that he agreed the Chase was open in Nazi-occupied Paris for business as usual with authorization from New York but that this was only in order to protect the Bank's French customers. I pointed out that the only French customers permitted to retain accounts in Nazi-occupied Paris were those who had elected to collaborate with the German Government. Understandably, Mr. Mills found himself unable to do more than repeat his previous statement.

This succession of events has been accompanied by some interesting matters in the continent of Europe. Synagogues have been burned and Jews attacked. It has come to light that a substantial portion of the two million, five hundred thousand pounds paid by *Stern*, the West German illustrated magazine, for the forged diaries of Adolf Hitler was paid into the treasury of the organization known as HIAG,† the mutual-aid society of former members of the Nazi SS. Indeed, a prominent member of HIAG's executive board, Herr Medard Klapper, personally received at least one hundred thousand pounds; he was allegedly a former member of Hitler's SS Elite Guard. It has also been revealed that personages in high places were responsible, in 1943, in the middle of World War II, for releasing Sir Oswald Mosley, head of the British Union of Fascists, from Holloway Prison, London, where he was being held under Regulation 18-B, used to permit arrest without trial of Nazi sympathizers and collaborators under wartime provisions. Hitler had already proposed that Mosley

† Hilfsgemeinschaft auf Gegenseitigkeit.

should be a leader of German-occupied England following German invasion and conquest.

Among those responsible for Sir Oswald's release were Lord Halifax, British ambassador to Washington, who had played a special role in attempting to bring about a negotiated peace with Hitler in 1940; Lord Winterton; and, disturbingly enough, Prime Minister Winston Churchill, who approved the decision of Home Secretary Herbert Morrison in a secret telegram sent from Cairo on November 21, 1943. The release allegedly infuriated Stalin, who, not without reason, saw this as an example of appeasement of the Germans in time of war.

Indeed, it has been a recurring feature of Soviet propaganda that very high-level collusion with Nazis has occurred before, during, and after World War II. Anybody who has read Solzhenitsyn or made even a cursory study of the wholesale subversion, policy of conquest, and mass murder of the Soviet Union must surely pause before considering seriously any statement that emanates from Moscow. However grievous though it may be to myself as the son of a Conservative British Member of Parliament, I am compelled to concur with the rapidly growing view that there has been in high places at various times in our history a concerted effort to give aid and comfort to Nazis, to avoid confrontation with them in the period before World War II, to bring about a negotiated peace with them during the war, and to restore them to power in the postwar period. The motivation scarcely needs stressing: in confronting the rapidly encroaching Communist Empire, it was felt that convinced subscribers to National Socialism would be desirable allies and adjuncts.

However, there is an inherent irony here. It is not insignificant that the operation of German spy master Reinhard Gehlen, who was brought to Washington in 1946 and trained as an American operative, was penetrated by the Soviets within two years, or that Charles Howard Ellis, righthand man of the British Security Coordination chief, Sir William Stephenson, was a Nazi-Soviet agent. Thus, the one logical (though not excusable) motive for using Nazis against the Russians is undermined by the fact that the Nazis and the Soviets, in collusion with British and American intelligence contacts, have combined in a kind of chess-playing club, trading off secrets, playing both ends against the middle, while the rest of the world is involved in hot, cold, or temperate wars. And the rot seems to be irreversible.

The personages who figure most prominently in this book have been responsible for encouraging national paranoias for reasons of their own. They have sought to secure alliances with Nazis simply because their so-called confrontation with the menace of Russian invasion has allowed them to indulge a persistent anti-Semitism along with the protection of their pocketbooks. It was the very essence of Hitler's philosophy that the Jews were responsible for the Russian revolution. Actually, the Jewish bankers led by Otto Kahn had little or nothing to do with the revolution, which was largely financed by the Morgan Bank—which was said never to have employed a Jew.‡ However, for the extreme right wing of the United States, represented in the secular arm most strongly by Senator Burton K. Wheeler of Montana, in the religious arm by Father Charles E. Coughlin of Detroit, and in the military by Colonel Charles Lindbergh, the Jews and the Communists were one.*

No doubt the Jewish/Communist menace is still discussed in the purlieus of clubland from Los Angeles to London. That there is no sub-stance whatever in this thesis has not troubled those who disseminate it.

Before giving a bird's-eye view of the pages that follow, it may be useful to describe the Roosevelt government vis-à-vis pro-Fascist feelings at the time. Roosevelt himself was, as is widely known, a consummate politician, holding in balance all of the conflicting forces that animated his Cabinet in order to secure prosperity for America in the Depression and uniform loyalty (or an appearance of that) in time of war. Exploring his prolific memoranda at the Franklin D. Roosevelt Memorial Library, at Hyde Park, is an inspiriting experience. Again and again, his sure judg-ment is an indication of executive greatness. It is true that some of his governmental appointments may seem dubious at best. But it has to be remembered that he himself was part of the financial elite and needed its support in order to achieve reelection to office. Therefore, he laced his Cabinet with moneymen who may not have been above moral reproach but could at least be controlled to a point, not least because the Chief Executive emphatically had the goods on them.

Taking it from the top, Cordell Hull, the Tennessee backwoods boy who became Secretary of State, was an able appeaser who gave diplomatic

‡ Antony G. Sutton, *Wall Street and the Bolshevist Revolution* (New Rochelle, N.Y.: Arlington House, 1974).

* The myth of widespread revolutionary Communist movements in the United States has largely been an invention of the extreme Right.

recognition to Vichy and successfully attacked General Charles De Gaulle for authorizing the invasion of the islands of St. Pierre and Miquelon, off the southern coast of Newfoundland, just after Pearl Harbor, when those islands were occupied by pro-German Vichyites. Under Hull's aegis, a number of Vichy figures, including the Duchess of Windsor's lawyer, Maître Armand Grégoire, were admitted to this country after Pearl Harbor, while De Gaulle was persona non grata and Jews were refused entry by the visa division, which was run by that old friend of Mussolini and former ambassador to Italy Breckinridge Long. That ardent supporter of Italy's invasion of Ethiopia notoriously interfered with cables from Switzerland in which the local legate advised him of the Jewish plight. This episode and others like it leave one with little room to find admiration for the Department of State in such matters.

One of the few more enlightened figures of the State Department, Sumner Welles, who strongly opposed any appeasement with fascism, was dislodged from the Department when a group of his enemies led by former ambassador to France William Bullitt determined his homosexual activities aboard a presidential train and exposed them to the President.

The picture at the Department of Justice was scarcely more encouraging. The Attorney General, Francis Biddle, a product of the Philadelphia Main Line with powerful financial connections, appeared often on radio and in the press condemning Nazi-American activities. Yet behind the scenes he failed to act on Nazis, soft-pedaling investigations and thus handicapping his supposedly autonomous inferior J. Edgar Hoover, who was hampered by him in many investigations, as Hoover's many memoranda at Hyde Park clearly show.

As examples of Biddle's behavior, it should be noted that he, instead of prosecuting Father Charles Coughlin when it was disclosed by journalist George Seldes that Coughlin was in the direct pay of the Nazi government, with affidavits to prove it, simply allowed the matter to rest, on the alleged ground that to expose Coughlin to trial would greatly aggravate the Irish electorate—a clear case of official cowardice. Conversely, when O. John Rogge proceeded against the Nazi agents and seditionists who figured in a famous trial of the 1940s, Biddle failed to give him satisfactory support; Biddle also yielded to pressure from Senator Burton K. Wheeler and had the other government prosecutor, William Power Maloney, actually removed from the case. Later, Biddle's successor, Tom Clark, fired

Rogge from the Department for exposing Nazi collaboration on Capitol Hill—under the influence of the selfsame Montana senator.

Biddle also failed to act in the matter of John L. Lewis, the labor leader who collaborated with William Rhodes Davis in support of the Nazi government, a matter dealt with fully in my book *Trading with the Enemy*. Biddle proved equally lax in the matter of Sean Russell, Quartermaster General of the Irish Republican Army, who, in collusion with Congressman Jim McGranery of Pennsylvania, was involved in a totally hushed up attempt to assassinate the King and Queen of England during their state visit to the United States in 1939. Biddle failed to prosecute the matter of the theft of Roosevelt's Victory Program, part of the war plan code named Rainbow Five, from the war room, a theft that helped precipitate Hitler's declaration of war upon the United States, and he flubbed the investigation into Hans Wilhelm Rohl, the German-American California building tycoon alleged to be involved in the leakage of certain strategic information vis-à-vis Pearl Harbor.

It would be tedious to enumerate here the many failures of action, displays of cowardice before the electorate, and lapses of judgment by which, lip service aside, Attorney General Biddle compounded the failure of the State Department to protect the United States from subversive pro-Nazi elements. I have preferred to exemplify the matter by illustration in the text.

As for J. Edgar Hoover, he emerges from documents with considerably more credit than his critics would wish.† His annotations on the numerous records in my possession, written in a curious, rounded, fourth-grade hand, indicate a stubborn, impatient, and relentless cop who was handicapped at every turn by several obstacles. First, the State Department, as any FBI veteran of World War II will readily confirm, interfered constantly with his pursuit of enemy agents. Again and again, he would be ready to close in, when the State Department, which, as Roosevelt said, was neutral in time of war (and he only hoped it would remain so) would step in and protect the accused. Hence, many enemy agents slipped through the mesh and made their way out of the country. It would be a logical deduction that the reason for this protection lay not only in a certain desire to bring about a negotiated peace with Germany, but also because, as in the present Barbie case, too many important names would

_____

† His role in the McCarthy era was, of course, entirely undesirable.

be exposed to public scrutiny in a trial held in the full glare of wartime publicity.

Hoover was also limited by his own boss, Biddle, as I have already pointed out, who persistently failed to supply him with necessary backing; indeed, Hoover was often in the humiliating position of reading crucial information in the columns of Drew Pearson and Walter Winchell before it reached his desk. He was further frustrated by the fact that his bureau staffs across the country were largely run by men who were ill trained in counterespionage and who simply prepared lengthy reports without supporting them with properly conducted interrogations. As an example, when, in 1943, Count Cassina, protégé of the unwitting Barbara Hutton and Cary Grant, was arrested as a German agent and disclosed that he was an eyewitness of an espionage mission to Spain involving Errol Flynn, Flynn was not even questioned on the matter and it was buried conveniently in the files. This was perhaps attributable more to incompetence than to guile, or even to Hollywood studio protection, but, along with many identical episodes, it raises more questions than it answers.

The Bureau was in essence a collection of cops playing at being secret agents, but so handicapped was the United States, both intellectually and politically, at the outset of World War II, that the President had to turn to any source in order to secure some kind of protection from subversion. Army and navy intelligence were seriously understaffed and suffered from inadequate training. Moreover, as in all countries, every branch of intelligence was jealous of its own discoveries and deliberately failed to supply information to the others. It was only through the single-handed efforts of that lone wolf of the State Department, Assistant Secretary Adolf A. Berle, that crucial information from Hoover and other sources passed up the line to the Oval Office via the hardworking General "Pa" Watson, the presidential secretary.

Fenced about on every side, the FBI chief did what he could to bring offenders to justice, although in the case of Sean Russell he allowed himself to be handicapped beyond the point that could be considered either necessary or desirable.

The record of Major Lemuel B. Schofield, Biddle's fellow Philadelphian and German-American head of the Immigration and Naturalization Service, was no better than that of his master. In *Trading with the Enemy*, I showed in great detail his persistent relationship, even after Pearl Harbor, with the Princess Stefanie Hohenlohe, Hitler's favorite half-Jewish honorary Aryan and agent of the German Government.

The princess came to the United States on several occasions, moving here permanently in 1940. Her purpose was to determine precisely which leaders of society might be favorable to the German cause and to try to make contacts that would lead to permanent peace between the United States and Germany. One of her contacts was Sir William Wiseman, former head of British Intelligence in the United States; another was Fritz Wiedemann, German consul general in San Francisco, and a third was Major Lemuel Schofield, head of the Immigration and Naturalization Service, her lover, a Philadelphia lawyer who, although she was an agent of the Third Reich and a friend of Adolf Hitler, became her financial support in the year of her arrival and assisted her at every turn. On November 26, 1940, at the Mark Hopkins Hotel, in San Francisco, she, Wiseman, and Wiedemann held a meeting toward preparing a negotiated peace between Britain and Germany.

During World War II, Major Schofield aided and abetted Stefanie Hohenlohe. He dropped deportation proceedings against her in May 1941; he was seen in public with her; he pretended that she had provided information on Germany in return for her immunity, which in fact she had not; and when Hoover had her imprisoned, Schofield visited her with gifts, money, and food and did his best to have her released. Roosevelt dismissed him over these treasonable activities in 1943, but Schofield did not waver. He returned to private practice and defended the White Russian Nazi contact Serge Rubinstein against the U.S. Government on draft-dodging charges and then, when the Princess Hohenlohe was released, installed her permanently in his home near Philadelphia.

Given this wholesale assistance to German causes in high places, it is hardly surprising that such figures as Senator Wheeler and Father Coughlin were able to survive World War II. Indeed, of those people I have dealt with, only Major Schofield got his comeuppance.

The two most dominating figures of the period in terms of pacification of the Third Reich were Father Charles E. Coughlin and Senator Burton K. Wheeler. Coughlin, born of pure Irish stock in Canada, was intensely devoted to the German cause. Burton K. Wheeler was born in Hudson, Massachusetts, the tenth son of a poor shoemaker. Oddly, he began his career as a radical, and supported the New Deal until he clashed with the President over the creation of the NRA. It was with the advent of war in Europe that this lanky, rumpled politician, cigar-smoking and wearing a dented Stetson, started to make trouble for President Roosevelt by doing everything in his power to prevent what he called "the ploughing under of every fourth American boy" in a potential conflict. Interestingly, Senator Wheeler's secretary of the 1930s, Fräulein Martha Valesky-Wiedemann, a German national, became after Pearl Harbor an assistant intelligence radio monitor in Berlin for SS leader Ernst Kaltenbrunner.

The America First movement, in which Senator Wheeler prominently figured, and which Father Coughlin supported, was—and is—portrayed as merely a well-intentioned collection of right-wing figures of both the Republican and the Democratic parties who sincerely if misguidedly did their utmost to keep the United States out of World War II. In fact, as a careful examination of German Foreign Office documents makes clear, the movement was directly supported both financially and politically from inside Germany itself. The go-between was the invaluable Hans Thomsen, German chargé d'affaires in Washington, whose numerous contacts on Capitol Hill I shall deal with in sum. The America Firsters went untouched by any investigation or prosecution even after the author John Roy Carlson (Arthur Derounian) exposed them in the widely read book *Under Cover*, published in the middle of the war.

Throughout the war, the so-called America Firsters continued to be vociferous in the House. Among others, they strongly defended Senator David I. Walsh of Massachusetts when he was discovered to have been consorting with German agents in a male bordello in Pacific Street, Brooklyn; and they stood firmly for Vivien Kellems, Connecticut manufacturer and political opponent of Clare Booth Luce when she was in breach of the Trading with the Enemy and Treason acts in corresponding with a German manufacturer in time of world conflict.

The record was no better in neutral Europe. In *Trading with the Enemy* I described how Leland Harrison, U.S. minister in Berne, Switzerland, not without the knowledge of the U.S. embassy in London, permitted Standard Oil of New Jersey to ship gasoline of enemy origin through Switzerland while at the same time precluding the purchase of freedom for Jews from the SS because of the conditions of the Trading with the Enemy Act.

Mr. Harrison emerges with even less distinction in his handling of U.S. intelligence operations in Switzerland. The OSS's Allen Dulles, without sanction from the White House, engaged, under Mr. Harrison's banner, in meetings with Prince Max von Hohenlohe, representing the SD, SS Intelligence, in Switzerland in 1942 to discuss a negotiated peace with Germany which would leave Hitler dead or in prison while a new Fascist government, composed of the rags, tags, and bobtails of the Nazi hierarchy, would rule in his place.

The purpose of this proposed surreptitious alliance, which was in direct conflict with the principle of total surrender laid down by Roosevelt and Winston Churchill, was allegedly to arrange a *cordon sanitaire* against America's ally that indispensable bugbear the Soviet Union, whose potential menace seemed paradoxically greater after it defeated Hitler at Stalingrad. Subsequent to that defeat, Nazi-Allied peace meetings notably increased. Similarly, Dulles made arrangements with SS General Karl Wolff in order to secure the surrender of Italy and the security of German armaments as a potential force against Russia. General Donovan (at that time Colonel) of the OSS cannot be absolved from his own arrangements, many of them conducted despite the express disapproval of the chief executive.

Shortly before Pearl Harbor, Walter Schellenberg, the head of SD Amt VI,‡ became an American communications executive. The reason for his special role in peace negotiations with the Allies assumes new significance when it is known that Colonel Sosthenes Behn, chairman of ITT, appointed him a board member in Germany for the duration of the war in order to secure ITT's German holdings and those in German-occupied territories from nationalization by the German Government. In view of the fact that he was a paid director, authorized by the board in New York, as explored most fully in my book *Trading with the Enemy*, it is not surprising that he had a vested interest in helping his American contacts toward a separate peace. Colonel Donovan's friendship with Colonel Behn is a matter of record; indeed, ITT's channels of communication were as useful to Donovan as they were to Schellenberg, and a continual exchange took place, at one stage resulting in the breaking of the U.S. diplomatic code by a team that included the monitors of the SD, one of whose number was the aforementioned former secretary of Senator Burton K. Wheeler.

Neither Schellenberg nor Donovan acted with authorization by either Roosevelt or Hitler in setting up wartime meetings in Sweden, Spain,

‡ The foreign intelligence section of the SD.

and Switzerland. At the end of the war, they did not go without their reward: Donovan was elevated to a generalship and Schellenberg was conducted to London for a job as an informer under British Intelligence (later, when his usefulness expired, he served a term in prison, presumably as a sop to popular feeling).

The reader innocent of such matters may well ask how, in the course of a war in which hundreds of thousands of their kinfolk died, it was possible for the intelligence services of the world to indulge in a series of bargainings, games, exchanges, and chess maneuvers while the supreme executives were unconditionally in the conflict. The answer lies in the very nature of secret intelligence and the fact that its leaders traditionally have been given excessive autonomy, which has led to their supragovernmental character.

While these undetected activities continued, the public had to be fed its sacrificial beasts. The hangman's noose at Nuremberg served to stifle not only the lives of its imposing victims, but also any public fear that full justice had not been done. Instead, starting with Hjalmar Horace Greeley Schacht and Emil Puhl, both of the Reichsbank, the international figures who had encouraged the aforementioned liaisons were effectively spared. This act of convenient mercy led directly to the history of postwar U.S.-Nazi collaboration, with which we are growing more familiar day by day.

First came the apparently necessary Operation Paper Clip, in which German scientists were imported regardless of their political background, to assist in space research and the munitions-building that led to the Cold War. General Reinhard Gehlen, head of Hitler's chief anti-Soviet intelligence operation in Eastern Europe, was flown to Washington to spend over a year being briefed toward the formation of a CIA-funded anti-Soviet operation in Germany. Later, General Adolf Heusinger, a mass murderer of Jews, was to be similarly honored by President John F. Kennedy, who made him head of the military force of NATO.

Nicolae Malaxa, the Romanian industrialist who had financed the Fascist Romanian Legion, popularly known as the Iron Guard, was pleased to enter the United States under the direct auspices of the State Department in 1946, having conveniently shifted his allegiance to the Soviet Union, with which, despite the imminent advent of the Cold War, the United States was actively conducting business. Similarly, the Nazi activist Viorel Trifa, who had, interestingly enough, been elevated to a bishopric without the inconvenient necessity of taking Holy Orders, was protected, aided, and abetted within the United States despite his alleged role in the violent pogrom in Bucharest by the Iron Guard in January 1941. And yet a third Iron Guard figure, Otto von Bolschwing, found a pleasant sinecure in Silicon Valley, with full CIA protection.

The foregoing is intended chiefly to orientate the reader: to show how the Barbie case is simply the latest in a long chain of incidents in which, with a combination of corruption, naïveté, and alleged fear of Communist invasion and takeover, major figures of American politics have nourished the convenient and lesser evil of nazism to confront the larger evil of communism. It is to show the danger incorporated in such a policy that I have undertaken the writing of this book.

✠✠✠✠✠✠✠ 1

Origins: The Bund

In December 1939, a significant appointment took place at the German embassy's ugly red brick building on Pennsylvania Avenue in Washington, D.C. Hans Thomsen, the handsome and personable, Norwegian-born former secretary of Herr Adolf Hitler, became chargé d'affaires, a post he was to retain until he presented Under Secretary of State Sumner Welles with Germany's declaration of war, on December 11, 1941.

Thomsen was authorized to pursue a policy that was clearly laid down by Berlin. This policy was to secure a lasting peace between the United States and Nazi Germany. To this end, Thomsen was supplied with very substantial sums of money, running, according to some accounts, into the millions of dollars. He succeeded in buying off congressmen and senators, underwriting literary agents and publishers, flooding bookstores with propagandist material, and issuing magazines and pamphlets. It was a remarkable venture in appeasement, and its purpose was ultimately and predictably cynical. Indeed, as late as July 12, 1941, five months before Pearl Harbor, that honest all-American Secretary of the Interior Harold L. Ickes was remarking that Thomsen was involved in peace proposals that involved not only figures of the American Government but the British ambassador, Lord Halifax, almost two years after Britain had declared war on Germany. The go-between at that time was the Philadelphia Quaker leader Malcolm Lovell, by definition a pacifist.

As Ickes remarked in his diary at the time, the negotiated peace which Thomsen and his like so aggressively sought, and which such figures as Colonel Lindbergh, Coughlin, and Wheeler wholeheartedly supported, would have been only a temporary arrangement. Hitler would have consolidated his gains and prepared for World War III, which he would have undertaken when he was ready. With Russia under his belt, he could easily have destroyed the British Empire. He would also have set the groundwork for a situation in which America would be a mere impotent neutral, rather like Sweden.

Thomsen had arrived in 1936 as special counselor to the embassy, with the advantages of fluent English, an impeccably Aryan and athletic physical appearance, and an attractive socialite wife, Bébé, who could give amusing parties in the nation's capital. He found a ready ear in the American social establishment. Anti-Semitism and fear of communism were two overriding concerns in those elevated circles. Money was of course the obsession of all concerned. Nobody wanted to get involved with a war in which his European investments would be cut off.

The public certainly wanted to stay out of the European conflict for as long as possible. Many Americans in 1939 were only a generation or two removed from European immigrants who had crossed the Atlantic by steerage in order to escape from the internecine conflicts, class struggles, and royal squabbles in which they were merely pawns in a game. They resented their humble positions and the fact that they became fodder for sword or cannon in one war after another. They came to the New World to escape war forever, to be able, through sheer grit and enterprise, to build their personal nest eggs and to secure peace, prosperity, and good health for their children.

Irish and German elements predominated in many areas. Indeed, if there was such a thing as a universally desirable American he might be said to be fair-skinned, tall, of athletic appearance, and redolent of Aryanism. The prejudices against Jews, Italians and Slavs were everywhere to be found. The Irish, too, carried with them a residue of bitterness: bitterness against the British, bitterness fed by ancestral memories of the great famines and the maraudings of the Black and Tans.

The vast majority of Americans had only a peripheral interest in European political affairs, if indeed they had any at all. The rise of Hitler to power and the subsequent displays of force against the Jews even in those prewar years was widely commented upon in the press in America but seldom raised an inkling of protest in the letters columns.

As war approached and Austria and Czechoslovakia fell to the jackboot, Americans at every level were saying to each other, and writing to the papers, that young Americans must never again be suckered into Europe's problems as they had been in World War I. They blamed President Woodrow Wilson and his propagandist activity following the sinking of the *Lusitania* in 1915 for the deaths of the flower of a generation in the trenches in France.

Even Roosevelt had to be extremely careful that the U.S. public, which was concerned only with being allowed to make money and to continue to enjoy its football and baseball games, its movies and radio and its automobile outings, would not get wind of presidential plans to involve his country somewhat unconstitutionally in the destruction of Hitler.

Thus, it can be seen that Thomsen arrived on fertile soil, and we shall learn more of his activities later on.

It is interesting that one of the chargé d'affaires's first targets was the fanatically pro-Nazi German-American Bund, which crystallized the feelings of a vigorous minority of Americans while greatly aggravating the majority with its torchlit street parades and struttings in uniform. The Bund was highly inconvenient, at least after Hitler showed his hand in Vienna and Prague. It was too overt, and turned many Americans from basic indifference to a sense of unease. Although communism was the real enemy and nazism was something of a joke, nevertheless when newsreels showed Americans dressing up in Nazi uniforms and beating up Jews on street corners, a basic American sense of decency was offended. And also, and perhaps more significantly, there was the uneasy feeling that sinister "European" goings-on were finding a foothold on the American mainland.

We might well ask why any number of United States citizens, both in the blue- and the white-collar classes, enlisted in the cause of the Führer as a kind of separate branch of the Nazi Army? The answer can be found in the mentality bred in certain circles by the Depression. A large number of malcontents, it was true, were drawn to join Communist cells; but many others blamed communism and the Jews for their plight and found consolation in joining paramilitary movements like the Bund.

These organizations, made up of scores of thousands of members, had their own bureaucratic hierarchy, their military leaders, their printing presses with garish posters, inflammatory pamphlets, and manifestoes of every description. They wore comic-opera versions of Gestapo uniforms, and in this guise some struggling factory worker could stand up straight and feel bold, striking, and handsome. Indeed, aside from the need to achieve visual uniformity, which has always appealed in countries of large population, there was always the sexual advantage of attracting the kind of women who were besotted by the idea of an affair with a man in battle dress.

The Bund was in essence a manifestation of a Nazi *internationale,* equivalent in organization and subversive purpose to the Communist Internationale, with which it was allegedly in perpetual conflict. The foreign organization of the Nazi Party was known as the Auslands Organisation, to be referred to throughout this text by its popularly accepted abbreviation, AO. The foreign section of the Nazi Party was at first under the direction of Hans Nieland, headquartered in Hamburg, followed by the appointment, on May 8, 1933, of the British-born Ernst Wilhelm Bohle, an assistant to Rudolf Hess (who was deputy to Hitler in that year). Hess directed Bohle in his activities.

Both Hess and Bohle were internationalists, determined to secure a Western Alliance against the Slavic and Jewish peoples, both of which threatened, in their view, its purity and internal security. Hess was born in Alexandria, Egypt, and Bohle in the British Midlands.

They were concerned about any activism in America that might cause disaffection against Germany. The Teutonia Association, formed as early as 1924, under the guidance of one Fritz Gissibl, included both Germans and Americans of German descent and lasted until 1932. It was replaced by the Nazi foreign section's trusted organization led by Heinz Spanknoebel of Berlin and set up in Detroit. Nazi cells were set up in New York City, Chicago, Cincinnati, Los Angeles, and San Francisco. But Spanknoebel's aggressive behavior and attacks on Jews caused him to be withdrawn to Berlin for briefing by Bohle in 1933.

In July of that year, the Association of the Friends of the New Germany was formed, later to be renamed The German-American Bund. Bohle had given orders to Spanknoebel and his adjutant Gissibl to play down aggressive nazism, but unfortunately for U.S.-Nazi appeasement, Spanknoebel proved to be uncontrollable. With no apparent authorization from the Nazi Party, he and his lieutenant took control of the United German Societies of Chicago and New York. German-Jewish members withdrew under pressure, and Spanknoebel launched a policy of mass meetings, German Day celebrations, church rallies under the aegis of Lutheran ministers, distributions of swastika stickers on buses and in subways, and every possible form of demonstration. In 1936, Gissibl stepped down, and a former auto worker, Fritz Kuhn, took over, forming the Bund.

Kuhn was born in Munich in 1896. Well educated up to university standard, he served four and a half years in the German infantry in World War I, rising to the rank of lieutenant. His brother Max rose to be a Supreme Court judge in the Nazi judiciary, a fact that proved helpful in giving Fritz Kuhn credibility in the German Government.

His leading officer was Gerhardt Wilhelm Kunze, a chauffeur from Camden, New Jersey, who later was to assume Kuhn's position, and who was, unlike Kuhn, a Nazi spy. Of Kuhn's other followers, Hans Zimmerman was a waiter, and Carl Nicolay a struggling poet who used the pen name Wilhelm Meister. Another close associate was James Wheeler-Hill, a White Russian despite his non-Slavic name, whose dream was to unite the White Russian groups that envisaged the overthrow of the Soviet Government. The White Russians formed a significant part of the Bund, but the majority was largely composed of Irish-American Catholics and German-American Lutherans.

Like so many other Nazi collaborators and sympathizers, Kuhn came from Detroit. Significantly, he had worked at the Henry Ford Hospital and the Henry Ford Motor Company; his anti-Semitic, anti-Communist position found its perfect place in the Ford empire. His era as American führer was launched on March 29, 1936, when he was elected leader in Buffalo, New York. The Bund was divided into fifty-five cells; Kuhn announced its formation from a platform bedecked with swastikas and Stars and Stripes. Officers were set up in various parts of the nation. Gauleiter Hermann Schwinn was in charge of the West Coast, George Froboese in the Middle West, Rudolf Markmann in the eastern states. G. W. Kunze became director of public relations, with headquarters in New York, where Kuhn had his office and home at 178 East 85th Street. It was decided to hold a national convention each year. The convention in effect gave Kuhn unlimited authority based upon an outright power of attorney.

Although the articles of the Bund constitution, laid down in New York in 1937, ostensibly called for allegiance to the United States and to the preservation of law and order, the organization was bent upon the wholesale subversion, subordination, and collapse of the U.S. democratic system from within. In this purpose, the Bund was as active as the Communist Party, which it condemned for precisely the same intention. It was better organized, centralized, and financed.

Soon each state had its leader. Each new member was subjected to a Gestapo-like inquiry to ensure purity of blood; all non-Aryans were excluded from membership. Propaganda was distributed, and information about German-American Nazi sympathizers was collected and forwarded to Berlin.

The problem was that many German-Americans or their parents had come to the United States to escape the very totalitarianism that Kuhn was peddling. He was frustrated by the fact that it was difficult to attract more members; the press, always eager for sensation, reported the Bund's activities in headlines and thus severely provoked the freedom-loving American public against it.

There was nothing illegal about the Bund's activities, since there was nothing in the democracy's statutes that forbade the forming of militias or the setting up of training schemes, whether fascistic or not. Nevertheless, the existence of the Bund's youth movement caused criticism across the nation. Many found it offensive to see in newsreels in their movie theaters five- and six-year-old children dressed up in brown or blue shorts or skirts, white blouses with Hitler scarves, marching in unison and heiling Hitler as they did so. These newsreels, and press reports, showed that the camps were run with rigid discipline and the children ate, slept, talked, and dreamed nazism just as the Hitler Jugend did. The children were trained to lie if they were asked where Bund meetings were held. They were taught pride in keeping themselves strong and healthy so that they could forge powerful links in the chain of pure and unsullied German genealogy.

One of their camps was near Grafton, Wisconsin, where there were ample grounds surrounded by wooded hills, and a river with excellent swimming facilities. At Camp Hindenburg, as it was known, tents were arranged in circles, surrounding a flagpole flying the flag of Hitler Youth: a white streak of lightning or half swastika on a black background. Next to it, the American flag fluttered cheerfully.

Other camps were situated near Philadelphia, at the Deutschhorst Country Club; at Efdend, near Pontiac, close to Detroit; and, the most elaborate camp of all, Siegfried, near Yaphank, Long Island. To a loud *"Achtung!"* delivered over the public address system, boys and girls would form into ranks, marching behind the German swastika to heil the arriving Bund storm troopers as they came in on the train from New York City. A band would blare a stirring German march at the depot, and then the children and youths would accompany their guests to the camp.

Kuhn or Nicolay would address the crowd with wild enthusiasm, whipping up feverish excitement. Special school lessons were given in the history of the German "race" and the Nazi Party. As soon as a new party song was sung in Berlin, it was repeated in the Bund camps.

The psychological appeal to young boys was strong. The uniform, the marching, the emphasis on physical fitness, and the opportunities to meet nubile girls encouraged membership and inflated the budding male ego. The sense of belonging to a pure-blooded club from which all those who were physically or racially inferior would be rigidly excluded had a strong appeal to the adolescent mind.

Many Bund members were trained in the use of rifles, pistols, and machine guns and were expert in demolition work. In 1936, Kuhn traveled to Berlin in connection with the Olympic Games, carrying with him over three thousand dollars which had been raised by the members from their Depression relief checks, since he was too cheap to take the money out of his million-dollar annual dues. He also took with him a Gold Book of German-Americans, a lavish, leather-bound history of the Bund with six thousand signatures in it. On August 2, 1936, Kuhn and his elite guard of storm troopers marched down the Unter den Linden, in Berlin, pausing at the Chancellery to meet Hitler. Kuhn was thrilled to look straight into the eyes of the Führer, who asked about Germans in America, thanked Kuhn for his fight against the evil American press, and asked eagerly about his plans for a trip through Germany. The Führer promised to ensure a warm welcome for the Bund in Munich, and in farewell said, "Go back and continue the fight."

The photograph of Kuhn shaking hands with Hitler caused widespread annoyance in the United States and resulted in a backlash at the German Foreign Office. Indeed, the result of the photograph, which represented Kuhn's greatest moment, was that ironically it helped to finish him. The new ambassador to Washington, Hans Dieckhoff, made clear, along with Hans Thomsen, that he would not encourage Kuhn, at least in public; messages went out to all consulates stating that there must be a policy of extreme caution in relation to Kuhn in the future.

German propaganda changed its character on the American continent. Instead of inflaming, it sought to soothe. It sought reassurance and comfort, rather than activism, in the American people. Kuhn's extravagant statements on his return about Hitler's "friendship" for him only annoyed Ambassador Dieckhoff and the German Government still further.

By late 1937, Ernst-Wilhelm Bohle had firmly decided to limit and finally withdraw the financial support of his AO organization of Germans abroad. But Fritz Kuhn obstinately continued his activities, arranging gala celebrations and rallies by day and by night to aggrandize himself and enhance his financial position. Ambassador Dieckhoff sought to control him; it was essential to encourage isolationism by any means possible.

In November 1938, there were about one hundred thousand Bund members and sympathizers. On November 7, a Jewish youth murdered the third secretary of the German Embassy in Paris; three days later, there was a pogrom in Germany—known as Krystallnacht, or the Night of Broken Glass—in which temples were destroyed, stores looted, and Jews sent to concentration camps or murdered. This outright declaration of war against the Jews of Germany proved to be disastrous for Kuhn. Although the American public was naïve about European politics, this butchery proved to be altogether too much, and the public suddenly became interested in the newly formed House committee under Martin Dies of Texas, which was empowered to investigate Nazi as well as Communist and civil-rights groups in the United States.

Kuhn began to panic. He had gone to Germany earlier in 1938 and had met with the diplomat Fritz Wiedemann, who was bent upon cementing alliances with the United States. Wiedemann warned him of his dangerous position and urged him to subdue himself. He told Kuhn that his lies, violations of confidential conversations, and causing of a severe rift between Washington and Berlin were reprehensible.

Unregenerate, Kuhn decided to embark on one last reckless gesture of defiance, both of official German policy and of everything America stood for. He decided to hold a supercolossal pro-American rally in Madison Square Garden on George Washington's birthday, February 22, 1939. The publicity for the approaching event was considerable, and there were long lines at the box office to buy tickets for this, the single most striking display of nazism in the history of the United States. Kuhn had a flair for showmanship: the stage was illuminated to striking effect. There was a huge painting of George Washington flanked by the Stars and Stripes; the swastikas were mounted on fires that leapt from glowing suns. About twenty-two thousand people were present at the occasion, and two thousand policemen were on hand to prevent rioting. The crowd sometimes cheered, sometimes booed; Kuhn audaciously compared Hitler to George Washington, abused the President, predicted that the Bund would assemble a million members within a year, poured scorn upon Jews as parasites and war profiteers, and called for a united Fascist front against communism. A Jewish activist named Isadore Greenbaum rushed through the storm-troop line and tried to hit Kuhn, who had him thrown off the stage. Kuhn personally netted thirteen thousand dollars from the rally.

This was simply a last display of self-indulgence, since already Kuhn's position was becoming untenable. In May and June, the Dies Committee subjected him to an interrogation in which he almost came to blows with his questioners, especially Alabama's Joe Starnes. Starnes was particularly annoyed with Kuhn and harassed him vigorously. Unfortunately, Martin Dies seemed not to see a significant difference between communism and nazism, socialism and national socialism, and provoked Kuhn's contempt for his ignorance. Kuhn fought determinedly on issue after issue, but there was no escaping the fact that the hearing was being reported in the press and that Kuhn's stance was singularly unpopular. Moreover, he was in trouble on another matter. He had been exposed shortly before when he had been charged with larceny for misappropriation of Bund funds. Even within the terms of his organization, he was unable to hold to the rules, and Kunze was waiting eagerly in the wings, despite the fact that Kunze himself was believed to be involved in the embezzlement.

In December 1939, Fritz Kuhn went to Sing Sing on a two-and-a-half-to-five-year rap. In the meantime, the German Government was changing its American emphases still further. Fritz Wiedemann became consul general in San Francisco and began plotting for an American-British-German alliance of purpose against Russia. The Propaganda Ministry, in Berlin, with the cooperation of the AO, set up the Transocean News Service, which got underway in the early months of 1939. The TNS was run by a German-American named Manfred Zapp, who had been a correspondent for German newspapers all over the world. With headquarters in New York City, he was amply funded by Thomsen; he used the Transradio consortium, composed of RCA, British Cable and Wireless, and Italian and French members, among other outlets.

Dr. Hans Borchers, German consul general in New York, was a keen supporter of Zapp. From the Transocean headquarters at 341 Madison Avenue, a stream of material flowed out to every part of the nation and to places as far afield as Latin America and South Africa, where Zapp had previously worked. By mid-1939, Zapp worked under the control of the German embassy and consulates, receiving finance from the AO, the Ministry of Propaganda, and the Foreign Office. The intention was to ensure the cooperation with the German Government of those who were pacifist, republican, and nationalistic. The pacifist Quakers—notably Malcolm Lovell—were encouraged to support the German cause, and although most were repelled by Hitler, there were those who were sufficiently duped to travel to Berlin with Zapp's encouragement to meet with various propagandists there. Money was poured into such useful organs as the Irish Catholic New York *Enquirer.* When money grew tighter from Berlin, the embassy directly financed Zapp.

Other monies were supplied by individual subscribers. Gradually, Transocean spread through South America; it became the chief propaganda agent of the Nazi government in Guatemala, Mexico, Havana, Ecuador, Chile, Argentina, and Brazil. Most of the material came straight from Berlin under the direction of a well-known Nazi agent; Zapp arranged Von Simon's travel to South America. Zapp was constantly presented with the problem of offering Transocean news to the American press. It had to be recast, revised, and rewritten in order to adapt it to American concepts and the reading habits of the American public. Transocean was up against Reuters and the Associated Press, which could offer far more words per day and also supplied more reliable and unbiased news. News of German origin was not welcome to most Americans. When Zapp managed to get airplay, Jewish listeners complained. More and more, he had to concentrate on selling the Transocean News Service through newsletters, trying to evoke enthusiasm for the German cause in Mexico and Central America. Zapp tried to develop his organization as a source for confidential information. He made useful contacts, including Lawrence Dennis (economic adviser to the Wall Street brokers E. A. Pierce), of whom more later. He also found a New York correspondent, August W. Halfield, who gave him information on financial matters. Another contact was James D. Mooney, of General Motors. Zapp obtained support from the Nazi sympathizer George Sylvester Viereck. But, more and more, it became clear that Zapp's was a process of preaching to the converted. The bulk of Americans were neither infiltrated nor impressed by Zapp.

More efforts were made through the German Library of Information, at 17 Battery Place, New York City. The German Consulate General was at the same address. Under the direction of Dr. Matthias Schmitz, *Facts in Review* was distributed to some seventy thousand people. It was a carefully assembled publication, whitewashing Germany under Hitler, that plugged, among other things, the political movement known as America First.

The Nazis and America First

On December 17, 1941, ten days after Pearl Harbor, Charles A. Lindbergh, the famous Lone Eagle and possibly the most celebrated of America's national heroes, addressed a meeting of fifty individuals of the America First Committee, assembled at the home of Edwin S. Webster, Jr., at 35 Beekman Place, New York City. Webster was New York secretary of the Committee. Lindbergh said that for years America had been speaking of the Yellow Peril; yet now we "are fighting on the side of the Russians and Chinese." He went on to say that the U.S. Government had "no plan and does not know for what it is fighting."

Lindbergh went on to say that there was "only one danger in the world, namely, the Yellow Danger"; that China and Japan in reality were "allied together against the white race"; and that Germany "could have been used as a weapon against this alliance" in collaboration with the United States. Lindbergh said that the ideal program would have included Germany taking over Russia and Poland in collaboration with the British as a bloc against the yellow race and bolshevism; but that, so he stated, "the British and the fools in Washington had to interfere." He said that Britain was "the real cause of all the trouble in the world today."

Lindbergh stated that now that the war was on, America First must be on the alert for the time when the American people, by reason of the lists of the missing and statements of war losses, realized they had been betrayed by the British and the Administration. He said that then America First would be "a political force" and could "negotiate peace with Nazi Germany."

No clearer statement could have been made of the position of the extreme right wing of the United States. America First was at the heart of the international plan to secure a lasting peace with the Third Reich. The philosophy was based on ideological as well as financial considerations: purity of race and the destruction of Jewry and communism allied with financial empire-building all over the world. In other words, a purpose identical with that of the German extreme Right.

The keynote speech of America First was delivered by acting chairman General Robert E. Wood on October 4, 1940, before the Chicago Council on Foreign Relations. General Wood contended that totalitarian states could not be destroyed by war and that a German-dominated Europe would not destroy our foreign trade. Intervention in the war must be avoided at all costs. General Wood was chairman of Sears Roebuck, whose president, Donald Nelson, was head of the War Production Board. The next in line at the War Production Board was William L. Batt, partner in Philadelphia with Hugo von Rosen, cousin of Field Marshal Göring in the SKF ball bearings company, which supplied Nazi-related companies in South America throughout World War II.

Other Board members included the national director and secretary, Douglas Stuart, whose magazine *Scribner's Commentary*'s income came from Stuart's Quaker Oats millions. Also on the board were the air ace Captain Edward (Eddie) Rickenbacker, Henry Ford, Alice Roosevelt Longworth, Mrs. Burton K. Wheeler, John T. Flynn, Kathryn Lewis, daughter of John L.*, Thomas N. McCarter, director of the Chase National (later Chase Manhattan) Bank, which kept open its branch in Nazi-occupied Paris during World War II, and the millionaire Chicago publisher William H. Regnery. A friend of the Committee was Colonel Robert R. McCormick of the Chicago *Tribune.* William J. Grace, who had Nazi connections, and Avery Brundage, chairman of the Olympic Games Committee, pro-Nazi and supporter of sending a team to the Hitler games in 1936, were others prominent in the organization.

The Committee published a monthly called *Equality* containing such

---

* For details of John L. Lewis's Nazi connections, see my *Trading with the Enemy* (New York:Delacorte Press, 1983).

articles as John L. Lewis's attack on conscription and Senator Wheeler's demand for protection of American youth from death overseas.

The Committee was nationwide. There were 250 chapters and 750 units throughout the country, with a total of five million members. America First was incorporated in New York, California, and Missouri. It was on behalf of the Committee that Senator Wheeler distributed one million copies of a congressionally franked postcard in 1941 discouraging men from joining the Army. A million dollars per annum poured into America First in 1941 to make its activities possible.

That money was received from Nazi sources—as revealed by J. Edgar Hoover in a secret memorandum to the President dated February 23, 1942 and now declassified at Hyde Park.

Hoover advised that the organization was far more dangerous than the Bund, that if Hitler had destroyed England, America First would have raised a rallying cry to have Roosevelt impeached and Lindbergh made President in a new grand alliance with Hitler. That Lindbergh was ideally placed for this position can be shown by the fact that he addressed the Canadian nation by radio in September 1941 stating that Canada had no business sending any men or arms to Britain. On September 16, 1941, in a speech at Des Moines, Iowa, Lindbergh stated that the world conflict was engulfing the United States because of "the British, the Jews, and the Roosevelt administration." He was seconded by Senator Gerald P. Nye on September 23, 1941, in an interview in the Chicago *Daily News* in which Nye charged that "foreign-born magnates of the Jewish faith" were responsible for anti-Nazi propaganda in films. On November 1, 1941, former Governor Philip F. La Follette of Wisconsin gave a speech in Washington, D.C., in which he called for a revolution by "fearless red-blooded Americans to overthrow the government." The America First Committee interfered with the armed services and encouraged troops to lay down their arms.

J. Edgar Hoover discovered a range of Nazi associations in America First. In December 1940, Manfred Zapp was known to be in touch with America First. On January 16, 1941, the FBI reported that the car belonging to Dr. George Gyssling, Nazi consul in Los Angeles, was seen parked outside the local office of the Committee.

On April 22, 1941, the Philadelphia *Ledger* announced that a local America Firster, Mrs. Edith Scott, was inviting women associated with a Nazi organization into the membership. Newspaper distribution tycoon

John B. Snow also distributed America First pamphlets. The American Legion exposed America First as being involved in subversive propaganda distributing leaflets via bookstores.

The Swedish tycoon Axel Wenner-Gren (see chapter 14) gave financial backing to America First. He was pro-Nazi and a supporter of a negotiated peace.

The Nazi publication *Free American* encouraged its readers to enroll with America First. The German American National Alliance, of Chicago, circulated Nazi propaganda appealing for contributions to America First. The FBI obtained copies of checks drawn by former or present Bund members for America First.

On June 16, 1941, Senator Wheeler and Congressman Hamilton Fish were reported by the FBI to be using the same mailing-list stencils used by the Bund.

On July 30, the FBI discovered that America First had formed a special unit for the investigation of Communists under the direction of the White Russian Nazi collaborator George Wrangell. Former Bund members also worked voluntarily with Wrangell to urge the parents of draftees and enlistees to fight the national defense program.

In September, FBI men questioned the arrested Nazi agent Friedrich Auhagen in his prison cell. Auhagen said that America First was an agency of the German Government, designed to distribute its political material. Hoover concurred with this conclusion.

Nor did the war itself do more than reduce the activities of America First. FBI agent and author Arthur Derounian (John Roy Carlson) discovered that there was little or no change in the activities of many figures of the organization after Pearl Harbor. Lists of members were kept in a safe in Detroit by the Nazi sympathizer Robert Vietig, an insurance man who was fond of using the phrase "You can't take Americanism out of the hearts and minds of the people." John L. Lewis remained deeply involved with the Committee. ACLU strikes were engineered in the war years. The Fascist Gerald L. K. Smith met with leading members secretly, as Derounian reported to his bosses.

Detroit, headquarters of Father Coughlin and Henry Ford, became more and more the focus of these activities. An organization known as the Committee of One Million raised money and preached negotiated peace in Europe. Derounian got a job with Garland Leo Alderman, of America First, and typed up twenty-five hundred names of members for new mailing lists. Father Coughlin helped to back the lists with his own personal assistance. Soon, Derounian discovered the continuing common denominator between groups pleading appeasement and defeatism. But by 1943 America First could not do much more than express its annoyance with the war.

✸✸✸✸✸✸✸ 3

The White Book

In their efforts to smear the Roosevelt administration, Hans Thomsen, at the German embassy in Washington, and the America Firsters on Capitol Hill were always looking for evidence that Roosevelt had intentions of war against the Third Reich. Such evidence emerged at the beginning of September 1939, when, after the German Army of Occupation marched into Warsaw, Nazi officials ransacked the Polish Foreign Ministry. They were delighted to find files relating to the Polish embassy in Washington and the Roman Catholic Ambassador Count Jerzy Potocki. In these files there were minutes of meetings between William Bullitt, at that time ambassador to France, and Potocki, the gist of which was that the President of the United States intended to push his people unconstitutionally into World War II.

In one report in November 1938, Potocki said that Bullitt "speaks vividly and interestingly. Nonetheless, his reaction to events in Europe resembles the view of a journalist more than that of a politician, for in his conversation he alludes to the entire scale of very complicated European problems." Potocki said that Bullitt's views were very pessimistic. He spoke of "the complete lack of war preparation" in Great Britain. He added that, in the opinion of military experts, the war "would last at least six years and would in their opinion end in the complete destruction of Europe, and with Communism reigning in all states. Undoubtedly, at the conclusion, the benefits would be taken by Russia. He spoke of Russia with contempt. . . .

"He talked of [Roosevelt] rearming the United States, France and England to cope with German power. He said it was the wish of democratic countries that war would break out between Germany and Russia. . . ." Clearly, Bullitt was expressing the desire of the right wing that Hitler destroy Stalin. Then came the crucial point in the memorandum. Potocki asked Bullitt whether the United States would take part in such a war, and he said, "Undoubtedly yes, but only after Great Britain and France had made the first move." It was this remark that was to plunge Roosevelt into one of the greatest crises of his administration.

There was another meeting between Potocki and Bullitt, in January 1939. Bullitt called at the embassy to say he was leaving for Paris on the twenty-first of that month with a trunk full of instructions, and directions from President Roosevelt, the State Department, and senators belonging to the Committee on Foreign Affairs. Bullitt would present Roosevelt's position to the French Government. The position was as follows: Roosevelt unambiguously condemned totalitarian countries; the United States preparation for war on sea, land, and air would be carried out at speed and would consume the sum of $1,250,000,000. Roosevelt said that France and Britain must stop all compromises with totalitarian countries and must not discuss territorial changes. Furthermore, the United States could give the assurance that it would leave the policy of isolation and be prepared to intervene actively on the side of Britain and France in case of war. America was ready to place its money and raw materials at the disposal of those nations.

Potocki reported to Warsaw on January 12 a picture of the political situation in the United States of America. Potocki announced that American public opinion expressed itself in an increasing dislike of nazism and of Adolf Hitler. The ambassador showed his hand early. He stated, "Above all, propaganda here is entirely in Jewish hands. Jews own practically 100% of the broadcasting stations, cinemas, press organs, and periodicals. Although American propaganda is somewhat roughshod, and paints Germany as black as possible—*they certainly know how to exploit religious persecutions and concentration camps* [italics supplied]; yet, when bearing public ignorance in America in mind, their propaganda is so effective that people here have no real knowledge of the true state of affairs in Europe."

The report went on to attack refugees from Germany and Czechoslovakia who inflamed American public opinion with anti-German abuse. An "artificial war panic" was being created. Roosevelt's attacks on fascism were intended to divert public opinion from domestic problems and the struggle between capital and labor. He hoped, the report said, to stampede the public into endorsing his armaments program.

Roosevelt simply "staged the menace of World War brought about by Hitler . . . while on the other hand, a bogie had to be found that would gabble about an attack on the United States of America by the totalitarian countries," Potocki wrote. The Munich Pact was described as a "godsend" to Roosevelt, because he lost no opportunity in translating it as France's and England's capitulation to German militarism. The report went on to discuss a "campaign of hatred" against Hitler launched by such Jewish intellectuals as Bernard Baruch; Herbert Lehmann, governor of New York State; Justice Felix Frankfurter; and Secretary of the Treasury Henry Morgenthau, Jr. These individuals were "linked with international Jewry by ties incapable of being torn asunder. . . . Jewry was able not only to establish a dangerous center in the new world for the dissemination of hatred and enmity, but it also succeeded in dividing the world into two warlike camps." The ambassador went on, "Roosevelt has been given the power to enable him to enliven American foreign policy and at the same time to create huge reserves in armaments for a future war which the Jews are deliberately aiming for."

Based on material supplied by the German embassy in Washington, this document clearly stated the position of a personage whom most Americans thought represented a country that was a bulwark against the Nazi threat.

The next document unearthed by the German authorities in Warsaw concerned a meeting in Paris in February (no exact day given) between Bullitt and J. Lukasiewicz, Polish ambassador in Paris. Bullitt had just returned from three months' leave in America when the conversations took place. Bullitt said that if there should be war between Britain and France and Germany and Italy in which Britain and France would suffer defeat, Germany would be a real danger to the United States. Thus, the United States would enter the war not from the outset but "only a certain time after the outbreak of war." Bullitt said, "Should a war break out, we shall certainly not participate at the beginning, but we shall finish it."

Bullitt then said that this point of view of Washington circles "lacks all idealism, and results entirely from a necessity of defending the real interests of the United States." Bullitt leaked secret intelligence by saying the President would send "airplanes to France, for the French Army was the first defense line of the United States." He said, "Speaking theoretically, the fear exists that Britain might possibly attempt with Berlin to force upon France, at a moment of tension, a compromise not reconcilable with her own interests. In such a case, France will be able to count upon the strong support of Washington. As far as Britain is concerned, the United States controls various and immensely important means of coercion. The mere threat to make use of them would suffice to cause Britain to withdraw from any policy of compromise at France's expense."

Bullitt went on to say, "The relation between leading American circles and Italy and Germany is negative, principally for the reason that, although they are of the opinion that the recent successes of the Rome-Berlin Axis, which undermine both the prestige and the authority of France and Britain as Imperial Powers, threaten almost directly the real interests of the United States, the foreign policy of Washington will counteract any possible further development of the situation in this direction."

Bullitt went on to talk of U.S. "means of coercion" of an economic nature that could be effective in Rome and Berlin; Lukasiewicz said that it was not clear whether the United States would be prepared to fight Germany and Italy for the French colonies, or to fight for certain systems and ideologies. Bullitt replied that Washington's attitude "would be solely determined by the real interests of the United States and not by ideological problems."

Lukasiewicz concluded: "One thing . . . seems certain to me, namely, that President Roosevelt's immediate policy will tend to support France's resistance, to stay the German-Italian pressure, and to weaken Britain's tendencies to compromise."

This report has to be understood in context. William Bullitt had originally been a Soviet enthusiast as ambassador to Moscow. He had changed, and had moved so far in the opposite direction that he had aroused the suspicions of Ambassador William E. Dodd in Berlin. One must go back to Ambassador Dodd's diary of February 12, 1936, referring to a meeting between himself and Bullitt in the German capital. At this meeting, Bullitt had condemned the cooperation between England, France, and the Balkan states, saying he cared "not a damn" for England and that Lord Lothian's appeasement policy was "dangerous." Later, on December 13, 1936, referring to a story by Drew Pearson charging that

Bullitt had been sent to Europe "to deal with the Nazis because he favors their policies" Dodd said that Bullitt had argued with the French for the defeat of the Franco-Soviet Pact and had "become attracted to Fascism before leaving Moscow." Dodd reported that on the previous day Marcel Knecht, editor and owner of *Le Matin*, had visited with him and had stated that Bullitt was working for an alliance between France and Germany. On November 18, 1937, Dodd remarked that Bullitt had listened without comment to Alfred Rosenberg expounding Nazi philosophy at a dinner in Bullitt's honor at the French embassy in Berlin.

A further document turned up by the Germans in Warsaw was a memorandum by Jan Wszelaki, Polish commercial counsellor, with a fellow Catholic Joseph Kennedy, ambassador to the Court of St. James's, on June 16, 1939. Wszelaki reported that, at the meeting, Kennedy stated that Germany seemed to have no alternative but war, could not abandon her positions, and "would not shrink from a conflict if pressed." He commented "on certain optimists who inclined toward the belief that Germany would be easily and rapidly conquered or who counted on a quick revolution in that country."

Kennedy emphasized the fact that the Western powers would be bankrupted "if the arms race continued for any length of time" but that Great Britain and the United States should "not discontinue or restrict their program of armaments." Kennedy said that the Poles were the only people in Eastern Europe whose armaments and military qualities could be relied upon with absolute certainty.

He asked what Poland required from Britain in the way of material and financial assistance. He said he would see the Prime Minister and Lord Halifax and press them to make a loan to Poland. He said that his two sons (Joseph and John) who had just traveled all over Europe would lecture on the subject at Harvard. He added, "You cannot imagine to what an extent my eldest boy, who has recently been in Poland, is able to influence the President. I should say that the President believes him more than he does me. Perhaps because Joe (Jr.) pictures the situation with such conviction and enthusiasm."

The German authorities in Warsaw rushed the documents to Berlin. They were published by the German Foreign Office on Ribbentrop's instructions on March 30, 1940, along with many other documents including conversations between Potocki and Bullitt in Washington.

German Foreign Minister Joachim von Ribbentrop read the documents at once. He instructed Hans von Moltke, former ambassador to Warsaw, to prepare a special White Book reprinting the conversations. On March 10, 1940, Von Moltke was finished editing and arranging; he had been greatly distracted by other work. Ribbentrop gave the documents to Mussolini, attacking the "Jewish plutocracy" of the United States working through "sinister" ambassadors for the ruin of the Reich. Soon after, Von Moltke gave the documents to Ernst von Weizsäcker, German undersecretary for foreign affairs, who said that the documents were too complicated for the ordinary reader and that they should be held back from publication until "there is a marked deterioration in our relations with the United States."

Apparently, Weizsäcker was overruled by Hitler, because the documents were published four days later. A chief motive was clearly to upset Roosevelt in the coming election. In a memorandum dated March 9, followed by a full-scale press conference, German Propaganda Minister Dr. Joseph Goebbels announced that the White Book would be published the next day, a Sunday, and predicted the documents would create a first-class political sensation, "since they in fact prove the degree of America's responsibility for the outbreak of the present war." Goebbels required that the first five documents be published in full accompanied by a commentary communicated by telephone from the Propaganda Ministry. Publication of the documents was "of supreme importance to the Reich and to the German people. Political organs writing for foreign countries, including even those serving southeastern Europe only, must also, wherever possible, print a photocopy of one page of these documents. . . .

"We inform you in confidence that the purpose of publishing these documents is to strengthen the American isolationists and to place Roosevelt in an untenable position, especially in view of the fact that he is standing for reelection. It is, however, not at all necessary for us to point out Roosevelt's responsibility; his enemies in America will take care of that."

The report of the German Foreign Office was published all over the world. It caused an immediate sensation. It showed conclusively that the American President planned to bring his country into war at a time when the majority of the population and Congress supported peace. Roosevelt had no alternative but to announce that the documents were forgeries, and Cordell Hull followed suit.

On March 29, 1940, German Chargé d'Affaires Hans Thomsen telegraphed the Foreign Ministry in Berlin that the matter had "broken like a bombshell." He quoted Cordell Hull's official communiqué: "The statements have not represented in any way at any time the thought or policy of the American Government, nor have they been made." This statement was reproduced in the Department of State bulletin.

Hans Thomsen had a busy night. The excerpts from the White Book, containing the documents including Joe Kennedy's statements, were published under headlines all over the United States. For twenty-four hours, news bulletins and radio commentaries discussed little else. Joe Kennedy kept silent. Roosevelt's and Hull's denials were followed by denials by Bullitt and Potocki, both of whom were hauled over the coals at the White House. They denied everything they were reported as saying; their official statements appeared in the New York *Times* on March 30. Thomsen pulled strings with isolationist newspaper owners and the documents were printed at great length. Thomsen exulted to Berlin next day, "Thus the widest publicity is achieved in America, and public opinion is informed." He talked of the "unusual haste of the disavowals" and that the government "feels that it is driven into a corner and that Roosevelt's foreign policy is being exposed." He referred to the fact that it was generally recognized that the publication could influence the 1940 elections.

The group that was closely connected to the Foreign Ministry of Germany acted at once. Senator Wheeler used the matter in speeches. He was trying for the Democratic nomination for President with backing from Thomsen.* Hamilton Fish and Robert Reynolds moved for an indictment of Bullitt and even for Roosevelt's impeachment; Thomsen decided not to distribute pamphlets containing the crucial materials from the embassy itself. This would only alert the public. Indeed, he pushed back the idea emanating from Berlin in cables that he should disseminate the documents on the ground that the American public would be suspicious if the material were known to be emanating from such a source. Instead, arrangements must be made for local publication.

Thomsen held several meetings with the wealthy publisher Ralph Beaver Strassburger. Strassburger was the owner of the widely circulated Norristown *Times Herald* and was pro-Nazi. The paper, emanating from Pennsylvania, peddled a line in German sympathies. Thomsen had known

* See *Trading with the Enemy*. German Foreign Office documents published by the U.S. Government Printing Office contain the actual evidence.

him from his early days in Washington and had dined at his apartment at the Waldorf Astoria. In fact, Strassburger had a double motive in courting the German Embassy. A racing enthusiast, he had substantial stables in France and ran his horses at Longchamps. He was concerned about the German invasion of France and secured a promise from Thomsen that his properties would not be touched; Thomsen assured Ribbentrop that Strassburger was emphatically not Jewish, despite his Jewish-sounding name. The response from Berlin was that his property was already secure, and Strassburger was so grateful for this German protection that he nominated Thomsen for membership in his club.

Strassburger's German connections were substantial. He had a substantial holding in the German electrical-appliance colossus Siemens and Halske, as well as in I.G. Farben. The judges for his Ralph Beaver Strassburger Prize for literature contributing to German-American relations were Dr. Joseph Goebbels, diplomat Franz von Papen, and propaganda press chief Ernst (Putzi) Hanfstaengel. He was a keen subscriber to Nazi periodicals. On a trip to Louisville to see the Kentucky Derby, he announced at the table of his private railroad car to eight Democratic senators, including the Democratic whip, Senator Boland, "The United States might still go on and prosper if Britain lost and Hitler won."

While negotiations were going on with Strassburger to publish the documents, the New York publishing firm Howell, Soskin, asked the German embassy if it could consider handing over the White Book for publication. The company received a negative response. But then Thomsen decided to reopen negotiations and sent Manfred Zapp, of the Transocean News Service, to approach Howell, Soskin, as an independent person, not revealing his German connection. The reason for this was that the embassy must not be linked to the arrangements. The utmost caution and secrecy must be observed.

On April 24, 1940, Thomsen reported to Berlin that the arrangements were further developed. He was satisfied that Howell, Soskin, had connections to the Republicans. They would bring out an edition to which the embassy would contribute an initial fund of three thousand dollars. On May 2, Zapp told Howell, Soskin, he could guarantee a circulation of ten thousand copies to useful contacts. Ribbentrop wired Washington that there must be a much wider distribution. In response, Zapp and the correspondent of the *Deutsches Verlag* took embassy money to the tune of one hundred thousand dollars and plunged it into the publishers. Moreover, arrangements were made for the author C. Hartley Grattan to write an introduction. Howell, Soskin, was very nervous about the sheer numbers Ribbentrop requested, since these exceeded those for bestsellers; they feared FBI action. To relieve them of the risk, Thomsen promised to arrange for organizations to acquire large numbers of the book via confidential agents. Then Thomsen contacted Strassburger, who in turn got in touch with Soskin and said that the Norristown *Press* would buy any excess copies of the books.

Finally, the Norristown *Press* entered into a contract actually to print the books for Howell, Soskin; Howell, Soskin, would then sell copies back to Norristown at a discount. On June 19, Thomsen telegraphed Berlin that fifty thousand copies had been bought and distributed; he added that "in this way the majority of the politically influential people, in particular all of the Senators, Representatives, and the entire press of the country are by now in possession of the Warsaw documents."

Strassburger printed seventy-five thousand copies, which went all over the country. In the meantime, Representative Jacob Thorkelson, of Montana, a frequent supporter in the House of Senator Burton K. Wheeler, read the documents into the *Congressional Record.*

There was only one problem. The American public was unimpressed by the documents. They were too serious and complex for mass consumption—and Roosevelt's popularity was unimpaired. *The White Book* (or *White Paper*, as it was known in America), did not impede him in the primaries or stumble him on his path back to the White House that November.

✠✠✠✠✠✠✠ 4

The Kennedy Connection

One individual quoted in full in *The White Book* was in 1939 enjoying an uneasy sinecure in London. Since early that year, MI5, the British domestic Counter Intelligence Service, had been keeping a careful check on the U.S. ambassador to the Court of St. James's, the ever-problematical Joseph J. Kennedy. In a unique example of the pot calling the kettle black, British Foreign Minister Lord Halifax, who continued trying to make peace with Germany into 1940, maintained a perpetual grumble to Washington that Kennedy was defeatist and dangerous in his political views. Certainly, Kennedy, who was not without financial interests in Germany and who was not precisely discreet in suggesting a negotiated peace with Hitler, was not the ideal choice for the London appointment.

In the spring of 1939, Kennedy was in touch with the ubiquitous James D. Mooney of General Motors, whose services to the Third Reich had been rewarded, as Henry Ford's had been, with the Order of Merit of the Golden Eagle from Adolf Hitler. Mooney, like Kennedy, was more concerned with protecting his business interests than anything else. Neither he nor Kennedy was particularly enamored of Hitler; they wanted to maintain the hegemony of the Western Alliance in order to protect their investments.

Mooney was obsessed with arranging for gold to become the general currency of the West, in order to eliminate currency restrictions in time of war. Early in 1939, he met in Berlin with Helmuth Wohlthat, a brilliant, young, American-educated German economist and right-hand man of

Reichsmarschall Göring. Wohlthat wanted to meet with Kennedy, who agreed to undertake a conference in Paris to discuss a U.S. gold loan to Hitler. Mooney also wanted to arrange a meeting between Emil Puhl, of the Reichsbank, and Kennedy to the same end.

Finally it was decided that Wohlthat alone would meet Kennedy. On May 3, 1939, Kennedy told Mooney by long-distance telephone that he would be willing to come to Paris for the high-level meeting; however, he would have to talk to President Roosevelt first. Roosevelt immediately forbade the trip.

Mooney chartered a plane in Brussels and flew to London. He went straight to the embassy from the plane and presented Kennedy with his plans for an American gold loan to Germany, a restoration of Germany's colonies, and a removal of embargoes on German goods, which concessions would lead to lasting peace in Europe. Once again, he urged Kennedy to see Wohlthat. Kennedy called Roosevelt again and again, but again Roosevelt refused him.

Then Kennedy stepped entirely out of line—which is why MI5 began to "cover" him. He directly disobeyed presidential orders by arranging for Wohlthat to come to London. The meeting between Kennedy and Wohlthat took place at the Berkeley Hotel on May 9. According to Mooney's report, Kennedy and the Nazi economist agreed on everything. But Roosevelt was very annoyed and stopped further meetings.

There matters rested for a time. In October, Kennedy made a very curious appointment. He hired as his most trusted code clerk, handling his own and Winston Churchill's confidential telegrams to the President, a highly suspect individual named Tyler Kent. Kent was under investigation by MI5 from the moment he alighted from the steamer that carried him from New York. MI5 would undoubtedly have warned Kennedy of the potential danger of Kent, had Kennedy himself not been under suspicion of collusion with Britain's enemies.

Tyler Kent was a nervous, good-looking man in his late twenties. Born in Manchuria in 1911, he was the son of a U.S. consul whose career lacked distinction. He spent his childhood and had his upbringing in Germany, Northern Ireland, England, and Bermuda; his education included Princeton, the Sorbonne, the University of Madrid, and George Washington University. He joined the Foreign Service in February 1934; he was appointed to Ambassador William Bullitt's staff in Moscow in that year.* He worked as a cypher and code clerk; during his employment, he became increasingly aggravated by his inside view of Roosevelt's foreign policy. He was sure he detected signs of Roosevelt's critical attitude to the Third Reich.

With great determination, Kent accumulated documents in Moscow and took them home to his flat. He made copies of these with a camera and burned the originals. Whether he sent second photocopies to German or Russian sources is unknown. He planned to join the International News Service in New York, which would give him a chance to publicize the contents of the documents—or so he later claimed.

Security in Moscow was so lax that his thefts went undiscovered. According to the British historian Nigel West, a specialist in intelligence matters, Kent was also enlisted at the time as a double agent by the Soviets, but this is insufficiently documented. When he traveled to London in October 1939, he was in possession of his numerous photocopies and his luggage went unsearched at the customs shed. He came under diplomatic immunity.

Once in Great Britain, he was alarmed to discover that Kennedy, in London, Bullitt, now ambassador to France, and the other diplomatic representatives of the State Department were exchanging views of the character displayed in the pages of *The White Book*. There was talk of plans for aggressive war if Britain should enter first. Kent saw visions of American colonialism. His well-educated mind became somewhat overheated. He began making connections in London.

Naturally, as a former diplomatic resident of Moscow, his first link was with the White Russian group that paralleled the clique led by Serge Rubinstein, son of the banker to the czars, in New York, allegedly to use them for the German cause and spy on them for the Russians. Admiral Wolkoff, commodore of the czar's fleet, was living in London, surrounded by other émigrés who dreamed of the accession of the Romanov Grand Duke Cyril to the Russian throne. The admiral, who owned a small cafe called the Russian Tea Room, in Harrington Road, eked out a living supplying tidbits to Nazi agents through the convenient entrepôt of that

---

* Bullitt's role was important in breaking off the Franco-Soviet Pact, which would have prevented Hitler from attacking France in 1940. He brought considerable influence on the Quai d'Orsay in the matter, to the great consternation of Ambassador William E. Dodd in Berlin and U.S. journalist George Seldes.

modest eating house. His daughter, Anna Wolkoff, was a somewhat unin-
telligent woman of pleasant appearance and raucous humor who fancied
herself romantically as a German agent. Another in this little clique was
Captain Archibald Ramsay, Conservative Member of Parliament for Pee-
bles and Southern Midlothian, who was a member both of the Anglo-
German Fellowship and of the more dangerous organization known as
The Link, which issued a periodical of inflammatory character entitled
The Anglo-German Review, which specialized in attacks on Winston
Churchill as First Lord of the Admiralty and on Anthony Eden.

Among the members of The Link were Admiral Sir Barry Domville,
former director of Naval Intelligence and vice admiral in charge of the
War College; Sir Raymond Beazley; Lord Redesdale; and Lord Sempill. A
typical view of The Link as expressed in its official journal (June, 1937)
was that Czechoslovakia was "a tumor in the heart of Europe . . . which
required a surgical operation to prevent it poisoning the lifestream of
Europe." When Hitler performed that surgery, The Link applauded the
accomplishment.

Tyler Kent himself joined The Link. He appears to have been its only
American member. Years later, his mother, in a letter to one of her
friends, described The Link as being an organization of "excellence, comparable to the English Speaking Union."

Greatly encouraged by the customers of the Russian Tea Room, Kent
busily began copying documents of seeming strategic importance and
handing them out to Anna Wolkoff and her father, the admiral. Other
copies went to Archibald Ramsay, M.P., who was busy developing an
organization known as The Right Club, which spread anti-Semitic propaganda. Anna Wolkoff divided her time between eagerly inspecting secret
documents at Tyler Kent's flat in Gloucester Place and affixing stickers to
walls and lampposts denouncing the European war as the work of the Jews
and the Communists. She also organized hostile demonstrations in a
movie theater when Winston Churchill was seen on the screen in the
Gaumont-British News.

Kent talked of taking the documents to the United States when he
would join Hearst's International News Service, which had Nazi backing.
But talk was all it was. In fact, had he released anything of the sort, he
would instantly have been subject to prosecution. Instead, he contented
himself with scattering documents before his confreres.

It is clear that MI5 warned Winston Churchill to be very careful;

that they had their eye on Kent and that all messages that passed through the embassy must be capable of scrutiny without the disclosure of official secrets. When Roosevelt began to correspond with Churchill by telegram, in October 1939, in the easily understood Gray Code, Kent felt his pulses racing. He was convinced he was on to some major conspiracy to drag the United States into war without benefit of congressional approval or that of British Prime Minister Neville Chamberlain. He asserted later on that one of the cables stated Churchill would soon take over the British Government and that he and Roosevelt together would rule the world. No such telegram ever came to light.

The telegrams that did pass through Kent's hands, and which he stole, with Churchill's knowledge, were few and far between. They were dated October 5 and 16, 1939, December 25, 1939, January 29 and 30, 1940, February 1, 1940, and May 18 and 20, 1940. Although Kent later claimed that the telegrams showed Roosevelt's unequivocal desire to aid and abet England, in fact the telegrams cleverly suggest the opposite. They include only the most cautious comments by Roosevelt, who reveals that he cannot offer the sort of help Churchill wants without the necessary congressional approvals.

Nevertheless, one of the Russian Tea Room group made sure that the documents were placed in German hands. The medium for the transition was the Count del Monte, an attaché to the Italian embassy in London; Italy was still not at war with Great Britain at the time. Direct evidence of a leak may be found in a "most urgent, top secret" telegram sent by Ambassador Mackensen of Germany, in Rome, on May 23, 1940, to Joachim von Ribbentrop, in Berlin. The telegram states, "I am reliably informed by an unimpeachable source that on the 16th of this month the American ambassador in London received telegraphic instructions from Roosevelt to deliver a message of reply to Churchill. . . ." The message quoted stated that it might be possible to give Britain forty or fifty destroyers of the mothball fleet, but that would be subject to the approval of Congress. Approval would be difficult to obtain and it was doubtful if the ships could be spared anyway. Antiaircraft guns would be supplied; favorable consideration would be given to the manning of and ammunition for the guns; satisfactory results had been achieved in the matter of steel supplies; and "as Churchill knew, the American Fleet was now concentrated at Hawaii. . . ."

Apparently, MI5 decided to act just after the last telegram was given to the Italian attaché. It is possible that Captain Maxwell Knight of MI5 had a plant in the Italian embassy who alerted him to the leak.

At all events, Knight's team went to Anna Wolkoff's flat and searched it, finding incriminating material. Then Knight himself, accompanied by the second secretary of the U.S. embassy and two Scotland Yard officials, arrived at Kent's flat on May 20. One of the Scotland Yard men turned the handle of the door and found the door locked. He knocked politely; this was England. A voice inside said rather feebly and, in the event, uselessly, "You can't come in." Inspector Keeble forced the lock and proceeded to enter with a search warrant. The team saw Kent in his pajamas, standing at the foot of his bed. His girlfriend was in an adjoining room. The MI5 and police ransacked the apartment. A closet contained a cardboard box with photographic negatives. A brown leather Gladstone bag was stuffed with copies on gray stationery including one dealing with foreign agents in America. There were other boxes containing documents: some fifteen hundred in all.

Kent was arrested and charged officially at Cannon Row Police Station. Without smiling—evidently he lacked a sense of irony—Kent stated that he had photographed the documents with a camera owned by a person named Hyman Goldstein. Apparently, he was not averse to dealing with the Jews he hated when assisting the cause of the Nazi government.

It is clear that the arrest of Tyler Kent was carefully timed to the accession of Winston Churchill as Prime Minister only a few days before. Churchill seized the occasion to arrest the Russian Tea Room circle, as well as Admiral Sir Barry Domville and the members of The Link. Most of these wound up in prison on the Isle of Man by the provisions of a special contingency allowing for the incarceration of known enemy collaborators without trial. It was unfortunate that President Roosevelt could find no equivalent provision in the U.S. statutes.

It was by now clear that Kent was a mere pawn in an international game. There was no question of his being brought to America until Roosevelt had won the primaries in the 1940 election. Therefore, he must be tried in Britain after several months of being kept incommunicado, and the charge must be a breach of the Official Secrets Act.

Thus, an American citizen not bound by the provisions of the Act, was improperly brought to trial at the Old Bailey before a jury in October 1940. In the meantime, he was held at Wandsworth Prison. More facts filtered through in the intervening months. Detective Sergeant Harold

Sutling revealed that he had found records of a visit made by Anna Wolkoff to Germany in July 1939 in which she had been received by the very prominent General Frank, right-hand man of the Sudeten Nazi leader Konrad Henlein. This gave "some idea of her importance and lent credence to the view that she was a Nazi agent." She was also found to have sent letters to "Lord Haw-Haw" (William Joyce), the British traitor who broadcast for the Germans directly to England during the war. Details emerged of her contacts with the Count Antoine de Laubespin, secretary of the Belgian embassy, and the Romanian embassy—names indicative of her range of connections. There were also descriptions of her meetings with the Count del Monte, of the Italian embassy, whom she saw frequently in restaurants in Soho and called in public "Mr. Macaroni." Her friend Hélène Louise de Munck spoke openly of her activities to her bosses: Mlle. de Munck was herself an MI5 agent.

At his trial, which was held behind sealed doors before a jury at the Old Bailey in October 1940, Kent was calm, controlled, and unregenerate. He gave his evidence coolly, stating that he had stolen the documents only in order to expose an improper presidential attitude, the use of an American code by a British First Lord of the Admiralty, and a general failure to preserve the American Constitution on Roosevelt's part. The jury took just twenty-five minutes to decide for the government. Kent reaffirmed his loyalty to the United States before he was dispatched to seven years' imprisonment at Camp Hill, a converted monastery in the southern part of the Isle of Wight.

Anne Kent never rested in her determination to clear her son's name. However, she scarcely went about it in the right manner. She enlisted virtually the entire Wheeler clique, and they in turn waxed vehement in Congress. This was scarcely calculated to bring about an act of mercy from the White House or Ten, Downing Street. She continually charged that the case was totally out of order and that her son was a victim of international politics.

This of course was correct, though for reasons different from those adduced by the inexhaustible Mrs. Kent; she kept up a barrage of denunciations and appeals for years on end. She became arguably the most boring person in Washington, and her voluminous pleading correspondence, now to be found in the ivied halls of Yale, makes exhausting reading.

Joe Kennedy was scarcely more helpful to the cause of history. In an interview with Henry J. Taylor in the Washington *Daily News* on September 5, 1944, he accused Kent of giving the secret messages to the Italian diplomatic pouch to go to Berlin. This was needlessly inaccurate. Furthermore, Kennedy improperly said that if the United States had been at war he would not have favored handing Kent over to Scotland Yard but would have recommended that he be brought back to the United States to be shot.

He would, in fact, not have been entitled to make any such recommendation. He deliberately lied that the Italian connection was established by MI5 when the Count del Monte happened to call Kent during the search of the Gloucester Place flat. He also asserted that the Kent matter had made it impossible to communicate to Washington by code. This nonsense was unsupported, since in fact Kennedy did communicate with Washington during the period in which he claimed communication was not possible. He communicated on the issue that Kent's trial in America would be highly inconvenient. No credibility can adhere to any of his statements on the subject, and it is clear that he simply wanted to distract attention from his own duplicitous role in London.

Kennedy's activities were in fact considerably worse than those of Tyler Kent. Indeed, Roosevelt was so concerned about his machinations that he even held a cabinet meeting, in December 1940, to discuss Kennedy's involvement in a negotiated peace plan with Germany. Part of the plan was to use Bernard E. Smith, the well-known Wall Street plunger, as a go-between in Vichy; according to reports sent to the President by J. Edgar Hoover, Smith met with representatives of Pétain and Göring in France toward the so-called "reconstruction" of Europe. Prominent Englishmen were also involved. Roosevelt was furious when he found out about this. He even asked the ambassador to Vichy, Admiral William Leahy, to stop Smith from meeting with Pétain.

Furthermore, Roosevelt became increasingly aggravated by Kennedy's defeatist statements to the press. He recalled Kennedy via Sumner Welles and secured his dismissal. When Kennedy attacked Lend-Lease, that was the last straw. There was a horrendous meeting with Roosevelt at his country residence, followed by a flushed and irritable Kennedy being driven around by Eleanor for two hours before his train departed, because the President could not endure his presence in his home.

In 1982, Kent was located and interviewed by Robert Harris of BBC 2's "Newsnight." He was living in a trailer park in Texas, still talking about the Jewish Communist plot to get America into World War II. More recently he has contributed an account of his activities to a publication entitled *The Journal of Historical Review*, published in Torrance, California, which also asserts that the Jews invented the Holocaust.

✠✠✠✠✠✠✠ 5

The Capitol Hill Conspiracy

On the morning of August 31, 1940, Harriett Johnson, the efficient and dedicated young secretary of Senator Ernest Lundeen of Minnesota, arrived late for work in the Capitol Building in Washington, D.C. She had been delayed by the worst thunderstorm of recent years. Lightning flashes blazed around the Capitol dome; thunderclaps followed her into the entrance lobby. Yet the storm, and her unaccustomed lateness, were not all that were troubling this serious and hardworking woman. For several weeks, she had been fighting off fears that her boss was in the pay of a leading Nazi agent: that he was receiving sums of money in order to distribute isolationist propaganda under his franking privileges through the offices of Congressman Hamilton Fish of New York.

Harriett was surprised to find that Lundeen had preceded her to the office. Normally, this mild, balding man with pale, fleshy features arrived, slightly flustered, around 11 A.M. But despite the storm he was already at his desk. And he was seated with his head in his arms, sobbing as helplessly as a child.

Harriett asked him what was troubling him. He replied only that he had gone too far, that there was no possibility of turning back. She sensed he was referring to his Nazi connection. But it was not until later that she realized the full significance of what the senator was saying.

Through sobs, Lundeen told Harriett that he had to fly to Minneapolis at once to see his wife, Norma, that he had something important to tell her. Harriett urged him not to take a plane that day; the storm was far too violent. But he insisted, saying that although commercial flights were grounded, he was taking a special government transport plane via Detroit that was leaving at 2:45 that afternoon.

Reluctantly, feeling tense, Harriett drove her boss to the airport. He said nothing during the entire journey, but occasionally his face would screw up and the tears begin streaming down his cheeks. When he boarded the plane, which was delayed by almost half an hour, Harriett had an overwhelming feeling that she was seeing him for the last time.

Unbeknownst to her, J. J. Pasci, a Federal Bureau of Investigation agent working directly under J. Edgar Hoover in the Bureau headquarters in Washington, followed Lundeen aboard. Pasci was under orders from his superiors to keep a check on the senator's movements. Just a step ahead of him, Lundeen bid Harriett a quick, nervous farewell and climbed onto the cramped Pennsylvania Central Airlines DC-3.

Harriett turned to leave. As she did so, she noticed, through the open doorway, some of the passengers locked in a struggle. It seemed that the senator was involved, but Harriett could not be sure.

Lashed by wind and rain, trembling with the reverberation of the summer thunder, the DC-3 taxied down the runway, splashing through puddles and lurching uncertainly on its wheels. The pilot, Captain Lowell Scroggins, managed to make a decent takeoff, but the plane still bumped around as it hopped over the Blue Ridge Mountains' foothills thirty-six miles west of the capital. Suddenly and inexplicably, Scroggins, who had thirty years of experience with this kind of weather, lost control; there was talk later on of an explosion. The plane went into a dive, plowed into a field, ricocheted, bounced forward a hundred feet, then burst into flames. Lundeen, the FBI man, and the remaining eighteen passengers were killed.

Back in the Capitol Building, Harriett Johnson had her worst fears confirmed two hours later. She heard the news of the crash over a crackling radio set kept in the mailroom when she was sending out letters that evening. She was shocked into tears. Later, although official reports denied the fight on the plane or an explosion, saying that the crash was an act of God, Harriett was not convinced.

She had an unpleasant night. Next morning, she did the unthinkable: she examined the locked files that the senator never allowed her to investigate. She discovered many documents which showed that Lundeen was indeed in the direct pay of the Nazis; that he was using his free mailing privileges to distribute isolationist propaganda financed directly from the German embassy and press office. While she pondered on which authority to report the matter to, she was amazed to receive a telephone call from Norma Lundeen, who seemed more afraid than upset by her husband's death and said she was coming to Washington at once. Next day, Norma, a tall, strikingly attractive brunette with a flamboyant taste in hats, walked unannounced into the office. It was clear to Harriett that Norma, who was known for her determination, had not merely battled through an ordeal of a night and a day of bumpy flying in a small transport plane in order to attend to her husband's burial arrangements. There was something in his office that, come hell or high water, Norma Lundeen had to have.

Harriett asked Norma, "What can I help you with?" Grimly, and without bothering to say good afternoon, Norma replied, "The Viereck files."

The files Norma was referring to were the secret files of letters and of instructions from, and financial transactions between George Sylvester Viereck, agent of the Nazi government in the United States, and Senator Lundeen. Harriett had no alternative but to hand the bulging folder over to Norma, who pushed it under her arm and left without another word.*

Harriett was having a hard day. She realized that what she had done could be misinterpreted as concealing important evidence of collusion with the German Government. Even though the United States was not at war with Germany, she knew that President Roosevelt's official attitude was opposed to Hitler and the conquest of free Europe and that the distribution of propaganda from a German source was certainly reprehensible or worse. After consulting with her associate secretary Phyllis Spielman, she decided, fighting against her intense loyalty to her dead employer, to bring the facts she knew to the attention of the FBI. Edward Tamm, of the Bureau, came to see her; in turn, he reported the matter to William Power Maloney, the determinedly liberal and highly charged special assistant to the Attorney General in charge of investigating Nazi propaganda activities.

As Maloney talked to Harriett Johnson, he felt a growing sense of excitement. He was delighted by what she told him. Now he had another important piece of a jigsaw puzzle he had been working on for several months: a puzzle that, as he fitted the segments together, presented an

* It is assumed that Mrs. Lundeen did not know the political significance of the contents.

unsavory picture of corruption and Nazi collaboration in both the Senate and the House. Maloney's researchers had traced the roots of infiltration of government to Hans Thomsen, chargé d'affaires of the German embassy in Washington, as well as to George Sylvester Viereck. But even Maloney did not know the full ramifications of the plot.

The conventional view, sustained by most Americans until this day, is that the isolationists in the Senate and the House were merely misguided, that in their desire to keep America out of the war, to protect young American boys from being killed, they meant well; that they were innocently oblivious of the real meaning of fascism in Europe and that they simply let the country drift toward Pearl Harbor without intending to harm their nation.

The true facts, as William Power Maloney partly determined them in 1940, were less palatable. In fact, some seven senators and thirteen congressmen, most of them directly bribed, others in collusion, aided and abetted the Nazi government by using their franking privileges—their stamped signatures on the letters in place of postage stamps—to distribute isolationist speeches, reprints of articles, and even books through the mail. Many of these were written, co-written, or edited by Viereck, with assistance from Berlin. Thus, the heart of the isolationist movement, which held America back from joining the war on Britain's side and greatly influenced the American public against the British and the Jews, can be said to have been a direct product of the Nazi Foreign Office and, by extension, of Hitler himself.

Chargé d'Affaires Hans Thomsen was, as we know, the direct instrument of Hitler in the matter of penetrating Capitol Hill. He had for several years been Hitler's private secretary, privy to all of the horrifying events that led to the Führer's rise to power.

Thomsen found valuable friends in the devious Assistant Secretary of State Breckinridge Long, former ambassador to Italy and an admirer of Mussolini, who had publicly endorsed Mussolini's invasion of Ethiopia. Useful contacts overseas were Ambassador to Belgium John Cudahy, Ambassador to France William Bullitt, and the ever-reliable Joe Kennedy, in London.

The Thomsens constantly entertained the press at conferences at which they praised Hitler over the cold buffet and talked of his intentions on Danzig and the Corridor, and of the dream of all international pro-Fascists everywhere, *Lebensraum*: "Coal, wheat, and a share of the world's goods." While the press basked in the Thomsens' hospitality, the ugly old red brick embassy on Massachusetts Avenue was a clearinghouse for secret agents.

An examination of the top-secret cables sent by Thomsen to his superiors in Berlin in 1940 and 1941 shows the single-minded purpose of the German Foreign Ministry under Ribbentrop in attempting to secure permanent appeasement by the United States in time of European war.

On June 13, 1940, Thomsen reported that it was necessary to take "literary countermeasures" against Roosevelt, and to this end he had made contact with the New York literary agent William C. Lengel. He proposed paying twenty thousand dollars for a total of five book projects: one by Theodore Dreiser, in which that author would warn the American people against intervention in Europe; one by Sylvia Porter, seeing the economic consequences of war with Germany from a woman's point of view; articles or books by the journalist George Creel; and works by the novelist Kathleen Norris and by the author-publicist Burton Rascoe. The sum was authorized (Miss Porter today says she had no idea where the money was coming from) and paid, but the authors malingered, and then Pearl Harbor canceled the books.

On June 15, Thomsen was reporting that "the Embassy entertains the closest relations" with the isolationists through a German agent unnamed. We have already observed Thomsen's role in distributing the American edition of *The White Book*. He sought funds on September 1 to discredit the liberal newspaper *PM* and was authorized to pay three thousand dollars to distribute a pamphlet attacking that publication. A total of one hundred thousand dollars was guaranteed in October as a "press war fund" to ensure support in political and journalistic circles.

In February 1941, Thomsen personally arranged for the German-American group in the Middle West known as the German-American National Alliance to back the America First Committee via German agents. A "well-known anti-Semitic woman writer" (not named) was induced by Thomsen to organize a flood of isolationist letters to Congress. The Peace Mobilization Committee, closely allied to Thomsen and the embassy, arranged demonstrations in various cities. One such demonstration, led by Irish agitators and organized by Thomsen, appeared before the White House on February 1. The embassy financed a women's march on Washington, accompanied by sensational publicity, that month.

On April 27, Thomsen reported to Berlin that a confidant of Colonel

Lindbergh had called on German military attaché General Friedrich von Boetticher and asked for a suspension of German press reports on Lindbergh's isolationist speeches. Thomsen wrote, "Lindbergh represents the best of the Americans, who are most important for us now and in the future. The contacts with him are maintained through a group in the General Staff which has the greatest importance as a counterweight against Jews and warmongers."

The *German Foreign Office Documents* are filled with telegrams like these, stating outright the financial, political, and personal links established by Thomsen with the isolationists.

Hans Thomsen's most significant contact, aside from Lindbergh, was George Sylvester Viereck, who received a total of well over a half million dollars in three years in order to bribe, corrupt, and undermine members of the Senate and the House, and to finance, distribute, and disseminate isolationist or pro-Nazi propaganda.

Bébé Thomsen felt uneasy with Viereck, as she did with most intellectuals. Viereck lacked the glamour that was expected in diplomatic circles, and most of his meetings had to be kept a secret, conducted in various hotels or private apartments around town, rather than at the embassy or the rented Vanderbilt residence. Certainly, Hans Thomsen could not visit with Viereck at the latter's Riverside Drive apartment, in New York, with its portraits of Hitler and Himmler on the walls. Thomsen, who shared his wife's love of glitzy social events, disliked the hole-and-corner atmosphere of his meetings with Viereck, and yet he appreciated Viereck's maze of underground activities.

Small, slight, scholarly, and coolly intelligent, with acute dark eyes sharply observing the world through rimless spectacles, Viereck looked like a research chemist. He was born in Munich on New Year's Eve 1884. He had a motive, in his blood, for assisting the German cause. He was, so far as is known, an illegitimate grandson of Kaiser Wilhelm I, who had led Germany into war against Great Britain in 1914. Viereck's consuming ambition was to restore the Hohenzollerns to the German throne. Following some early years as a publicist, Viereck moved to the United States in his mid-twenties and became an American citizen.

He achieved an early reputation as a poet in a tradition of romantic decadence. As early as 1910, in his book *The Confessions of a Barbarian,* he expressed a desire that Germany and America be one in the rest of the twentieth century. As magazine editor and tub-thumper for the German cause, he became an outright agent of Berlin in 1914.

He was exposed in a sensational incident in New York on July 24, 1915. Along with his German colleague in espionage and propaganda Dr. Heinrich Albert, he had been dogged for weeks by the famous American secret agent Frank Burke. That day, Burke followed Viereck and Albert onto a Sixth Avenue Elevated Railway train at Rector Street. Viereck left the train at Twenty-third Street, leaving with Albert a briefcase filled with plans of wholesale sabotage of American factories, for an invasion of the United States through Canada, and for espionage involving prominent figures. When Albert rose to leave the train at Fiftieth Street, he absent-mindedly left the briefcase behind. Burke made off with the plans, and next day they appeared on the front page of the New York *World*.

Although Viereck and Albert were engulfed in a scandal that helped deactivate them for the war's duration, neither saw the inside of a prison cell. In the 1920s, Viereck met with Hitler and urged upon the Führer his royalist sympathies. In an article in *Liberty* magazine in 1932, Viereck wrote that Hitler must learn with Mussolini that "political dictatorship and monarchy are not irreconcilable."

Viereck, who continued to write books, including *My First Two Thousand Years: The Autobiography of the Wandering Jew* and the aptly entitled *Spreading Germs of Hate*, often visited his alleged grandfather, the Kaiser, in exile at Doorn, Holland. Viereck was delighted that the Kaiser's son was in the Gestapo. This drew him closer to Himmler, whom he identified more and more as a royalist. He was impressed by the fact that Himmler secretly worshiped at the tomb of King Henry I of Saxony, holding midnight services with capless head bowed in prayer.

Carrying the endorsement of Hitler, Himmler, and Dr. Goebbels, Viereck in 1932 went to work for the New York public relations firm Carl Byoir & Associates, joining Standard Oil press agent Ivy Lee there in pushing pro-nazism. In 1933, Viereck arranged for the German Railroads Information Bureau, an espionage organization sheltering under the camouflage of a tourist body, to enter into a $108,500 contract with Byoir. By the mid-1930s, Viereck was working directly for Nazi consulates, which were headquartering espionage activities throughout the United States. He published a book called *Germany Speaks*, ghosting the text by one Herbert S. Houston. He traveled to Berlin to ghost-write the introduction for Hitler himself—for which the Führer was duly grateful.

The book bore witness to the strivings of the New Germany, praising Hitler's regime in the most fulsome possible terms. Viereck also contributed to Father Charles Coughlin's flagrantly Nazi magazine *Social Justice*, and he supplied many articles on Germany to *Liberty*, with the blessing of its helpful owner, William Randolph Hearst. In 1939, he traveled to Munich and was signed up as American correspondent of the newspaper *Neueste Nachrichten*. He also made a deal with German intelligence organizations to use his correspondent role as a front. Back in New York, he accepted a substantial contract on September 24, 1939, with the German Library of Information, at 17 Battery Place; he was to write regularly for *Facts in Review;* he began by praising Hitler's action in invading Poland and helping to retrieve the ancient German Empire.

With Europe at war, Thomsen began financing Viereck from a special account opened at the Chase National Bank. Viereck was funded also by Hansen Sturm, chairman of the Romanoff Caviar Company, a White Russian organization bent upon restoring royalty in Europe. A third source of funds was General Aniline and Film, third-largest manufacturer of motion-picture and still-photography materials in the United States. Soon, Viereck went beyond simply contributing to magazines; he began working as an assistant to the head of the German Library of Information and personally supervised the distribution of ninety thousand copies biweekly of *Facts in Review* to schoolteachers, religious figures, and lawyers. He also gave money to the Nazi-American Fellowship Forum and to the German-American Board of Trade *Bulletin*. Viereck soon had a quarter of a million people redistributing Nazi propaganda. Much material came on Japanese vessels from Hamburg via Russia in order to avoid the British censors in Bermuda. Some materials were sent in packages within legitimate packages in case they should be discovered by customs officials. By mid-1940, as much as twenty thousand pounds of propaganda were being imported per month.

When Viereck needed additional money, he turned to Rafael Trujillo, Fascist dictator of the Dominican Republic. And soon Viereck realized that he would have to circumvent censorship by distributing violent, seditionist, and anti-Semitic materials through the U.S. Government itself.

His main contact with Congress was the press agent Prescott Dennett, a smooth and skillful young man who had built a small but flourishing business by handling awkward image problems for various politicians and who had a network of connections in the right-wing press. Dennett was not particularly political, but he knew the value of a dollar. Viereck met with him in the Riverside Drive apartment with Hitler's portrait and in hotel rooms in Washington, D.C. He arranged for Dennett to accept mailbags filled with reprinted speeches that Viereck himself had often written or edited. These speeches appeared by arrangement in the *Congressional Record* and were then offprinted in large quantities and circulated either through various Nazi printing and publishing companies or directly from the Senate and House mailing rooms free of charge. In this way, they were not subject to interference by the Office of War Information.

Viereck's first major governmental contact was Ernest Lundeen. Lundeen was secretly pro-Nazi and anti-British, a fact he zealously preserved from his decent secretary Harriett Johnson. The Vierecks were frequent visitors at Lundeen's home, and on one memorable occasion were entertained at dinner with the president of the German Red Cross, the pro-Nazi Duke of Saxe-Coburg. Viereck made a deal with Lundeen whereby he would pay the senator thousands of dollars at a clip and at the same time write speeches for the senator filled with isolationist propaganda. Lundeen always made sure that the Nazi checks he received for the speeches and their reprint in the *Congressional Record* were made payable to specified dummies in order to launder their sources. One of the most inflammatory of the speeches was "Lord Lothian Against Lord Lothian," an attack on the British ambassador, who had moved from an appeasement line to a more loyal British position.

Lundeen received money not only from Viereck but from the German-American Board of Trade and the Steuben Society. He not only repeated the pro-Hitler resolutions of the Society in speeches, but he also had them published in the *Congressional Record* and circulated through his frank. Viereck used Nazi money to hire Lundeen as chairman of the so-called Make Europe Pay War Debts Committee, designed to distract Americans from focusing on German aggression and demanding that a hard-pressed Britain repay its World War I debts in this new time of war. Warming to his theme through 1940, Lundeen, regurgitating Viereck, made even more hysterical demands. He insisted that America should annex all Britain's islands in the Caribbean in repayment for World War I loans. He enlisted the aid of other keen anti-Britishers, all of them under Viereck's thumb and in direct receipt of money from Germany, among them Senator Robert Rice Reynolds, of the North Carolina tobacco family, and Congressman Martin L. Sweeney of Ohio. Sweeney went on the air and read a Viereck speech, "The 100 Families That Rule the Empire." Prescott Dennett had arranged the broadcast.

Viereck began to make publishing deals for senators and congressmen with the Nazi Siegfried Hauck, president of the German propaganda publisher Flanders Hall, of Scotch Plains, New Jersey. Among those contracted by Flanders Hall directly, and financed by the German embassy, the Romanoff Caviar Company, and Rafael Trujillo of the Dominican Republic, were Senators Burton K. Wheeler, Rush D. Holt of West Virginia, and Gerald P. Nye of North Dakota, and Congressmen Jennings Randolph of West Virginia and William Stratton of Illinois. Rush D. Holt, an impassioned speechmaker, known as the boy senator, led the pack. Indeed, so flagrant was his published work that it actually was sent by Viereck via Lisbon for forwarding to Berlin for approval by former German ambassador to Washington Hans Dieckhoff, who was now in charge of American affairs under Ribbentrop at the Foreign Office. The book was returned with extensive changes. Holt unhesitatingly accepted the changes, and the book, entitled *Who's Who Among the Warmongers*, was accepted by Flanders Hall. Holt also completed, under Nazi financing, a book entitled *The British Propaganda Network*, which disclosed secret information on Whitehall's newspaper battle against Germany.

Just before publication, Holt, who by now had received several thousand dollars from Viereck, panicked and decided to take his name off the two volumes. Instead, he had them printed under the name of the Japanese espionage agent Ralph Townsend. He made up for his cowardice by circulating a quarter of a million copies of a slanderous speech against Roosevelt, paid to the tune of three thousand dollars by the German Government through Viereck. In a letter to Berlin on September 1, 1940, Hans Thomsen announced this example of outright collaboration.

As the occasion of Roosevelt's 1940 election approached, Viereck's activities increased still further. Under his direct guidance and financing, Senator Wheeler used his frank to distribute twenty thousand copies of Ambassador Joe Kennedy's *Step Out of War* and Mississippi Congressman John E. Rankin's *America and the War*. Senator Stephen A. Day of Illinois distributed ten thousand copies of *America's Opposition to War*. Senator Gerald Nye distributed an identical number of *No Further Towards War*. At the Republican convention in Philadelphia in June, fifty isolationist congressmen received a total of fifty thousand dollars in order to influence the delegates in favor of isolationism. Moreover, Stephen Day was paid thousands to form a Republican committee that published a "Keep America Out of War" advertisement in the press. On June 25, the first advertisement appeared in the New York *Times* signed by Representatives Samuel B. Pettingill, Harold Knudsen, John J. O'Connor, and Hamilton Fish, and Senators Edwin C. Johnson, Bennett C. Clark, David I. Walsh (under investigation for consorting with Nazi agents), and the inescapable Burton K. Wheeler and Rush D. Holt. It should be noted that certain of these figures were Democrats.

As time went on, it became clear that these activities might easily be stopped. Therefore, it was necessary to centralize them and ensure that the mass of propaganda would emerge from only one office under the Capitol dome. Viereck consulted urgently with Thomsen and with Prescott Dennett, and the result was a decision to use the office of the prestigious New York congressman Hamilton Fish. Fish could not only be relied upon since he was allegedly in receipt of funds from the Romanoff Caviar Company, Hansen Sturm, and Rafael Trujillo; he was also an old friend of Viereck's, who had actually prevented the Dies Committee from calling Viereck in, in 1938. Fish had leased his house at 55 East 77th Street, New York, to Nazi consul general Hans Borchers, Gestapo leader in New York; he had visited Ribbentrop in Germany in 1939 and had discussed cementing of U.S.-German relations; and he had traveled to Oslo in Ribbentrop's plane to discuss Hitler's imminent invasion of Poland with the Swedish Nazi collaborator Axel Wenner-Gren.

Fish introduced Viereck to a second secretary, the small, frail Britisher George Hill, who was identified in court later on as a Gestapo agent. Fish later protested that he had no idea of the arrangements made between Viereck and Hill. However, State's Attorney William Power Maloney and FBI boss J. Edgar Hoover thought differently.

Viereck arranged with Hill that Fish's locked storeroom be used to house the heavy bags of mail containing franked propaganda. Other bags in Fish's storeroom contained booklets and books for distribution throughout the country. In all cases, the envelopes carried Hamilton Fish's stamped signature in place of a postage stamp. Many of the reprinted speeches were passed through the America First Committee, which itself was in receipt of funds from the German embassy. Viereck paid Hill directly, and so did Lundeen, to ensure his complete cooperation and that he would not turn his coat and report the redistribution of material to the authorities. No less than five hundred thousand copies of congressional propaganda helpful to the Germans poured out of Fish's office in a period of a year. There were speeches by Senator Reynolds assailing Churchill, by Senator Clark denouncing Britain as a whole, and by Senator Nye calling for retroactive provisions against Britain. The activities continued until 1941. When the Germans sank the U.S. vessel *Greer* in September of that year, Thomsen wrote to Berlin (September 11, 1941) ". . . in order to demonstrate the danger and the insincerity of Roosevelt's foreign policy by using the *Greer* incident, in accordance with instructions, and through suitable contacts, I got in touch with several of the leading interested senators, numerous congressmen, various journalists, and suitable organizations, some of whom gave me reason to expect that they would press for a Congressional investigation." On September 12, Thomsen reported that his "influence" on such figures as Senators Nye and Clark had paid off. A full investigation was to take place under another useful contact, Senator Walsh of the Senate Naval Affairs Committee. It was only through Roosevelt's direct intervention that the *Greer* incident was not finally subjected to this Nazi-supported inquiry.

William Power Maloney became more and more annoyed by these activities as evidence started to pour onto his desk in the form of numbers of leaflets, books, and reprints. Maloney, a stubborn man of great integrity, with a square jaw and a bulldozing physique, worried his subject like a terrier with a bone. He had worked for three successive United States attorneys for the Southern District of New York and had attained fame exposing rackets in Reno. He had made a specialty of looking into mail fraud. He was aided by a direct-mail specialist and ultra-American liberal, the plump, bespectacled Baltimorean Henry Hoke, who hated all Nazis.

Despite the erratic behavior of Attorney General Francis Biddle, Maloney managed to secure an open mandate from Roosevelt to untangle the threads of the Capitol Hill conspiracy. He began by swearing in a reliable grand jury in September 1941 and subpoenaed over two hundred witnesses, including Viereck, Congressman Fish, Senator Holt, and Prescott Dennett. He also subpoenaed Harriett Johnson to tell her story of Lundeen's death, just over a year earlier.

Classified for many years, the hearings were transcribed on ten thousand pages at a cost of a hundred thousand dollars. Viereck was indicted on October 8 as a foreign agent who had failed to be open and frank in terms of his motives and activities when registering, three years earlier. He was easily broken down under Maloney's withering examination, admitting his activities in full. On October 24, George Hill was indicted for perjury for denying he had known Viereck and for pretending he knew nothing about the mailings from Congressman Fish's office. Much to Maloney's annoyance, he could not obtain an indictment against any of the senators and congressmen involved; instead, the small fry were fed to the wolves.

Not content with being let off the hook, Burton K. Wheeler, Rush D. Holt, Hamilton Fish, and the others tried to have the indictments quashed. They denounced William Power Maloney as a publicity hound. Fish denied any knowledge of Viereck's Nazi connections and said that neither he nor Hill had the faintest idea how the mailbags had found their way into his office. He even said that they had never been in the storeroom but had been found in the corridor and hallway outside it. He stated that they could not have been put in the storeroom anyway, because it was always locked, and that even if Hill had accepted them, he did not have a key. Later, Fish said that it was true Prescott Dennett had suggested franking certain speeches, but that Hill had told Dennett this was against the law. Fish had asked Hill to pick up the franked speeches from Dennett's office.

Actually, as William Power Maloney knew, the bags of mail in Dennett's office were eighteen in number and crammed with propaganda; five minutes after Dennett was served with a subpoena to appear before the grand jury, he had panicked and called Hill, who had boldly sent truckmen from the mail staff of the Capitol Building to pick up the bags and bring them to him. Maloney proved unable to establish conclusively whether Fish knew this.

Fish managed to avoid his own subpoena until two days before Pearl Harbor, and Maloney charged him with such evasion. George Hill himself tried to stay his own trial by charging that Maloney was so prejudiced he was incapable of handling the case. Hill continued to lie, allegedly under instructions from his attorney, former Congressman John J. O'Connor of New York. But at the communion rail of his Episcopalian church one Sunday, Hill changed his mind and decided to disclose what he knew to Maloney.

Maloney was overwhelmed with work preparing Hill's trial. Fish clashed bitterly with Maloney in court, again denying any knowledge of

Hill's collusion with Germany and protecting his former employee to the end. The eighteen mailbags were opened, and three House post-office employees testified to their removal from Prescott Dennett's office. The evidence was conclusive, and Hill was found guilty of perjury on January 15, 1942. Unregenerate, Fish said, after the frail little man in his crumpled brown suit was led off to a jail cell: "I am very sorry to hear that Hill, a decorated disabled veteran of the World War and a clerk in my office, has been convicted of perjury on two counts, neither of which—if he had admitted the charges—constituted a violation of law, nor did either of these charges impugn his loyalty or his patriotism. Mr. Hill is of English ancestry, his mother and father having been born in England, and he has no use whatsoever for the Nazis. As a disabled combat veteran, he had an obsession against our involvement in the war before we were attacked at Pearl Harbor." The New York *Times* dutifully recorded these words without comment.

On February 6, attorney John J. O'Connor made a surprise call on Maloney and offered a proposal, the details of which have never been made public. Maloney threw O'Connor out of his office.

On February 7, Hill was sentenced to serve from two to six years in prison. Maloney said before the judge, "This man is still shielding George Sylvester Viereck, a sworn enemy of the country. Mr. Hill has made no effort to show his good faith or any repentance to tell the truth and come clean. He has not shown that he wishes to do his duty as an American citizen." The judge asked Hill if he had anything further to say. Hill did not reply.

Maloney proceeded enthusiastically but in a state of near exhaustion after night-long sessions of work to prepare for Viereck's trial. He was astonished when without warning Judge Allen T. Goldsborough summoned him to his chambers and said, "Be ready for trial, under me."

Maloney was furious. He was nowhere near ready with his documentation, and Goldsborough wanted to begin the trial only two weeks later. "I'm worn out," Maloney said. "I'm entitled to more time." Maloney also objected to Goldsborough's handling the case, as he associated Goldsborough with the extreme right-wing elements in the government.

Goldsborough said, "You can have two more days. But only two. The case goes to trial exactly when I've scheduled it and I'm going to try it. You might as well get it through your head once and for all that no other judge in this court can try this case except me and the trial will begin whether the government is ready or not."

Maloney was again upset. He remembered how one of Viereck's attorneys, Daniel F. Colahan, had constantly bombarded the court, demanding that Goldsborough try the case. Maloney left the meeting with Goldsborough and swore out an affidavit giving details of the meeting. He demanded that Goldsborough step down, and Goldsborough refused, claiming that the affidavit was legally insufficient to sustain the plea. However, Maloney at last had a very angry Judge Goldsborough removed. The trial went ahead under Letts.

Maloney made a strong impression on the jury. He told the ten men and two women the whole story of Lundeen and Viereck's association. A chief target was Hamilton Fish. Maloney shouted at Fish on the witness stand, "Is it a coincidence that the views expressed in Viereck's works are similar to those you have as a congressman?"

Fish screamed, "The man who made that statement lied!"

"Are you referring to Mr. Viereck?" Maloney asked.

"No, sir!" Fish yelled. "I'm referring to you! I do not think I should come here and be insulted!" He turned to Judge Letts and said, "Do I have no rights? I've been in Congress for twenty-two years and not a piece of Nazi propaganda has gone out of my office to my knowledge or consent. I have had no connection with George Sylvester Viereck and I know him only as an American citizen. I am unaware that he is registered as a German agent. His acquaintance with me was the same as Franklin D. Roosevelt's."

Maloney leapt to his feet. "That statement is a public insult!" he cried. "I ask that it be stricken from the record! Congressman Fish, you would know Nazi propaganda if you saw it, would you not?"

"No!" Fish screamed back. "I wouldn't know Nazi propaganda if I saw it, because I don't know anything about it!"

Asked by Viereck's counsel about his background, Fish described his gallant service in the war and that he had been decorated. "And some of these attorneys were not!" he said, glaring at Maloney. "And no one has questioned my patriotism and no one will!"

Asked whether he had introduced Viereck to Hill, he said, "I don't have any recollection of it, but Mr. Hill says it happened and I'm not quibbling about that." He charged that Hill made a private business of circulating speeches and that he had nothing to do with it. He denied any knowledge of who received the speeches or paid for them.

Norma Lundeen, looking as attractive as a movie star, seized her moment. After answering routine questions by Maloney, she suddenly turned to the jury and, without warning, delivered an impromptu address, announcing that her late husband was not on trial, that she had never seen German embassy correspondence in her husband's office, and that she did not know that Viereck was un-American. It took considerable pressure on Maloney's part to have her step down from the witness stand.

Prescott Dennett was called as a witness for the prosecution but, astonishingly, got away with pleading that his answers might incriminate him and was excused on the spot.

On March 13, 1942, after only two hours of deliberation, Viereck was sentenced to two to six years and fined fifteen hundred dollars in costs. In his summation, Maloney directly charged Hamilton Fish with collaborating with the enemy and referred to him as "that windy warrior who cowered in his tent while his poor, unfortunate clerk took the rap." Viereck delivered a patriotic speech running to over a thousand words after the verdict was given. Maloney interrupted to protest violently when Viereck compared Lundeen and Roosevelt. Viereck said in closing that he wanted to see cooperation between Germany and the United States in a negotiated peace, and that he could not deny his German blood. He said, "Like Luther, here I stand—I can do no other." The statement, intended to be heroic, carried a tinge of irony: Lutheran ministers were working as German secret agents at the time.†

On March 20, Judge Letts suddenly cut Hill's sentence in half. He told Hill that he considered him, based on Maloney's sworn statements, "a dupe who had been misled." Maloney seized the occasion to launch another attack on Fish, saying, "Those who advised Mr. Hill to do what he did should be substituted in his place."

A year later, Viereck's conviction was reversed in the Supreme Court. Both he and Hill were suddenly at large.

One would have thought that the matter would now be closed, since Maloney had clearly exposed the plot and discretion would surely have been the better part of valor. However, Senator Wheeler, Congressmen Fish and Clare Hoffman, and others continued as usual, once again using

† See Chapter 10, "The White Russian Nazis."

the franking privileges—after Pearl Harbor, with, predictably, no intervention from the Attorney General. Since it was scarcely possible to continue distributing propaganda under the franking privileges directly from
the Capitol Building, such organizations as the Republican Nationalist
Revival Committee and the National Economic Council were used.
When thirty-three pro-Nazi seditionists were tried, later in the war, the
aggressive senator and congressmen called for the removal of William
Power Maloney as prosecutor and distributed speeches defending these
"persecuted Christians," under their franks, via a Colorado publication
called *Western Voice*. *Western Voice* was edited by Harvey Springer, a
fundamentalist minister in Englewood who virulently attacked the Jews,
charged the Federal Council of Churches as being Communist-domi-
nated, and called the flagrant Fascist Gerald L. K. Smith "a real man of
Christ," as well as inviting Smith to give a sermon in his church.

Prescott Dennett became a private in the U.S. Army Air Force while
at the same time using free-mail soldier's privileges in 1943–44 to distribute fifty thousand copies of a bulletin attacking Maloney as a "courtroom Napoleon" and demanding that the Army raise money to help the
Nazi seditionists. Soon after this, Senator Wheeler arrived on the panel of
the Senate Judiciary Committee and asked Francis Biddle to remove Maloney from the sedition case. Biddle crumbled as usual, and Maloney had
to step down.

The direct-mail specialist Henry Hoke took over where Maloney was
forced to leave off. He was appalled to discover that not only was the
volume of freely distributed propagandist mail not reduced by executive or
legal action in time of war, but was in fact vastly increasing by 1942. He
prepared no less than fifty case histories and bound them up into a large
dossier entitled *So You Don't Believe It?* addressed deliberately to a public
that was naïve and refused to credit that such goings-on could occur after
Pearl Harbor. The dossier was circulated privately and reprinted through
Hoke's own channels of distribution for his mail services, but (significantly) he was unable to have any portion of it reproduced in the *Congressional Record.*

Among those franked, freely distributed publications he exposed as
emerging from Washington sources in 1942–44 were *America Preferred,*
which charged Roosevelt with bringing famine to America and named the
Jews as the enemies of society. *America Speaks* reprinted more statements
by congressmen and senators discussing the "hogwash" of the Atlantic

Charter, the socialism of the New Deal, and the importance of Hitler. *Bible News Flashes*, edited by Pastor William D. Herrstrom, another fundamentalist of use to the Third Reich, had a headline reading, "God Is Not a Jew." "No one ever said he was in the first place," Henry Hoke added in a footnote in his file. Yet another publication was *The Broom*, edited by the Romanian-American C. Leon de Aryan, the ideally named propagator of such poisonous doctrine as "The Jews are at the root of the world's ills" and "Congressmen Nye, Wheeler, Fish and Hoffman are great men."

Joseph P. Kamp's many publications included *Native Nazi*, a violent attack on Maloney and the Department of Justice. Gerald L. K. Smith's fascistic *The Cross and the Flag* actually started publication three months after Pearl Harbor with endorsement from Senators Reynolds and Nye, who praised it to the skies in public. Backed by various industrialists, Smith rallied a staggering one million people to support the idea of a negotiated peace with Hitler and came close to winning a seat in the Senate from Michigan in spite of his anti-American stance. His favorite phrase was "When chaos comes, I'll be the leader!" Yet another fundamentalist minister, Gerald B. Winrod, of Wichita, Kansas, published *The Defender*, beginning in 1942, which attacked Jews as the anti-Christ; it was partly owned by Senator Reynolds, with support by Gerald L. K. Smith. Howard B. Rand's *Destiny*, the flagrantly Nazi organ of the Anglo-Saxon Federation, stated that the Anglo-Saxons, not the Jews, were God's chosen people and the true Israelites, and that of all Christ's disciples, only Judas was a Jew.

All of these papers, many of them distributed under franking privileges, were listed by Henry Hoke in his special dossiers, but he was unable to obtain results with the Attorney General in having them put out of business. He was deluged with letters, phone calls, and menacing personal visits insisting that he should say no more on the subject either privately or in print. His friends also were threatened. He was charged by printers, direct-mail business figures, and experts in mail selling with having misused his business for the purpose of conducting a vigilante program. His reply was that he presumed these critics were aware that Pearl Harbor had taken place. There was no reply.

Hoke continued until 1945. He drew up maps showing the extent of isolationist penetration. He made lists (obtained through contacts) of subscribers to the subversive publications. He hammered away at the Dies

Committee, convinced that it had been forced to lay off Nazi investigations after Pearl Harbor and concentrate only on communism at the time when it should have been most concerned with Fascist activities. He noted the fact that in several wartime speeches Goebbels praised Martin Dies specifically by name. In desperation, Hoke and friends of Maloney turned to the one organization that most Americans even of the right wing tended to trust: the American Legion. Contrary to statements in the left-wing press, the Legion played an important part in exposing fascism during the war. At a national convention on September 23, 1943, the Legion charged that Hamilton Fish had directly abused the congressional franking privileges by permitting them to be used by "certain groups and individuals including George Sylvester Viereck and the America First Committee to disseminate propaganda inimical to the United States." The resolution concluded with a request to Attorney General Francis Biddle to "take such action and steps as are necessary . . . to put an end to the abuse of the franking privilege . . . and to take court action, if necessary."

Fish issued a reply denouncing the charges as false and "manufactured lies." He categorically refused to even consider the charges, and Hoke sent out a circular stating that "if Fish denies responsibility for what happened in his office, then he shouldn't have that office. . . . When Fish claims to constituents that the exposé of the franking scandal is a campaign to 'smear me politically', he deliberately distorts the truth. No political opponent set up the propaganda mill in Fish's office. . . . No political opponent forced Fish to introduce his friend and 'great American' George Sylvester Viereck to his 'poor clerk secretary' George Hill. The real truth is that Fish has been protected by his political opponents, who didn't want to be accused of using this disgraceful mess as a weapon for votes." Actually, of course, the truth was that William Power Maloney and Attorney General Biddle were unable to prove Fish's knowledge of the matter and that Hill never implicated his boss directly.

6

Close-up on Sedition

Maloney now turned his attention to the important matter of securing an indictment against the most strongly fascistic intellectual in the pro-Nazi American movement: Lawrence Dennis. Significantly, Dennis was opposed to the flagrant and irrational Nazi groups headed by Fritz Kuhn; instead of adhering to Himmler and Hess, he owed much to Alfred Rosenberg. Although he did not entirely concur with Rosenberg's extremist support of the theories of a restoration of the ancient Norse gods and a renunciation of the Catholic Church, he believed in Rosenberg's adherence to a vision of world Fascist power which would join with a newly established United States of Europe and crush the Soviet Union. More than any other of his kind, Dennis was an American who had worked out his thoughts and feelings into something approaching a philosophy; and he was in direct contact with German agents.

Dennis had been employed by the State Department on several foreign desks; by 1938, he had become a special economic adviser to E. A. Pierce and Co., a prominent firm of Wall Street brokers. His State Department and business connections placed him ideally at the center of the Nazi plan to influence Capitol Hill.

Dennis, whose favorite and most widely quoted remark was "I do not believe in democracy. . . . I'm in favor of the revolution of Nazism," was, predictably, a close friend of Senator Wheeler. He constantly played on Wheeler with flattery, support, and contributions siphoned from German agents. He was a keen advocate of negotiated peace with Germany. He wrote a book entitled *The Coming American Fascism*, which was filled with propaganda against Jews and labor unions and looked forward to a glorious alliance with the Führer. He contributed extensively to *The American Mercury*, an extreme-right-wing magazine that peddled a line of appeasement.

In April 1936, Dennis traveled with S. J. White, a partner in E. A. Pierce, to Europe to establish major Nazi connections. Just how much importance the German Government attached to Dennis may be judged by the fact that he was entertained by Rosenberg at several meetings and made useful liaisons with Ernst (Putzi) Hanfstaengl, Nazi Party foreign press chief, who was to turn up in Washington, D.C., during World War II; Hans Dieckhoff; and the invaluable Friedrich Auhagen, who was to become a Nazi agent in America.

Dennis wrote glowingly to his wife of his experiences, describing his indoctrination course at the Amerika Institut, in Berlin. He was received warmly at the Propaganda Ministry; Hanfstaengl offered to help him publish *The Coming American Fascism* in translation, a promise that was kept. The excited Dennis even met Mussolini and exchanged understandably similar views. He gloried in the Nazi Party Congress and wrote to his wife on September 9, "Leaving now for Nuremberg . . . where the world will be told where it gets off." The Führer personally took him with friends to lunch and a tour of the city. His host was Ulrich von Gienanth, who was soon to become (at Dennis's suggestion) propaganda attaché at the German embassy in Washington.

Entirely delighted by his indoctrination, Dennis returned to the United States. He established his position in a network of Nazis including George Sylvester Viereck, Manfred Zapp, Hans Thomsen, and Auhagen. More and more in the mid-1930s, Dennis hoped for a palace revolution or coup d'état that would eliminate Roosevelt; he saw Major General George Van Horn Moseley as the solution to America's problems. He was praised consistently in the German press as a savior of decent Americanism.

In March 1939, Auhagen, with Dennis's support, began the American Fellowship Forum in New York City, a collaborative pro-Nazi organization that published the magazine *Today's Challenge*, with contributions by Senator Lundeen and Congressman Fish, among others.

Dennis's chief contact was Charles Lindbergh. When Lindbergh spoke at America First Committee meetings in Chicago and New York City in 1941, Dennis was on the platform. Lindbergh's pronouncements strongly resembled Dennis's, leading some to believe that Dennis directly fed propaganda statements to America's hero. As examples, Dennis wrote that wars are fought between right and right, not between right and wrong; Lindbergh said that the war in Europe was "not so much a conflict between right and wrong as a conflict between differing concepts of the right." Dennis said that the issue of the redistribution of territory and resources was one that had ultimately to be determined by power; Lindbergh, that there was no adequate peaceful way for a nation to expand its territory and add to its colonies. The Dennises claimed friendship with the Lindberghs and credit for the gist of his speeches. When Anne Lindbergh published her fascistic book *The Wave of the Future*, in 1939, Eleanor Dennis stated (and it was not denied) that her husband had given Mrs. Lindbergh the idea of writing it.

On December 23, 1940, Dennis wrote to a friend of his in Greensboro, North Carolina: "I spent hours Saturday with Lindbergh. I am now working on something to be run under another name in his *Scribner's Commentator* and to be reprinted for the [Verne] Marshall No War Committee, which he is the prime mover of." On December 27 of the same year, Dennis advised another correspondent that *Scribner's Commentator* was a Lindbergh creation. It was one of the most flagrant Nazi publications in the United States.

William Power Maloney worked heroically to secure an indictment against Dennis. He hoped to bring down with him all of the other pro-Nazis who surrounded Dennis by charging them outright with sedition. After Pearl Harbor, Maloney brought about a series of grand-jury hearings following the George Hill indictment. Maloney dragged out thousands of magazines and subpoenaed letters and miscellaneous documents that conclusively showed Dennis and several others to be directly connected to German agents and money sources. However, Attorney General Francis Biddle failed to act on Maloney's urgent suggestions and seemed to do everything to throw obstruction in his path. The congressmen who had so strongly denounced Maloney's treatment of Viereck and Hill raised a violent hubbub against Maloney even after Pearl Harbor.

When, on July 21, 1942, the grand jury was compelled by the weight of evidence to indict Dennis and twenty-seven others in Washington, D.C., Maloney, instead of being hailed as a public hero, was widely vilified across the country. He was accused of being a "persecutor" and a "mocker of justice." The pamphleteer and Fascist propagandist Joe Kamp, later the familiar of Senator Joseph McCarthy, issued a booklet naming Maloney as "a stooge for the international Jewish bankers." Prescott Dennett (ironically, serving in the Army) appealed for funds to fight "the courtroom Napoleon," using the free mailing privileges accorded to members of the armed services in order to do so. The sedition case was declared to be "a Jewish plot" in Kamp's and other circulars, and Wheeler was frequently in Biddle's office demanding that Maloney resign from the case.

When Biddle objected to this kind of pressure, Wheeler announced that he would blow the whistle on the Department of Justice. Whatever he had on the Department is unknown. But it must have been quite substantial, because Biddle literally dismissed Maloney without warning in 1942 and made it clear that he would not be invited to act even in a consulting capacity to his successor. Thus, the most passionately loyal of American patriots was shafted by Nazi sympathizers with the approval of the Attorney General. It should be pointed out that several of the defendants were already serving prison terms for offenses that even Biddle could not hide.

The sedition case was taken over by the correct, precise, and meticulous O. John Rogge, a most experienced and accomplished lawyer who was more middle-of-the-road and cautious than the fiery Bill Maloney. Rogge knew that every effort would be made to show that pursuing the sedition matter at all was a contravention of the American constitutional right of free speech. He was so weakened from the start that he did not feel empowered to act upon wartime security measures, nor could he even take action on sedition and subversion alone; he had to prove that the defendants had actually been paid agents of the German Government, and he had to contend with every effort to obstruct his examination of the appropriate documents in Maloney's files. Indeed, the Department of Justice itself prevented him from getting access to some of the crucial evidence; from the moment he began work, the right-wing press, headed by the Chicago *Tribune* and the Washington *Times-Herald* delivered an onslaught against him. Anyone who thought that war with Germany and the deaths of Americans at the front would alter the views of the extreme right wing vis-à-vis the case in hand was sadly mistaken. It is estimated that only one quarter of the ten thousand pages of crucial testimony taken in the three years and four months of the grand-jury hearing were even allowed to be introduced into the courtroom when, after innumerable delays, the case at last began.

Rogge's most formidable adversary was Senator William Langer of North Dakota, who frequently visited Viereck and other defendants who were in the District of Columbia jail on charges of collaboration. Langer accompanied the defendant Elizabeth Dilling to meetings with other indictees and appeared in the Senate violently attacking Rogge and attempting to clean up the image of the other defendants. He stated that they had children serving in the Army or that they were on "our side" in World War I. He carefully omitted every damaging detail.

When the sedition case began, in the spring of 1944, Langer engaged several of the defendants to address franked envelopes in the courtroom with Langer's signature, containing propaganda which defended them and went out to an audience of many thousands of people. This was done openly; only the extreme left-wing newspapers mentioned it.

The trial began in the U.S. District Court for the District of Columbia on April 17, Chief Justice Edward C. Eicher presiding. The charge was that the defendants sought to overthrow the U.S. Government and set up a Nazi state, in part by means of demoralizing the American armed services with propaganda methods. Rogge charged that the defendants were "equivalents of Quisling in Norway and Laval in France." It was probably a mistake to have included the flagrant Bundists with the others. It would have been better to bring in the Reverend Gerald L. K. Smith, who shared Dennis's propagandist activities in his journal *The Cross and the Flag;* Joseph Kamp; and the invidious Merwin K. Hart. By restricting the case to inflammatory materials and distributions, Rogge was left in a perilous position, extremely vulnerable to the twenty defending counsel, who decided from the beginning to turn the trial into a blatant example of attempted suppression of free speech.

One of the defendants, Edward James Smythe, was a fugitive from justice when the trial began, and had to be brought back under arrest from a point near the Canadian border before the hearing could get underway. Smythe's attorney, James J. Laughlin, had the nerve to read in court a letter from this escapee asking for Judge Eicher's resignation from the case as "a New Dealer." Not surprisingly, the judge declined to accept this recommendation. A commotion was caused in court by one of the defendants, Mrs. Lois de Lafayette Washburn, who continually invoked her namesake in protesting her active suppression and fought with photographers, raising her arm in a Nazi salute. Amusingly, the counsel for Kunze and Viereck asked that their clients not be associated with Mrs. Washburn in the judge's mind.

Edward James Smythe was arraigned before the bar on April 19 bound by ten thousand dollars bail. He engendered a violent argument among the twenty defense attorneys, who also argued that the press should not be admitted. Judge Eicher tried in vain to reason with the hubbub and then fled the courtroom. This delayed the impaneling of the jury for several hours. There was a fight between Smythe's attorney (Laughlin) and FBI witnesses on the matter of Smythe's disappearance and the Bureau's pursuit of him to the border. Quarrels were to mark the trial from that moment on, turning it rapidly into a circus. Smythe was sent to prison, where sympathizing senators led by Wheeler and Langer sent him money and gifts of foods.

On April 23, Laughlin called Henry Ford and Charles Lindbergh as witnesses for Smythe, saying that his client could "not safely go to trial," whatever that might mean, without those distinguished personages present to support his case. He suggested that President Roosevelt stop the trial, because it would cause "racial and class hatred," and he swore out an affidavit seeking to disqualify Judge Eicher as prejudiced against the defendants. He also added the names of Francis Biddle and Martin Dies to the proposed *defense* witnesses.

At a parallel hearing, Laughlin was charged with contempt of court, found guilty, and fined one hundred and fifty dollars; he was then allowed to return to the case. In his testimony, he made clear that the people mentioned as prominent defense witnesses had themselves been of overt assistance to the causes supported by his client and for that reason his client could not be declared to have done anything wrong. This persuasive point of view was perhaps the only note of honesty sounded by counsel for the defense in the entire proceedings.

Stung, Henry Ford made an official announcement in which he said, "This attempt to link my name with those who are charged with disloyalty to our country is a malicious attempt on their part to obscure their alleged misdeeds and has no basis in truth or in fact." Mr. Ford neglected to mention the fact that he was simultaneously authorizing the continuance of his factories in occupied France to build trucks for the German Army.

The first part of April was taken up with impaneling the jury; juryman after juryman, jurywoman after jurywoman, were dismissed because of various degrees of prejudice in one form or another. Elizabeth Dilling and Lawrence Dennis fired their attorneys, and Mrs. Dilling hired her former husband to defend her. Albert Dilling sought congressional investigation of the trial on the grounds that it was impossible for it to be fair in time of war. This suggestion was ruled out by Senator Pat McCarran, chairman of the Committee on the Judiciary, on May 3.

Events took another turn the following day, when defendant Elmer J. Garner, editor and publisher of an anti-Semitic newspaper, was found dead in his furnished room. There was no suggestion of foul play. Another defendant, the evangelist Gerald B. Winrod, stated loudly at the next day's hearing that he insisted he officiate at the funeral service. This was allowed.

The same day, Viereck learned that his son had been killed while fighting with the U.S. Army in Italy. Needless to say, his counsel used this fact to obtain sympathy for his client, who had so clearly represented that very political position which his son had given his life in fighting.

Every attempt was made to show that the trial was the result of a Jewish conspiracy personally engineered by Roosevelt and that the defendants simply echoed the views of distinguished Americans such as Henry Ford. Restored to the case, Laughlin stated on May 5 the embarrassing fact that Ford had contributed financially to Mrs. Elizabeth Dilling and her cause. Ford remained silent on the matter.

Judge Eicher held two other defending attorneys in contempt as the trial went on, thus further confusing the issue, as those attorneys no doubt intended. By May 15, after six weeks, the jury was still not selected. The following day, a frustrated Rogge, at last seeing twelve jurors before him, said loudly, "Let's get to trial!" The final jury included several Knights of Columbus, the ultra-right-wing Roman Catholic activist group. Apparently, the exhausted Rogge could not succeed in showing that these jurors would be prejudiced.

Lawrence Dennis opened the trial by petitioning (as his own attorney) that Prescott Dennett, Smythe, and Mrs. Washburn be sent to mental hospitals for examination and severed from the case. Clearly, he was concerned that Dennett might prove to be a damaging witness, since he had handled much of the direct propaganda links to Dennis from Berlin; the others had to be eliminated because they also would say too much. The judge did not allow the motion and the hearing was continued. Rogge gave an eloquent address to the jury, stating that he would prove the defendants were involved in a Nazi conspiracy to destroy democracy.

The majority of those accused and their attorneys made so violent an uproar of objections and foul language that it was almost impossible for Rogge to be heard. It was obvious that they were seeking to so prejudice the jury that they would bring about a mistrial; the theory was that so much time and money would have to go into arranging a hearing that the matter would be dropped. Rogge made clear above the din that the conspiracy was a real one, that the evidence was concrete, that the accused had advocated pogroms, blood oaths, and hanging people from lampposts. He stated that they would soften the social structure by propaganda, terrorism, abuse of democratic privilege, mutiny, and revolt; that they would seize power by provoking a Communist revolt to which theirs would be a counterrevolution.

On May 18, to loud applause from his fellow defendants, Lawrence Dennis delivered a high-powered address to the jury, calling Rogge's outline of the government case "corny, false, fantastic, untrue, unprovable, and unsound." He claimed that the trial was "a Roosevelt administration fourth-term conspiracy" and "another Dreyfus case," in which the government was "trying to write history in the heat of battle." He said, "Pearl Harbor did not suspend the Bill of Rights;" again and again he shrewdly played on the jury's innate love of free speech. He said that he could not defend himself against the government's charge unless he was permitted to show that the government was involved in "a world Communist conspiracy." It was clear that he wanted to name the Communist sympathizers in Roosevelt's Cabinet, but the judge would not let him.

Dennis made another interesting statement. He said that he had resigned from the State Department because he had criticized South American policy.

Albert Dilling spoke warmly of his former wife's career as an anti-Communist whose works had been reprinted and circulated by the Daughters of the American Revolution and whose book *The Red Network* had been enthusiastically recommended by the *Army and Navy Register*. Mr. Dilling said that he would show that the B'nai B'rith had conspired for her indictment and represented "a worldwide, anti-Christian, pro-Communist secret Jewish fraternal society against civil liberties and the gentile majority."

The issue of the trial again became muddied when Fritz Gissibl, of the German American Bund, arose from the political mortuary to identify certain of the defendants as bundists or Bund sympathizers. This again threw the attention of the jury off the crucial issue of propagandism. Another issue that upset the orderly process of the trial was the matter of introducing documentary evidence. This should undoubtedly have been ironed out in advance. Laughlin again indulged in trial antics by going to Fort Myer, Virginia, to defend a client in a court-martial while knowing perfectly well that civilian attorneys would not be admitted to that hearing.

Although every effort was made to prevent the introduction of documents, Rogge succeeded in introducing the first of four thousand exhibits on May 25, but he seriously miscalculated. Instead of introducing propagandist magazines, literature, and letters from Germany showing the American propagandist connections, he started with documents relating solely to the Bund, an issue thoroughly thrashed out already. Since the German Government itself had disowned the Bund and Rogge's purpose was to establish more subtle and authorized connections, this process of Rogge's was redundant, futile, and nonexpedient. Rogge was on stronger ground when he moved on to show how various leagues and associations had striven toward the establishment of Germanism in the United States, but again he had been distracted by a side issue. Indeed, the only advantage in dredging up the Bund was to show that its bookstores had sold the works of some of the defendants, including Mrs. Dilling. It was far more important that he present the books themselves, and other supportive documentation of most recent date, to establish the defendants' outright sedition.

On June 2, Laughlin again upset the proceedings, by calling for a mistrial on the interesting basis that he had just been indicted in Baltimore for falsifying records in a bank-robbery case. He added that this unfortunate circumstance would prejudice the jury against his clients. He also said that he had been charged with falsifying records of the Florida state prison. Judge Eicher overruled the demand.

Every time that new evidence was introduced, the defense lawyers became hysterical and screamed objections. And each day, Rogge sank deeper into a quagmire of his own making as he tried to discredit the Bund. The heat of the Washington summer grew more and more insufferable; four of the witnesses were excused either because of the heat or because of related illnesses. Another delay was caused when Rogge's assistant broke his spectacles; it became obvious to all that Judge Eicher was wilting not only from the heat but from the constant struggle to quiet down the battery of defending attorneys. It was a peculiar irony that almost all of those attorneys, who had done everything in their power to throw the trial into disarray instead of properly and decently obeying the rules of jurisprudence, were lawyers supplied by the state.

After two and a half months, neither defendants nor prosecution had managed to present a satisfactory case, and the press omitted the few controversial elements in the evidence. The central issues remained untouched. Judge Eicher was compelled to take the unusual step of restricting each cross-examination to three minutes after Laughlin deliberately consumed forty minutes with a prosecution witness, a Los Angeles customs collector who had brought with him a list of fifty thousand names of recipients of enemy propaganda including Mrs. Roosevelt. The collector had waited seven weeks to give his evidence. Laughlin threw the court into another uproar when he stated that each defending attorney should receive copies of fourteen volumes of names of two thousand pages each, which would have resulted in making eight hundred and forty thousand letter-page photostats. That was enough for Eicher. To gusts of uncontrolled laughter, he said soberly that that would be impossible.

Another unfortunate event took place. On June 13, the Supreme Court reversed a conviction of the alleged seditionist Elmer Hartzel, a Pennsylvania economist who had been sentenced to five years' imprisonment on a charge of issuing Nazi propaganda to the armed forces. Laughlin said that the decision of the higher court should prove to Judge Eicher that "We have the case licked." The irritated judge had to listen to the defense argue for a directed not-guilty verdict on the basis of the Hartzel decision. Meanwhile, the bundists kept appearing on the stand, proving nothing new.

Rogge moved on quickly to the issue of General Van Horn Moseley, stating that several of the defendants mirrored the Christian Front intention to place Moseley in the White House. But, by now, both press and public were beginning to lose interest in the case. Eicher firmly silenced defense attorneys when they became notably repetitious and out of order, and he fined Albert Dilling two hundred dollars (his seventh imposition since the trial began) for his untoward tactics. He penalized Laughlin the same amount when Laughlin conducted an outrageous examination of FBI undercover man William A. Bockhacker. He asked Bockhacker, rudely, "How long have you been a spy?" When Bockhacker said his religion was Protestant, Laughlin demanded a detailed explanation.

The defense attorneys ganged up as a club known as the ECC or Eicher Contempt Club and had badges made up with the initials which they wore on lapels or neckties. The badges carried stars according to the number of fines received. The attorneys twiddled them as they walked in the courtroom, for the benefit of the reporters. Eicher chose to ignore these gestures, since he clearly knew that they were intended to cause so severe a disruption that all would have to go for separate contempt trials and the proceedings would come to a halt.

But finally Eicher was unable to endure Laughlin any further, and he told him that he would have to withdraw from the trial. Laughlin was forced to leave. He immediately filed a formal protest with the Circuit Court of Appeals, but that tribunal deferred action. As a result, he turned up at the counsel table the next morning, July 6, and again was ejected from the court. Another lawyer, Henry H. Klein, refused to appear at all for his clients, and every effort made to get him back into court on behalf of defendant Colonel Eugene N. Sanctuary failed. Immediately, other lawyers again called for a mistrial, since Laughlin's clients were now deprived of counsel.

Laughlin filed an impeachment petition against Judge Eicher. Eicher designated new lawyers for Sanctuary and for Laughlin's clients. In the judge's chambers on July 10, Eicher had a conference with Edward L. Smythe and his new counsel, M. Edward Buckley, and O. John Rogge and Joseph W. Burns (his second). What took place at the conference was not disclosed. But the result was that Smythe was suddenly released on a thousand dollars bond, perhaps because he wanted to obtain new evidence for his defense. He was accompanied by two federal marshals. Meanwhile, attempts to declare a mistrial continued.

By July 12, Bund matters were still being discussed and Rogge had not moved on the propaganda matter. Robert Noble, one of the defendants, behaved with such unruly lack of control, rejecting his lawyer out of hand and making statements out of order, that his case was severed from that of the other defendants, as he had hoped, and he had to have a new trial separately. Another defendant, David J. Baxter, was also severed, because he was too deaf to hear anything that was going on in the courtroom. New York lawyer Henry H. Klein was cited in contempt. Defendant James True was absent for weeks because of illness.

At long last, late in July, Rogge reached the crucial propaganda/ seditionist issue, citing leaflets and other materials that showed an attempt to incite anti-Americanism in the armed services. One document emanating from George Deatherage talked of the fight against Jewish communism taking place in the streets. Rogge produced copies of a German-American newspaper filled with Nazi propaganda after Pearl Harbor. But unfortunately the proceedings were disrupted yet again when one of the defending team turned from grilling a prosecution witness to fly with coat flapping down the aisle to catch a woman as she passed the door and tell her he was the only lawyer who could handle her divorce case, reemerging in the court triumphantly waving a two hundred dollar retainer check.

On July 25, after fourteen weeks, Rogge started in on General Van Horn Moseley and the plot to overthrow the government. Despite a barrage of screams, yells, and beatings of fists on tables, he pressed on, producing letters by William Dudley Pelley to Moseley stating such things as: "The weapons are in our hands to hurl this overseas crowd of subversionists out of our country. . . . I am carrying in my head, my dear General, information of so colossal a character that I feel it should be shared by at least four other men besides myself: namely Henry Ford, Col. Lindbergh, Senator Wheeler and yourself. . . . I am already in contact with Mr. Ford and [am] leaving for Detroit in the morning to see him again." Ford naturally denied any knowledge of this matter and so did Moseley.

Rogge was warming up at last. He produced a letter from Colonel Sanctuary to Pelley discussing "a special deal" whereby Roosevelt won the 1936 Catholic vote. Albert Dilling said that introducing this was designed to prejudice the seven Catholic jury members. Several attorneys said they, too, were Catholic and that the introduction of the statement was a disgrace. Another letter came directly from the Amerika Institut, in Germany, to Pelley.

Evidence showed that George Deatherage had made his home near an army camp in West Virginia, where he entertained officers and infiltrated their minds with thoughts of Fascist revolution. Absentee defendant James True was discovered to have talked with Deatherage about killing the President. Rogge also showed the defendants' connections to the White Russian Fascists. Further documents came from Los Angeles, stored in the Deutsches Haus by Hermann Schwinn.

The death of a district-court judge brought about yet another delay; the press by now was relegating the case to the most obscure back columns. By late September, very little evidence was being introduced, while defense lawyers were being prosecuted on contempt charges. On October

6, Roosevelt condemned "Silver Shirts and others on the lunatic fringe," and immediately counsel again sought a motion for mistrial because the President's statement could influence the jury. This, despite the interesting fact that the jury was not permitted access to newspapers and radio and was two-thirds Republican. When this effort failed, Dennis issued a statement saying, inter alia, "We challenge the right of the President or any other Federal official to use free time given him over the radio to denounce a defendant in this trial during the course of the trial. I hold that this Executive intervention is the last straw." Some defense attorneys called for the case to be deferred until after the 1944 election; no doubt they hoped that Thomas E. Dewey would be elected.

An interesting witness turned up on October 11. Former Nazi official Hermann Rauschning testified that Hitler had told him personally that the unity of the United States could be paralyzed in an internal revolution and had laid down the plans. On November 30, Edwin P. Banta was found guilty of being a traitor to his country in a court of special sessions. He was charged with a conspiracy to destroy the sedition case. This was a step forward, but, sad to say, on the same morning, Judge Eicher, exhausted, had died of a heart attack in his sleep. He had made his way through 3 million words in almost eighteen thousand pages weighing more than one hundred fifty pounds. Rogge had called thirty-nine out of a total of sixty-seven witnesses. There had been five hundred motions for mistrial or directed verdict, a total of $1,220 in fines for seven defense lawyers, and one death and two severances from the trial.

Associate Justice James M. Proctor polled defending counsel immediately; they naturally asked for a mistrial. After one week of deliberation, he granted them a favorable decision, on November 27. And there the matter rested. Despite the massive testimony and documentation, the case was closed, and all except those bundists already in prison were free.

Rogge was left with many weeks of unused evidence in his hands. Included in this was massive material showing how defendant Gerald B. Winrod was directly in the service of the German Propaganda Ministry, had distributed a massive amount of propaganda against the Jews, and was a chief figure in propaganda distribution of other kinds. Elizabeth Dilling was shown to have heiled Hitler at the Nuremberg party congress and to have associated with members of the Luftwaffe; she had conducted a campaign to help Hermann Schwinn. An enormous amount of evidence had been collected on Edward James Smythe, showing that he was linked to every branch of the German diplomatic corps and had brought together the Bund and the Ku Klux Klan in meetings in 1940. He had been on record as saying, "I look upon Hitler as the second Jesus Christ of the modern world." But none of Rogge's evidence of sedition and collaboration was of any use.

With the war over, government interest waned—to the combined joy of Senators Wheeler, Langer, and Nye and the other Fascists on Capitol Hill. Rogge traveled to Germany as special assistant to Attorney General Tom Clark, who replaced Biddle when Biddle became a member of the judicial team at Nuremberg. In interrogating Herbert von Strempel, formerly first secretary of the German embassy in Washington, Rogge learned that Lawrence Dennis was a paid Nazi agent who had received fifteen thousand dollars from the embassy to publish his *Weekly Foreign Letter*. Rogge realized that he and Maloney before him had been right to single out Dennis as the first target; he tried desperately to attempt a new trial of Dennis and the seditionists. But already it was clear that the more important American enemy, Russia, was beginning to preoccupy everybody's mind. Even when Rogge denounced Senator Langer for having attempted to aid and abet the enemy, few people seemed interested.

Rogge embarked on a lecture tour in October 1946 to tell America of the still existing Nazi danger in its midst. Among those he named directly were Burton K. Wheeler, Lindbergh, and William Randolph Hearst. Wheeler, according to Rogge, went to see President Truman and demanded that Rogge be removed from office.

On the night of October 25, Rogge flew from Washington, D.C., enroute to Seattle, the first leg of his tour. He had been given official leave of absence and permission to undertake the tour.

The plane was scheduled to stop at Billings, Montana; he intended making a side trip to Missoula to see friends. But due to severe weather conditions the plane had to continue to Spokane, where it stopped, apparently without refueling.

With a storm beating at the aircraft, a hostess came up to Rogge and said all of the seats had been sold and he would have to leave at once. Feeling very annoyed, puzzled, and confused, Rogge made his way down the gangway and across a rainswept tarmac to the airport building. An official was waiting for him. The official said that a "Mr. Savage" of the government was coming to see him and he must wait. Rogge had never heard of anybody by that name. After about an hour's wait, Rogge's plane took off and the person calling himself Mr. Savage appeared. By now, it was obvious that the choice of Spokane as a landing place had not been accidental.

Savage produced a badge; he identified himself as an FBI man. He handed Rogge a letter. The letter was not signed but bore the name Tom Clark. It stated that Rogge was fired as of that instant and there would be no question of appeal. Shocked beyond words, but knowing all too well why he had been punished, Rogge listened in amazement as the FBI man asked him to hand over all Department of Justice papers, documents, and materials in his possession. "This is all I have!" Rogge said sharply. He handed his Department of Justice parking shield to Savage.

He returned to private practice. Like Maloney before him, he realized that the forces of American fascism were too strong for liberals like himself. Already, the path was firmly paved for the Cold War and the McCarthy Era.

7

The Father of
the Little Flower

Throughout the sedition trial, the defendants were continuously supported by Father Coughlin. If any single building could be said to have been the center of fascism in the United States, it was his Shrine of the Little Flower, in Royal Oak, a suburb of Detroit. The shrine was thought out in terms resembling those of a Cecil B. De Mille spectacular, combining in equal measure the vulgar and the ecclesiastical. It was fashioned in the form of a large, somewhat phallic tower of marble and granite, the profanity of which was more or less relieved by a colossal figure of Jesus Christ impaled upon a crucifix. Apparently, the moral significance of this impalement, which Father Coughlin symbolically performed whenever he opened his mouth, was lost upon him, as it was upon his followers and the Bishop of Detroit.

Across the street, Coughlin established the Shrine Super Service station, which not surprisingly supplied the useful products of Shell and Standard Oil of New Jersey. The profits flowed directly into the Father's well-lined pockets. Within the station, there was a thriving hot-dog stand which peddled crucifixes, prayer books, Coughlin-signed leather-bound copies of the Vulgate, swastikas (which were more expensive but no less popular) and reproductions of the Iron Cross, First and Second Class—which were not only purchased by men. On a separate newsstand were copies of Coughlin's Nazi periodical *Social Justice* and of *Mein Kampf*, the *Life of Pope Pius XI,* and Alfred Rosenberg's *The Myth of the Twenti-*

eth Century—despite the fact that the Rosenberg doctrine of pagan worship of the ancient Norse gods was entirely unacceptable to the Vatican.

Coughlin's history is instructive. On October 5, 1930, he began broadcasting his unique blend of distorted Christianity, puffery for the Third Reich, and support for the rapidly rising Nazi Party. He appeared on the Jewish William Paley's CBS radio network, rapidly gaining an audience of millions. At his peak, he employed a staff of one hundred, which diligently worked in the bowels of his sanctified edifice sorting out the influx of mail. On January 4, 1931, he preached an inflammatory gospel on behalf of the international fraternity of money; he gave a speech, written by Congressman Louis McFadden of Pennsylvania, spinning out a party line that the Treaty of Versailles was the cause of the world depression. When CBS sought to censor him, he went on the air to denounce the network and told his listeners that his speech had been cut. Thus, severely reminded of the Bill of Rights, an embarrassed Paley had no alternative but to allow Coughlin airplay.

Coughlin continued to invoke Jeffersonian principles of free speech in order to issue a series of broadcasts which were in contradiction of Jeffersonian ideals. He bragged of Hitler and Mussolini as leading exponents of Christianity. One article in his magazine *Social Justice* on April 3, 1939, read: "The Rome-Berlin Axis is serving Christendom in a peculiarly important manner." Peculiar was right; but Coughlin seemed oblivious to the cosmic absurdity of his statement. So humorless was the priest that he had his editor, the ubiquitous E. Perrin Schwartz, chastise liberal journalist George Seldes for having had the nerve to say that *Social Justice* was a Fascist publication. In the same issue, the priest pronounced the dictum that Hitler was the person who had rectified the injustices of the Treaty of Versailles. How Coughlin managed to reconcile these two statements in the same issue, only the God he constantly invoked could answer.

Coughlin recommended that the United States become a Fascist corporate state in which by some mysterious osmosis "democracy would be perfected." He did not specify who would be President but that scarcely seemed necessary in the circumstances. No doubt Wheeler or a papal representative in the White House would have greatly appealed to his readers. Having absorbed his views on the excellence of Hitler's conquest of Europe, they were presumably ready for anything. And the circulation of this publication had reached an estimated one million a week by 1940. At times, Coughlin's pages followed on Hans Thomsen's dispatches with alarming speed. When the British vessel *Athenia* was torpedoed off the coast of Ireland, just before war broke out in Europe, *Social Justice* repeated the Hitler-Ribbentrop line that the British had sabotaged the vessel to provoke the United States into the war—as the sinking of the *Lusitania* had done in World War I.

A regular contributor to *Social Justice* was one "Leon Hamilton," whose real name was Father Jean Baptiste Duffee, of the Franciscan Friars Church of New York. Duffee wrote many political articles for the magazine; he arranged the Father Coughlin birthday ball at Prospect Hall, in Brooklyn, arranged by Coughlin's fanatical Christian Fronters, on October 25, 1939. Duffee was the contact between Coughlin and Boris Brasol, author and White Russian forger of *The Protocols of the Learned Elders of Zion.* Coughlin reprinted the *Protocols* in *Social Justice* at a time when Brasol had obtained an appointment as special assistant to New York State Senator Frederic Coudert. Coughlin circulated the *Protocols* through the publishing house owned by William Dudley Pelley (leader of the Gestapo-like Silver Shirts), who had served with the Japanese in Siberia in 1918 when he became convinced that Jews were financing the Russian revolution.

In the primaries before the 1940 election, Coughlin spread venomous anti-Roosevelt propaganda, charging the President with being Jewish and encouraging the Christian Fronters to paint Semitic noses on posters of his face wherever they found it. On November 20, 1938, Coughlin wrote a glowing account (repeated on CBS and in a public speech) of the reasons for Nazi ill treatment of Jews; regurgitating the canard that Jews were Communists, he said, "Nazism was conceived as a political defense mechanism against Jewish Communism, and was ushered into existence as a result of the same." The speech was approved most earnestly by Dr. Goebbels and Hitler; Archbishop Edward Mooney tried to have Coughlin make a retraction, but Pope Pius XII stepped in and gave Coughlin support. A week later, Coughlin charged that Jewish bankers had financed the Russian revolution—a main theme of *Mein Kampf.* On his CBS radio program, he poured scorn on the Jewish musical figures Jascha Heifetz, Mischa Elman, and Fritz Kreisler, and added for good measure, "I bet that Einstein fellow eats with his knife and is fooling everyone with his relativity theory. Someday the Jews will get what's coming to them. Just wait and see."

Coughlin repeated Dr. Goebbels's speeches verbatim. As an example,

Goebbels said in a speech that winter, "On the 26th of December, 1918, one of the Socialist members of the Reichstag, the Jew Dr. Oscar Cohn, declared that on the fifth of the previous month he had received four million rubles . . . for the purpose of the German revolution." Coughlin repeated this word for word. In other speeches, Goebbels described the shooting of hostages by Communist terrorists in 1918 and in 1919 under the Bolshevik regime of Béla Kun.

Coughlin wrote on April 11, 1939, in a round robin to subscribers: "AntiChrist is riding high, wide and handsome. Meanwhile, the Jews of America have not condemned Communism. Meanwhile, the government of America is fostering relations with Communistic states."

Archbishop Spellman was under a bombardment of demands to stop the Christian Fronters. But despite the fact that almost all the Christian Fronters were Catholic, Spellman did nothing whatsoever about them.

At several of Coughlin's speeches in 1940, the cry from the audience came: "Kill the Jews!" He continued to praise General Franco, Hitler, Mussolini, and Tojo. He proposed Wendell Willkie for President, since, despite Willkie's pro-Semitic stand, he was considered to be suitable because he hoped to bring down Roosevelt. He suggested Lindbergh for Vice President. He described the conflict between Roosevelt and Willkie as "Marxism versus Americanism." He was greatly embarrassed when Willkie repudiated Coughlin and his one million readers for their fascism; and he was even more devastated by Roosevelt's triumph in the November 1940 elections. He violently attacked the Civil Service Commission for opening the ranks to Negroes and Orientals; he not only published articles denouncing the Commission but even inveigled the famous Father Flanagan of Boys Town into supporting his racist position. By a peculiar irony, the Jewish Louis B. Mayer, a member of Frank D. Buchman's Moral Rearmament movement, of which Himmler and Hess were also members, made a sanctimonious film about Father Flanagan, carefully omitting the fact that Flanagan was a leader of anti-Semitism under Coughlin.

Monsignor John A. Ryan, liberal leader of the Catholic hierarchy, and Alfred E. Smith, famous Catholic layman and onetime governor of New York, denounced Coughlin as a liar and seditionist, and Coughlin in turn called for a new Führer, not named but indirectly disclosable as Senator Burton K. Wheeler, who could discipline these dissident Catholics. Coughlin worked for his close friend Henry Ford, whom he had forgiven for pouring a fortune into Soviet Russia, in setting up a "company union" that would break up the labor unions in Detroit. Coughlin worked closely with work bosses Harry D. Bennett and John Koos in inviting Homer Martin, head of the United Automobile Workers, to dine at the Shrine of the Little Flower.

Coughlin's terrorists engaged in sabotage in U.S. Army camps and encouraged protests against lengthening of service. The U.S. Army chief of staff, General George C. Marshall, charged Coughlin directly with collusion, duplication of Nazi phraseology, and expressions of bundist philosophy as shown in the documents produced by Army Intelligence showing infiltration in the ranks, but nothing was done. Simultaneously, Wheeler was distributing propaganda to the troops under his franking privilege and was never punished for it.

Coughlin's influence spread to Hollywood. He backed the KGOR radio fanatic G. Allison Phelps, who broadcast daily a poisonous doctrine of anti-Semitism and used the offices of North Carolina's Senator Robert R. Reynolds as a source of information in Washington. Coughlin also supported Nazi-connected motion-picture writer/director Russell Mack, who was in turn paying Phelps for his Nazi activities.

Coughlin attacked Roosevelt's Jewish supporters, including Justice Felix Frankfurter, Bernard Baruch, and Secretary of the Treasury Henry Morgenthau, Jr. Lend-Lease was a particular object of his hatred, along with the repeal of the Neutrality Act. *Social Justice* continued as usual after Pearl Harbor. Three months later, on March 16, the paper stated that Hitler's destruction of the Jews was entirely in order. In another issue, the paper attacked the U.S. Government for sending food parcels to England and Russia when American children were "on the edge of starvation." The American alliance with Russia was most blisteringly attacked. Firm predictions were given that Hitler would win the war. The Nazi propaganda broadcasts in Berlin were picked up by Coughlin in the basement of the Shrine of the Little Flower and carried with him to the tower, from whence he delivered his hortatory broadcasts. Dr. Seuss parodied him in *PM;* Seuss showed Hitler leafing through *Social Justice* as Germany's leader called the good father in Detroit. The caption read, "Not bad, Coughlin . . . when are you going to start printing it in German?" Coughlin compared such attacks to Christ's crucifixion.

Coughlin played a significant role in the matter of the Spanish rescue-ship mission. In April 1940, the Spanish Refugee Relief Committee in

New York was advised that the French Government had ordered all Spanish Loyalists in French concentration camps back to Spain. The Relief Committee picketed the Vichy Consulate in Manhattan to protest what would virtually have been a death warrant for 150,000 men and women. The New York police, on orders from Mayor LaGuardia, broke up the picket line and arrested the picketers. Influenced by Coughlin's agents and representatives of Frederic Coudert, Boris Brasol, and others in the Coughlin circle, the press, headed by *Social Justice*, and even the liberal New York *Post* condemned the picket as a Communist plot, with the result that public feeling turned against the Loyalists. When Mrs. Eleanor Roosevelt wrote a column in the *World-Telegram* favoring aid for the refugees, the column was killed. A committee, formed ad hoc under Helen Keller, managed to raise thirty thousand dollars for a rescue ship, and the National Maritime Union offered to sail the vessel free from France. However, the State Department, under pressure from the ever unhelpful Breckinridge Long, would not permit the refugees to land at a United States port, so they were sent to Mexico.

Mrs. Roosevelt uncharacteristically yielded to pressure and withdrew from the rescue ship, endorsed by the New York *Times*, which had already denounced the voyage as Communist-inspired. The *Times*, with perhaps unconscious irony, announced that Eleanor had withdrawn because she wanted to work instead with the Red Cross, which the same week was sending substantial food shipments to General Franco while declining to take an interest in the Loyalist rescue mission.

Coughlin also zeroed in on Paul J. Kern of the Civil Service Commission, who was trying to remove barriers of race, color, religion, and politics in the hiring of government employees. Coughlin and the Christian Front began a campaign against Kern and the CSC, condemning the appointment of Jews to the New York City police force while at the same time filling Commissioner Valentine's ranks with Coughlinites.

Coughlin, after Willkie's defeat, nominated Martin Dies for President, a curious choice in view of Dies's investigation into Nazi activities. However, Dies's targets largely consisted of Communists and the German-American Bund activities that were already discredited in Berlin.

Although Monsignor John A. Ryan exposed Coughlin in the pages of *Commonweal*, the father of the Little Flower remained uncondemned by the Pope, Archbishop Spellman, or any other leading figure of the Catholic Church. And he enjoyed the support of Colonel McCormick in the

Chicago *Tribune*, who would soon leak state secrets concerning a planned American attack on Germany and occupied Europe.

Coughlin was very much behind New York State Senator Frederic Coudert, of Coudert Bros., employer of Boris Brasol at the time. Established by the New York legislature as the result of lobbying by Coughlin and his associates, the Coudert Committee started up in 1940. It launched a full-scale campaign against teachers at New York colleges, rooting out Jews and alleged Communists through a barrage of lawyers, propaganda material, and disruptive tactics in the American Federation of Teachers. Taking up the cry of *Social Justice* that the City College of New York was the focus of Jewish communism and a poisonous influence on American youth, the committee succeeded in suspending thirty-five teachers at that institution on the basis that they were of Semitic race and "Red" persuasion. Not only were the teachers suspended, they were hailed with threatening anonymous letters and postcards filled with disgusting language. One teacher's son was seized by Christian Fronters and his forehead was branded with a swastika. The schools were covered with anti-Semitic slogans and stickers, and fights were encouraged between blacks and Jewish students. "Our efforts were proved to be fruitful," *Social Justice* complacently announced.

The Coudert Committee introduced questionnaires demanding to know religious affiliation before appointments were made. When the teachers' union went to the American Education Association, under Dr. Milo F. McDonald, and the Teachers' Alliance, under Francis S. Moseley, they might as well have dropped their petitions into the Grand Canyon. Both McDonald and Moseley were contributors to the Coughlinite weekly *The Tablet*, a rabid racist periodical, while the Education Association's own publication *The Signpost* condoned the Christian Front and condemned its opponents. Both publications trumpeted the splendors of the Coudert Committee.

Despite a constant outcry from the Jewish press, backed up by careful documentation of the Coudert activities, the New York legislature and government did not intervene. The keen Coughlinite Timothy Murphy, a teacher at Gompers Vocational High School, was accused in sworn statements by thirteen teachers of brutality to Negroes and Jews, the use of students as spies on teachers, and distribution of Christian Front propaganda among young boys. Coudert even went to the extent of setting up star-chamber hearings under attorney Paul Windels, a supporter of

Coughlin, who interrogated teachers and students on their racial backgrounds and religious beliefs without giving them benefit of counsel. Formerly Mayor LaGuardia's attorney, Windels, was approved by the mayor and his Board of Education appointees. The star chamber compelled and coerced its victims by processes of intimidation to give testimony whereby teachers would be convicted. Simultaneously, Windels was allegedly mulcting the city of New York out of one and a quarter million dollars in payment of advertising contracts for the Independent Subway.

The Committee even succeeded in obtaining teachers federation membership lists, which it published in the Hearst paper the *Journal-American* along with smears of one member after another. Immediately afterward, New York radio stations banned the union's radio program, "The Truth About the Schools," and when one station dared to run it, the Coudert Committee subpoenaed the managers and forced them to yield up a list of the actors and technicians. This action, and further action against the suspended teachers, resulted in a public meeting at which Coudert's supporters sang "The Star-Spangled Banner."

In all of these activities, Coudert was completely supported by the *Protocols'* Boris Brasol. Brasol was head of the United Russian National Organizations of America, a coalition of all anti-Semitic, pro-Nazi, and pro-Japanese Russian White Guard groups in the United States. Before the Russian revolution, Brasol had been one of the leaders of the Black Hundreds, a czarist organization devoted to terrorism. Coudert had his own Fascist connections. One of his partners was Paul Fuller, secretary and director of Coty perfume, which had founded the Fascist newspaper *L'Ami du Peuple.* François Coty had subsidized the Fascist organization known as Croix du Feu. Fuller was attorney to the anti-Semitic Prince Louis II of Monaco, grandfather of Prince Rainier. As chairman of the Chapultepec Land Improvement Company of Mexico, Frederic's father constantly attacked land reform in Mexico. On May 25, 1941, Frederic Jr. wrote a letter to the New York *Herald Tribune* asking for understanding of the Vichy regime and Pétain's struggle to rescue France. In this, he entirely reflected his friend Coughlin's views. Coudert Jr. defended attempts to annex the French treasure seized from the Belgians; he claimed that the annexation was legal—a claim sustained also by Adolf Hitler.

Coughlin sent his business editor Leo Reardon to Berlin to see Hitler in an attempt to make Hitler give a public statement that he did not oppose the Christian faith. Hitler was too busy to see him but told Ribbentrop he much admired him, and Ribbentrop entertained Reardon in style. He referred Reardon back to Fritz Hailer, German consul general in Detroit, who became Coughlin's chief contact with the German Government.

Coughlin's influence spread into Ireland itself. By the late 1930s, the Christian Fronters and the IRA both came under the Abwehr, and Coughlin sent money, propaganda material, and IRA slogans to Irish sympathizers in the United States. He also sent coals to Newcastle and preachments to the converted in shipments from Royal Oak to Dublin.

Neither the government nor the Vatican moved against Coughlin until April 1942 and even then did nothing to bring about his prosecution as an agent of the German Government. Roosevelt insisted over Biddle's objections that *Social Justice* must be suspended, but that was as far as it went. Attorney General Francis Biddle did nothing except inform the Postmaster General that he should consider suspending *Social Justice*'s second-class mailing privileges. The basis for such suspension was that the paper violated the 1917 Espionage Act by obstructing the war effort; no mention was made of the fact that Coughlin was personally guilty. Even in this time of war, there was a solemn meeting held at which distinguished legalists sat around discussing the matter of the mailing privilege. Coughlin disdained even to appear at the hearing and denounced it as the work of Jews and Communists while blatantly announcing that his whitewashers were wrong and he was solely responsible for every word the magazine published. To ensure that this statement reached the largest audience, he gave it to the New York *Times* on April 21, 1942: Hitler's birthday.

Coughlin's contempt for Biddle was absolute. He went to see him in Washington, telling him that threats to end publication of *Social Justice* should be called off or alternatively it should stand trial for sedition. Biddle, nervously, wavered and Coughlin screamed at him with Hitlerian intensity: "You, sir, are nothing but a goddam coward! You should have been a street cleaner . . . you have no courage. You were born a coward and you're still one!"

Biddle then acted most typically. Instead of having an independent liberal member of the Cabinet deal with the matter, he engaged Leo T. Crowley, an extreme right-wing Papist who, as alien-property custodian, was protecting Nazi-American interests throughout the war. Crowley agreed with Biddle that there must be no grand-jury indictment of Coughlin. Nor must the press stand trial. The Catholic electorate would be provoked. The best procedure was to have Archbishop Edward Mooney of Detroit tell Coughlin that if he did not suspend *Social Justice* he would risk being defrocked by Rome. Actually, no authorization for this had been received in Detroit from the Vatican.

One of Father Coughlin's chief proselytizers was a young St. Louis man named Martin James Monti. Like many Nazi sympathizers, he was inducted into the Army; he served in the Air Corps, hoping to find a way to obtain intelligence for the Axis. In 1944, he was in India and arranged a transfer to Italy. On October 13, he stole a P38 photoreconnaissance aircraft from the U.S. Army air base near Naples and flew it across the lines to the German air base in Milan. He gave himself up to the German command and offered to be of service to them. He told them that Father Coughlin had personally inspired the mission.

He was transferred to Berlin, where he broadcast to American troops and civilians by shortwave on an English-speaking program entitled "The Round Table Conference." Frequently mentioning Coughlin as his guide and inspiration, he regurgitated the pages of *Social Justice* by stating that Russia, not Germany, was America's real enemy and must be crushed; that the Jews had instigated World War II; that GI's were being recruited by the Soviets to join them as agents. In the spring of 1945, Monti was rewarded for his pains by being made a lieutenant of the Elite Guard of the SS.

After the fall of Germany, Monti was apprehended, court-martialed for desertion, and charged with the theft of the P38. Since his action was clearly treasonable, the normal punishment would presumably have been death. However, it is not surprising to learn that his activities were rewarded with a fifteen-year suspended sentence and reenlistment as a private at Mitchell Field, Long Island, where he rose to the rank of sergeant in 1946. The Cold War was imminent, and Nazi sympathizers were being amnestied, excused, and encouraged.

✠✠✠✠✠✠ 8

The Plot to Kill
the President

Along with Charles Lindbergh and Martin Dies, a popular nominee of
Coughlin and other Fascists for President of the United States was Major
General George Van Horn Moseley, commander of the Third Army before his retirement in 1938. He was to become the focus for a most
audacious plot to bring about a coup d'état against Franklin D. Roosevelt.

Moseley, who was sixty-four in 1939, lived at the grand old Biltmore
Hotel in Atlanta, Georgia, surrounded by black-and-Jew-hating southern
colonels who gathered in the lobby with its potted palms or in the fumed
oak of the cocktail bar.

Throughout 1937 and 1938, a stream of miscellaneous visitors arrived
at the general's suite of rooms to discuss plans for the liquidation of
Roosevelt and a takeover of the government. Among the first and most
persistent of these callers was the engineer and builder Captain James E.
Campbell, who had served under Moseley.

Campbell feared that his business ventures were threatened by
friends of false color who were secret Communists. In this matter, he
enjoyed the concurrence of his closest friend, Dudley Pierrepont Gilbert,
son of a well-known architect. The two men spent much of their time
traveling the country to investigate without authorization striking union
members in factories to see if they carried Communist Party cards.

Through Campbell's influence, many officers of V Corps, to which
he belonged, began similarly investigating liberals, whom they called fellow travelers. Gilbert supplied his friend with news clippings that pur-

ported to support the theory that a Communist revolution was afoot: a revolution that could be put down only by a Fascist counterrevolution and a new President. In turn, Campbell conveyed these ideas to the then Brigadier General Moseley, who carried them into the upper reaches of army circles.

Campbell acquired a convenient Deep Throat, a waiter at the Harmonie Club, on East Sixtieth Street in New York City, who served table at secret meetings of various Jewish and liberal figures including Justice Felix Frankfurter. The waiter used the name George Rice. He told Campbell that indeed a Communist revolution was imminent and that the group of prominent figures that he served were busy discussing it. The Communists would begin by paralyzing industry through the CIO with a series of violent strikes. They would then "attack government bonds and cause damage to banks and insurance companies." They would seize communications and would enlist the twelve thousand members of the Lincoln Brigade, which had done service for Loyalist Spain. Furthermore, one hundred thousand Spanish Loyalists in Mexico would be summoned to the cause. The rebels would then seize communications and overthrow the government by force. Most of the names Rice supplied to Campbell were Jewish.

Gilbert and Campbell took their information supplied by Rice to G2: Army Intelligence. The intelligence officers told them that when previous information of this sort had been forwarded to the White House, it had been deliberately lost or thrown away. Frustrated, Gilbert and Campbell took their material to General Moseley, who inflamed members of the military establishment in the matter.

Gilbert's paranoia over the Communist menace clearly had a pathological origin. He engaged Campbell to build a house for him, a barricaded miniature fortress in the wilds of western Kentucky, where he could hide behind thick walls with a gun when the "revolution" took place. When someone threw a brick through his car window as he drove through a mining town during a strike, he attributed it to a Communist attempt on his life. He became convinced that Kentucky would be one of the few safe places to live when the Jewish establishment on the East and West coasts of America would take over on behalf of the Soviet Union.

Gilbert paid more and more money to Rice for tips obtained allegedly in the private dining room of the Harmonie Club. He would meet the diligent informer at the Waldorf-Astoria or the St. Moritz Hotel. Rice would hand him a sheaf of notes in longhand, and he would sit at a public lobby desk and copy every word. Rice would then take the original and flush it down a toilet.

Rice provided more and more sensations for Gilbert to give to Campbell and Campbell to give to Moseley. One of these stated that a Communist in Roosevelt's Cabinet had leaked military and naval secrets to the Soviet Union. Another stated that many army and navy leaders had been forcibly retired without pensions because they had suspected communism in Washington, D.C.

Rice further advised his friend that the purpose of the Communist conspiracy was to involve the United States in war. The Russians and the Jews wanted an alliance to take place against Hitler, which would be followed by the Red revolution.

Rice found a willing audience in Gilbert and the others when he stated that Father Coughlin was the only true savior of democracy. The trio, followed by Moseley, were convinced that Kuhn, Loeb, the Jewish banking company, had financed the Russian revolution. They supported the widespread distribution of the Brooklyn *Tablet*, a Roman Catholic newspaper which regurgitated anti-Semitic mythology. They disseminated articles in the *Tablet*, supported by the endorsements of Coughlin and the bishop of Brooklyn, that Communists had caused the victory of Congressman Maury Maverick in Texas and the advancement of the career of the columnist Heywood Broun.

Campbell secured his position with Moseley by entering into contracts with him to distribute prophylactic sheaths through Moseley's army contacts to the rank-and-file, with a cut in the deal for the now major general. Campbell secured the support of the manufacturer James F. Cooke by giving him the contracts for the French-letter boxes. Campbell obtained a foothold in G2 by reporting companies for smuggling goods to Loyalist Spain. He also reported Juan Negrín, the Loyalist leader, for going to Mexico "to raise an army of 200,000 communists to invade Texas and Arizona."

Campbell drove thousands of miles to enlist in the cause all of the various Fascist cells that had sprung up across the nation, many of them supported by well-to-do women who apparently did not realize what they were getting into. One of his most important contacts was the engineer George E. Deatherage.

Deatherage was the self-appointed Führer of a Fascist organization known as the Knights of the White Camellia. The Knights had first emerged in 1867, in the days of reconstruction after the American Civil War. They had gone out of business, and most of their activities against Negroes and Jews had been efficiently assumed by the Ku Klux Klan. Deatherage re-formed the Knights in 1934 and raised a considerable sum of money, much of it at the Harvard Club, in order to ensure the continued existence of the organization.

Deatherage had his headquarters at College Hill, St. Albans, West Virginia. He kept in constant touch with Gilbert and Campbell in New York and western Kentucky, and with Moseley in Atlanta. In 1937, he directly connected himself to the Nazi government, drawing his military American confreres into the web. His chief contact was Manfred von Killinger, Nazi consul in San Francisco. He also worked closely with the German propagandist leader Johannes Klapproth and the British Nazi Henry Hamilton Beamish, who commuted between London, Southern Rhodesia, and California.

In 1936, Deatherage formed the American Nationalist Federation, an organization that pledged support in the coming counterrevolution against the alleged Communist uprising. The support would come from all of the Nazi cells, which would mean several hundred thousand who would flock to the Confederation's swastika flag. Deatherage's right-hand man was the White Russian Vladimir Kositzin, who would bring in the White Russian Fascists.

Deatherage kept in close touch with Berlin and with Ulrich von Gienanth, military attaché at the German embassy in Washington. When Deatherage asked Von Gienanth how Hitler got started, the military officer told him that it was also with a small amount of money, a brewery headquarters, and propaganda leaflets. Von Gienanth made clear that the German Government disapproved of the German-American Bund because of its flagrant public activities. He encouraged Deatherage to follow a policy of developing anti-Jewish feeling, saying that there was ten times more of that in the United States than there was in Germany before Hitler's rise to power.

Both Von Gienanth and Hans Luther, of the German embassy, visited Major General Moseley and discussed coming prospects with him. Deatherage felt that there was an advantage in encouraging the Bund, because its scores of thousands of members could be enlisted in the counterrevolution. At lunch with the Bund's Fritz Kuhn at the Harvard Club in 1938, Kuhn pledged him five hundred Bund groups.

Deatherage grew bolder as World War II approached. He began writing speeches for Moseley and circulating propaganda directly through Moseley's clubs and army affiliations. Although Moseley apparently had doubts about heading up a counterrevolutionary government, he did not hesitate to deliver anti-Semitic speeches of Deatherage's authorship well into 1939.

On December 29, 1938, Moseley regurgitated a Deatherage address in Indianapolis. It was a virtual repetition of an earlier speech he had given at the New York Board of Trade, which had been cheered by the assembled bankers and industrialists.

He began his speech with a lie: that he had no ghostwriter. He charged all liberals with being radicals and Communists. He talked of an unlimited right to carry arms, as the pioneers did; but he said that "Communists, CIOs, and . . . murderers" must not be allowed to carry weapons. He said, "Remember that, in all history, before an internal enemy attempts to destroy his victim, he first disarms him by the operation of law."

He complained that the President forbade the Army to investigate communism. Discussing the President's policy, he said, "Is this bungling going to lead us into war, while communism is left free to destroy us at home?" He said, inter alia, that "the one thing that is preventing the spread of communism in the Far East by the Russian Government is a long line of the breasts of Japanese soldiers who are holding those communistic ways back." This statement was greeted with applause. He attacked Great Britain violently; he attacked the idea of bringing in Jewish refugees from Europe, adding as a footnote that he had many friends among the Jews.

Moseley began to hint of the Deatherage plan at the end of his speech: "And, finally, gentlemen, remember that there is not a single Red, not a single Pink, in the Army nor in the Navy! They stand clean. They stand supreme. Given the right orders from the Commander-in-Chief, they would meet every emergency. They can protect us individually as citizens in our local communities. They can protect us nationally as a government. Will the right orders come down under the present administration?"

Moseley gave another speech before a meeting on national defense at the Bellevue Stratford Hotel in Philadelphia on March 28, 1939. He said that the war now proposed "is for the purpose of establishing Jewish hegemony throughout the world. We must recognize that fact. The Communists have forced us to state it frankly."

He referred to an address given recently in Atlanta to a Jewish assembly in which the speaker had said that the Jews were being organized to force the Roosevelt administration to compel Hitler to reinstate Jewish refugees in Germany to their former status, even at the cost of war. Moseley added that the speaker had been encouraged by the President and his First Lady.

Moseley denounced such a scheme and repeated that Kuhn, Loeb, had financed the Russian revolution, that Trotsky visited representatives in the United States, and that the Versailles Treaty was a mistake. The speech continued in like vein. Moseley referred to the visits of German ambassador Hans Luther to his home and indicated that he concurred with Luther's statement that "Hitler desires peace, but . . . Germany must have elbow room in Europe for her development, and . . . the powers must not interfere with Hitler as he reshapes Middle Europe to the advantage of the German people."

He added that world war was part of the world plan of the Communists and that Nazism was useful in the matter. "The Fascists and the Nazis in America have only one mission, as I understand, and that is to see to it that the Communists shall not take possession of this nation. In fact, the finest type of Americanism can breed under their protection as they neutralize the efforts of the Communists. How, then, can we lick communism? First, by exterminating from the life of this nation all traces of the New Deal, the principle backers [sic] of communism. But that is not all. We must go to battle against the Communists themselves."

He accused six million Americans of being Communist sympathizers, led by eighty thousand members of the Party. He said that they had plans to take over the principal cities and that efforts must be made to prevent this revolution from taking place. He wanted a bill to allow the Army a free hand in the matter. He clearly supported the idea of a military government, though he stopped short of suggesting that he himself could take charge of it.

The general delivered a third speech in Springfield, Illinois, on April 26, 1939. In this address, he condemned Roosevelt outright as an arbiter of a divided world and charged England and France with building "a steel ring around Germany in Europe." He hypocritically stated, in case some-one should throw a brick at him, that he held no brief for "Mr. Hitler, Mr. Mussolini, and the Mikado." But more honestly he added, "We must admit that the success of the National Socialists in Germany saved that country from communism." He similarly approved the political actions of Mussolini and Emperor Hirohito.

He stated that whereas there was no danger from Germany, Italy, or Japan, there was danger from labor leaders Harry Bridges and John L. Lewis. There was a peculiar irony in this, showing that the general was less than well informed: Lewis was involved in making deals with the Nazi-collaborator oilman William Rhodes Davis at the time.

He wound up the speech with an inflammatory charge that the Jews were whipping up war fever and that all of their attacks on Hitler were simply intended to bring the country into ruins. He reiterated Hitler doctrine by stating that it was necessary to adopt selective breeding, steril-ization, and the elimination of the unfit as well as all Jews from the American body politic. He did not specify where he proposed sending the Jewish population; presumably, he either had concentration camps in mind or supported the theory of George Deatherage and others that the Jews should be shipped off to the island state of Madagascar, a suggestion also made by no less an authority than Adolf Eichmann.

In May 1939, Moseley, Deatherage, Campbell, and Gilbert appeared before the House Committee on Un-American Activities. The chairman was Martin Dies of Texas; the board entertained such strange bedfellows as the ultra-liberal Jerry Voorhis of California and the notorious J. Parnell Thomas, who later became the scourge of the Hollywood Ten. The Com-mittee heard the witnesses out and scored them chiefly on anti-Semitism, leaving their anti-Communist remarks aside. Reference was made to such predictions by Deatherage in print as "the gutters will soon run with the blood of the Jews." Moseley was questioned directly on the matter of the current controversy about admitting children of Jewish families from Ger-many as refugees. Moseley replied, "I don't think the Jews expect to get the Congress of the United States to make any definite changes in the immigration laws. They are closed, I hope, for all time."

The effect of the Dies Committee hearing, and its attendant public-ity, was that it was difficult for Campbell, Gilbert, and Deatherage to operate in the matter of the proposed coup d'état. The banner of intended revolution passed into the hands of the leaders of the Christian Front movement, with Father Charles Coughlin presiding behind the scenes.

The Christian Front movement, which had developed simultaneously with the German-American Bund, was in every way more insidious and powerful. Whereas the Bund after 1938 operated without much support from the German Government, the Christian Front was indirectly encouraged by Himmler, Hess and Ernst-Wilhelm Bohle. Whereas the Bund had a substantial percentage of Irish Catholic membership, the Christian Front was almost entirely Irish-American. In view of the careful approach toward Hitler by Pope Pius XII on his assumption of the papacy in 1939, it is not surprising that the scores of thousands of Christian Front members felt not entirely out of order in pursuing their activities. The movement was divided up into units of twenty to twenty-five men each, under Coughlin's specific direction: a device resembling that to be found in the SS. The Front took over from Deatherage in 1940, absorbing his American Nationalist Federation in a consuming alliance of purpose. The difference was that whereas Deatherage's ANF was made up largely of the lunatic fringe in the blue-collar class of unemployed, the Christian Front had in its membership an extraordinary number of police, members of the National Guard, White Russians, and expatriate Irish Republican Army militia. What had seemed a mere pipe dream in the minds of the Bund or the trio supporting Moseley for President now became something approaching a possible political putsch movement. A coup d'état at this stage was not entirely outside the bounds of possibility. And once again, General Moseley was first choice as the nation's leader.

Yet the problem now was that the Christian Front became too overt in its activities, as the Bund had. Its members were constantly beating up Jews in subways and on buses, on street corners and in parks, while at the same time forcibly distributing *Social Justice*. They openly denounced the President under the protection of the free-speech regulations they would have been the first to abolish under the new regime.

In 1940, J. Edgar Hoover became seriously concerned when he got wind of the formation of a group of extremist Christian Fronters that called itself The Sporting Club. This group was determined to rally three hundred thousand Irish-American members in the police and the National Guard to seize the White House and place Major General Moseley in the Oval Office. On the face of it, this plan might have seemed unrealistic, but, given the hatred of Roosevelt in certain circles, it is at least understandable. The question for Hoover was, How would this "revolution" be pulled off? He intensely disliked Roosevelt; his backdoor visits and constant stream of memoranda were not marked by any real warmth. But he was a policeman first and foremost, and he resented the presence of seditious and rebellious elements in the police force. He often clashed with police leaders, since he in many ways was in a position to override them on the investigative level. The wholesale graft and corruption in the New York Police Department aggravated him unendurably, and he was always looking for ways to seek out evil.

He appointed his trusted New York bureau chief Percy Foxworth to be in charge of the case. Foxworth hired an informer who could be relied upon because of his impeccable Irish background, devout Catholicism, and appealing, robustly healthy appearance. His name was Dennis Healy. He had been a boy bugler and machine gunner for the Irish Free State Army in its war against the Black and Tans. At the time he joined the FBI, he was working as a junior engineer with the New York Central Railroad. Among his acquaintances was another railway man, the tough, stocky, loudmouthed German-American Claus Gunther Ernecke, who had become a self-appointed Nazi agent in the mid 1930s. Both Healy and Ernecke had served in the National Guard.

Healy pretended to be pro-Nazi and asked Ernecke to arrange for him to join The Sporting Club. Healy was to report on his findings to Foxworth every week. In his first conversations with Ernecke, Healy determined that the leaders of The Sporting Club and also of the newly reformed Christian Front Revolutionary Council were John (Jack) Cassidy and William Gerald Bishop.

On September 7, 1939, Healy attended his first Sporting Club summit meeting, with Ernecke, at Erasmus Hall High School, in Brooklyn. Ernecke introduced Healy to Cassidy, Bishop, and the others present as a future machine gunner for the group whose political affiliations could be relied upon. Cassidy made little impression on Healy: he was somewhat nondescript: a businessman playing soldier. But Bishop was riveting: extremely handsome, well built, cultivated, and distinguished-looking, he had all the appurtenances of a first-class con man.

Through the meeting, at which plans for the coup d'état were discussed, Healy scribbled notes with a tiny stub of pencil on his sleeves. He discovered a great deal then and at immediately subsequent meetings. He was disturbed to learn that Bishop and Cassidy had allegedly obtained the support of Brigadier General Alexander E. Anderson, Lieutenant Colonel Martin H. Meaney, and Captain John Prout of the National Guard Infantry in their plans against the President. This was serious if true and undoubtedly made the matter a top priority for the FBI.

Healy learned more and more about Bishop—most notably that Bishop had pull at a high level in the Department of Justice. Bishop had a most fascinating background. Born in England to unmarried parents, he had seen his mother arrested in Vienna in World War I as a suspected spy. He had been involved in anti-Communist Nazi activities in that city at the time of Hitler's first emergence. Forbidden passports by both Britain and Austria due to a suspicion that he was a double agent, he traveled for years under the alias of William Arneck.

Despite his handicaps, Bishop, with his chiseled features and slender physique, had an attraction that carried him over many obstacles. In London, he worked as guide and companion to Captain Gerald Lowry, the first British officer to be blinded in World War I. He joined the Spanish Foreign Legion but was twice cashiered out of it; he claimed to have worked as secretary to the young Francisco Franco. Drifting to New York in the early 1930s, he worked as dishwasher, jam salesman, and CCC camp worker until he enlisted in the Christian Front, in 1938.

Only a renegade Englishman could have joined an Irish nationalist group, so Healy had no respect for Bishop. Gradually, by talking to Bishop, Cassidy, Ernecke, and the others, Healy learned that the purpose of The Sporting Club was identical to Deatherage's: to provoke a Communist uprising, thus managing an excuse to cause a counterrevolution. First, the Club would bomb the Communist newspaper *The Daily Worker*, in New York City, and Communist cells, and arrange for police contacts to arrest Communists at street corners. Union meetings would be disrupted with anti-Communist confrontations. The hope was that this activism would so inflame Earl Browder, Communist nominee for President, that there would be a general outbreak of Communist demonstrations. By showing a military force in opposition, the Christian Front would obtain widespread public support and then would rally three hundred thousand men, including Deatherage's American Nationalist Federation, and all the other National Guardsmen.

It became clear to Healy that the time was ripe for this mini-revolution. There were millions who were seething with resentment at the Depression and the long unemployment they had suffered. He decided to discover more. He invited the members of The Sporting Club to meet at his house in Manhattan, where he served pheasant and wine while FBI agents hid in the cellar with telephonic bugging devices supplied by Ma Bell, listening for proof of subversion through the chatter and the clink of glasses.

Healy was told that he would be tested on his ability with a machine gun. He attended a Sporting Club target practice at Narrowsburg, Long Island, at which he was shocked to see an enormous target consisting of a portrait of President Roosevelt blown up and caricatured out of all proportion. He had to steel himself to riddle it with machine-gun bullets. At one stage in the afternoon, a Sporting Club member brought a replica of a big Jewish nose and put it over the President's. The men gleefully shot it off.

Next day, Cassidy told Healy that twelve congressmen would be murdered the instant the new government took over. He dare not ask for the names. Later, Bishop told Healy that when the government was overthrown there would be a full distribution of American gold to Hitler. This was the dream of the Führer and his Economics Ministry: to overcome the problem of varying currencies by making gold the one medium of transaction in a conquered Europe.

Bishop and Cassidy began gathering more members. In November, two thousand five hundred rallied to the cause, five hundred of them on the New York State Police force alone. Bishop secured the support of the National Guard's Captain John Prout to obtain ammunition.

Guns also were promised. Bishop gradually revealed himself as a German agent; Ernecke was, of course, another; and a third was alleged to be Michael Vill, who turned out to have a brother in the German High Command. Vill had been with Hitler at the Beer Hall Putsch and had been the maker of bombs for the SA, the Nazi Party terrorist arm. He was a member of the Catholic Youth of the Hitler Youth Movement.

On October 21, 1939, a young newspaper reporter named Gertrude Wilbert working in Narrowsburg went to the Peggy Runway Lodge for a drink with her boyfriend. While they were in the barroom, Bishop came in with two other members of the Front. One of the Fronters performed a vulgar imitation of the crippled President giving a Fireside Chat; he announced that Roosevelt was "incompetent" and that the government would soon be overthrown and replaced by "men of my caliber." Bishop mentioned that the government and press were controlled by Jews. The man said, "You exterminate rats, therefore you should exterminate Jews."

Young Gertrude Wilbert was disgusted. She turned on Bishop and said, "You guys sound like members of the Nazi Bund." Then she and her boyfriend left the bar.

She reported the matter to the *Delaware Valley News*. This was highly inconvenient for Hoover, but fortunately very few people read the item. There was no public repercussion, and the secret meetings of The Sporting Club continued.

In late November, Prout handed over the first fifteen hundred rounds of ammunition to Cassidy at Fort Dix. Apparently, support was assured from military, police, and other official sources. It was intended to hold off on the actual bombing of Communist headquarters and organizations for a year or two, when the plans could be completely achieved. But Hoover didn't feel like waiting. He decided to bring the leaders in.

Early in December, William Gerald Bishop was strolling along a street near his home in Brooklyn when one of Hoover's agents called his name. Turning on his heel, Bishop saw a man with a hand stretched out in greeting. He shook it, whereupon the agent overpowered him, pinned his hands behind his back, and marched him into an automobile. "We've got you dead to rights, Bishop. There's no use denying anything," the FBI man said.

Agent Percy Foxworth raided the house and found dynamite fuses and bombs everywhere; Bishop said he was using the stuff for "blasting tree stumps." He mentioned his Department of Justice contacts, but they seemed to be unable to help—until, it seems, later on. He told many lies, including one that he had been shot in the foot by Pancho Villa's soldiers while fighting against the Mexican revolutionary. He denied he was a Gestapo agent.

Foxworth arranged for an accused diamond merchant, who had been charged with smuggling, to be placed in the cell with Bishop. In return for his release, the merchant pumped Bishop for information; this concurred with Healy's reports, and there was an addendum. Significantly, Bishop named his high-level contacts in the Senate and the House, all of whom he said he had met. It made up a typical rogue's gallery of familiar names: Senators Reynolds of North Carolina and Vandenberg of Michigan, the inescapable Senator Wheeler, and Representative Jacob Thorkelson of Montana.

The FBI swooped on Cassidy's home. Copies of letters to Berlin were found in Cassidy's house, stating that a Communist revolution was imminent; that the Administration was failing to investigate Communists because of Communists in the government; that "a ring of steel" would be flung around Washington, D.C.; that thirty thousand rounds of ammunition was promised from Fort Dix; and that the Department of Justice contacts would be helpful along with those in the Army. Cassidy carried in his wallet a photograph of the leader of the Silver Shirts, William Dudley Pelley, and a list of 470 policemen in New York who could be relied upon. He admitted on interrogation that he had in mind Moseley for President and Brigadier General Anderson and Lieutenant Colonel Meaney as heads of the Army.

It was determined that the business address for the Front was a post-office box in New York City, but its headquarters was at the Paulist Fathers' Building on 59th Street near Columbus Circle. No mention was made of Father Coughlin when the arrest of the ringleaders was announced. Indeed, Coughlin was neither brought in for questioning nor called in as a witness in the subsequent trial, and Moseley, Anderson, and Meaney were also left untouched by the scandal. They denied any knowledge of the matter, and there it rested.

The Federal District Court trial of The Sporting Club, under Judge William F. Campbell, began in April 1940. The defending counsel was former magistrate Leo J. Healy, who was not pleased that Hoover's informer was his namesake and never stopped mentioning the fact throughout the hearing. Leo Healy was a contentious and arrogant extreme right-winger who greatly relished challenging Hoover head on. He had convinced himself by the time the trial started that Bishop and Healy were both Communists, deliberately planted in the Christian Front to act as agents provocateurs in order to discredit and ruin the Front. In discussing the matter with his witnesses, most of whom were the defendants, he had decided on a line in which each would state in turn that Bishop alone had suggested and promoted the idea of the counterrevolution. This would effectively cast doubt upon Healy in the eyes of the jury, since the implication would be that he and Bishop had worked together. This fabrication was unfortunately all too typical of legal practice at the time.

The questioning of the jury had its unintentionally funny aspects. Each juror was asked if he read magazines or newspapers which would deal with the Christian Front activities, and each replied that he did not. How a person who did not read the news could be presumed to judge such a case remains a mystery. The members were asked if they had heard of the

Irish Republican Army and they said that they had not. They were asked if they were members of the Communist, Socialist or American Labor party and whether they were affiliated with related organizations, including the Lincoln Brigade and the Friends of Loyalist Spain. They replied in the negative. They were asked if their feelings would be hurt if anti-Semitism were discussed. Jews were excluded from the jury; none was asked if he was a Roman Catholic or had Nazi affiliations.

Father Coughlin zigzagged in the pages of *Social Justice*, sometimes claiming, sometimes disclaiming, responsibility for the Christian Front. The trial violently divided Right and Left, Protestant and Catholic, and the press as a whole did not help Hoover, by pooh-poohing the entire conspiracy as a kind of Graustarkian misadventure that no one could take seriously. This kind of skepticism over the seriousness of Nazi activities did not occur when Communist activities were mentioned. The American Civil Liberties Union also handicapped Hoover by stating that the trial was "on the borderline of being oppressive."

Magistrate Healy compelled his namesake to admit that he had posed as anti-Semitic to obtain information, and that he had taken part in street fights to preserve his cover. The former magistrate dragged Dennis Healy through days of grueling cross-examination, trying unsuccessfully to prove he was a Communist and agent provocateur. Even Dennis Healy's action in writing names on his starched cuffs was greeted with contempt. The magistrate said, "Have you read detective stories in which the sleuth did that?" Dennis Healy replied that he had not.

Dennis Healy became so ill from exhaustion and strain that on two occasions he had to be helped from the courtroom. But he did manage to make it clear how seditious The Sporting Club was: that its stance was that any war against Germany would be Jewish; that the members would never fight against Hitler and would fight for the Führer when the time came. Magistrate Healy cleverly played on the jury, knowing the traditional American dislike of those who blow whistles, inform, or name names. He tripped Healy up in several minor lies that had the effect of discrediting his more important evidence. The ill and shattered witness for the prosecution soon realized the price that was to be paid for exposing Nazism.

On April 12, the call went out for Claus Gunther Ernecke to take the stand. There was no response. Like the other defendants, Ernecke was out on bail of seven thousand five hundred dollars (the total bail for the defendants came to a figure none of them could have met, leading one to conjecture whether Father Coughlin may have raised it).

Magistrate Healy told Judge Campbell that Ernecke was not the type to jump bail; he said that the German agent had been terrorized by threatening letters, had muttered, "Somebody will get me," on several occasions, and had been unavailable on the telephone when the counsel had tried to reach him. He must have been murdered or kidnapped.

At 9:15 the following morning, Michael O'Neill, caretaker of the Brooklyn apartment house where Ernecke lived, entered the Fronter's cold-water flat and found him missing. After a search of the building, he discovered him hanging in the cellar. The only marks on the body were the impression of the noose and a slight burn on the right hand from a steam pipe. Neither the FBI nor the police ever disclosed the contents of the suicide note. In court, Magistrate Healy could not resist a melodramatic statement: "I hope Dennis Healy is satisfied now. This act, if committed by Ernecke, is not an evidence of guilt, but of a broken heart. A broken heart because a friend such as he considered Dennis Healy should do what he did to him!" The coroner brought in a verdict of suicide.

Next day, Dennis Healy was back for another blast from his namesake. He was made to look bad for those very things which in a more rational atmosphere would have made him look good: for receiving money from the FBI to entertain the members of The Sporting Club and to buy a gun, ammunition, and an automobile. Magistrate Healy's sustained attempt to smear an FBI informer went on and on, with only occasional interruptions by the prosecuting attorney and the judge. A counsel for one of the defendants tried to use against Healy that he had worked for the British as a secret agent in Ireland and that this somehow invalidated him as a witness.

On April 18, the FBI's Peter J. Wacks, Percy Foxworth's liaison with Healy, took the witness stand and corroborated every word Dennis Healy had said. He stated that Healy was a loyal American and had volunteered to be an informer at considerable risk to himself. Again and again, Wacks confirmed that The Sporting Club had had the outright support of Brigadier General Anderson and Lieutenant Colonel Meaney and that the National Guard and police had offered their full support to the conspiracy. He produced tapes in court showing that the Christian Front was on the verge of being turned into a full-scale militia. He described the defendants giving the Nazi salute to Cassidy.

Wacks was followed by Special Agent Charles A. Gannon, who testified from FBI records that Ernecke and Bishop were paid German agents
and that it was possible Bishop held the rank of major in the Abwehr. He
also revealed that defendant Michael Vill had a long record of Nazi activities.

Special Agent Arthur M. Thurston had the many high explosives and
bombs in Bishop's house carried into the courtroom, and showed films of
four or five Sporting Club members in target practice. Despite every effort
of Magistrate Healy, who struggled to prevent the introduction of prima
facie evidence, such evidence became overwhelming. There was even a
confession by defendant John Viebrock of the planned revolution, naming
Father Coughlin; and another by eighteen-year-old William Bushnell, Jr.,
who stated that he had been trained in bomb throwing for activist purposes.

One defendant, Macklin Boettger, stated that Representative Jacob
Thorkelson of Montana was a member of the Fronters' Action Committee. Asked about this by the New York *Times*, Thorkelson burst out laugh-
ing. He said, "The notion that the sixteen defendants could overthrow the
government with thirteen rifles is insane." He said that the "fiasco" of the
trial was that it was "a childish attempt to shield the Communists" and
that he thought fascism "milder than Communism."

It emerged during the course of the trial that William Bishop was
even more seriously connected to Germany than had generally been supposed. He was actually a member of the American National Socialist
League and—here the plot really thickened—a member of Alfred
Rosenberg's Edda Kulturbund, a mystical antireligious society that called
for the resurgence of the ancient gods. It emerged that Bishop was a plant
by Rosenberg's foreign intelligence group.

Under oath, Captain Prout of the National Guard admitted he had
arranged for Bishop to receive ammunition. Bishop's testimony was a
disaster. U.S. Attorney Harold M. Kennedy totally discredited him, forcing him to admit he had bought British and French war medals in a store
and that much of the rest of his statements was inaccurate.

With the evidence concluded, Judge William F. Campbell, on June
12, denied defense motions to dismiss the charge of conspiracy, except for
that against one defendant, Alfred J. Quinlan. But he still held Quinlan
on the count of conspiracy to steal ammunition. Magistrate Healy could
not resist saying in his final address to the jury that there were no myster-

ies in the case except "who was backing witness Dennis Healy," saying characteristically that if his clients were guilty of the charges against them they should be "taken down and shot in the street." The magistrate merely repeated that all his clients were concerned with was protecting the country against communism.

U.S. Attorney Kennedy was by contrast very subdued. He said, in measured tones, "You don't refer to a cancer as a little cancer. There is no such thing as a slight case of murder . . . how do you deal with a program of this kind? Should you wait until you have to deal with it under martial law?"

The jury left the courtroom to weigh no less than one million, five hundred thousand words of testimony and the difficult issue of deciding where sedition, and plans to overthrow the government, took over from the God-given right of American free speech. The prosecuting counsel had not clearly delineated the precise nature of the conspiracy, and the failure to bring in George Deatherage as a witness for the prosecution was a serious one. Moreover, the absence of Coughlin and Moseley, Meaney and Anderson from the hearing was troubling. It was hard, in the circumstances, to give a picture of the seriousness of the matter. And there was another problem for the prosecution: According to Albert E. Kahn's liberal newsletter *The Hour*, Mrs. Helen Titus, the forewoman of the jury, was the cousin of Coughlin's right-hand man, Father Edward Brophy.

Precisely what happened when the jury was locked up has never been disclosed. Later, Mrs. Titus claimed that all members except one wanted a complete acquittal, which seems almost incredible in the circumstances. If the statement is true, it indicates a remarkable example of heroism and Americanism on the part of the holdout.

The jury was taken to a nearby hotel; relatives arrived with clothing, medication, and toilet gear, depositing the articles at the front desk. All next day, the jury continued to wrangle; at 10 P.M., they asked the judge for an early adjournment of deliberations, as they could not face sitting up until midnight. They had become exhausted listening to the evidence reread to them by the court reporter.

By 11:25 P.M. on the third day, they still had not reached a decision. They had to argue in suffocating heat without air conditioning in those mid-June days when New York had the atmosphere of a fever swamp. The sound of riveting in a nearby elevator shaft was so deafening they had to be moved to another room.

That afternoon, they asked the judge for various exhibits, including William G. Bishop's scrapbook and a manifesto against foreign wars. At 6:30 P.M., an impatient Judge Campbell offered further services if necessary, but these were not called upon. The arguments dragged on until the weekend. By 11:25 P.M. on Saturday, June 23, Campbell closed the court for the weekend and they retired to their hotel.

At 5:39 P.M. on Monday, after a miserable weekend in an airless hotel, after twelve days of trial and five days of deliberation, Mrs. Titus stood before the court and declared ten of the defendants innocent of the counts of conspiracy to overthrow the government and steal government property. She declared that there was a disagreement on the count against Bishop, Boettger, Viebrock, and Prout. The eighteen-year-old William Bushnell, Jr., was declared innocent on the second charge; the jury disagreed on the first. Cassidy and four other defendants left the courtroom free men. The crowd of two hundred cheered them with "Good luck!" and "Hooray for our side!"

Father Coughlin announced the acquittal on the front page of *Social Justice*. He hailed the verdict with the correct prediction, "The result of all this will be that the Christian Front movement will emerge vigorous and more potent than ever."

In January 1940, Attorney General Robert H. Jackson inexplicably nolle-prossed (in other words, declared no further action on) the remaining defendants. Prout was separately court-martialed for improperly supplying ammunition from Fort Dix but was acquitted outright. Bishop was threatened with deportation but was finally excused also.

The Christian Front movement celebrated by bombing synagogues in Manhattan and Brooklyn. Once more, Jewish women and children were afraid of taking to the streets. Pearl Harbor made no difference. Coughlin remained silent when asked for a comment on the Japanese surprise attack—the only major public figure apart from Senator Wheeler to do so.

On January 21, 1942, John Cassidy, joint leader of The Sporting Club and codefendant in the trial, obtained admission to the state bar of New York. Protests by Jewish groups were useless, since a commission had already decided on his admission.

It was obvious that somebody in a high position was helping Cassidy. The many Jewish lawyers in the bar association seem to have had no power in the matter.

Perhaps as a sop to the public, Attorney General Francis Biddle closed down *Social Justice*, Coughlin's inflammatory magazine, four months after Pearl Harbor. It is believed that Roosevelt insisted on this action in view of the publication's overtly seditious content in time of war, and it is also believed that he summoned Archbishop Spellman and insisted that the Church disown any connections with Coughlin in the interests of the war effort.

Be that as it may, the Christian Front continued throughout the war and never ceased to scheme toward an overthrow of the government. J. Edgar Hoover kept pressing to disrupt its activities in the face of intolerable odds. He settled on his favorite target, the New York City police force —where the nest of Christian Fronters remained intact. He planted a hardworking Armenian-American journalist, Arthur L. Derounian, who was looking for material for a book, in the circle of Fronters in Brooklyn, under the pseudonym John Roy Carlson. Carlson knew that the same powers led by Moseley, Wheeler, Nye, Vandenberg, Walsh, and the others on Capitol Hill still existed in time of war. Focusing on the police, he was convinced that the Coughlinites had a new leader in patrolman James L. Drew, of Brooklyn's Liberty Avenue precinct.

Like Dennis Healy, who was by now in hiding, Derounian was a brave and decent patriotic American. He dared to pose as a Fronter and a police contact, meeting with Drew and reporting that Drew was directly connected to the Christian Front's new reincarnation, The Christian Mobilizers. When he went to Drew's house, he said, he found that Drew's son had distributed *Social Justice* before its demise, and that the cellar was filled with aggressively seditious literature, including Nazi pamphlets.

He said that Drew was a close associate of the alleged German agent Herman Fleischkopf, who wrote pro-Nazi books under the pseudonym of Ernest Elmhurst. Elmhurst addressed secret Christian Mobilizer meetings. In his apartment on Staten Island, from which he would sally forth on Sundays to dig clams, he allegedly had swastikas decorating pictures of an American Indian and a Minute Man. A garish coat of arms showed the American Eagle with its claws resting on two swastikas. The walls were crowded with Nazi books.

Derounian accompanied Elmhurst on a clam-digging expedition one Sunday and pumped him expertly, learning that the Mobilizers were spies —observing ship movements from Staten Island's vantage points. Discussions at meetings included comparisons of Hitler with Jesus Christ, Elmhurst saying that Hitler had been criticized because he had opposed the money changers—i.e., the Jewish bankers. At one meeting of the group at the drugstore next to the New York *Times* offices on Forty-third Street, almost perversely chosen, there was a discussion of where to put Nazi stickers in public places.

As a result of Derounian's charges, Hoover contacted Commissioner of Investigations William B. Herlands, to whom Derounian had also been reporting, and they exchanged dossiers. They conferred with Police Commissioner Valentine and he suspended Drew from duty on May 21, 1943. Explaining his action, Valentine stated to the New York *Times* that evidence collected in the past year proved that Drew had been associated with persons who were engaged in un-American and antiwar activities and were contributing funds to four seditious organizations. He also stated that Drew was contributing to the defense of three figures in the trial of pro-Nazi American seditionists then in progress: the Japanese spy Ralph Townsend, Elizabeth Dilling, and Charles B. Hudson.

The decision was made to have the patrolman appear before trial commissioner Michael A. Lyons at police headquarters. After several postponements, the private hearing took place, in July. Derounian was interrogated by Arthur Talley, Drew's attorney, who grilled him in an effort to prove that a liberal organization to which he belonged, the Friends of Democracy, was controlled by Jews. Derounian stated that eight of the thirty-nine directors of the Friends were Jewish and that there was no prejudice involved on his part.

Despite Talley's objections, thousands of anti-Semitic pamphlets, stickers, and books found in Drew's garage were introduced into the courtroom. Derounian was forced to give his home address and telephone number in open court, without demur from the police commissioner and despite a plea that his family would thus be endangered. It was cold comfort to him to learn that he would be given police protection day and night.

After the evidence of Drew's guilt was presented and both sides rested their case, Third Deputy Police Commissioner Michael A. Lyons reserved decision and sent the matter up to Commissioner Valentine. He recommended that Drew be restored to duty—which he was. And this despite the fact that he admitted connections to Nazi sympathizer Joseph McWilliams and that he was contributing to the defense fund of Elizabeth Dilling.

On December 21, after no less than five months of deliberation,

Commissioner Valentine dismissed all charges against Drew, who was totally exonerated; his pay was reinstated back to the first complaint. Commissioner of Investigations Herlands was furious and stormed into the office of Mayor Fiorello LaGuardia. He returned to his office to issue a statement to the press branding Valentine's action as "a major defeat on the home front." In other words, he came to the edge of saying that Valentine was aiding and abetting an enemy.

Herlands minced no words. He said that he had "never pulled punches whether the persons concerned were in the Administration or not" and did not "propose to start now." He said the Valentine decision was contrary to all evidence and public policy. It seemed likely that the mayor had endorsed the Valentine judgment. Despite the fact that Herlands submitted a 54-page report to the mayor including 245 pages of testimony and numerous exhibits, LaGuardia did not intervene.

On December 27, 1943, Valentine gave Coughlin and The Christian Mobilizers a Christmas gift by stating that his decision was final. He stated, when asked if the case might be reopened because of Herlands's complaint, "In my forty years in the Police Department, I don't know of a single Commissioner who ever reversed his decision. Is the decision fair? I made it. Are Christian Front elements in the Department supporting Drew? That's the bunk."

With great effort, William B. Herlands brought the matter back to LaGuardia, who was compelled, in the face of much Jewish criticism, to set up an unofficial board to investigate the matter.

The board consisted of former Court of Appeals Judges Frederick E. Crane and Edward R. Finch and former Police Commissioner George V. McLaughlin. The Committee sat on the matter for a few days and on January 11 upheld Valentine's decision. The Mayor stated that the case was closed. ("That's finished. What else can I do? When three such men reach a unanimous decision, who am I to question it?")

Councilman Peter V. Cacchione, of Brooklyn called for Drew's outright dismissal. Majority Leader Joseph T. Sharkey demanded LaGuardia make a statement clarifying the situation. A meeting of 250 citizens of Brooklyn declared a committee to fight Drew, and Representative Emmanuel Celler demanded a reexamination of the evidence.

LaGuardia appeared with Drew on his weekly radio broadcast from City Hall on January 17. Drew reaffirmed his innocence and said he was sorry his case had brought "sorrow to the Mayor and to Valentine," and he disavowed any anti-Semitism. LaGuardia further whitewashed the matter by having one Catholic, one Jewish, and one Protestant policeman tell him on the program that there was no religious bias in the department. LaGuardia stepped far beyond his mayoral position in stating that he was satisfied with Drew's disclaimer and that it was "heartbreaking" that the impression had been created of discrimination in the department. However, it is most significant that only three days earlier, Valentine had amended the police-department regulations to preclude members from associating knowingly with persons engaged in subversive activities or to join organizations that fostered racial and religious hatred. It might well be asked why any such general order was introduced just over two years after Pearl Harbor unless the Drew case had made it necessary.

Herlands was not satisfied. He conferred with Rabbi Stephen S. Wise and at a rally against anti-Semitism at Carnegie Hall on January 18, Wise, with Herlands's permission, severely criticized LaGuardia's action. So serious did the matter become that on January 18 the New York City Council unanimously adopted a resolution calling on LaGuardia to make a statement clarifying the Drew matter beyond a reasonable doubt. Councilman Louis Cohen, Bronx Democrat, stated that LaGuardia's act in having Drew on his talk to the people was an outrage and turned his stomach. He called LaGuardia disgraceful and in a unique show of hands the entire council in one voice demanded the investigation. But it never took place.

How can one explain LaGuardia's actions in the matter? Perhaps only on the ground that he was very uneasy about provoking the police force, and that he was mindful of the importance of supporting the Irish elements in local government, which might stand behind an Irish-American. Like Francis Biddle, he placed expediency before patriotism; no further comment seems desirable, at least in the absence of any evidence against LaGuardia.

On January 26, the Third Avenue Realty Corporation, representing citizens' groups, filed a suit to compel a court review of Valentine's final judgment. The petition stated that Valentine's action was "arbitrary, capricious, unjust and wholly and utterly against the weight of the credible evidence presented at the hearings, and without basis or foundation in the record and without support in the evidence whatsoever, and contrary to the public policy of this state."

Third Avenue Realty's attorney Irwin Slater further stated that the result of the clearance was the recent wave of attacks of vandalism and sacrilege against Jewish synagogues and vicious assaults on Jewish children. There was no arguing with that: The Christian Mobilizers had struck again. It was obvious that LaGuardia and Valentine had given several hundred Coughlinites on the New York police force carte blanche, as *The New Republic* had said on January 3, to indulge in unpatriotic and un-American activities.

Somebody brought pressure to bear at a high level and Third Avenue Realty withdrew its suit. Disgusted, Commissioner of Investigations Herlands asked LaGuardia to accept his resignation on February 6, 1944. Ironically, LaGuardia stated in accepting the resignation that Herlands had written "[a] brilliant and shining chapter in the hard fight for decent and clean government." With those noble words ringing in his ears, Herlands returned to his domestic hearth.

The Attempt to Kill
the King and Queen
of England

That Father Charles Coughlin was in the direct pay of the German Government is scarcely surprising in view of the fact that the Irish Republican Army, which he so vigorously supported, was itself, like the Ukrainian groups, directly financed by the Abwehr.

Coughlin was also involved with the IRA Quartermaster General Sean Russell, the single most dynamic force in the Irish nationalist movement. Born in Dublin in 1890, this former cabinetmaker not only enjoyed Coughlin's unstinting support but also that of the Irish-American congressman James P. McGranery of Pennsylvania.

Vigorous, stocky, and muscular, Russell was distinguished by a wild brush of rapidly graying hair that stood up from his head like the mane of a lion. His sharp, shrewd, inquiring eyes stared out of a nest of wrinkles; his high forehead, aquiline nose, and square jaw indicated a formidable combination of intellect and will. His broad shoulders and muscular, craftsman's hands inspired confidence in his followers. His genial manner and somewhat schoolmasterly charm suppressed his true nature, which was vengeful, severe, and jesuitical.

His hatred of England was harsh and unyielding. Thus, in the 1930s, he found a ready reception in the Coughlinite/Christian Front movement in the United States. He consistently supported Coughlin's stand on isolationism, a negotiated peace with Hitler, and refusal to help Great Britain. On St. Patrick's Day each year, he sent good wishes to the American-Irish association to celebrate not only their patron saint, but the anniversary of the British evacuation of Boston as well.

Russell's closest U.S. connection from 1934 on was with the semisecret society known as Clan-Na-Gael, which diligently followed the policies laid down by the IRA and which, in common with the Christian Front, promoted terrorism, ill treatment of Jews, and anarchism directed against the Roosevelt administration.

Jointly inflamed by Coughlin and Russell, the Irish-Americans joined such organizations as the Knights of Columbus and the Ancient Order of Hibernians in order to infiltrate the ranks of the right wing in a direct pursuit of the Nazi cause. They were opposed to American foreign policy and uniformly denounced, both in their meetings and in the pages of their magazines, Lend-Lease, the Atlantic Charter, and the undeclared war in the Atlantic. They were devotedly opposed to the Soviet Union as well as to Great Britain. They demanded the removal of American troops in Northern Ireland, believing the presence of those troops to be indicative of the British policy of partition.

While officially criticizing these extremists, the Vatican did little or nothing to discipline the motley collection of Irish-American priests and higher-ranking ecclesiastical officials, including Coughlin, who unhesitatingly took up the Fascist cause. This self-sanctified ecclesiastical neutralism was forgiven by Russell and his terrorist adherents out of necessity more than anything else. The Vatican's name was irresistibly convenient for the invocations that preceded Russell's public meetings.

Convinced they were authorized by God and the Pope, Russell's Irish extremists found little to admire in the Roosevelt Cabinet. They fastened their hopes after 1938 upon a convenient group of Irish-American congressmen and upon three egregious figures who had the capacity to attract constant attention. These were Postmaster General James A. Farley, whose public persona of broad-beamed, genial all-Americanism and private finaglings in the field of German-American collusion made an unhappy contrast; Joseph Kennedy; and John Cudahy, ambassador to Eire and later to Belgium. Always, the thoughts of the Irish-American factions turned to Berlin as well as to Dublin; among the first to grasp the potential value of the Irish faction for the Third Reich were West Coast German-American Bund leader Hermann Schwinn and Nazi counsul general in San Francisco Fritz Wiedemann.

On August 22, 1936, Sean Russell, who was urgently in need of funds, began a nationwide tour of the United States in order to raise the sum of one million dollars for his planned bombing campaign against the British people. As a plank in his platform, he proposed a unilateral revolution against the British Government. He was, of course, acting without authorization from the Irish Free State Government, and Irish intelligence had him under a constant-watch order. American chargé d'affaires in Dublin James Orr Denby sent reassurances to the U.S. State Department on Russell, which enabled the IRA leader to act freely in America.

While in the United States, Russell stayed in the Bronx (care of a relative, Mrs. McCormack), traveling on a visitor's visa issued some four years earlier in the name of John Russell. State Department memoranda of the time indicate that that department was in a state of confusion about Russell's political orientation. The memoranda indicate that Russell had "pronounced Communist views" and that his purpose in being in the United States was "to contact Communist organizations." The State Department's muddle can be partly explained by a device used by the IRA. During the Spanish Civil War, it had backed the Loyalists with money and personal aid in order to obtain information behind the lines that would be of use to the Nazi government.

A similar device no doubt had inspired the Australian actor Errol Flynn, who named his son for Russell; Flynn was traced, by agents of MI6, to a meeting with Russell at a hotel in Lisbon in May 1938. Flynn had pretended to bring one and a half million dollars from such members of the Anti-Nazi League of Los Angeles as James Cagney and Fredric March. No such sum had been supplied. Flynn used his fame and public support of the Loyalists to obtain intelligence which he then supplied to the Fascist agent Bradish Johnson in Paris. At a meeting with Russell in Lisbon, Flynn promised financial help and contacts in America.

Drawing his money from such useful high-level contacts, Russell obtained his first million-dollar goal in 1939 and launched a series of bombings in England. Agents set off explosions in factories in Liverpool; near Euston Station, in London; and in houses in Manchester, Hammersmith, and Tottenham Court Road. One bomb at Victoria Station blew up a cloakroom and fatally injured a honeymoon couple. These acts of terrorism received the unqualified endorsement of U.S. Irish organizations.

In the early spring of 1939, Russell returned to the United States again for two purposes: to raise more money and to cause the deaths of King George VI and Queen Elizabeth of England as they crossed by train from Canada to Detroit. Scotland Yard and British Intelligence were concerned over the visit; early in May, as Russell headed for Los Angeles, Victor Mallet, counselor at the British Embassy in Washington, was in close touch with Pierrepont Moffat, State Department chief of the Division of European Affairs, on the matter. The Department of Justice was asked to instruct J. Edgar Hoover to create problems for Russell—but notably failed to act.

Russell's contacts in Los Angeles included not only Errol Flynn but the director John Ford, who had achieved great fame with his pro-Irish film *The Informer*. Yet another California contact was the Irish writer Ella Young, former lecturer in mythology at Stanford University, who published fairy tales, and poems in Gaelic and English, and reworked Irish legends, which were published by Russell's East Coast associate the printer Joseph McGarrity, who was head of the Clan-Na-Gael.

Richard B. Hood, special agent in charge of the FBI Bureau in Los Angeles, determined that McGarrity joined Russell at the Hayward Hotel in downtown Los Angeles on May 17. That same day, Ella Young sent the two Irishmen a telegram from her home in Oceano, California, requesting them to visit her. Thomas J. Devlin of the Los Angeles *Examiner* and Officer J. S. Koehn also kept their eyes on McGarrity and Russell, along with British vice consul Lionel Holiday. Hood was obliged to tell Holiday that he was on instruction to do nothing about Russell, but simply to watch him.

On May 18, Holiday again warned Hood that Russell and McGarrity were expected to "do harm" to the King and Queen. That same day, Dr. John H. Lechner, of the American Legion's Los Angeles public relations committee, called all city editors in that city and told them he had a most important announcement and that he was holding a press conference immediately. At that conference, he introduced the reporters to a Dr. Alfred A. Dinsley of Montrose, California, who allegedly specialized in cancer research. Dr. Dinsley declared that he was "a British Secret Service Agent with the designation F-10" and that he was able to state categorically that Russell was in the country to dispose of the royal couple. He gave a detailed account of Russell's movements. Unfortunately, although his statement appeared in the early editions next day, his veracity was denied by the British consulate. It was pointed out that no such designation as F-10 existed and that had Dr. Dinsley been a British agent he would have been subject to criminal prosecution under the British Official

Secrets Act for having disclosed the fact. Thus, Dinsley was ridiculed; and the effect of this was to deactivate whatever interest the FBI might have had in the matter. A possible explanation of this mysterious episode is that Russell and McGarrity engineered it in order to render absurd the potential charges against them.

However, they were scarcely helpful to their own cause by openly discussing the reception they would give to the British monarch and his wife within the hearing of a Hayward Hotel employee, who reported their conversation to the FBI. Not that this mattered, since the FBI continued to do nothing and Russell was still not brought in for questioning.

On that same day, May 18, Norman Kendal, assistant commissioner of the Metropolitan Police Office of New Scotland Yard's Special Branch, wrote to the State Department referring to Russell's reported presence in Los Angeles. However, instead of calling for Russell's direct investigation or questioning, the letter stated with disturbing coolness:

> Information has been received that this man is in the United States of America for the dual purpose of raising funds to finance the present campaign of sabotage and to instigate hostile demonstrations by Irish Republican elements there during the visit of Their Majesties the King and Queen.
>
> This information is forwarded as the Commissioner knows it is the desire of the United States authorities that the visit should pass off without any untoward incident, and he would be grateful if, in the event of Sean Russell leaving the United States of America, the name of the ship on which he leaves, port of arrival in Europe, etc., he could be notified.

Apparently, British Intelligence had not alerted Scotland Yard or MI6 that the purpose of the mission was to kill the royal couple. Indeed, the appearance of Dr. Dinsley resulted in Richard B. Hood of the Los Angeles FBI stating in a telegram to Washington that the story was purely a hoax. However, the same day that he was denouncing it as such, Nathanael Peiper of the FBI in San Francisco reported to J. Edgar Hoover that his office had bugged a meeting in San Francisco between Hermann Schwinn, Fritz Wiedemann, and Russell in which the details of the bomb plot were discussed. The purpose was "to waylay the Royal couple in

Detroit as they crossed from Windsor on the train." The FBI apparently preferred to follow Hood, and still did very little. The Los Angeles newspapers bent over backwards to correct any impression that Dr. Dinsley might have given of Russell's true purpose.

However, the State Department, in an unaccustomed burst of pro-British concern, kept in touch with the British consuls on the matter on the American West Coast. The reason for this interest was the temporary presence in the State Department in 1939 of a very remarkable person. George Messersmith had been United States consul in Berlin and Vienna and ambassador to Cuba, and was currently in an interregnum on a special desk prior to replacing the aging Josephus Daniels as ambassador to Mexico. Anti-Nazi, he took a great interest in all activities which opposed Britain and the Roosevelt administration, and he knew from his background in European affairs of the Irish-Nazi connection. Where the FBI and the Department of Justice fell down, he took up the slack. He and his associate Avra Warren performed their own intelligence action in the matter, keeping in touch with stringers on the Coast.

Russell's movements were closely followed in San Francisco. He was found to be in touch with both Harry Bridges, Australian president of the West Coast maritime union, and the alleged Communist activist Harrison George. It is clear that these contacts were simply blinds to confuse consular and State Department investigators.

Great concern was expressed by the Royal Canadian Mounted Police in the matter of border control. So concerned were the Los Angeles *Examiner's* reporter Thomas J. Devlin and police officer J. S. Koehn that they offered to go to London to testify to their anxiety at their own expense. At the same time, the Woman's National Organization of Ireland, the Cumànn-Na-Mban, publicly protested the cooperation of British and American police against Russell. George Messersmith continued to keep an eye on Russell's movements, with little or no help from the Department of Justice. The royal couple continued to tour Canada; bombs, found in pieces after exploding in movie theaters in Liverpool, England, were discovered to be of American origin.

On May 25, 1939, S. T. Wood, of the Royal Canadian Mounted Police in Ottawa, cabled Hoover asking for photographs, descriptions, and measurements of Russell to be cabled to them at once so that Russell could be intercepted in the event that he tried to cross the border. On May 31, the British Home Office rather desultorily laid out possible plans to extradite Russell, who was at Butte, Montana, that day. Russell was at the Finlen Hotel there, contacting nationalist circles. Via his own spies, not the FBI's, Messersmith determined that Russell left the following day for the Middle West or the East—on either the North Coast Limited or the Olympian. The intelligence service was slack and the police failed to search the trains. To confuse matters still further, when Inspector Carnak, acting head of the Criminal Identification Division of the Royal Canadian Mounted Police in Ottawa, contacted FBI agent W. W. Banister through his Edmonton, Alberta, office, Banister said that Russell had never been in Butte at all. This was entirely incorrect.

Avra Warren and George Messersmith requested that the Chicago authorities keep Russell under "constant and extraordinary surveillance" when he arrived there on June 2. Indeed, they even considered obtaining Russell's detention; at that moment, aided by the ineptitude of the FBI, the IRA leader was moving about freely in that city, preparing for his journey to Detroit. Also on June 2, the State Department was advised by Post Office Inspector Cooney in Butte that Russell definitely had stayed there at the Finlen Hotel. So much for FBI efficiency.

Russell was kept under surveillance by Messersmith's and Warren's special agents at the Morrison Hotel. Messersmith was in a highly ambiguous frame of mind. He wrote to Warren on June 2, "This [close surveillance] is I feel all we should do for the next few days still. I realize your preoccupations which I share, but there are the definite dangers that we will do more harm than good by having him taken into custody or detained now.

"If he is detained on the ground that he has not made legal entry or for some such reason, he has the right to a hearing, and if this should be delayed there is no doubt that various Irish-American groups in this country would become very vocal. We would have all sorts of people saying that the man was being detained in custody and not being given a hearing promptly.

"The undesirable publicity which we would raise through detention at this moment would, I believe, assume serious proportions. All in all, I think the wise course is to have [Russell's] movements carefully followed so that we can lay hands on him at any time this may seem desirable."

Actually, had the FBI chosen to make known the details of the planned assassination discussed in San Francisco to the State Department and to the newspapers, the ill effects of Dr. Dinsley's press conference would have dissolved and the public would have been in a mood to accept Russell's being taken in for questioning. Despite the residual isolationism of the American public even after Hitler's conquest of Austria and Czechoslovakia, most Americans felt affection for the British royal couple and would have reacted strongly to a widely publicized announcement that the couple's lives were in danger. However, the FBI's position became uncomfortably clear in a letter written by Hoover to Messersmith on June 5, 1939. It stated categorically, "It has been necessary for me to decline this specific request for investigation from New Scotland Yard because of the fact that this Bureau has not been requested or authorized to conduct any investigation concerning the protection of the persons of the King and Queen of England." Why not? Francis Biddle had not supplied the authorization.

The truth was that just as all departments were nervous of taking action against Father Coughlin, so they were jittery about Russell. The public in any democracy represents the ultimate power. Without the primary evidence of the tapes of the San Francisco meeting, and with the election looming the following year, the Administration clearly dared not provoke the Catholic electorate.

Except for Messersmith, who on June 5 forced the Immigration Department to move against Russell in Detroit. McGarrity had joined Russell there while the royal couple progressed to the border, greeted by cheering crowds. The citizens of Windsor, many of them working in automobile factories across the border in Detroit, gathered in thousands on the Ambassador Bridge as the heavily guarded royal train chugged toward its destination. Whether the royal couple was advised of the danger is unknown. But just before the train reached Detroit, Russell was already in prison along with McGarrity, and his Irish Free State passport was impounded. For some reason, McGarrity was released immediately and returned to his hotel. Immediately Russell's apprehension was known and the royal couple proceeded safely to Niagara Falls; three congressmen, James P. McGranery of Pennsylvania, J. Joseph Smith of Connecticut, and Martin L. Sweeney of Ohio gathered around them seventy Irish sympathizers in the House and decided on the spot to take action against the government in the matter. The three congressmen went to see Roosevelt, who promised to take the matter up immediately with the State Department. The congressmen jointly stated that if Russell was not released at once the seventy to seventy-five appropriate figures of Congress would see to it that the royal couple's visit to Washington was subject to their mutual boycott.

On June 7, there was a confrontation in the House. Representative Sweeney said firmly, "Mr. Sean Russell, a prominent Irish citizen, was here upon a lecture tour. He was minding his own business. It just goes to show the influence of the British Government in the United States when the Justice Department on the request of Scotland Yard arrests a man like this. I shall insist that the State Department give an adequate explanation of this outrageous affair."

The Clan-Na-Gael put up $4,000 bail. If bail was forfeited, McGarrity would guarantee that McGranery would return it to the Clan.

In a last-ditch effort to keep Russell in bondage, Messersmith pulled strings to have the bail increased to $5,000, which McGranery was able to raise overnight. Immigration released Russell from his cell in Detroit; the special bond covering his release was worded very peculiarly indeed. Instead of containing the proviso desired by Messersmith that Russell leave the country at once, it stated that he depart within "a reasonable period of time," for the interesting reason that the British were stopping ships in Bermuda and "there is some fear that he would be apprehended by the British who have Criminal Processes outstanding against him." Why that fear should be entertained by the Department of Justice can only be conjectured.

Sean Russell came to Washington, and a party was given in his honor by his supporters, including Senator Wheeler. Among those present was Garth Healey, secretary of the Irish embassy, who had helped in the matter of the bond. On June 10, Sean Russell went before U.S. Immigration Inspector Leland W. Williams for a hearing on a deportation order engineered by Messersmith and Avra Warren. They were acting on the technicality that Russell disguised the nature of his occupation and purpose of visiting the United States, as well as his real name in applying for his nonimmigrant visa.

Russell joked with reporters about his pleasant stay in Detroit and reasserted an earlier statement that his presence in that city at the time of the royal visit was "purely coincidental."

Letters poured into the State Department demanding that Russell be better treated. The FBI, having made their token move in Detroit, could do no more. When a representative of the Attorney General's office was asked late in June about the Sean Russell case, that representative knew so little about it that she asked the FBI to inform her what had been done. The answer was noncommittal.

The bond on Russell was continued until April 1940. On July 21, the Irish Republican Army formally declared war on England; at a meeting supported by Russell at a house in the Bronx, McGarrity stated that the war would not be over until the British Government recognized the Republic of Ireland, withdrew troops from Irish cities, ceased to influence Irish politics, and set free those men and women in English jails charged with the recent bombings. Those present at the meeting said that if one prisoner was sentenced to death or died in his cell it would guarantee support for the IRA to blow up "power stations, post offices and/or government buildings in England." They reasserted their conviction that the Republic of Ireland, proclaimed in 1916 and formally ratified by the Irish people in 1919, was the only legal government of the state of Eire.

At the time, German support of the Clan-Na-Gael and Sean Russell was even more overt. Despite this fact, nothing was done about Russell. Indeed, clearly confident that nothing would interfere with his operation as war rapidly approached in Europe, he returned to open activism in the United States. Neither the State Department nor any other branch of government continued to keep an eye on this dangerous terrorist after his bond was lodged. Even Messersmith had been deactivated. On August 11, 1939, Messersmith wrote in a memorandum that the British embassy had asked Pierrepont Moffat whether Russell was still in the country. Messersmith was obliged to reply that he did not know.

The same morning, Avra Warren determined that Russell's passport, which had been held for only two months at Immigration headquarters in Detroit, had been delivered under the table to Russell's attorney. The official in the Labor Department said, based on what information was not made clear, that if Russell did not leave the country on a false passport before the genuine passport was released to him, he would leave the country that week or the following week. The Labor Department official, a Mr. Tom Fitch, said he would try to learn whether Russell left from New York City—it would be difficult to learn if he had left from another port. Fitch went on to say there was no way of telling whether Russell had already left the country on a false passport. It would only be possible to determine that "if the consular officer before whom he appears on his arrival abroad to make arrangement for the cancellation of the bond at Detroit is wide enough awake to find out when, how, and from what port and under what name he left the United States.

"The Department of Labor indicated that arrangements had been made with Russell's attorney for Russell to appear before an American consular officer abroad and make arrangement for the cancellation of his bond." Apparently, neither Fitch nor anyone else had bothered to ask Russell's attorney whether his client was in the country.

Or even picked up a copy of a daily newspaper. Russell's appearances at public meetings were recorded extensively that August. At a mass rally in Chicago, attended by ten thousand people, of the Irish American National Alliance, he stated to loud cheers that the bombings in England were totally justified and part of "the most enjoyable war I ever fought." He said, "And this is a war! It's a war against the English yoke. The bombings are a frontal attack in a full-fledged modern war. But this is a new kind of war, because it has been waged against the nation instead of against its people. It is the most humane and the most skillful warfare in history. I've had my real fighting and liked it as well as any man, but this is the first war I was ever in where soldiers have an opportunity to show that they can think instead of kill.

"We can destroy bridges, railways, buildings and public utilities. . . . Prime Minister De Valera and the Irish Parliament are compromisers. They deal with the enemy. The bombings are being carried out by our army and they will continue."

Russell continued his tour uninterrupted and uninvestigated. When a routine press inquiry came into the FBI on August 29, W. W. Banister, of Hoover's office, simply referred to Russell's visit to Butte and gave no further references. However, the report of the inquiry was significantly headed SEAN (JOHN) RUSSELL: ESPIONAGE, thus acknowledging that the FBI had full cognizance of his activities.

On October 3, Irish police and customs men in Dublin seized a cache of arms worth over $1,000,000 secretly imported from the United States and also $100,500 in cash. Russell had raised this matériel and money. The matter was of so much concern to the State Department that Cordell Hull personally sent a telegram marked SECRET to the American legation in Dublin stating that if these articles had been exported to Ireland this would constitute a violation of the law. It was clear that in fact the export was illegal and it was also clear that Hull's office had not been briefed, because the cable indicated the belief that Russell had left

America. Again, merely opening a newspaper would have established his continued presence in the country.

In fact, Russell remained in the United States until April 1940. He continued to raise money for armaments while official memoranda went to and fro questioning precisely where he was. One might have legitimately assumed that the FBI and the State Department would have made it their business to find out. In August 1940 he was said to be staying with the Reverend Richard Collins in San Francisco, and on December 10, 1940, the FBI reported upon censored letters sent by an alleged friend of Russell, Anna Griffin of San Francisco, to an alleged mistress of his, Aine O'Farrelly, at that time interned in Mountjoy Jail, in Dublin. On December 30, Hoover was asking where Russell was in a memorandum to his office in San Francisco, and in February 1941 his requests became more urgent. In July 1941, he insisted on hearing from agent E. J. Connelley in New York what was going on, writing, "Imperative this case receive attention. Submit report without fail in ten days." He was still wondering about Russell in 1943. He was asking whether Russell was in the country or had died in Lisbon, as had been reported.

The fact was that Russell had left the country in April 1940, operating under direct instructions from the Abwehr under the protection of Congressman McGranery, who had obtained work for him as a fireman on the ship SS *George Washington*, bound for Genoa. According to some sources, he got aboard in the disguise of a blind musician. Almost a year later, Errol Flynn's Nazi associate and friend Dr. Hermann Erben was to leave America for Japan and China with Errol Flynn's help, also disguised as a musician. Russell went straight to Germany with the approval of Admiral Canaris, chief of the Abwehr, and he was installed in the home of a bank director near Berlin, where he was trained very carefully under the guidance of German agent Franz Fromme. He was given a course in sabotage in a laboratory run by Ribbentrop's special adviser on Ireland, Dr. Edmund Veesenmayer, and he watched commando units of the Brandenburg Regiment in full training with explosives and joined them in their operations. Ribbentrop very much admired Russell; he encouraged him to bring about a coup d'état against De Valera and the British in Northern Ireland. In return for this cooperation, Russell arranged for the release of his close friend and IRA associate Frank Ryan, who had been imprisoned by Franco during the Spanish Civil War. Canaris talked to Franco; Ryan was allowed to escape from prison, where a car was arranged by Wolfgang Blaum of the Abwehr headquarters in Madrid.

Ryan went to Berlin, where Russell conferred with him; Russell forgave Ryan for his activities for the Loyalists, and together they made arrangements to leave for Ireland.

Russell and Ryan were given the use of a U-boat which sailed from Wilhelmshaven on August 8, 1940, at around the time the head of the Federal Bureau of Investigation and the Secretary of State of the United States were wondering which part of America Russell was in. A day and a night after leaving Wilhelmshaven, Russell was seized with stomach pains. Conditions on the U-boat were cramped, airless, and primitive and the doctor was unable to do very much. Russell died in a matter of hours. The question is why? Is it possible that a British secret agent was on board the U-boat? Was Ryan acting as a double agent, and was he still loyal to his Communist sympathies? Did Loyalist elements or perhaps Russian intelligence inspire him? Could he have killed his old friend? And there is another question: why did the U-boat captain, on leave in Berlin soon afterward, prove to be so careless that he was knocked down and killed by a car?

The official medical verdict given by the German Admiralty was that Russell had died of a perforated ulcer. This is unlikely. If that were the case, the condition would have been advancing for some time, and at the age of fifty Russell would not have been fit enough to become involved in special commando training in Berlin just a few weeks earlier. Moreover, any man who worked for the Abwehr, especially on so crucial a matter as subversion in Ireland, would have had to undergo an unusually strenuous examination, equivalent to that required by the Gestapo, before undertaking the long journey. It is doubtful whether Russell would have risked the venture if he were suffering from severe stomach trouble.

Since Ryan was nothing if not loyal to Russell, the only remaining possibility is that a British Intelligence contact killed Russell. Certainly, British Naval Intelligence is known to have had plants all through the German Navy; it would have been a comparatively simple matter to poison Russell's food or drink.

On March 23, 1943, the United States District Court for the Eastern District of Michigan filed suit for a retrieval of the $5,000 bond supplied by the United States Fidelity and Guaranty Company on behalf of the Irish-American activist Clan-Na-Gael and finally guaranteed by

Congressman James McGranery, who would stand to lose the full amount if the government won. McGranery called Henry Schweinhaut, special assistant to the Attorney General, Criminal Division, on March 25, saying that he had paid premiums on this bond at the rate of $100 a year since it was supplied. Greatly agitated, McGranery said, "The FBI investigated Sean Russell and their reports have him dead at least three times, including reports he died in Germany, that he was murdered by the British at Gibralter, and that he died at Lisbon, Portugal. They don't know if he's dead or alive."

That McGranery knew of these reports only goes to show that he had contacts in the Washington bureau, contacts who undoubtedly had aided him and his fellow congressmen in their protection of Russell. McGranery misinformed Schweinhaut that Russell had left the country on the SS *Conte di Savoia,* whereas in fact, as we know, he had sailed on the *George Washington.* This can only have been a deliberately misleading statement on McGranery's part. Indeed, Schweinhaut and his associate Lambert O'Donnell, an attorney in the Criminal Division, both felt that McGranery had gotten Russell out of the country in order to evade the British authorities. Schweinhaut felt that although the burden of proof of Russell's leaving the country rested with the defense in the action to forfeit the bond, he did not feel that the bond should be forfeited if Russell, from the information available, appeared to have left the country.

In a later FBI report, it was stated that the Bureau would remain "inactive as usual" in the matter and would not investigate whether Russell had left the country or not. Even in 1943, neither Immigration nor (allegedly) the British authorities were able to ascertain Russell's whereabouts.

The case of Michigan versus the U.S. Fidelity and Guaranty Co. was dropped. Then, on June 21, 1944, James J. Conaty, executive treasurer of the Clan-Na-Gael in Boston, was seized by a fit of conscience—or perhaps by a fit of annoyance with McGranery. He swore out a statement that McGranery had put Russell on the ship himself in disguise; he had first placed him there as the blind musician, and had later placed him as a fireman with the aid of a Nazi agent who was a member of the crew.

Despite this sworn statement, McGranery was not brought in for questioning. On August 31, 1948, there was another interesting development. James Brislane, second in command of the Clan-Na-Gael, filed a complaint in the U.S. District Court for the Eastern District of Pennsylvania, charging that Congressman McGranery was chosen as a trustee of $5,000 and the money was placed in his care to secure the alien bond which had been issued on behalf of Sean Russell; that on January 20, 1944, the government voluntarily dismissed the case against Sean Russell, that this dismissal released the bonding company from its liability, that following this, Brislane and other officials of the Clan-Na-Gael made demands on McGranery to return the money entrusted to him but that McGranery had wrongfully refused and continued to refuse to return all or any part of the money entrusted to him. The complaint asked for a judgment of $5,000 plus interest from January 20, 1944, and costs.

On September 30, McGranery filed an answer specifically denying the allegations made in the complaint, asserting that neither James Brislane nor the Clan-Na-Gael had any claim to the money; that the money belonged to the estate of Joseph McGarrity, who had died in 1940, and that in view of the fact that the money belonged to the McGarrity estate, the executors of that estate should be made party to the litigation.

The case went to trial on March 28, 1949. During the hearing, the entire IRA-Nazi-Russell-McGarrity-congressional connection was raked over. It was revealed that Russell's attorney Thomas F. Chawke had told McGranery and McGarrity early in 1940 that the bond had been forfeited in January because Immigration was not satisfied that Russell had left the country. Chawke was afraid that he would be called upon by the bonding company to put up the $5,000, for which he was secondarily responsible.

The trial revealed that McGranery had signed a receipt on February 29, 1940, indicating that he had received of Joseph McGarrity on behalf of the Clan-Na-Gael the sum to be held in trust for bail. If the bail was not forfeited it was to be returned to Clan-Na-Gael. The end of the matter was that McGranery was found guilty on March 29, 1949, but was let off with a modest fine.

The result was that despite the fact that both American and British intelligence were aware of the Nazi connections of the Clan-Na-Gael and the Irish Republican Army, both organizations continued to flourish throughout World War II. Encouraged by the ineptitude of officialdom in the Russell matter and the overt (before Pearl Harbor) and covert (after Pearl Harbor) support by McGranery until the showdown over the money, the IRA did not cease its activities, and the Abwehr retained its connections with that organization well into the war.

✠✠✠✠✠✠✠ 10

The White Russian Nazis

Alfred Rosenberg was the chief inspiration for the American White Russian groups led by the Organization for Rebirth of the Ukraine, better known as ODWU, and the Ukrainian Hetman Organization, or UHO. The concern of these organizations, which were keenly supported by Boris Brasol, was the recapturing of the Ukraine from the Soviet Union. Meetings of the Control Commission of the Ukrainian National Organization were held at 83 Grand Street, Jersey City, and were heavily attended by leaders of the Ukrainian community. By 1940, the association had a membership of forty thousand people, all operating under former leaders of the White Guard, a terrorist Czarist organization that committed acts of violence, murder, and despoliation in Poland and the Balkans. The directing body, or Provid, which worked directly with the Abwehr and with the Auslands Organisation (AO), had a string of special liaison officials, bound to their duties by a sacred oath, who threaded through free nations spreading their doctrines and subversive plans.

In the late 1930s, terrorist leaders of the ODWU, including leaders of the German Army specializing in espionage operations, arrived in the United States and were granted residency when many Jews had difficulty in squeezing through the needle's eye of the State Department Visa Division. By 1940, following a series of clandestine meetings across the nation, the leader of the ODWU in the United States was Monsignor Ivan Buchko, of the Ukrainian Catholic church at 22 East Seventh Street, New York. Despite the fact that his activities on behalf of the Nazis had resulted in his removal even from countries like Argentina and Uruguay, he was admitted back to the United States and had no further problems with either Breckinridge Long, of the Visa Division, or Major Lemuel Schofield, of the Immigration and Naturalization Service.

The hetman was particularly influential in Detroit. It is not surprising that a special assistant to Harry Bennett, of Ford Motor Company, was one of the hetmans at a time when Bennett was working closely with Coughlin to infiltrate unions. The German-American Bund under Gerhardt Wilhelm Kunze paid funds into the UHO, and the reliable German Library of Information, at 17 Battery Place, supplied much propaganda material for distribution. A keen admirer of the UHO and the ODWU was Joseph P. Kamp, the proselytizer, editor and publisher, and sponsor of the Nazi Sympathizer Major General Van Horn Moseley, who later became a supporter and intimate friend of Senator Joseph McCarthy of Wisconsin.

Meanwhile, leaders of the ODWU and the UHO besieged Hitler with telegrams of approval of his every move. The organizations had contacts in the Army.

In late 1940, the Organization of Ukrainian Nationalists moved to Rome, where a correspondent of the official Ukrainian Fascist newspaper *Svoboda*, of Jersey City, was the paymaster of funds supplied in the United States. All members of the organization in Germany were in the Gestapo or the Regular Army from the moment war broke out in Europe. They kept up constant contact with their American associates. The Ukrainian Catholic diocese gave support to the organization; and when a representative went to New York City as an auxiliary authorized by Cardinal Spellman, he actually began promoting the ODWU and the UHO through Catholic journals. The organizations raised substantial funds to subvert the large number of Ukrainian-Americans who were opposed to their activities.

The Ukrainian Mutual Aid Society held a meeting in New York City on October 19, 1940, demanding the ejection of the ODWU and the UHO from Ukrainian circles. The members insisted that unless the Ukrainian National Association purged itself of all pro-Nazi elements they would split off permanently from the UNA. Letters were drawn up, signed by all members, insisting on the outlawing of the extremists. They were backed by the liberal newspaper *PM* and by Albert E. Kahn's weekly newsletter *The Hour*.

In December 1940, with the matter not resolved, a member of the British appeasement group which was lobbying for negotiated peace with Hitler made contact with *Svoboda*'s editor, in Canada. The paper had been banned there. The agent told him that he represented Lord Halifax, who was shortly to become British ambassador to Washington; about a month earlier, at a meeting at the Mark Hopkins Hotel, in San Francisco, Sir William Wiseman, of Kuhn, Loeb, had discussed with the Princess Stefanie Hohenlohe and Nazi Consul General Fritz Wiedemann Lord Halifax's role in a negotiated peace with Germany.*

Boris Brasol was in support of the Fascists. On January 26, 1941, he published in the newspaper *Rossiya* an open letter to Radio Station WEAF in New York City attacking the Fred Waring orchestra for ruining the old Russian national anthem to the commercial "Forty million Americans are smoking Chesterfields." Brasol condemned the jazzing up of the hymn as part of a Bolshevik plot and threatened a Russian-American boycott of the well-known brand of cigarette.

In March 1941, the Ukrainian press service in Rome increased supplies of propaganda to the United States. In one bulletin, it bragged that ODWU members in Argentina, operating directly under the Nazis, had sunk several British ships. Other missives from Rome attacked the ODWU critics in *The Hour* and *PM*. But Albert E. Kahn, of the former publication, obtained a document in booklet form with photographs showing a UHO convention in Berlin in which the members gave the Nazi salute to a portrait of Hitler. Publication of this information caused embarrassment in Berlin, since the organization was not thought to be as widely exposed as the German-American Bund. There was talk in Nazi circles of disbanding it; but on April 5, Kahn charged that Ukrainian Fascists were responsible for the sabotage of the Pennsylvania Railroad Cleveland-to-Pittsburgh express which caused the death of five persons.

Other organizations supported the Ukrainians. These included Romanian groups connected to the Iron Guard. Support also came from the Armenians, in the form of the Tashnags, or Armenian Revolutionary Federationers, who had made a deal with Hitler that he would put them in power when he invaded their Soviet-controlled country. A Tashnag had stabbed to death Archbishop Leon Tourian, primate of the Armenian Church in America, when he was celebrating Mass in New York on

---

* See *Trading with the Enemy*, p. 194.

Christmas Eve 1933, charging that the archbishop was a Soviet secret agent.

The Tashnags had financial and personal links to the Irish and White Russian groups. As early as March 15, 1938, the ODWU organ *The Nationalist* extended an invitation to all Armenian revolutionaries to coordinate their activities with the Ukrainians, and that collaboration continued until the early 1940s. Like the Ukrainians, the Armenian terrorists falsely claimed the support of the whole of their national community.

That same month, instead of discrediting the ODWU and the UHO, Nazi Germany issued instructions for Ukrainians to step up their activities. Under orders from Berlin, they infiltrated agents into every industry and the Army, Navy, and Coast Guard, until finally they matched the Irish in being instruments of Nazi subversive efforts.

By July 1941, Ukrainian organizations were financed from Berlin and American sympathizers to the sum of $6,000,000. Through their recording secretary, they retained contact with the Berlin headquarters. They denounced Winston Churchill and Roosevelt for joining forces with the Soviet Union.

All through that summer, Ukrainian fifth columnists spread out across the United States filming roads, bridges, factories, and military and naval locations. Virtually the whole of Pittsburgh, with its mills, railroad yards, and river barges; Detroit and the bridge to Windsor, Ontario; and Lockheed and other airplane plants in California were filmed by the underground groups. By October, they had a grasp of the whole American defense system. They were aided by Lithuanians who supervised the distribution of Nazi materials in Lithuanian-language dailies bitterly attacking the Red Russians and calling for all Lithuanians to stand shoulder to shoulder against the Soviet Union. The organization worked very closely with the Quisling-type regime in Lithuania, the puppet government set up under the Nazis. The Lithuanians were particularly active in distributing leaflets condemning Germany's enemies in the matter of the invasion of Russia.

The Ukrainians had friends everywhere. Even so distinguished a publisher as the Yale University Press published a book, Michael Hrushevsky's *A History of the Ukraine*, which praised the German Ukrainian fifth column in the most extravagant terms and praised Hitler outright. A venomous stream of manifestos poured out of ODWU headquarters as Hitler became an increasing threat to the United States and Roosevelt waged an undeclared war in the Atlantic. It was not until after Pearl Harbor that at last the Jewish Henry Morgenthau, Jr., Secretary of the Treasury, ordered the freezing of the Ukrainian funds.

Another supporter of the White Russian Nazis was an executive of the Romanoff Caviar Company, chiefly known in intelligence circles as a source of money for isolationist congressmen and senators.

A major figure of the White Russian movement in the United States was Count Anastase Vonsiatsky, popularly known as Annie. He embodied his role of Nazi to the hilt. He had huge shoulders, powerfully muscled arms, and a barrel chest; he was over six feet tall and weighed over two hundred pounds. He had an enormous head, and he liked to dress in uniform of brown shirt, thick, studded leather belt, riding breeches, and leather thigh boots. His office was decorated with maps of the world, showing the czarist empire before it was destroyed by the Soviets, pictures of the Romanoff royal family, photographs of their slaughter at Ekatarinburg, and ship models of the czarist fleet.

He had a large following—and a small battalion of armed followers situated in Thompson, Connecticut. His favorite remark to visitors of his own persuasion was "America First does good work. It is a must when Hitler wins. Your Senators Wheeler, Nye, and D. Worth Clark will save your America for you Americans. And Lindbergh is great! And Father Coughlin!" Vonsiatsky saw this group correctly as the forerunners of the Fourth Reich, when America would join with Germany in the New Dawn of racial purity. In common with other White Russians, he dreamed of the restoration of royalty in Europe. He wanted to see Romanov Grand Duke Cyril on the throne in Moscow and St. Petersburg and the Gestapo-employed sons of the Kaiser put back in Berlin. If Hitler opposed this scheme, he must be deposed in favor of Himmler. Unfortunately, with its necessary concern about communism, the Roosevelt government initially proved lax about prosecuting the White Russians; J. Edgar Hoover, so often handicapped in other areas, had to fight through red tape to investigate the count and his cohorts.

Anastase Vonsiatsky was born in Warsaw, Poland, on June 12, 1898, of a family that was devoted to the hegemony of royalist power in Europe. His parents had pictures of the British Queen, and the Kaiser, and the Czar, all of whom were related, framed on their bureaus alongside each other. At the age of eighteen, the huge and vigorous, brutal youth did the only thing possible for a man of his athleticism and virility: he enlisted in the White Russian Army. He was the toast of the Yalta barracks in 1920 for his fanaticism and for his numerous conquests of attractive young women. Smoking a cigar, roaring with laughter, telling dirty jokes, his booted feet propped up on a chair and a large glass of vodka in his hand, he was adored by everyone.

When the Germans seized the Crimea, Vonsiatsky became a soldier of the puppet government. Too idle now that his services with the bayonet or a rifle were not called for, he and his friends filled the time raiding homes of alleged Communist suspects. They took their victims at gunpoint by horse cart to a house that had once belonged to the czar and tortured to death those who did not have the money to buy them off. When a local newspaper had the temerity to complain of their activities, Vonsiatsky and his friends wrecked the offices.

In the autumn of 1920, the count, driven out of Russia by the revolution, joined thousands of White Russians who took refuge in Constantinople and then in Paris. He starved for a time, and collapsed in the Paris back streets; taken to a hospital, he was found to be suffering from severe malnutrition. His huge body had shrunk to 150 pounds; he lay so exhausted in his hospital bed he could not raise his hands to eat. A very rich woman, the clever, sophisticated Marion Stephens, divorced wife of a Chicago lawyer and daughter of department-store millionaire Norman B. Ream, visited the hospital to disburse sums of money and gifts to the patients. She stopped longer than usual at the count's bedside; even in his emaciated state, he attracted her, and she told the hospital supervisor that she wanted him moved to a private ward at her expense. She nursed him back to health; he proved enormously grateful. The fifty-five-year-old woman and the twenty-two-year-old man began an intense and impassioned romantic relationship.

With $50 million at her disposal, Marion Stephens was ideally placed to back the count's dream of welding together the White Russians of the world into the so-called All-Russian National-Socialist Labor Party, which arose in the United States simultaneously with Hitler's nascent Nazi Party. Even with that amount of money, it took six years to find all of the White Russians in exile in America and the Latin American countries and to enlist them in the cause.

Back in the United States, the count and Marion gave interviews to the press in her favorite city of Philadelphia. In several of them, Marion announced that Vonsiatsky would work his way up through the Baldwin

Locomotive Works, to learn the business gradually, and without special assistance from her. She stated that when the czar's government was restored, as it rightfully should be, Anastase would be the company's representative there. The count lied cheerfully to reporters that he was as rich as his protectress—or would be if it were not for the fact that the Russians had confiscated his lavish estate in southern Russia.

On February 4, 1922, the count and Marion were married in an elaborate society wedding in the Russian Orthodox faith at St. Nicholas Cathedral in New York. Encouraged by contacts in Berlin, the count quickly gave up his job with the locomotive company and he and Marion devoted all their time and money to their holy crusade against Moscow. He linked up with Fascist parties in Italy and Spain that could be relied upon to bring about the invasion and defeat of Russia; by 1929, he had traveled so extensively toward his purpose, staying with Marion in royal suites in the world's finest hotels, eating and drinking prodigiously, that he had already spent $1 million.

Financially aided by Herbert Hoover, who longed to see a restoration of the czars because the Bolsheviks had seized his Russian oil fields in 1919, the count lived for a time in Paris, where he published an inflammatory magazine, *The Sentinel*, with the subheading: *The Organ of the Russian Military in Exile*. In 1934, he surfaced again, first in Berlin and then in Tokyo, where he helped found the Japanese White Russian spy network. He traveled to Shanghai to confer with the legendary German agent Ignatius Trebitsch-Lincoln, now in the disguise of a Buddhist monk as Abot Chao-kung. He then proceeded to Harbin in Manchuria, a major White Russian center, where he addressed secret meetings and was appointed the world *vojd*, or leader, of White Russia. Had his dream of the restoration of the czars come true, he would undoubtedly have been made prime minister of the new Russia under Hitler.

The count proceeded to Budapest, Belgrade, and Bucharest to set up organizations that would aid the Nazis when they attacked the Soviet Union. Back in Connecticut, the count financed and supplied the police with tear-gas bombs to disrupt factory strikes. He established a White Russian magazine, boldly called *The Fascist*, and the Russian National Fascist Revolutionary Party, which joined forces with the Bund and received the approval of Senators Wheeler and Nye.

On May 21, 1939, the count addressed a Bund rally at Camp Siegfried, Yaphank, Long Island, at which thirty thousand young Americans of pure Aryan blood, dressed in Gestapo uniforms, saluted banners portraying Himmler and Hitler. The count, in the black-and-silver uniform of the Death's Head Brigade, stood beside another White Russian, the English-sounding James Wheeler-Hill; he screamed at the crowd, "It is a great honor to be at the side of your brave leader, Fritz Kuhn!"

As war approached, the count helped the Ukrainians to set up a spy ring of White Russian, German, Lithuanian, Latvian, and Estonian agents working in factories, plants, and ship docks across the country. They were ordered to leak information in their own networks for transmission to Berlin. On one of several visits to Germany after war broke out in Europe, the count conferred with Alfred Rosenberg in Berlin on the combination of all Germanic peoples in a master race. The Union would consist of 100,000,000 people subjugating all other races in slavery. Rosenberg's office in Berlin contained a map of the ancient German empire showing how much had been taken from it by marauders over the centuries; the count was inflamed by the vision Rosenberg presented of Hitlerian reconquests of the continent.

Like George Sylvester Viereck, the count made a special point of visiting with the Kaiser at exile in Doorn. He also met the Kaiser's sons, one of whom was the chief salesman for the Ford Motor Company in Europe. The count also met with, and found a willing ear in, the anti-Semitic Henry Ford himself, and, of course, Harry Bennett and John Koos.

Travel became increasingly difficult as the war went on. Vonsiatsky decided to center his activities entirely in Thompson, Connecticut. His mistake was to be too overt in his efforts to unify the various scattered anti-Semitic, Nazi, Fascist, and other patriotic groups under his leadership. Marion Vonsiatsky made the mistake of boasting at a party in New York that her husband was born on the same day as Peter the Great and was destined to rank with Napoleon and Hitler in the world's history.

J. Edgar Hoover and General Sherman Miles of Army Intelligence decided to keep an eye on Vonsiatsky and his movements. The count and Wheeler-Hill were followed everywhere, and their conversations were bugged. Federal agents determined that Wheeler-Hill would be Vonsiatsky's second-in-command and foreign minister after Hitler invaded Russia; and this was at a time when Germany and Russia were in alliance. Agents followed the count to meetings with the Japanese ambassador in Washington. Plants in the embassy taught them that already Japan was being

involved in intrigues on behalf of the Third Reich. Vonsiatsky also continued to work closely with Serge Rubinstein, whose chief contact was the
locally resident Tujusakuru Kasai, of the Japanese Diet.

At his estate in Thompson, the count built a combined fortress and
arsenal on the two hundred rolling acres on a promontory overlooking the
sea. The fortress was of white stone, with walls two feet thick, and machine guns bristled everywhere; the arsenal contained large supplies of
tear-gas and hand grenades. Although the people of Thompson regarded
the count as something of a maniac with dreams of glory that led him to
pantomime the Führer, he was in fact, as J. Edgar Hoover knew, poten-
tially dangerous to American security.

It occurred to the FBI chief in New York, the hardworking, bullet-
headed Percy Foxworth, that it would be difficult to bring the count in
unless some Russian-speaking person could be made to penetrate his circle. Just when Foxworth was wondering whom to hire for the job, the
ideal person materialized out of nowhere. This was Alexei Pelypenko, a
lean, rangy, secretive Roman Catholic priest of Ukrainian birth and Polish
adoption who hated the Nazis for their invasion of Poland and turned
against them after working as a Nazi contact in Argentina.

Born on February 12, 1893, at Kovalivka, in the Ukraine, Pelypenko
was originally ordained a Greek Orthodox priest at Luck, Poland, in 1915,
then traveled to Warsaw. Clever and accomplished, he was a master of
several languages; and from 1933 to 1937 he taught young Nazis at the
College of St. Andrew, in Munich. The Gestapo suspected him of being a
double agent but had no proof—he was given three days to leave the
country. In order to avoid prosecution, he arranged for an assignment in
Rome, where he made connections to Italian Intelligence. He was then
assigned to Prague to assist in the arrangements for the German invasion
of Czechoslovakia, and in August 1937 he joined his daughter Hala, who
was being trained at the French college in Buenos Aires, Argentina.
Pelypenko attached himself to the chief of the Gestapo in South America,
and to the German embassy. Because of his links to White Russians and
the German Government, he joined the international plot to assist
Ukrainians in starting a revolution on the day when Germany would invade Russia. However, the action of the Moscow government in moving
into East Poland and stopping the German advance and the signing of the
pact between Hitler and Stalin caused him and his fellow Ukrainians to
lose faith in the Germans' carrying out their part of the agreement. He

and his colleagues felt that they should throw their lot in with the British and work for the formation of a bloc of Slavic states, including Yugoslavia, Czechoslovakia, Romania, Bulgaria, and "Ukrainia." These colleagues knew that it would be necessary to have British and American support to form the bloc and defend the area from Russian aggression. They also felt Turkey and Greece could be used as a buffer against Russia.

Pelypenko decided to cease being a German agent and use the confidence the Nazis had in him to help the Allied cause. He wrote to the FBI in Washington from a new location, in Valparaíso, Chile, in 1940, stating that he would like to work underground in the United States. He was invited to come at once.

Arriving at the beginning of 1941, he revealed that the Nazis and the Japanese had designs on the Panama Canal. He said that the Polish army stationed in Iran was being trained to attack Russia; that Turkey would be brought into the fight against Russia; that the Soviets were furious with Washington for not closing down Count Vonsiatsky's activities; that Russia would be very dangerous after World War II; and that no official secrets must be given to the Russian ambassador.

Pelypenko told Military Intelligence officers of G-2 on March 18, 1941, that Nazis were coordinating German, Japanese, Italian, and Spanish spies on the American West Coast through the Ukrainian and other White Russian groups under Vonsiatsky. He gave the army men lists of names of White Russian spies; and he revealed that a White Russian who had assassinated the Polish Minister of the Interior in 1935, was being imported to assassinate President Roosevelt. Because of this disclosure, contacts in South America succeeded in liquidating the killer.

Pelypenko was briefed at the FBI headquarters in Washington under conditions of great secrecy and proceeded to New York at once. He dared not attempt to go to Thompson, Connecticut, without first infiltrating himself into the count's White Russian circle. He carried with him the impeccable credentials of his birth certificate and of his discharge papers from the White Guard. He also carried photographs of the late czar and czarina, and of present members of the Russian royal family. He could also show that he subscribed to Vonsiatsky's *The Fascist* and to the German-American Bund. His Roman Catholicism might have been a problem, except that Father Charles Coughlin was also close to the count. He could explain his conversion from the Greek Orthodox Church by claiming that he had had to assume a Catholic cover to work for Nazi Germany in Rome.

Armed with a letter of introduction, Pelypenko traveled to Thompson. He made his way through looming Gothic iron gates up a long driveway to the gloomy mansion, where the butler directed him to his room. He joined the count and his now elderly and fragile wife at dinner at a candle-lit table with servants hovering, waiting to obey every request. To Pelypenko, it all seemed almost too theatrical to be true.

Vonsiatsky told Pelypenko all he wanted to know. He described his network of contacts in every branch of the armed services. He told the priest of his Intelligence liaison, Wolfgang Ebell, at El Paso, Texas, who helped all German agents into Mexico. He described how he sent messages via shortwave through San Francisco and Nazi Consul Fritz Wiedemann to Japan and thence to Germany, thus bypassing British censorship in Bermuda. He rejoiced in the fact that the Japanese were able to transmit secret messages from Hawaii because Roosevelt had unwisely taken the power of intercept away from army and navy communications and given it to the inefficiently run Federal Communications Commission. Even at that stage, there were inklings in what Vonsiatsky said of the plans against Pearl Harbor.

Pelypenko was surprised to learn that Gerhardt Wilhelm Kunze, who had just taken over as head of the German-American Bund, was not merely a Nazi sympathizer, as the public believed, but in fact a Nazi agent financed directly from Berlin. Pelypenko learned that Kunze was a direct contact to Japan and Germany through linkups in Mexico. Kunze preferred Mexico because the telephone companies there were partly controlled by ITT and partly by Swedish interests and both owners were in the pockets of the Nazis. The count said that Kunze would shortly be going to Mexico to give messages to Japanese submarines lurking off the Pacific coast. There was a Mexican fisherman there who ran a fleet of boats and was presently being bribed to carry agents out to the submarines.

The count bragged of his future as head of All the Russias and as supreme master of America; he received weekly instructions from Foreign Minister Joachim von Ribbentrop.

The count told the priest that there would be a meeting of the leaders of the White Russian conspiracy in Chicago, at a suite at the

Bismarck Hotel, in June 1941. The host would be Chicago Bund leader Otto Willumeit.

Pelypenko, through a secret contact in New York, reported the gist of the meeting to Percy Foxworth, of the FBI, who in turn alerted his Chicago bureau chief. The meeting at the Hotel Bismarck was bugged. It was attended by the Lutheran clergyman Kurt Molzahn, of Philadelphia; Otto Willumeit; Wolfgang Ebell, of El Paso; Gerhardt Wilhelm Kunze; and Vonsiatsky himself. It was agreed at the meeting that Kunze would leave for Mexico as soon as convenient. First, he was to go into hiding. He was to resign as head of the Bund.

Followed by agents, all operating under orders from J. Edgar Hoover, Pelypenko had a meeting with Otto Willumeit at the German-American Bund headquarters at 2855 North Western Avenue, Chicago, on June 20, 1941. Willumeit advised him that he should proceed at once to Detroit, where he should contact Father Charles Coughlin, who was definitely part of the plot. Pelypenko was startled: he had thought of Coughlin only as an isolationist. Pelypenko determined that Friedrich Beyer, Baltimore hardware merchant, carried messages to Coughlin from the German embassy's Hans Thomsen, in Washington.

Feeling very tense, but excited at the prospect of meeting the most famous religious figure of his time, Pelypenko continued to Detroit, and thence to Royal Oak, where Coughlin's Shrine of the Little Flower church was situated.

As he approached the church on the warm afternoon of June 21, the priest remembered Willumeit's last words: "Father Coughlin collaborates with our friends in Detroit and receives financial support from them. You will learn all the details from our Consul Hailer there." Indeed, it was Fritz Hailer who had confirmed that Pelypenko would be safe in seeing Coughlin because he was one of the collaborators. When Pelypenko had asked, "Do you work with the Father much?" Hailer had replied, "We do."

Pelypenko went into the church; he was given a message by a priest that Father Coughlin was waiting in his house next door. Coughlin opened the door of the house himself. The priest exuded hospitality as he ushered the tall, angular Pelypenko into his comfortably furnished living room.

Since Pelypenko spoke almost no English, the two men conversed in Latin and Greek. Pelypenko told Coughlin he had come from South

America, that he had worked with Christan Zinsser there, and that he had joined conspirators in Chicago. America's most famous priest was delighted. "Good!" He beamed. "Come and join us for dinner."

Pelypenko walked into the dining room, where he was intrigued to see five other priests at the table. The entire conversation was conducted in Latin. Over the brandy and cigars, Coughlin told his visitor, "Your Russian background is very useful. I am sure you have a great deal of information concerning Jewish and Communist leaders which I can use against them in this country."

Pelypenko promised to supply the good father with as much material as he could. Coughlin said he wanted to collect anything possible in the way of anti-Semitic propaganda.

A further meeting took place on June 28. Coughlin again was at the door of his house with a smile and a handshake. As Pelypenko walked into the living room, he noticed that the famous Father Xavier, of the Franciscan seminary in Detroit, was there. Father Xavier spoke fluent Russian and acted as interpreter to avoid conversation in classical languages. Coughlin repeated that he wanted anti-Semitic material as he took the small amount Pelypenko had brought. He said, "Our people can amply compensate you. And let us all find ways to attack President Rosenfeld [sic]. He is a warmonger who is trying to embroil us in a catastrophe. He is a hireling of the Jews."

Now Coughlin really opened up. He revealed to the astonished priest that he was a coordinating link with all subversive groups in the country: that he was connected to the whole White Russian Nazi group under Vonsiatsky, that he was in direct touch with Ukrainian terrorist groups in Detroit, and that he was linked to John Koos, the Nazi Ukrainian working for Henry Ford.

Coughlin didn't stop there. He described the support he was giving to Stephen Fik, editor of the Vonsiatsky-financed Nazi magazine *The Fatherland.* He disclosed links to Gerhardt Wilhelm Kunze and Canadian Nazi agent Gerhardt Tunlich. Referring to the summit meeting of the Nazi conspirators in Chicago, Coughlin said, "That is excellent. I am happy to hear there are men who are willing to risk their lives for a cause."

On August 7, after several more meetings, Pelypenko was driven to the depot by Father Coughlin's driver with a letter of introduction from his host to Hans Thomsen's Washington right-hand man, Kurt von Heyden. They met at the Harrington Hotel, in the nation's capital. Von

Heyden said at the meeting, "I am glad you talked to Coughlin. Certainly he is our man. We give him help financially and we give him material to use. Cooperate with Coughlin and help him in every way. That way you will help Germany."

Pelypenko reported to his FBI contact on Coughlin, but the FBI did nothing either then or later. Coughlin reached an audience of many millions a day on perhaps the most popular radio program of its kind in the nation. He welded together the enormous Catholic faction, and even the liberals and supporters of Roosevelt attended to his words. In a sense, his flagrant anti-Semitism and admiration of fascism protected him from disclosure as a secret agent. Who would believe he could be working directly for the Third Reich when he not only had no cover but was so overt in his sympathies? Surely he must just be an innocent, well-meaning figure of the extreme right?

As war with America grew nearer, the German Government became more and more uncomfortable with the German-American Bund, and Pelypenko discovered at various meetings across the country that Kunze was under orders to disappear. On November 13, Kunze was already in hiding from both the American authorities and the loudmouthed Bund members before proceeding to Mexico. His Bund deputy, George Froboese, who had served under Fritz Kuhn, called a meeting of the Bund's executive committee in November 1941. Froboese dismissed Kunze on the spot. Vonsiatsky told Pelypenko of this event. Just before Pearl Harbor, Kunze slipped across the border. At a meeting in Chicago, Pelypenko, Molzahn, and Kunze met with Vonsiatsky to discuss the arrangements whereby Molzahn would concoct a fake passport for Kunze to cross into Mexico. Molzahn had considerable help through the Lutheran Church printing office, which specialized in false documents.

Chicago Bund leader Otto Willumeit drove Kunze to Seattle, Portland, and San Francisco, reporting back to the count as he did so. In turn, the count kept Pelypenko informed. All along the road from Seattle to San Francisco, Kunze showed the Chicagoan the weaknesses of American coastal defense, spots for possible landing parties from Japan, and the distances between naval units. The two men proceeded to the Sacramento River dam; Kunze explained that a break in that dam would inundate a hundred square miles of the country. Kunze held meetings with loyal White Russian Nazi contacts working in Bay Area aircraft factories near Oakland.

The spies proceeded to Texas, Kunze pointing out oil fields and pumping stations on the way. They met Wolfgang Ebell in El Paso and crossed the Mexican border to Juárez, where a local German brewery owner was a contact. Kunze proceeded to Mexico City. Pelypenko was present in Vonsiatsky's office at Thompson when a letter arrived from Kunze postmarked December 8, 1941, one day after Pearl Harbor. The letter revealed that the count had given Kunze twenty-eight hundred dollars in traveling expenses. The letter read, "Rosenfeld has his war at last but it will cost him his head." It went on, "Please send all the money you can to Ebell. Rosenfeld finally has what he thinks he wants but before long he will have it in the neck. If the Japanese war had waited a few weeks more, I would have been in Japan. As it is, I shall have gone on in another direction by the time this letter reaches you. There can be no going back for me anymore, and the farther away I go, the more difficult it will become to send me money."

Kunze was referring to the fact that he was planning to be picked up by U-boat off Mexico and taken to Germany.

Early on the morning of June 16, 1942, Kunze slipped out of a small port on the Gulf of Mexico called Boca del Río. Two fishermen were rowing. The tall, pale man with the Hitler mustache looked calm. He didn't realize that another fishing boat, seemingly engaged only in an early catch, was in fact being used as an observation post by two Mexican agents working with the FBI.

As the periscope of the U-boat emerged from the water, the second fishing boat cut across the route of the first. The Mexican police boarded the Nazi's fishing boat and arrested Kunze on the spot. Caught redhanded, he turned coward and began admitting everything. The policemen ferried him back to shore and, in handcuffs, he was flown to Washington for further questioning.

Pelypenko's aid had undoubtedly brought Kunze to justice. After two more months of gathering information, J. Edgar Hoover closed in on the gang. A squad of FBI men invaded the Thompson estate and grabbed Vonsiatsky. They also rounded up Kurt Molzahn, Otto Willumeit, and Wolfgang Ebell.

Vonsiatsky's bravado crumbled under close interrogation. He agreed to plead guilty. So also did Willumeit, but Molzahn decided to fight his case. Kunze, after saying he had no money for the defense and asking for a legal-aid attorney, changed his mind and decided to plead guilty also. He said in court in Hartford, Connecticut, on July 21, 1942, "I had to plead guilty. The trial will be nothing but a circus and I would have no chance at acquittal under the circumstances in these times."

Vonsiatsky was sent to federal prison for five years. But Willumeit and Ebell were held in Hartford County Jail to be used as government witnesses at Molzahn's trial.

The trial opened on July 28, 1942, Molzahn being charged directly with spying for Germany. Nervous and self-conscious, he was dressed in his clerical clothes. The day was so hot and humid that the jurors, in a state of near collapse, had to be brought down from the jury room, where they were waiting; it was situated in a small penthouse on the sun-baked roof of the Federal Building.

The prospective jurors were asked whether their verdict would be swayed by the fact that America was at war with Germany or that Molzahn was personally the recipient of gifts from the Kaiser. Not surprisingly, several prospective jurors were excused on the grounds of prejudice. On July 29, Special Assistant Attorney General Thomas J. Dodd gave a picture of the conspiracy at the Bismarck Hotel in Chicago, in El Paso, Texas, and in Philadelphia; but no mention was made of Detroit, and indeed the name Charles Coughlin never once emerged throughout the entire trial. It was unpleasantly obvious to the conspirators that they were small fry; that the one really big fish in their midst was going to go unpunished. If they did mention his name under interrogation in their cells, nothing was done about it. Dodd referred to "a wealth of information on the U.S. Army and Navy on both the Atlantic and Pacific coasts, which the conspirators had given to Molzahn and which he had conveyed to Hans Thomsen in Washington."

On July 30, in the still stifling courtroom, a sweating Alexei Pelypenko testified for the government. Through a Russian interpreter, he described the procedures he had undertaken in order to help the government. He also revealed the shocking fact that instead of being awarded a medal and his American citizenship, he had been held in a grim Immigration detention home at Fort Howard, Maryland, because he had overstayed the period allowed in his passport visa. It is probably germane to observe as a footnote to this extraordinary disclosure that Major Lemuel Schofield, director of immigration and naturalization, was the lover of the Nazi agent Princess Stefanie Hohenlohe, who was being given special privileges in her own imprisonment at the time. J. Edgar Hoover's failure to aid Pelypenko can only be described as disgraceful.

As the prosecution's account of religious figures involved in espionage grew more and more intriguing, few if any members of press or public noticed that the most crucial evidence of all—involving Coughlin—had been winkled out of the prosecution's case. Molzahn was condemned to a lengthy prison term, and even after his release did not blow the whistle on the priest. As for Pelypenko, nothing further was said about him in the papers, and it is only now that declassified documents disclose the reward he received from the American Government. He was imprisoned and then released providing he left the country at once. But where could he go in the middle of a war? And even if he could travel, what would he use for money? The government had given him nothing. He was rearrested by presidential warrant on March 30, 1943, and was interned by Attorney General Francis Biddle on July 13, 1943, at Ellis Island for the duration.

✠✠✠✠✠✠✠ 11

The Theft of the Victory Program

A persistent fallacy maintained by historians, and recently repeated by Professor Gordon Craig in *The New York Review of Books,** is that no reason can be adduced for Adolf Hitler's decision to declare war upon the United States following the Japanese attack on Pearl Harbor on December 7, 1941. It had been pointed out that his avowal of loyalty to the Tripartite Pact, signed in Berlin on September 27, 1940, and assuring support to the Japanese, called for action on Germany's part only in the event that Japan was attacked by an aggressor nation. Since Japan had acted as the aggressor in the matter of Pearl Harbor, and indeed without the knowledge or assent of the Third Reich, Germany's obligation was not mandatory.

A careful consultation of Hitler's speech of December 11, 1941, leaves no doubt as to the reason for his declaration of the existence of a conflict with the United States of America. First the Führer carefully summarized the long list of deliberate provocations in which Roosevelt, in contravention of international law, informed Great Britain of the movements of German steamers, ordered other vessels to be shadowed, opened up the Red Sea for supplies to the British Army, blocked German assets in America when no state of war existed, closed German consulates, allowed the U.S. destroyer *Greer* to engage in a maneuver against U-boats, permitted a similar incident in the matter of the destroyer *Kearney*, seized the German steamer *Odenwald*, and in every other manner fought an un-

* July 21, 1983.

declared war on the Atlantic.† Finally, Hitler disclosed the last straw: "With no attempt at an official denial there has now been revealed in America, President Roosevelt's plan by which, at the latest in 1943, Germany and Italy are to be attacked in Europe by military means. In this way the sincere efforts of Germany and Italy to prevent an extension of the war and to maintain relations with the United States in spite of the unbearable provocations which have been carried on for years by President Roosevelt, have been frustrated. Germany and Italy have been finally compelled, *in view of this* [italics supplied] and in loyalty to the Tripartite Pact, to carry on the struggle against the United States and England jointly and side by side with Japan for the defense, and thus for the maintenance, of the liberty and independence of their nations and empires."

Anyone casually examining this text, in an effort to understand Hitler's seemingly inexplicable move in plunging his nation into war, thus helping to spell his own doom in the wake of his impending failure in the invasion of the Soviet Union, might assume that the plan to attack Germany and Italy in 1943 had been made public by Roosevelt in order to provoke the Führer most drastically, probably at the instigation of Winston Spencer Churchill. Be that as it may, the plan, known as the Victory Program, a part of the Rainbow Five overall war plan, was a top-secret proposal, under lock and key in the War Department, available only to the supreme chiefs of staff, and arguably the most highly classified document in the possession of the White House.

How, then, was it leaked, thus coming to the Führer's attention? In order to answer that question, it is necessary to move back several months to the plan's actual inception.

Overriding the numerous objections raised by the isolationists and Hitlerites on Capitol Hill, the President, mindful of his special relationship with Winston Churchill and the more belligerent elements in the British Cabinet, had embarked, early in 1940, upon a program of industrial mobilization and military procurement on a scale that most grievously aggravated his numerous critics. At first, his program was, or was passed off as, purely defensive in character, as well as serving the not inconsiderable advantage of giving a boost to the economy. However, by 1941, the development of combat operations in continental Europe rendered the

† Hitler, of course, quite neglected an equal number of infringements by the German Navy.

increased arming of the United States no longer simply a convenience but a most urgent necessity. Roosevelt took it upon himself to drive such reluctant figures as Secretary of Commerce Jesse Jones to improve production and to unstop inconvenient bottlenecks. On March 11, 1941, the Lend-Lease Act was passed, which called for slightly over seven billion dollars of Treasury funds for use in military and defense aid and assistance to those nations at war with Nazi Germany.

Intelligence sources disclosed Hitler's immediate plans to destroy his alliance with the Soviet Union by an illegal onslaught on its territories. The danger to the United States was clear, since the collapse of Russia would take Hitler all the way to the Pacific, where he and Japan would present a two-pronged threat to the Hawaiian Islands. Army planners began drawing up extensive expenditure programs under the 1940 Munitions Program, and Congress was constantly badgered for budget increases as the isolationist ice floe began slowly but surely to crack. Throughout the spring of 1941, the Office of Production and Management called for full-scale army economic mobilization based on a strategic general plan. On May 21, chief of staff General George C. Marshall asked WPD, the War Plans Division, to set about a clear-cut strategic estimate, and shortly thereafter the President specifically asked for a considerable raising of the sights. Major General James H. Burns, Harry Hopkins's right-hand man in Lend-Lease, prepared memoranda to the Secretaries of War and of the Navy on April 2, 1941, urging a totally committed program of munitions production. Following the German attack on Russia, Roosevelt, on July 9, 1941, seconded Burns's memoranda, issuing a presidential edict, couched in the form of a request, seeking even more strenuous efforts toward a coordinated plan for what amounted to national wartime measures. Harry Hopkins visited with Marshal Joseph Stalin in Moscow in August—a great provocation to Hitler and the isolationists—obtaining from the Soviets a long list of munitions requirements. There can be little doubt that the President's desire to accommodate the Soviet Union helped provoke the events I shall shortly describe.

On September 11, 1941, the Army summarized its estimate along with naval requirements in a secret joint report buttressed with appendixes, maps, charts, tables, and secret data on strategic assumptions and purposes, potential military objectives and targets, and estimates of military strength. Known as Rainbow Five, this remarkable document, running to some seventeen pages originally but greatly expanded thereafter, called for an outright defeat of Nazi Germany in 1943, for which an appropriation of one hundred and fifty billion dollars would be required. U.S. Army ground forces would be required to a total of 216 divisions, 61 of them armored; 51 separate motorized divisions; and half a million men for antiaircraft artillery units. It may be necessary to repeat that this was quite the most important single document in the possession of the chiefs of staff and of the White House.

The architect of Rainbow Five was Brigadier General Leonard T. Gerow, chief of the War Plans Division. Secretary of War Stimson had handed the responsibility to General Marshall, who in turn passed it to Gerow. Gerow selected as his instrument of execution of the Victory Program Colonel Albert C. Wedemeyer, who in the 1980s was to be resurrected from the military mortuary to serve as special military adviser to President Ronald Reagan.

Colonel Wedemeyer had an interesting history. His father's parents were born in Germany, and he himself had been educated in part at the German War College, in Berlin. He rented his apartment in the German capital from a member of the Nazi Party, Gerhard Rossbach, and during his sojourn became a great friend of General Ludwig Beck, chief of the German General Staff. His introductions to Beck were arranged by Lieutenant General Friedrich von Boetticher, German military attaché in Washington. He corresponded regularly with his German contacts until the advent of World War II in Europe.

He was friendly with Charles Lindbergh and acted as his interpreter in German uniform when the Lone Eagle visited various Nazi factories and army posts, and he was a keen supporter of General Robert Wood, the head of America First. Rightly or wrongly, he was regarded by the German embassy in Washington as part of the pro-German military clique in the War Department. There is no question that he was a convinced isolationist who sincerely believed that the United States was not obliged to commit itself to war on behalf of Great Britain.

Wedemeyer was in his soul opposed to the purpose expressed in the very Victory Program to which he was assigned. Precisely why Roosevelt instructed him to draw up the plan, and then why Wedemeyer chose to execute it, can only be regarded as a joint execution of executive duty which overrode personal considerations.

Wedemeyer worked scrupulously on the Program. Five typewritten draft copies, meticulously numbered and registered, were sent by him to

Secretary of War Stimson, Assistant Secretary of War John J. McCloy, chief of staff George Marshall, and chief of the War Plans Division Gerow, with one copy retained by Wedemeyer. In the meantime, the inevitable rumors flew around Washington of the existence of the program. Clerks had made mimeographed copies of the crucial document and there is no record that they were subjected to a careful security check. Though they were strictly forbidden to examine the documents, one or other of them may have wanted to engage a listener in interesting conversation in the War Department Canteen and given more than a hint of the contents.

The numerous memoranda of Hans Thomsen and Boetticher to Berlin at the time indicate that a series of contacts had been established in the General Staff, centering upon the War Department itself. Members of this group held meetings at the home of former American military attaché in Berlin Colonel Truman Smith. Although pro-German and a sympathizer of America First, Smith had the ear of General Marshall. He also was closely connected to Rear Admiral Stanford C. Hooper, another isolationist, and needless to say, to Colonel Lindbergh. Yet another member of the group was Lieutenant Hubert L. Allensworth, of the Army Air Corps, who, it seems, was privy, along with his superior General H. H. (Hap) Arnold, to details of the Program.

The chief contact of this group on Capitol Hill was Burton K. Wheeler of Montana. According to FBI files, Wheeler had access through various leaks to privileged documents; in those days of lax security, senators were able to get their hands on any number of classified documents and make use of them as they saw fit. Boetticher met Truman Smith, Wedemeyer, and Major Alford J. Williams, of the Marine Corps Reserve and the Scripps-Howard newspaper chain, on several occasions, using certain journalists as an outlet. Admiral Hooper even supplied Wheeler with classified navy documents stating that the Germans had "no capacity for launching an air invasion against the United States," a fact which a high school knowledge of aviation would have established. Wheeler in turn handed over the information to George Sylvester Viereck, who in turn handed it on to Boetticher.

In view of this continuous series of leaks at a high level, it is not surprising to note that on October 20, 1941, Eugene M. Duffield, Washington staff correspondent of *The Wall Street Journal*, announced the existence of the Victory Program in his column, although he proved unable to give details of it. He described it as "A newly executed munitions schedule which Washington and London expect will beat Hitler." He went on to discuss the program's forecast of the military, business, and financial necessities for the coming war to defeat the Führer. He quoted the program by name and said that it called for a commitment of more than 65 percent of the nation's effort by 1943. He referred to the involvement of Donald Nelson of Sears Roebuck as head of appropriations, and his catalogue of supply priorities and allocations, and he referred to hints given in public by Stacy May, war production research chief, just back from England, toward the target of fifty billion dollars in armaments. Warming to his theme, Duffield discussed plans to push tank production to two thousand or three thousand a month, to schedule production of seventy-seven thousand or eighty thousand planes, and again he repeated the crucial date of 1943. As it happened, since he was basing his report (in "This Week in Washington") on random sources and had not apparently had access to the Victory Program or Rainbow Five itself, the government let the matter pass. However, it is disturbing to think that not a single member of the War Department was called to the White House for an accounting of this most serious leak. Perhaps, though there is no evidence at Hyde Park, the President thought that if the story went without official comment it would vanish in the night. If that was the President's feeling, it was justified, since not even the German embassy seems to have included it in its daily dispatches to Berlin.

This omission was evidently disappointing to the clique of isolationists in the War Department, because one member of that clique took the matter into his own hands. Each night, the War Department closed its doors and the papers in the Rainbow Five files were secured.

On the night of December 3, 1941, an officer attached to the War Plans Division decided on his own account to consult some of the documents at home. It was a simple matter to unlock the steel cabinet and remove the large expanding folder of several hundred pages. That he was not authorized to do so is indicated by the fact that he found it necessary to wrap the file in heavy brown paper, to make it look like a parcel for mailing.

He went to his home and from there placed a call to the reliable Burton K. Wheeler, who had actually asked to see the Program, according to Wheeler himself.

Later that evening, the officer arrived at Wheeler's house. Wheeler asked him, "Aren't you afraid of delivering the most secret document in America to a senator?"

"Congress is a branch of government" the officer replied. "I think it has a right to know what's really going on in the executive branch when it concerns human lives."

Wheeler asked the officer to leave the document with him. With mounting excitement, he read the pages, infuriated to discover that everything *The Wall Street Journal* had hinted at was concretely true. He was maddened by the fact that Roosevelt's promises of keeping America out of the war, promises which had helped him defeat Wheeler in the Democratic primaries of 1940, were shown to be mere eyewash. Wheeler correctly concluded that the document was a prospectus for winning a world war. He believed, without a scrap of evidence, that a very high official had authorized it to be brought to him.

At first, Wheeler thought he should take the document to the Senate Foreign Relations Committee, but in view of the committee's record of support for Roosevelt, he was afraid it would be buried. Instead, he decided to call an old contact, Chesley Manly, Washington correspondent for the Chicago *Tribune*, who was a key contact of the German embassy and could definitely be relied upon to make the best use of the material.

Meanwhile, before he actually proceeded, and during the course of a restless Thursday morning, December 4, it appears that nobody noticed the absence of the crucial document from the file. This is curious, since presumably the contents of the cabinet would have undergone a check. The fact that the document was included, if included it was, in the morning prospectus does lead one to question whether somebody in a very high place indeed knew the young officer would take it.

Wheeler at last made up his mind and called Chesley Manly. Manly, of course, was delighted. A scoop of this kind was unique; and at the time, the *Tribune* was feeling threatened by the very first appearance that day, on its own territory, of a rival newspaper, the Chicago *Sun*, financed by the department-store owner Marshall Field. Mandatorily, the story had also to appear in the Washington *Times-Herald*, not only because that paper was affiliated with the *Tribune* but because material of this kind was grist to its owner, Captain Patterson. By a fluke, it was turned down at the city desk of the affiliated New York *Daily News*.

The Washington bureau of the Chicago *Tribune* advised the *Tribune*'s managing editor, J. Loy Maloney, that a hot story was about to come in. But when Maloney received Manly's version of Wheeler's leak, he felt uneasy. After all, to release a state secret bordered on treason and was perhaps in breach of the existing Espionage Act of 1917. In view of his unease, Maloney felt he had to take the matter to his boss, Colonel Robert Rutherford McCormick, whom one wag dubbed "the greatest mind of the fourteenth century."

McCormick provided a willing audience. Tall, stern, immaculately tailored, the sixty-one-year-old newspaper tycoon was one of Roosevelt's most persistent critics in the Fourth Estate. His crusades against Roosevelt were quite inflammatory, couched in language more suitable for a fishwife than a newspaper publisher. In 1940, he tried to swing Wendell Willkie to an isolationist position, called the Lend-Lease bill the work of a "dictator," and charged the President with coming from "a stock which never fought for the country and now betrays it." He supported Wheeler in the Democratic primaries and expressed the conventional hope that when Germany invaded Russia the two powers would destroy each other. He was a keen admirer of Colonel Lindbergh and defended Japan's atrocities in China, using as analogy the Monroe Doctrine. Assuming the mantle of prophecy in an October 1937 editorial, he stated that Japan could not attack the United States, since "even our base at Hawaii is beyond the effective striking power of her fleet." In short, he was the ideal person to whom Maloney could address his plea for judgment, and McCormick instantly ordered the story to go front page.

The story appeared on Thursday morning, December 4, 1941, headed FDR'S WAR PLANS! GOAL IS TEN MILLION ARMED MEN; HALF TO FIGHT IN AEF. PROPOSES LAND DRIVE BY JULY 1, 1943, TO SMASH NAZIS; PRESIDENT TOLD OF EQUIPMENT SHORTAGE.

The story went on:

A confidential report prepared by the Joint Army and Navy High Command by direction of President Roosevelt calls for American Expeditionary Forces aggregating five million men for a final land offensive against Germany and her satellites. It contemplates total armed forces of ten million, forty-five thousand, six hundred and fifty-eight men. One of the few existing copies of this astounding document, which represents decisions and commitments affecting the destinies of peoples throughout the civilized world, became available to the *Tribune* today. It is a blueprint for war on a total scale unprecedented in at least two oceans and three continents, Europe, Africa and Asia.

The report expresses the considered opinion of the Army and Navy strategists that "Germany and her European satellites cannot be defeated by the European powers now fighting against her." Therefore, it concludes, "If our European enemies are to be defeated it will be necessary for the United States to enter the war, and to employ a part of its armed forces defensively in the eastern Atlantic and in Europe and Africa." July 1, 1943, is fixed as the date for the beginning of the final supreme effort.

Both Lloyd Wendt, in *Chicago Tribune: The Rise of a Great American Newspaper*, and Burton K. Wheeler, in his memoirs, *Yankee from the West*, say that the article, which continued overleaf for several thousand words, did not contain classified information. These disclaimers are erroneous. The information supplied was indeed classified top secret, and its release was a matter of the gravest danger to national security.

On the morning of the story's publication, the War Department was in an uproar. Not a soul entered the building without a copy of the Washington *Times-Herald* gripped firmly in his hand. Apparently the only personage in the entire government who had failed to read the paper on that fatal day was Albert C. Wedemeyer, who walked into the Munitions Building at 7:30 A.M. to find his secretary, greatly agitated, handing him a copy of the paper. The hubbub of conversation around him, emanating from a score or so of high-ranking army officers, ceased abruptly as he scanned the pages. Every eye was upon him. He was horrified by what he read. He was still more distressed when his secretary started to cry and the atmosphere became charged with suspicion. After all, he was the only man in that room with contacts with America First, Lindbergh, the German embassy, and Burton K. Wheeler. Wasn't it likely that he was responsible for the leak? However, he was somewhat mollified when his superior, General Gerow, assured him of his complete support. "J. Edgar Hoover had already been instructed by the President to investigate this matter," Gerow said. "You have my complete confidence. This breach of security is not a matter of guilt in the War Plans Division. Of that I assure you I am certain."

Assistant Secretary of War John J. McCloy took a different view. Indeed, he summoned Wedemeyer to his office and instead of suggesting he sit down, shouted at him, "There's blood on the hands of the man who did this!" However, he did not quite bring himself to charge Wedemeyer directly with an act of treason. He simply announced that when the guilty person was discovered he would be court-martialed. Back in his office, Wedemeyer faced a very unpleasant situation. Hoover had dispatched his number-one man, Edward Tamm, to the office, and Tamm was standing by an open filing cabinet while Wedemeyer's secretary was sobbing into her hands. One of Tamm's men was holding a copy of the Victory Program. The same passages were underlined in red by Wedemeyer as appeared in the newspapers. When Leonard Mosley, author of *Marshall: Hero for Our Times,* a biography of General George Marshall, interviewed Wedemeyer in 1982, for the purposes of his book, Wedemeyer gave an explanation of this. He said that he had looked at his copy of the plan before the FBI's visit, compared it with the newspaper's account, and underlined the passages appearing in both the plan and the newspaper. The problem was that he had stated elsewhere he had not seen the paper that fatal morning before entering the War Department. No doubt memory was failing him in old age.

The FBI focused upon General Newton Cavalcanti of the Brazilian Army, currently on a visit to Washington.

In the State Department files of the National Archives and Records Service, in Washington, the following record appears:

CAVALCANTI, General Newton. Rio de Janeiro, Brazil. Confidential. Subject is Director of the Motor-Mechanization of the Brazilian Army and is presently visiting in the U.S. for the purpose of investigating U.S. Army mechanization. He is reported to have spoken derogatorily of U.S. Army mechanization as compared with developments along the same line in the German Army. SUBJECT's pro-Nazi leanings have been known in Rio for some time. MID Cognizant. ND-7, 10; FBI. STATE (Wash.) December 29, 1941.

Another object of Hoover's suspicion was Senator David I. Walsh, senior senator from Massachusetts and chairman of the Senate Naval Affairs Committee. Walsh was under constant surveillance because of his frequent appearances at **a** male bordello at 329 Pacific Street, Brooklyn. He also frequently conversed with one William Elberfeld, an officer in the German Army who regarded Hitler as God and who spent as much time in the dubious Pacific Street institution as the senator himself.

Despite subsequent disclaimers, Wheeler was also closely analyzed on the day following. However, he enjoyed so charmed a life that he was never once subjected to questions, perhaps lending some credence to widespread beliefs‡ that Roosevelt deliberately leaked plans to Wheeler himself.

On December 4, Hans Thomsen cabled Ribbentrop in Berlin a "most urgent" message, which ran as follows:

> The publication on December 4 in the Chicago Tribune and the leading isolationist newspaper, the Washington Times-Herald, of the secret report of the American High Command to the President about the preparations and prospects for the defeat of Germany and her allies, is causing a sensation here.

Thomsen continued, saying that the report was doubtless an authentic war plan: that it refuted the old thesis that a war of starvation against Germany would suffice and it disclosed that "the elimination of the Soviet Union as a fighting power by the summer of 1942 at the latest and the collapse of the British Empire are soberly included in the calculations of the American General Staff so that the publication of the document will hardly cause any special rejoicing among the Allies."

This telegram found its way to Hitler's desk. In the meantime, Burton K. Wheeler ironically announced that he personally would conduct an investigation into the leak—a sure way of concealing its source. In the House, Congressman George Holden Tinkham obtained immediate permission from the members to reproduce the report in the *Congressional Record.* Roosevelt refused to answer questions on the matter at his official press conference at the White House, resisting particular pressure for a denial of the veracity of the document from Congressman William P. Lambertson of Kansas. Roosevelt dispatched the reporters to the hard-pressed Henry L. Stimson, who said, "The story is wanting in loyalty and patriotism. . . . What would you think of a general staff which did not

‡ Shared by Wedemeyer and certain of his colleagues to this day.

investigate and study every conceivable type of emergency which might confront it? What do you think of the patriotism of a man or a newspaper which would take these confidential studies and make them public to the enemies of the country?"

By now, the weekend was upon Washington, and even those most hard-pressed obeyed tradition and went home. On Sunday, they were rudely awakened from their pleasant somnolence by news of the Japanese air attack on Pearl Harbor. The theft of Rainbow Five suddenly seemed insignificant, and even when Hitler made its release the main plank in his platform for declaring war on the United States four days later, not a person noticed it.

However, Pearl Harbor or no Pearl Harbor, J. Edgar Hoover was having a field day and would not be shaken off. No doubt he would not have made his findings known to the public even if he had gotten to the bottom of the matter, but he kept pressing against Wedemeyer while failing to grill Wheeler or Walsh or Cavalcanti. Edward Tamm was put in special charge of the case. He asked again and again, on the Monday after Pearl Harbor, what security methods Wedemeyer had used to protect the Victory Program. Tamm's assistant Joseph Genau also cross-questioned Wedemeyer, chiefly in order to ascertain evidence of "guilt" in his general demeanor.

General Sherman Miles of G-2 (Army Intelligence) ordered Colonel J. T. Bissell and Captain Lowell J. Bradford, of his limited staff, to join the questioning. Again and again, Wedemeyer went over the list of names to whom copies were supplied, and it emerged that many had access to duplicated documents. The reports by Tamm were deliberately unfavorable to Wedemeyer. He was charged in them with confusing dates, showing unease, and falling back "upon the old adage that 'I could not remember' and seemed to be thinking of excuses for himself and his actions." An anonymous letter, addressed to Stimson and signed with the initials "OSA," appeared, saying that Wedemeyer "thinks and says Hitler is a savior and after America is taken over by the people and National Socialism is established here, the present injustices in government will be swept away. These are certainly not trustworthy men to have on our defense commission and our war plans and may account for the serious 'leak' of last week. Surely the President or General Marshall should investigate these officers' real feelings."

A Colonel Scobey, of the War Department, told Tamm and his

officers that Wedemeyer was a member of America First. He also charged General Wood, General Westerwell, and Congressman Tinkham with leaking to Wheeler information on American troops in Iceland, also an issue in the Hitler Declaration of War speech. He added that the Iceland leak was from five carbon copies of a report and mentioned that he had "a report from Colonel Wedemeyer which stated that there was no [other] officer present when the stencils were mimeographed."

On February 19, 1942, Captains Bradford and Sernau interviewed Assistant Secretary John McCloy on the matter. McCloy, while not specifically repeating his charges against Wedemeyer, said he thought that he "might be responsible."

Wedemeyer was subsequently cleared. Stimson repeatedly confirmed Wedemeyer's undivided loyalty and dedication to his country. There is no need to differ with that opinion today.

The inquiry cast light on the lack of security in the Munitions Building. In a letter to me, Brigadier General Carter W. Clarke, who was then chief of a section of G-2 with "the euphonious title 'Safeguarding Military Information,'" stated that the security arrangements in the Munitions Building were comparable to those "in a herd of billy goats." He pointed out that in September or October 1941 three junior lieutenant colonels ransacked IN and OUT trays, unlocked desk drawers and unsecured safes, and garnered "a bounteous harvest of classified documents. Next morning, all of the documents were returned to their embarrassed custodians."

There was no check on people entering or leaving the Munitions Building, nor was there a signed IN and OUT book. General Clarke says that he personally took material home at night unchallenged as he was finishing a cryptographic course. Furthermore, Clarke says, G-2 itself vis-à-vis the Munitions Building was a "pathetic, amateurish, bumbling, unfunded little group playing at counterespionage," which failed "miserably." When General Sherman Miles of G-2 intruded into the War Department, he was accused of meddling and, according to Clarke, "harshly castigated, especially by certain chiefs of branch who considered themselves divinely anointed."

One possible solution to the mystery may be found by reference to William Stevenson's *A Man Called Intrepid*, the highly questionable authorized biography of Sir William Stephenson, wartime chief of British security coordination in New York, whose two senior right-hand men, Sir

William Wiseman (Sir William Stephenson's precursor as British Intelligence chief) and Charles Howard Ellis, both had Nazi connections.

In that book, Sir William, through his biographer, addresses himself to the matter of the theft of the Victory Program. He states that the Program "purported to forecast U.S. Government plans to enter the war," that the Program was dispatched by radio to Berlin and was "duly decoded in England." But "the fact was that the Victory Program was a plant." The "Political Warfare Division of BSC [British Security Coordination] concocted the Victory Program out of material already known to have reached the enemy in dribs and drabs, and added some misleading information. . . . A young U.S. Army captain delivered the bogus Victory Program to the Senator, claiming he did this out of concern for the American people. . . ." Referring to Hitler's declaration of war, Stephenson is quoted by his near namesake as saying, "Hitler helped us achieve what Congress might have prevented. Under the U.S. Constitution, only Congress could declare war. . . . Wheeler had been made an instrument of justice. By supposedly leaking secret war plans he tripped a wire in Hitler's mind."

It is implied in *A Man Called Intrepid* that Sir William was authorized to leak the plan. However, what he leaked was not, as he says, a fake —but the real article. Was Roosevelt responsible? A minute inspection of the appropriate files at Hyde Park shows that Roosevelt was sending secret memoranda to Stimson and others as late as the spring of 1942 asking for information on the continuing investigation of Wedemeyer. Were these blinds?

Another possibility suggests itself. Charles Howard Ellis was Stephenson's right-hand man. It is possible that he deliberately informed Sir William that the Program was false, in order to plant it on behalf of his *Soviet* controls? Nothing more likely exists than that the Russians would want to distract the Germans with war against the United States, to draw them away from their already invaded territory. It would be a typical stroke of Russian Intelligence. It would also explain (since Ellis was also a Nazi agent) how information on the leak reached the German embassy *before* it reached the *Tribune* and why Senator Wheeler would trust his emissary, since his secretary was now in the Berlin radio receiving office.

All this must of course be speculation at the moment. The only alternative is to believe that Sir William Stephenson willingly abstracted the *authentic* Victory Program, the most important single document in the possession of the United States Government, and leaked it to the enemy, on presidential and prime-ministerial orders.

The Pearl Harbor Plans

Deliberate or not, the theft of the Victory Program was certainly the greatest security breach of its time—with one arguable exception. That was the FBI-alleged presentation of the plans of the secret military installations of Pearl Harbor by an American citizen, Hans Wilhelm Rohl, to a Nazi agent, Ulrich von der Osten, for transmission to Louis Siefken, German spy master in Shanghai, for forwarding to the Japanese in Tokyo.

Rohl was born in Lübeck on September 26, 1886. He began life as a humble laborer, working for various mining and construction concerns in South America. He came to the United States in October 1913 from Chile and worked as a foreman in a Nevada copper-mining company. Later, he settled in Sacramento and worked for various construction companies. In 1925, he married the American Floye Adams Hubert and became a resident of Los Angeles.

Apparently backed by a wealthy uncle in the Hamburg-America Steamship Company, which was deeply involved in espionage, Rohl built the successful Rohl-Connolly Construction Company, with Thomas E. Connolly, of San Francisco. The concern's commitment was to build installations, headquarters, and emplacements for the United States Army. Connolly was headquartered in San Francisco and Rohl in Beverly Hills.

Rohl was a yachtsman, who owned, successively, the *Pandora*, destroyed mysteriously by fire in 1933, the *Ramona*, and the *Vega*, which was extremely famous along the California shoreline. She was 125 feet long, was Diesel-powered, and carried a crew of sixteen. She had black silk

Chinese sails and a black-painted hull with gold-plated portholes and in-laid-marble bathrooms.

Rohl consistently concealed the fact from inspectors that he was not an American citizen; there was a limit on vessel sizes sailed by non-Americans, but Rohl greased palms and got away with it. On January 21, 1938, he dropped anchor in Honolulu after sailing through the Panama Canal and lied on Immigration manifests that he was born in Kansas. This was actually a basis for deportation if discovered.

In the mid-1930s, Rohl became associated with a certain Captain Theodore Wyman, Jr., whose birth records in Kansas City Rohl improperly assumed. Wyman and Rohl became intimate friends; they frequently attended night clubs, and when they arrived, so famous were they that musical numbers were performed for them by the orchestra and singer. Rohl staged orgies for Wyman in a luxurious suite at a downtown Los Angeles hotel, and they were prominent fixtures at the Los Angeles Athletic Club, the Los Angeles Country Club, the California Club, and the Hollywood Country Club. The Rohls lived at the Talmadge apartments, on Wilshire Boulevard, later moving to a fine house on Fremont Place. Wyman was frequently present, driven by a soldier-chauffeur in an official army car. The two men talked constantly of building hangars, runways, and landing fields, particularly in San Diego. Wyman was a drinker; he was obnoxious, loud, and insulting and would pour whiskey on the floor along with burning cigarettes. But Rohl accepted him because of his ability to secure army contracts.

Another member of the circle was Werner Plack,* who was a champagne salesman attached to the German consulate. They would go together to the Swing Club, at 1710 North Las Palmas Avenue, Hollywood, a fashionable night spot and pickup joint. Plack excited much suspicion because of his connection with the consulate. Plack was always visiting the Swing Club with Rohl and Wyman; on one occasion when they arrived together, the orchestra leader stopped the music and the floor show and the girls and band players sang, "Here comes Bill. Here comes Bill. Here comes Bill Rohl now!" Everyone laughed and stared as the celebrated trio took a table and were joined by nubile girls.

In 1939, Major Wyman, as he was then ranked, went to the Hawaiian Islands to take charge of the construction of secret installations near

_____
* Died in Berlin in 1983.

Pearl Harbor for the U.S. Army Air Corps. These installations included gun emplacements, airfields, underground ammunition storehouses, aircraft warning systems, and hangars and other buildings. This multimillion-dollar contract, one of the largest until that time, was naturally awarded to Rohl. This was totally illegal. Only American citizens were entitled to be involved in top-secret projects.

The job was begun according to contract on December 20, 1940, just short of a year before the Japanese attacked. Constant conversations took place between Rohl and Wyman in the many months following the signing of the documents. Only Wyman and Rohl and top-level figures in the War Department had the secret plans. Security was preserved under Army Intelligence provisions.

Furthermore, Rohl and Wyman engaged Japanese superintendents, carpenters, electricians, and builders in the company known as Hawaiian Constructors. Many of these were not American citizens. This also was an infringement of the law and a potential security risk.

They built hangars, tunnels, dugouts, and the military headquarters of Hickam Field. And this was at a time when Roosevelt was fighting an undeclared war in the Atlantic, Germany was involved in a Tripartite Pact with Japan, and relations between America and Japan were strained to the limit.

Rohl frequently visited Pearl Harbor and Hickam Field. According to a presently well-known film historian who was working his way through college in 1941 as a mate/steward on Errol Flynn's yacht the *Sirocco*, many conversations took place in the saloon between Flynn and Rohl when they would meet at the isthmus of Catalina Island. Plots to leak the secret plans were discussed with Flynn.

The work at Hawaii went on. And it was deliberately delayed, witnesses testified at hearings, to the point of internal sabotage. Tunnels were never closed up or properly protected—tunnels housing U.S. Army headquarters in front of Red Hill, overlooking Pearl Harbor. So incensed were the foremen and electricians, true Americans all, that they put bombproof shelters in by pooling their own money when Rohl and Wyman refused to do so. At night, Rohl and Wyman would go to the headquarters of Hawaiian Constructors at Alexandria Hall and join Japanese prostitutes at parties. Often, Wyman was drunk for weeks at a stretch. So poor was the work that several members of the staff reported it to G2, but nothing was done.

Certain Immigration officials in Los Angeles became nervous about the fact that Rohl had unsatisfactory papers. He had to be rushed through citizenship at once. On August 29, 1941, John J. Kingman, brigadier general and acting chief of engineers in the War Department, wrote to the indispensable Lemuel B. Schofield, head of Immigration and Naturalization and lover of the Nazi spy Stefanie von Hohenlohe, mentioning that Rohl was involved in important defense construction at Honolulu, was "possessed of outstanding ability, excellent judgment and resourcefulness for the management of difficult construction work," and that his services were "of vital importance" for defense. Major Schofield, not surprisingly, acted at once. Despite extreme pressure on him to deport Rohl, he went ahead and granted him his citizenship, based on the fact that he had an American wife.

Meanwhile, there were others who objected. The Hollywood producer Sy Bartlett charged Werner Plack with being a Nazi, and they had a fistfight in a Hollywood night club. Soon after, Plack departed for Berlin, where, among other activities, he was responsible for the Nazi broadcasts of the celebrated author P. G. Wodehouse, who was completely whitewashed after World War II despite Plack's sworn statements on the matter to the U.S. Government and the fact that Ribbentrop supported him from his special budget in Paris on orders from Hitler.

Right up to Pearl Harbor, the work was being finished. The plans were carried to New York by a person or persons unknown as early as March 1941. They were given to the well-known Abwehr secret agent and spy master Major Ulrich von der Osten, for transmission to Louis Siefken, of Abwehr, in Shanghai. Von der Osten was a favorite of the Abwehr chief Admiral Wilhelm Canaris. He was first heard of in Spain in 1935, when he assisted General Franco in his intelligence work for the Spanish Civil War under the pseudonym of Don Julio López Lido. With headquarters in a convent, Von der Osten enlisted many powerful secret agents, including, by oversight, Kim Philby, who was working as London *Times* correspondent in Spain and was in fact a Communist spy.

Canaris transferred Von der Osten to New York City to link up with local networks of agents. He worked closely with the important American spy Kurt Frederick Ludwig, who controlled a secret radio, eight special agents, and a number of mail drops in Europe. With instructions from Shanghai, Osten traveled to New York via the Middle West and checked into the Hotel Taft, a hostelry in midtown Manhattan. Under Osten's control, Ludwig, who was born in Fremont, Ohio, and used the special code name Lothar, prepared a number of strategic reports. He established that four thousand men were leaving for Greenland on the SS *America* and that a contingent of Flying Fortresses was going to England under Lend-Lease, and he described British, Norwegian, Polish, and Dutch ship movements.

Because Ludwig had spent some time in Germany and had a touch of a German accent, it was felt unwise for him to attempt to obtain detailed military information for Berlin. So Osten and Ludwig hired an American girl named Lucy Boehmler, who had not a trace of accent, since she had come to America at the age of five. She traveled constantly, to airports and other defense facilities, power stations, factories, and plants. She supplied her bosses with a stream of information on cargoes, bombsights, airfields, army movements, and the latest developments in bombers and fighter aircraft. American security was almost nonexistent, and Lucy Boehmler was an attractive and buxom young woman; all she had to do was turn up as a tourist with a camera and an amusing Bronx accent and the boys took care of her and showed her everything.

She wrote letters as a tourist with a typewriter on one side of heavy bond stationery; the reverse contained messages written with a toothpick in invisible ink. She made the ink with white pills contained in an aspirin bottle and dissolved in water in various hotel bathrooms.

Everything seemed to be going swimmingly, and the theft of the plans of the secret installations of Pearl Harbor and Hickam Field was the ultimate coup. Von der Osten sent one copy to Siefken but unwisely kept the other in his room at the Hotel Taft.

On March 18, 1941, he and Ludwig were walking through Times Square trying to deal with the very heavy and lethally fast-moving traffic. Suddenly a taxi came conveniently out of nowhere and struck Osten, who fell, mortally injured, against the curb. Ludwig snatched Osten's briefcase and ran off with it but neglected to clean out the room at the Taft. When police broke into the room, they found the copy of the plans with an annotation in tiny handwriting that read, "This will be of interest to our yellow friends." The police handed the material over to Percy Foxworth of the FBI New York Bureau. Twenty-four hours after Osten's death, a clerk at the Spanish consulate claimed the body at the morgue, carrying Osten's passport with the name Julio López. Foxworth immediately determined that the Spanish consulate was involved in the cover.

Two New York detectives were waiting at the Taft to see who would turn up. There was a knock at the door. It was Lucy Boehmler. She pretended she had made a mistake, but the detectives followed her to a Swedish restaurant and then to a lodging house, where they identified her contacts as members of the Ludwig spy ring. Hans Thomsen was shocked and furious when he found out. He had begged Canaris not to allow anything of this sort to happen. As part of the negotiated peace plans, he wanted no possible hint of espionage or sabotage to be going on.

FBI agents and New York police found out the addresses and phone numbers of the Ludwig ring simply by following the unsuspecting Lucy Boehmler. They were also aided by a furnace man, Walter Morrissey, who worked at the German consulate general, at 17 Battery Place. Morrissey noticed documents relating to Ludwig. He was supposed to throw them into the fire while members of the consular staff watched him, but instead he tossed the papers into the grate in such a manner that they choked the wind out. Then he would toss on a few shovels of burning embers. When the Nazis left, he dragged out the half-burned documents and handed them over to Foxworth's team.

Simultaneously, the British Censorship Office in Bermuda found letters with invisible-ink messages stating that Osten's death was caused by Jews and that it was fortunate that Osten had relayed the bulk of the information about Pearl Harbor to Siefken. The letter was signed by "Joe Kessler," Ludwig's new alias.

Ludwig tried to have Thomsen authorize his return to Germany, but Thomsen wanted no part of him. The FBI followed Ludwig as he made his way to the West Coast to take a Japanese ship to his controls in China; shortly before he could board ship he was seized, in Spokane, Washington, where he tried to bribe his way out of prison with fifty thousand dollars raised from contacts in the Argentine branch of Abwehr. But he did not succeed; he stood trial and was imprisoned for the duration of the war.

There were a series of investigations into the Pearl Harbor disaster, including a California Un-American Activities senatorial investigation, proceedings before the Army Pearl Harbor Board, and a House Military Affairs Committee investigation of the national war effort. All the facts were discussed at great length, and indeed it was disclosed at the California hearing that the Japanese Government had access to the Pearl Harbor plans. Reference was made directly to the specifications of the Rohl-Wyman contracts and that these were identical with those found in Von der

Osten's possession. However, nothing was done. Indeed, the Rohl-Connolly company went on simultaneously, building top-secret installations in Alaska and the South Pacific. The fact that Rohl had lied about his immigration and been awarded a government contract when he was not a citizen was ignored. Moreover, nobody informed on Errol Flynn, and of course Flynn never volunteered his personal knowledge of the matter. And there it rested for good.

✴✴✴✴✴✴✴ 13

The Windsor Plot

The Duke of Windsor's infatuation with nazism is well known. Because he was not noted for his intelligence, his precise role in collusion has always been left vague. An examination of the facts shows that he played an important part in conspiratorial arrangements before and during World War II.

In February 1941, the well-known journalist Fulton Oursler interviewed Windsor at Government House, in Nassau, the Bahamas, and published the results in *Liberty* magazine on March 22. Windsor gave the game away when Oursler asked him what his views were on a negotiated peace. The duke answered that he approved of such a peace, thus totally defying Winston Churchill's published statements that only total surrender of Germany would be considered by the British Government. Referring to the hated Versailles Treaty, in which Germany had been stripped of her resources, Windsor told Oursler, "It [the peace] cannot be another Versailles. Whatever happens, whatever the outcome, a New Order is going to come into the world. . . . It will be buttressed with police power. . . . When peace comes this time, there is going to be a New Order of Social Justice*—don't make any mistake about that—and when that time comes, what is your country going to do with its gold?" Churchill was very annoyed about this.

The Windsors were enchanted with their 1938 visit with Hitler and

* The title of an inflammatory Nazi magazine then in circulation in the United States.

their tour of Germany; the Duchess was seen handing a bag full of money to a Gestapo officer on the border of Austria.

The Duchess of Windsor's lawyer in Paris, Armand Grégoire, was an early member of the Nazi Party who also represented Ribbentrop and William Randolph Hearst. His partner was Bruno Weil, another fascistic figure who represented Nazis. Weil had been active in forcing Jews to vote for affiliation to the Third Reich in return for immunity from imprisonment. It is not surprising that the indispensable Breckinridge Long issued a visa for both of these gentlemen after Pearl Harbor, when he denied passports to Jews.

While the Duke's close friend Nazi collaborator and industrial-systems expert Charles Bedaux, of New York, was busy undermining France in preparation for Vichy and the establishment of full-scale collaboration with Hitler, Windsor by 1940 had become a member of the British Military Mission with the French Army Command. Neville Chamberlain and Winston Churchill were aware that Windsor's Nazi connections were far more serious than a mere "confused sympathy" would indicate.

On May 3, 1941, J. Edgar Hoover sent a memorandum to Roosevelt's Secretary, Major General "Pa" Watson, which read as follows: "Information has been received at this Bureau from a source that is socially prominent and known to be in touch with some of the people involved, but for whom we cannot vouch, to the effect that Joseph P. Kennedy, the former Ambassador to England, and Ben Smith, the Wall Street operator, some time in the past had a meeting with Göring in Vichy, France, and that thereafter Kennedy and Smith had donated a considerable amount of money to the German cause. They are both described as being very anti-British and pro-German.

"This same source of information advised that it was reported that the Duke of Windsor entered into an agreement to the effect that if Germany were victorious in the war, Herman Göring through his control of the army would overthrow Hitler and would thereafter install the Duke of Windsor as the King of England. This information concerning the Windsors is said to have originated from Allen McIntosh, a personal friend of the Duke of Windsor, who made the arrangements for the entertainment of the Windsors when they were in Miami recently. It is further reported that it is the intention of the Windsors to visit in Newport, Rhode Island, and also in Canada during the coming summer."

When Windsor asked Chamberlain for a more important job, the

Duke was frozen out. Mortified, he committed himself to the appeasement group in England which remained part of The Link and included Montagu Norman of the Bank of England, and Lord McGowan of Imperial Chemical Industries. In January 1940, Count Julius von Zech-Burkesroda, Nazi minister to The Hague, sent a special emissary to London to ask Windsor to tell the British Government that it was useless to try to change Germany politically and that Windsor should help bring about a negotiated peace. Windsor was fascinated. He secretly conferred with the Nazi messenger. Since he knew the messenger had arrived in the country for a clandestine purpose, this amounted to an act of treason in time of war.

On February 18, Windsor disclosed to Zech-Burkesroda's emissary the details of a secret meeting of the Allied War Council. Windsor revealed that the council had discussed in detail the situation that would arise if Germany invaded Belgium. The council members had discussed the discovery of a German invasion plan found in an airplane that had made a forced landing in Belgium.

The Windsors traveled from Paris to Spain. Walter Schellenberg, of the SD AMT VI, selected Eberhard von Stöhrer, the six-foot-seven, genial German ambassador to Spain, to contact them. He was one of I.G. Farben's most trusted agents, on the payroll of the Farben account at the Stein Bank. A man of great sophistication and flair, he had been first secretary of the German embassy in World War I, organizing sabotage in Catalonia against pro-Allied factories. He was also involved in a plot against the then Prime Minister, Count Romanones, who led the pro-Allied faction in Spain. As a result, he had been withdrawn by the German Government in 1917. Back in Spain in 1934, Stöhrer undertook a dangerous mission for Farben's General von Faupel, head of the International Falange. He made connections with the multimillionaire former smuggler Juan March, whom he backed politically in order to bring about the Franco revolution. He contacted generals, using the plump, dandyish General José Sanjurjo as an agent of the Nazi government. Sanjurjo pulled together the master plan that led to the Spanish Civil War. Stöhrer organized the straggling rank and file of the Falange, most of whom were hired killers drawn from the scum of the Spanish slums into a cohesive and dangerous terrorist organization that eventually overran Spain with guns and explosives.

Sanjurjo made the mistake of saying to too many people that he was weary of serving the "bankers and speculators" and that he would not knuckle under to I.G. Farben. On July 17, 1936, dressed in a uniform designed for him in London on Hitler's orders, Sanjurjo boarded a Junkers plane in Lisbon for a secret mission on behalf of the Falangists. Within minutes of takeoff, a time bomb in the baggage compartment blew Sanjurjo and the plane to bits. Undoubtedly, Stöhrer engineered the death —the first major casualty of the Civil War.

Von Stöhrer worked closely with Falangist leader Miguel Primo de Rivera, who was financed by I.G. Farben and took over in Spain when Faupel was transferred to Latin America to take over Brazilian and Argentinian espionage in collusion with the Bayer-Sterling group and lay the groundwork for the Nazi invasion of those countries, planned for March 1942.

Primo de Rivera was no less fanatical a Falangist. His involvement in every form of terrorism, subversion, and espionage against Allied interests had become notorious throughout Europe by 1940.

On June 24, the Windsors dined with Sir Samuel Hoare in Madrid. He had taken the precaution of not inviting them to stay at his house, which, ironically, adjoined the Nazi embassy, with only a thin wall separating the two buildings. Each country's intelligence men could spy on the other's.

The following night, the Windsors dined with Primo de Rivera at the Hotel Palace. Ribbentrop cabled Stöhrer to have the Windsors detained by refusing them an exit visa. The Spanish Government would cooperate in the refusal; it was essential that the suggestion not seem to come from Germany. Stöhrer replied that the Spanish Foreign Minister had agreed to comply.

On June 30, German Minister Schmidt sent a teletype to his protocol department making sure that Ambassador Otto Abetz should keep the Windsors' house in Paris under surveillance to see that it was not damaged by the French underground. Windsor was advised that the Berlin Foreign Ministry was protecting his property. His large account at the Banque de France was also preserved by the Nazis.

On July 2, Stöhrer advised Ribbentrop that the Windsors were about to go to Portugal to confer with the Duke of Kent, who was there in connection with the Lisbon Jubilee celebrations and was himself a go-between to Hitler. In a conversation with the Spanish Foreign Minister, Windsor said that he would return to England only if his wife were recognized as a member of the royal family. He bitterly attacked Churchill during the discussion.

The Windsors proceeded to Lisbon. It is evident that Churchill wanted to get them out of the country as soon as possible.

The elegant banker Ricardo de Espíritu Santo e Silva became the host for the Duke and Duchess in Lisbon. Upon their arrival, the British ambassador to Lisbon handed the Windsors a cold and impersonal letter from Winston Churchill advising them that they were to proceed immediately to take up the post of governor and first lady in Nassau. This was a particularly unfortunate choice of location. The Bahamas were already a focus of Nazi intrigue. The dominant financial group in Nassau included the Fraternity leader Axel Wenner-Gren and a new recruit, the wealthy landowner Harold Christie. Christie had introduced Wenner-Gren to a scheme for industrializing Mexico in preparation for a German takeover.

On July 10, 1940, Walter Schellenberg received a call from Ribbentrop. Ribbentrop said the matter was too urgent and important to be discussed on the telephone. Schellenberg was to go to the Foreign Ministry at once.

At the meeting, Ribbentrop praised Windsor as "one of the most socially aware and right-thinking Englishmen I have ever met. . . . The marriage issue was a pretext to remove this honest and faithful friend of Germany." Ribbentrop said that friends in Spain had conveyed to him that the Duke "still entertains the same sympathetic feeling towards Germany," and hated the constant presence of British Intelligence men. Ribbentrop told Schellenberg that Hitler wanted to offer the Duke a minimum of fifty million Swiss gold francs to be deposited in his account in that country. Schellenberg must go at once to bring back the Windsors, even if it involved using force. At the end of the meeting, Hitler called on the telephone. Ribbentrop handed Schellenberg a second earpiece so that he could listen in. Hitler said, "Schellenberg should particularly bear in mind the importance of the Duchess' attitude and try as hard as possible to get her support." Schellenberg made immediate plans to fly to Madrid.

In a cable dated July 11, German Minister in Lisbon Huyningen-Huene reported, "The Duke is convinced that if he had remained on the throne of England, war would have been avoided, and he characterized himself as a firm supporter of a peaceful arrangement with Germany. The Duke definitely believes that continued severe bombing would make England ready for peace."

This was the result of a conversation between Huyningen-Huene and Windsor at Espíritu Santo e Silva's house. Huyningen-Huene was a brilliant career diplomat. He was not prone to exaggerations or distortions. Therefore, the last sentence of the telegram has to be taken as genuine.

The German Government's chief concern as it sent Primo de Rivera to Lisbon was that the real reason for the Windsors' return might slip out: a peace conference with the Nazi leaders. Because British Intelligence was constantly following the Duke, there must be a fake arrest in which he would be interned as a member of the British Expeditionary Force who was illegally present in Spain. While Windsor was under "arrest" the plan would be made clear to him. He would be offered sanctuary, probably in his favorite city of Granada, until such time as a negotiated peace with England could be achieved.

On July 15, Primo de Rivera met with the Windsors in Lisbon. Windsor told the arch-Falangist that Churchill had made it clear in a very "cool and categorical" manner that he must leave Europe at once. Indeed, if he did not, he would be court-martialed. However, the Duke told Rivera, he had pleaded with Churchill for a few weeks' grace to obtain some of his effects from Paris. Churchill had agreed.

With the consent of the British Government, the Windsors sent their maid to Paris to pick up some things, and Otto Abetz approved the arrangements despite the fact that Britain was at war. William Bullitt helped. He flew to Lisbon for a meeting with the Windsors on July 20, on his way back to the United States. Whether or not he was part of the overall scheme is uncertain.

Rivera had further meetings with the Windsors. The Duke, restless and nervous, said he felt a prisoner in Portugal, surrounded by British agents. He was afraid of Queen Elizabeth, the wife of George VI, whom he blamed for intriguing against him and the Duchess over his brother's head. He uneasily asked Rivera on July 21 how he could cross back into Spain clandestinely without being seized by MI6—British Foreign Intelligence.

On July 22, Walter Schellenberg flew to Madrid for meetings with Stöhrer. He had details of plans to get the Windsors into Spain. He engaged a Japanese secret agent to infiltrate the Espíritu Santo e Silva house and bribe the servants to supply every detail of the Windsors' private conversations.

On July 23, a special agent of the Nazi government acting on behalf of Stöhrer gave the Windsors the plan. They were to be invited on a hunting trip in the mountainous borders of Spain. They would walk from their car to a preordained spot. By apparent accident, a secretary of the Spanish Ministry of the Interior in the pay of the German Government would meet them there and invite them to visit an estate on the Spanish side. But how could they get across? Winston Churchill had ordered the British ambassador to Portugal to confiscate the Duke's passport. The answer was that a Portuguese frontier official had been bribed. In case there was trouble (for instance if British agents tried to interfere), Rivera would be waiting with a small contingent of Falangist soldiers all of whom were fanatically devoted to Hitler.

The Duke pulled strings in the British embassy to have his passport returned, with, incredibly, a visa allowing him to travel to Spain.

Winston Churchill was drastically concerned. In the middle of the London blitz, the embattled Prime Minister had to make an immediate decision. He sent Sir Walter Monckton, a great friend of the Windsors, to Lisbon to try to persuade the duke that he should remain loyal to Great Britain and not become part of a Hitler conspiracy.

Monckton begged the Windsors not to cooperate with the German Government. On July 20, the duke told a Nazi emissary that he had decided to go on to the Bahamas. He added, "I had hoped to help negotiate peace. But I dare not at this time carry on negotiations contrary to my government and thus unleash propaganda from my opponents which would wreck my prestige in England. I will consider taking action from the Bahamas instead."

Stöhrer suggested to Ribbentrop that Rivera make a last and desperate effort to change the duke's mind. Rivera was to say that England would soon be defeated and King George would be exiled. The duke would be powerless to intervene from a British colony.

The same day Stöhrer sent the telegram, Ribbentrop sent another, suggesting that the duke's host in Lisbon should make a further statement to him. Germany would clear the way for any desire of the duke and duchess; if they would be willing to cooperate and return to the English throne, they would have their wishes satisfied; if they went to the Bahamas, they would surely be imprisoned.

On August 1, the Windsors were booked to go aboard the *Excalibur*, sailing for Bermuda, where they would change ships for Nassau. Nazi ambassador in Lisbon Huyningen-Huene and Walter Schellenberg made a desperate last-minute effort to secure the Windsors' cooperation. They offered them a personal protective service, security for the automobile journey, and a complete cover for the passage across the border guaranteed by the chief of Portuguese counterintelligence. Despite the fact that the counterintelligence chief was working with Scotland Yard, he could be bought.

However, Huyningen-Huene cabled Berlin, Sir Walter Monckton was proving influential. Huyningen-Huene plucked every string: He warned the Windsors they might be in danger from Jewish émigrés on the ship. He arranged with the customs people to confiscate the guns of the four Scotland Yard detectives who had been sent to cover the Windsors. He had the wife of a Portuguese official tell the duchess her husband would be fired if anything happened to the royal couple. He sent a bouquet of flowers with an anonymous greeting card containing a warning of imminent problems during the crossing.

The ship was delayed for hours while the Windsors tortuously wrangled over what they should do. At the last minute, Huyningen-Huene was in the Windsors' cabin with a personal appeal from Portuguese Premier Salazar. Finally, the duke bade farewell to his host, Espíritu Santo e Silva. He gave his game away completely. He repeated his conviction that if he had been king there would never have been a war with Germany. He said that disobedience to Churchill at the moment would disclose his intentions prematurely and bring about a scandal. If England would consider Germany's offer of negotiated peace, he would make himself available at once at any sacrifice. He gave Espíritu Santo e Silva a code word. The moment the banker cabled the word, Windsor would return at once. "I express this with a firmness of will and an expression of admiration and sympathy for the Führer," Windsor concluded.

At last the ship sailed. Contrary to the picture painted by successive biographers, who have omitted the most damning passages from the German records, it is clear that the duke was merely afraid of what the consequences would be if he fulfilled the plan laid down by Himmler and The Fraternity; he had no twinges of loyalty in those last hours. Indeed, on August 15, in Nassau, he cabled Espíritu Santo e Silva indicating that he was ready to receive the code word.

It was never sent. By this stage, it was clear that the Windsors were drastically exposed to danger. In the Bahamas, they could easily be disposed of by British Intelligence if they tried to return. They were no longer "protected" by Nazis.

However, they were soon surrounded by a powerful Fascist clique headed by Axel Wenner-Gren, the vacuum-cleaner king, head of Electrolux Industries.

✠✠✠✠✠✠✠ 14

The Sphinx of Sweden

Wenner-Gren was among the richest men in the world in 1940. His involvement in the Stockholm Enskilda Bank, Bofors Munitions, and SKF ball bearings had made him more millions. Born in a small Swedish town in 1881, tall, lean, with ice-blue eyes, he began his career as a salesman for Swedish Lux, an electric light bulb manufacturer. By 1911, he had become general agent for the company. Three years later, he had acquired control of the small and struggling Electrolux Company and had married a pretty American opera singer, Marguerite Liggett. In 1919, he snapped up a patent for a primitive vacuum cleaner that, by 1928, became the largest-selling cleaning device in the world. That year, he obtained a patent for a gas-powered refrigerator; by the mid-1930s, he was already a millionaire. He aided the Krupps, Göring, and I.G. Farben's Hermann Schmitz in evading the terms of the Versailles Treaty, setting up German munitions factories under the Bofors cloak, in Sweden. He obtained the safety-match empire of the millionaire tycoon Ivar Kreuger, who had committed suicide when ITT called in its options.

Wenner-Gren acted as a free-lance political agent, operating as an intermediary between Göring and Prime Minister Chamberlain of Great Britain in order to secure a negotiated peace.

In 1939, at the International Chamber of Commerce meeting in Copenhagen, Denmark, Wenner-Gren presented a plan to ensure the continuing assistance of German, Japanese, British, and American cartel agreements throughout World War II. Ribbentrop and the isolationist senator Hamilton Fish were present.

Wenner-Gren owned the *Southern Cross,* the largest private yacht afloat. Three hundred and twenty feet long, with a gross displacement of two thousand tons, the vessel was sumptuously furnished and paneled in mahogany and pine. Howard Hughes had sold her to Wenner-Gren for $2 million in 1937. She had the finest radio equipment available and carried rifles and machine guns. Among her better-known passengers were Greta Garbo, Gaylord Hauser, and Lord Lothian.

Just before war broke out, Wenner-Gren had an urgent meeting with Göring at Göring's mansion Karinhall. He was to leave at once for the United States and try to set up arrangements to stave off war. On August 31, 1939, he sailed around the stormy north coast of Scotland headed for New York and Nassau with a giant cargo of gold, supplied by Göring for the use of Nazi agents overseas. As the luxury vessel chugged down the Scottish coast, the watch reported that the Canadian liner *Athenia* was sailing on the same course for America.

Suddenly there was a loud explosion. A torpedo had slammed into the *Athenia*'s hull. Flames burst from her side. Passengers swarmed on the decks and struggled into the lifeboats or plunged into the icy sea.

It is possible Wenner-Gren radioed Berlin that the British had sunk the ship deliberately in order to provoke a war. It was years before documents disclosed that Germany was responsible.

To make himself seem a hero, Wenner-Gren picked up some three hundred survivors. But he quickly transferred them from his luxurious vessel to the already overcrowded British freighter *City of Flint.* He radioed New York that he had bravely snatched Americans from the ocean, thus earning congratulations from President Roosevelt—though not, be it noted, from Winston Churchill.

In Nassau, Wenner-Gren founded the Bank of the Bahamas, connected to the Stein Bank of Cologne, and bought a six hundred-acre, sandy, flyblown estate on Hog Island. He poured $1 million into turning it into one of the most luxurious resorts on earth. Calling it Paradise Island, he dug canals and built delicately sculptured bridges. Unfounded rumors had U-boats sheltering in the canals for refueling. In February 1940, Göring cabled Wenner-Gren by code, asking him to step in and settle the war between Russia and Finland. Wenner-Gren flew to Washington. He had an urgent meeting with Roosevelt which was chiefly concerned with discussing a negotiated peace with Germany. Sumner Welles was on the same ship that Wenner-Gren took to Europe. It was widely believed that Wenner-Gren spied on the American under secretary of state, who was sounding out Hitler and Göring on Roosevelt's behalf.

In Nassau, Wenner-Gren was among the first to greet the Windsors when they arrived, in July 1940. He took them on a voyage to Miami on the *Southern Cross* so that the duchess could go to the dentist and served them a lavish meal including a multicolored ice-cream replica of the yacht.

Wenner-Gren held $2,500,000 of the Duke of Windsor's money in the Bahamas and Mexico, because British subjects, even members of the royal family, were not permitted to shift their cash. Swedish nationals, on the other hand, were allowed to move their money around at will. When Wenner-Gren was threatened with blacklisting, he shifted the money to the Banco Continental, in Mexico City, for investment on behalf of the Windsors. He constantly held over the duke imaginary threats that the Germans would again try to kidnap him and perhaps exchange him for Rudolf Hess. Thus Wenner-Gren insinuated into the duke's mind that if he continued to prove helpful to the cause of nazism, he would not be touched. The duke's collusion in the money leak was, to say the least, illegal; and so were his communications with Mexico when British diplomatic relations with that country had been discontinued.

Wenner-Gren concurred with the Windsors' hatred of Bolshevism and the feeling that the war was a mistake. He believed the free world should enter into an alliance with the Nazis. Avra Warren, of the State Department, received a memorandum from a member of his staff on January 25, 1941, reading, "The most recent information I have regarding Mr. Wenner-Gren indicates that he is in constant and close touch with the Duke of Windsor and that both of them are seeing a great deal of prominent and influential American businessmen, particularly from the mid-western states, where a strictly commercial point of view would appear to prevail in business circles with regard to relations between the United States and Germany. There would appear to be certain indications that Wenner-Gren, as well as the Duke of Windsor, is stressing the need for a negotiated peace at this time on account of the advantages which this would present to American business interests. . . ."

The scheme encompassed a number of prominent figures in the Bahamas and North America. Among these were John J. Hastings, a former New York state senator who had helped to build the New York City subway. Hastings was in league with oilman William Rhodes Davis; Ed Flynn, Democratic boss of the Bronx and chairman of the National Democratic Committee; Ben Smith, the Wall Street promoter; and the White Russian Serge Rubinstein. A probably unwitting partner in the conspiracy was the multimillionaire Sir Harry Oakes, a Canadian gold and industrial tycoon who was the Windsors' host before they moved into Government House. Oakes was a loudmouthed, unstable, and vulgar upstart with few social graces. But his immense wealth ensured him a place at the table of the wellborn.

An addition to the scheme was the land promoter Harold Christie, who owned much of the Bahamas. He became very close to the Windsors. At Government House, he introduced Wenner-Gren and Harry Oakes to the pro-Nazi General Maximino Camacho of Mexico. William Rhodes Davis, Christie, Oakes, Camacho, Flynn, Smith, Hastings, and Wenner-Gren jointly bought up the Banco Continental, in Mexico City. The syndicate invested enormous sums in the Compañía Petrolia Veracruzana in conjunction with the Japanese Government. The Compañía supplied Japan with oil, platinum, and other rare metals to assist in its preparations for war. The Compañía syndicate cornered the market in hemp, copper, and mercury to prevent these crucial raw materials from going to the United States to help in American war production.

All of these activities were recorded in scores of State Department, Treasury, and FBI memoranda which poured onto Cordell Hull's overcrowded desk in the 1940s. American Intelligence began to close in. Yet not one word of these schemes appeared in the press.

Shortly after Pearl Harbor, Henry Morgenthau, Jr., under great pressure from Ambassador to Mexico George Messersmith, blacklisted Wenner-Gren and forced him to leave the Bahamas for Mexico City. To quote a Messersmith memorandum to Hull dated March 1, 1943, "There is no doubt whatever that Wenner-Gren was convinced that the Nazi government would be able to carry through [its] domination. . . . He was willing to sacrifice every principle and ally [himself] with the Nazi government with the thought that [he] would benefit by the domination of [that] government. . . . Mr. Wenner-Gren's activities in Mexico have not been such as to show any friendship for the United States . . . [they] are entirely out of accord with the best interests of the United States. . . ." Messersmith made similar statements about ex-Senator Hastings and the other conspirators.

Messersmith discovered that the syndicate was financing Maximino Camacho to bring about a coup d'état against his brother, President Ávila Camacho of Mexico. FBI investigators traced Wenner-Gren to an archaeological mission at Inca ruins, in Peru, in 1942, where he was located in meetings with German agents. It was believed he was setting up a network of political and economic contacts in that country to ensure that it would become part of the Third Reich.

In 1942, Wenner-Gren began to use funds from Mexican Electrolux to invest in every aspect of Mexican business, including bullfighting, football teams, race tracks, furniture factories, construction firms, agricultural developments, six haciendas, a stock farm, and a large estate in Cuernavaca. This money earned interest that was turned over to the consortium. He built a magnificent house, called El Rancho Cortez, at Cuernavaca, set in lush, tropical gardens. In a report prepared for private circulation, the author Stanley Ross stated, "In a 60 foot long dining room . . . the 20 foot long mahogany table is inlaid with the sword and firearms of Hernando Cortez. . . . Wenner-Gren's guests are served with culinary perfection turned out by the former chefs of the *Southern Cross.* And dinner is nostalgically topped off with sherbet in sculptured forms of the famous yacht, resting on a sea of ice lit up by a green bulb, and miniature likenesses of the crew molded in marzipan."

There was a private zoo including hundreds of rare birds, monkeys, pumas, leopards, sloths, and snakes, and a parrot whose favorite expression was "God bless America!" During the years after Pearl Harbor, the consortium members would drive up to the heavy iron gates in front of the great white stone house near Chapultepec Park. The servants were in livery matching that used by Göring; a blond young man in naval uniform always greeted the arrivals. Gobelin tapestries similar to those at Göring's Karinhall hung from ceiling to floor. Ross described "grilled windows that burnished the lustrous mahogany collector's pieces, and played from one polished piece of silver to another. There was silver everywhere: silver trays, bowls, platters and plaques; and several pairs of fine old Spanish stirrups that must have weighed about five pounds each, intricately carved." Everywhere in the house there were elephants, the Electrolux trademark, in gold, silver, ivory, and wood. Many of them had been bought from the estate of Florenz Ziegfeld and none had the trunk down (a symbol of bad luck).

It was in this opulent setting that the negotiated-peace team met frequently throughout the war. A topic of conversation was not only the planned coup but removing Wenner-Gren from the U.S. blacklist. The group was constantly frustrated by the obstinate Ambassador George Messersmith, who knew all about Wenner-Gren's Nazi connections from the years in which Messersmith had been consul general in Berlin. He was determined to keep Wenner-Gren on the Proclaimed List of enemy associates indefinitely and bombarded Washington with streams of reports. A typical report read: "Mr. Wenner-Gren's activities in Mexico have not been such as to show any friendship for the United States. . . . He [looks] upon Mexico as a field of exploitation and the invitation of General Maximino Camacho came at an opportune moment . . . he has been following practices in Mexico which are entirely out of accord with the best interests of the United States. . . ."* It was Wenner-Gren who brought in yet another member of the consortium, Ed Flynn, Democratic boss of the Bronx, who was also the lawyer for Serge Rubinstein. Ed Flynn in 1943 was put up as ambassador to Australia. Morgenthau, Ickes, Messersmith, and other liberals violently opposed the appointment. Australia was a highly strategic region in the Pacific war and was destined to be General MacArthur's headquarters. Flynn lost the job after a senatorial inquiry into his connections with the group in Mexico and his other involvements, including underground activities with the gangster Dutch Schultz and an interest in a brickmaking company that involved kickbacks. Flynn, aggravated by losing the post, spent much of his time in the last two years of the war in Mexico, helping the consortium.

The consortium's plans were wrecked because of an event that occurred on the night of June 20, 1943, when a violent tropical storm exploded over Nassau. Sir Harry Oakes had a quarrel with a Nazi member of the consortium†; it was clear that he had lost interest in any complicity with the group.

Lady Oakes was in Bar Harbor, Maine, for the summer vacation. Oakes gave a dinner party for eleven people that June 20, followed by Chinese checkers. He asked Harold Christie to stay overnight, perhaps because he was afraid of something or somebody. Christie moved into a bedroom separated from Oakes's by another bedroom and a bathroom.

While Oakes slept, somebody stole into his room and attacked him

---

* June 13, 1943.

† Name withheld because of the Privacy Act of 1974.

with a mysterious four-pronged implement. It could have been a golf club with the head broken off or a winch lever. There was a desperate struggle. Oakes was a powerful man and fought fiercely for his life. But the intruder was stronger. While Oakes was temporarily weakened, the visitor threw the contents of an insecticide can over his body and set it on fire. Then the killer sprinkled feathers over the burning man and struck four severe blows to the head, which killed Oakes.

Allegedly, the struggle, the screams of the burning victim, and the violent blows of the murder weapon did not awaken Christie. Later, Christie said he had woken up twice in the night, once because of the thunder and once because of the sound of mosquitoes. This statement laid him open to grave suspicion.

The Windsors' equerry, Major Gray Phillips, brought word of the murder to Government House in the early hours of the morning. The Duke's first move should have been to call London immediately and get the Foreign Secretary out of bed. He should also have called Lord Halifax, the ambassador to Washington. He should have gotten hold of Scotland Yard, which had representatives in Bermuda; Sir William Stephenson; and the Federal Bureau of Investigation, the last to be authorized to assist in such matters in wartime. He did none of these things. Instead, he told his personal staff that the Emergency War Powers Act would be exercised and that no word of the crime would be disclosed to the world. It was too late. Christie had broken the news to a friend and it was already on the wire services.

Windsor continued to act most questionably. He called Miami. He summoned two members of the police department, Captain Edward Melchen and Captain James O. Barker, neither of whom was authorized by the FBI to investigate cases of this kind during wartime. Instead of reporting to J. Edgar Hoover, the two men bypassed him completely and rushed to Nassau, where they took a fingerprint off a screen, bloodstain samples, and fragments of hair. The FBI laboratories in Miami were available and excellently equipped. But the two men, apparently on Windsor's instructions, flew the samples to New York City, where tests were made by Dr. Alexander Wiener, of the Chief Medical Examiner's Office. Hoover was furious. He made clear in report after report that the Miami Police Department had acted with gross impropriety. In a letter to his Miami bureau chief, A. P. Kitchen, dated October 4, 1943, he wrote, "In the future, be particularly alert for any facts or circumstances that give further evidence of an uncooperative attitude on the part of the personnel of the Miami police department."

In New York, Dr. Wiener, who was a friend of Sir Harry Oakes, announced that the fingerprint found on the paper screen in Sir Harry's bedroom was that of Sir Harry's son-in-law Alfred deMarigny. However, as Hoover's recently declassified reports make clear, the method of lifting the fingerprints from the screen was totally improper and the fingerprint was a forgery. The screen was covered in a complicated pattern, which should have shown up in the print. The fingerprint was clear.

Hoover conducted his own investigation. One of his informants revealed in a long and detailed letter that a prime suspect in the case was the aforementioned nameless Nazi, who hated Oakes and constantly threatened his well-being. This linked the murder clearly to the Nazi group that surrounded Sir Harry, but Hoover was powerless to intervene. DeMarigny was brought to trial for murder.

The witnesses perjured themselves over and over again. The detectives lied about the fingerprints. Harold Christie told an absurd story of coming into Oakes's room in the morning and finding his friend lying on the bed. Despite the fact that the body was badly burned and lay face down, he said that it lay face up and that he did not know Sir Harry was dead. He even said that he put a glass of water to Oakes's mouth and that Oakes swallowed it. This was ridiculous in view of the fact that rigor mortis had long since set in.

Throughout the trial, Alfred deMarigny behaved in a peculiar fashion. Instead of looking like a man fighting for his life, he smiled, yawned, stared at the ceiling, and propped his feet on the bars of the dock. He gave the impression he was waiting to start a tennis game. How can this be explained? Only by the probability that he knew he would be acquitted.

Inevitably, the jury found for the defendant. But there was a curious addendum to the verdict. DeMarigny was required to leave the Bahamas immediately. Only a direct order from the governor could have made such a deportation legal. There was no reason for it. If Alfred deMarigny was innocent, why did he have to leave the island? One can only assume the Duke of Windsor was responsible, since he issued the deportation order himself.

The Duke of Windsor's complicity in this matter can scarcely be doubted. The Oakes family has its own explanation. The late Lady Oakes insisted that the murder was committed by a voodoo priest who lived on one of the "out islands," the outlying part of the Bahaman group. She said that Oakes was having an affair with the priest's wife. The presence of the feathers on the body and the burning have all the appearance of a voodoo ritual, she alleged. She claimed that had the Duke arrested a black and tried him for murder, there would have been a revolution that might have stretched through the whole Caribbean region. But it would be a logical deduction that a member of The Fraternity put this idea in her mind. Hatred of blacks was of course part of the racist psychology of the Nazis.

Another theory has been that the murder was committed by the Mafia, which wanted to set up a gambling empire in the Bahamas and was blocked by Sir Harry at every turn. The theorists claim that Oakes was murdered outside the house and brought to it in a station wagon and that the fire was devised to remove details of the "outside job" and make it seem that Sir Harry had upset a kerosene lamp in the night. But there is no reference to this possibility in any of the FBI files, and there is to date no documentary evidence to support the theory.

Where does that leave us? With a third possibility, hinted at strongly in Hoover's memoranda: that Oakes had threatened to expose the Nazi group to British Intelligence in Bermuda and New York and the FBI in Washington. This would explain why the Duke of Windsor went to such extraordinary lengths to avoid calling these agencies.

The FBI files on the case have been drastically censored. FBI officials admit that most of the documents that have been withdrawn contain British reports which are of so sensitive a character that they still fall under the British Official Secrets Act. This could mean, of course, that they are extremely damaging to the Duke of Windsor.

15

The Man Who Used Cary Grant

One of the celebrated motion picture star Cary Grant's most important films was Alfred Hitchcock's *Notorious* (1946), in which he played an FBI agent in South America after World War II, investigating and uncovering a Nazi headquarters in Buenos Aires involved in obtaining strategic uranium deposits for use in a future war. By unfortunate happenstance, in real life the same star became the victim of a prominent Nazi agent himself.

That agent was a member of the International Falange, headquartered in Buenos Aires in World War II.

That Spanish pro-Nazi organization, run by General Wilhelm von Faupel, was a fanatically anti-Communist organization that swirled about Europe and Latin America, infiltrating many United States businesses, in particular the shipping company in New York known as García & Díaz, the address of which, at 17 Battery Place, New York, was identical with that of the German consulate. Like North-German Lloyd and the Hamburg-America Line, García & Díaz provided a constant flow of espionage traffic across the Atlantic as well as supplies for the notorious Compañía Transatlántica Española, the international Spanish organization of secret Nazi agents.

Falange funds were extremely lavish, flowing as they did from such organizations as the Spanish industrial empire of Río Tinto and the all-embracing Banco Alemán Transatlántico, chief organ of the Hitler economic regime in South America.

Headquarters of the Falange in New York was the Club Isabel y Fernando, run by José de Perignat, with seven hundred members, of whom one hundred formed a fanatical Fascist core.

The Falange in New York also operated out of the Ritz-Carlton Hotel, where Juan Cárdenas, an important diplomatic official, presided over the activities of the Casa de España. The Casa also functioned at the School of Franciscan Fathers, in Manhattan, where links were made to Father Coughlin, the Christian Front movement, and Merwin K. Hart, a Fascistic figure who publicly supported America First.

Yet another in the group was the Marquesa de Cienfuegos, who was born plain Jane Anderson, in Atlanta, Georgia, and was understood to be a Franco agent. She was a close friend of Archbishop Spellman and of Monsignor Fulton J. Sheen, of the Catholic University of America, who described her as "one of the living martyrs" because of attacks on her by Loyalists during the Spanish Civil War.

She gave enormously popular lectures attacking the Reds in Spain; later, she turned up conveniently in Berlin, where she made broadcasts to the United States in dulcet southern tones after Pearl Harbor. She talked often about the Jewish-Communist plot to cause the war.

When Juan Cárdenas became Spanish ambassador to the United States, the Falange was headquartered at the embassy in Washington and at the consulate in New York. Further connections were established all over the country. Magazines appeared regurgitating hard-line propaganda. John E. Kelly, a U.S. Army Reserve captain, knitted the Christian Front still more firmly to the Falange.

Yet another connection was General Franco's and Errol Flynn's close friend the Marqués de Aguiar, who moved between Washington and Berlin, where he attended Nazi congresses. Another figure with a Hollywood connection was the young and handsome nephew of the Duke of Alba, ambassador to the Court of St. James's. Count Carlos Vejarano y Cassina, also known as Count Nava de Tajo, who first emerged as a keen supporter of General von Faupel and Generalissimo Franco during the Spanish Civil War.

Vejarano suffered from a painful spinal condition which required periodic osteopathic attention. His father, honorary Spanish vice consul in St. Jean de Luz, France, persuaded Carlos to resign from the Franco command and make his way to Berlin, in April 1938, to have treatments. It was necessary for Vejarano to report to the Franco embassy in that city to receive orders and to give reports on his general condition. During one of these visits, in May, he determined Errol Flynn's Nazi connections.

Despite the recurring pain in his spine, Vejarano was charming, energetic, and handsome and very much in demand by women. Drawn to the Nazi form of government, he made contact, in the spring of 1940, with German members of the international set in the then fashionable holiday resort of Biarritz, in southwestern France. There the raffish social circles swirled around the beach, the yacht club, and the expensive hotels. One of his contacts was the playboy Michael Farmer, erstwhile husband of the screen actress Gloria Swanson. In Biarritz, Vejarano often met with a certain Nazi Major Wurmann, who was the head of the Abwehr in southeastern France. Like Walter Schellenberg, Wurmann would try to attract individuals who could penetrate the United States. Wurmann's right-hand man, Captain Richard Weiss, suggested to Vejarano that he travel to New York to seek to influence prominent socialites through his title and good looks and urge them to call upon their congressmen for a negotiated peace in Europe.

Vejarano agreed. He traveled to Paris in July 1940 to make further contacts. Weiss felt it would be a good idea if he worked with a woman. Weiss suggested the lovely Marie-Thérèse Perrière, who was bilingual and considered an ideal prospect. One evening, Vejarano called Marie-Thérèse and asked her to come at once to his suite at the Hotel Lancaster. When she arrived, she found him seated at a desk in his suite, surrounded by documents in German. He said that these made up the contents of a dossier which reflected damaging information on her and that on the basis of the material she could be "sent to a concentration camp." She would be freed from this unpleasant possibility only if she would agree to accompany Vejarano on his mission to the United States.

Marie-Thérèse was not impressed. She had already made plans to travel to New York under more satisfactory auspices. However, she wanted to find out what Vejarano was up to. He became very attracted to her, but she refused to respond to his advances; meanwhile, she determined his Nazi connections. It was clearly a trick to inveigle her: the worst that could be said of her was that she had been married to a Jew.

In further conversations with the Abwehr, Vejarano made the necessary arrangements to proceed to New York. Back in Biarritz, he was informed by Weiss, his control, that espionage schools were run in New York and Chicago; one of them operated under the aegis of the chef of a leading New York hotel. The token sum of one thousand dollars would be paid to Vejarano, who was not promised any further income. It was agreed that his father would be able to receive information through the Spanish diplomatic bag in Washington, in his role as vice consul in St. Jean de Luz. The letters would not only contain information showing who could be relied upon in New York to press for a negotiated peace, but would also supply information on any threats to the network that centered upon García and Díaz in New York. This would enable the Abwehr to retain a foothold even when America came into the war.

Vejarano set sail for New York City, arriving via Havana on the SS *Marqués de Comillas* on November 22, 1940. His father and aunt supplemented the Abwehr stake, which was given him in laundered money via García and Díaz aboard ship. Purser transactions were not subject to British search at that time.

In New York, Vejarano linked up with the Falange through Marcelino García and Manuel Díaz. Soon after that, he met with the socialite Sir Charles Mendl, who spoke of American problems and of the fact that soon Britian would draw the United States into war. Since Mendl knew the Roosevelts and was said to be connected to British Intelligence, this was considered to be useful information, so Vejarano conveyed it to his father through the diplomatic bag for reading by Captain Richard Weiss.

He met *Vogue* fashion editor Bettina Wilson and the John W. Cutlers. Mrs. Cutler confirmed Sir Charles Mendl's statement that America was being dragged into the war. Again, this was useful to the Abwehr. Vejarano met more and more prominent figures. He learned of the secret arrangements between Roosevelt and Churchill for a U.S.-German war; of the character of Lord Halifax and his desire for appeasement; and of those pro-Nazis who could be specially valuable in New York. In 1941 he met and fell in love with the beautiful Wilma Baard, daughter of a Hudson River barge captain. She had been in the headlines when she staged a satirical coming-out party intended to parody the most famous coming-out party of the 1938 season, that of the heiress Brenda Frazier. Accompanied by various barge captains and their friends disguised as wealthy uncles, Wilma was presented to Society, not all of whose members appreciated the joke when it was disclosed.

However, Wilma, though of modest background, looked stunning, and this counted for a great deal. She and Vejarano moved through a fashionable circle, none of whom guessed, any more than she did, the true character of her lover. Their June 1941 wedding was elaborate and well attended.

Sir Charles Mendl introduced the young Spaniard to his close friends the movie moguls Harry Warner and Darryl F. Zanuck, of Hollywood; Vejarano also made contact with Edgar Ausnit, the Romanian millionaire, of whom more later.

Bit by bit, he learned who in Hollywood were isolationists and who were not. One of his contacts was Errol Flynn; another, the sister of Hamilton Fish. He learned that many of Fish's relatives had not voted for the isolationist congressman and disapproved of his political beliefs. As a result, he withdrew his connection from them. He also made contact with the raffish Count Youka Troubetzkoy, an adventurer who very much resented the Roosevelt administration. Later, FBI files show, Troubetzkoy was to use Errol Flynn to try to get out of army service.

Vejarano also became friendly with the Woolworth heiress Barbara Hutton, who sent food via García & Díaz to a friend of hers in Spain who was a cousin of Vejarano's. Hutton gave Wilma Vejarano a ring insured for ten thousand dollars and a five-thousand-dollar check to pay for a difficult operation. Vejarano's and Hutton's mothers had been at school together; the Count had known Barbara originally when she was married to Count Reventlow.

The Vejaranos traveled to Hollywood at Barbara Hutton's expense in April 1941. They remained there until February 1942. They moved from the Beverly Hills Hotel to an apartment on Wetherly Drive, in West Hollywood. There Barbara Hutton introduced them to her future husband Cary Grant, who was at the height of his career following his triumphs in *His Girl Friday* and *The Awful Truth*. It can be assumed that Cary Grant and Barbara Hutton, Sir Charles Mendl and his wife, Lady Elsie, had not the slightest suspicion that the handsome young Spanish nobleman they saw constantly was a Nazi agent. Interestingly, the FBI kept the whole group under constant surveillance without disclosing the facts to any of the group's members. Meanwhile, Vejarano never ceased to correspond with his father, conveying the attitudes of Hollywood toward the Axis: who was sympathetic and who was not. Barbara Hutton, as one of the wealthiest women in America, and Cary Grant, who shared with her a circle of prominent friends, had access to all the Hollywood executives (some studios, notably Universal, had kept open their Berlin branches even when Europe was at war.) But the general attitude was in total defiance of the existing isolationist stance, and indeed Senators Wheeler and Gerald P. Nye of North Dakota belligerently attacked the studios via House Committees for making anti-German propaganda films, overlooking the fact that the British market was crucial to America and that powerful propaganda pictures were very attractive to a beleaguered English public.

Vejarano managed to make a living teaching Spanish to Cary Grant and Barbara Hutton over many months. Grant also arranged a screen test for him.* When Grant and Hutton were married, they often made a foursome with the Vejaranos, inevitably picking up the check. Questions about Vejarano's background were set aside. It was typical of Cary Grant that he had no more than a superficial interest in politics, and it surely never occurred to him that the nephew of Hitler's supporter the Duke of Alba would have to be a Fascist and a danger to American security. Even Sir Charles Mendl, who should have known better, seemed to think nothing of Vejarano's history and incorrectly told the FBI in one interrogation that the Duke of Alba was "unquestionably pro-Ally"† and that in his opinion the kinship would have "considerable influence in shaping Vejarano's sympathies." Moreover, Sir Charles continued, he would consider him to be loyal, and that, because he was married to an American citizen, "no suspicion could attach to him." Such foolishness seems incredible. But it was not uncommon in Hollywood social circles.

Despite the records flooding the desk of J. Edgar Hoover and his New York and Hollywood associates, Vejarano was called by the draft board for army service as a registered alien and actually was brought in for a physical and classified 4C on the basis of his spinal fusion. This again was unhappily typical of the times. The Nazi collaborators Serge Rubinstein and Errol Flynn were both brought in under the draft regulations,‡ and among others Joseph Lieblein, of the German-American Vocational League, a full-scale Nazi organization, was actually allowed to enter army service.

Furthermore, like Errol Flynn, Vejarano was given his citizenship in

---

* F.B.I. Report: Carlos Vejarano y Cassina, Espionage. 12/6/1943.

† When the duke appeared in the spectators' gallery of the House of Commons in 1942, Churchill said, "There is an enemy in our midst!" And the duke left.

‡ Rubinstein dodged the draft; put on trial for this, he was defended by Lemuel Schofield, whom Roosevelt had fired as head of Immigration because of his affair with Princess Hohenlohe.

1942; his marriage to Wilma Baard automatically secured it. According to Frank Angell, formerly of the FBI bureau in Los Angeles, many agents were reported by the FBI but the State Department stepped in to protect them.*

The file on Vejarano grew larger every day. J. Edgar Hoover became increasingly irritable with the delays in securing satisfactory information. Why Sir William Stephenson of British Security Coordination did not alert British Intelligence in Los Angeles, via his contacts there, among them Sir Alexander Korda and Cecil B. DeMille, to advise Cary Grant of the danger of his association with an enemy agent is totally inexplicable.

Cary Grant actually managed to secure a job for Vejarano in the advertising division of Columbia Pictures, at its New York office, when Vejarano traveled to Manhattan three months after Pearl Harbor to have medical treatments, paid for by Barbara Hutton. ("It is believed that Vejarano's connection with Barbara Hutton and Cary Grant may be of interest to you," wrote the FBI's L. L. Laughlin to his superior D. M. Ladd.) Vejarano's job at Columbia would have caused its manic chairman, Harry Cohn, to have apoplexy if he had known his true identity. As it was, those who appreciate irony can enjoy the fact that Vejarano was supplying Spanish sound tracks to movies transmitted to Latin America which were violently attacking and parodying the very Nazis for whom he worked.

The press kept silent on Vejarano and his close relationship with the Grants. It is possible that the studio publicity chiefs were tipped off by Hoover, though the FBI files (uncensored portions) do not show that. Otherwise, why would they have kept secret what could have been consid-

---

* I have touched on various reasons for the State Department protection in these pages. However, it perhaps should be pointed out at this moment in the narrative that the crucial figure in charge of immigration, Breckinridge Long, was the fly in the Democratic ointment in the Department. He was in charge of the Visa Division. He was a former friend of (as well as ambassador to) Mussolini, and an enthusiast for the Italian invasion of Ethiopia, who blocked crucial information reaching him from Switzerland on the plight of the Jews and left more than half a million empty places on the immigration quota list while Jews died in the European camps. No record is blacker in World War II than Long's—or that of his colleague, Major Lemuel Schofield, head of Immigration and Naturalization. They were joined in their malfeasance by Charles Howard Ellis, assistant to Sir William Stephenson, the famous "Intrepid." Ellis was in charge of the British Passport Office as consul general in New York. Ellis, who handled all immigrants from England (or even via England—including Errol Flynn and the Princess Hohenlohe) was a self-confessed Nazi agent who later joined the Soviets. Sir William Stephenson had tried futilely to whitewash him in two books, *A Man Called Intrepid* and *Intrepid's Last Case*.

ered a friendship between innocent parties? Somebody at least must have been suspicious of Vejarano, who continued to use the Grants for money and position.

Soon the inevitable happened. Vejarano was offered a job in an organization that had powerful Nazi connections: Sterling Products, which maintained intricate commercial liaisons with associated I.G. Farben organizations in Chile during the war. He left Columbia Pictures and was trained at the Sterling headquarters to go to Chile. Meanwhile, the FBI did an exhaustive job of checking out his background. Page after page of documents, reports, and elaborate interrogations were piled one on another but never properly coordinated with the Treasury's reports on Sterling.

It was decided that Wilma Vejarano was just a pleasant, stupid girl who was totally innocent of nazism. Vejarano's references, Nat Springold and Frank Rosenberg, of the same studio, and Cary Grant, were apparently not questioned.

The pursuit continued. Then, in November 1943, almost two years after Pearl Harbor, when all the damage had been done and he had sent all his reports to mail drops in Spain, Vejarano was at long last brought into the New York FBI headquarters and admitted everything.

Still the friends were apparently not told. It was only when he panicked and advised Cary Grant and Barbara Hutton of his plight that anything serious took place. Instead of checking the facts with Cary Grant, J. Edgar Hoover stood back while the horrified Hutton urgently called her uncle, former U.S. ambassador to the Soviet Union Joseph E. Davies, asking him to defend and protect Vejarano, who appeared to be falsely accused.

It came as a considerable shock to her when Davies flatly refused to take the case. Davies must have called Hoover and found out the truth. But even he didn't tell his niece and her husband.

On Davies' advice, Mrs. Grant turned to the distinguished New York attorney Milton S. Gould, who vividly recalls to this day her concern in the matter. Gingerly, he agreed to take up the case. He soon established that Vejarano was a Nazi spy. He was compelled to tell (at very long last) the couple whom he represented the unpleasant truth. Nevertheless, he still proceeded on the instructions of Barbara Hutton, who engaged him to defend Vejarano. One has to assume that Cary Grant did not approve of this arrangement.

Using Barbara Hutton's money, Gould managed to switch the charges from espionage, which would have meant death, to failing to register as an agent of a foreign government. What Cary Grant's feelings must have been at that time is almost inconceivable. If it were discovered that, no matter how innocent his role, he had befriended a Nazi spy in time of war and that his wife was paying money to defend that spy, he could have been in a most dangerous position vis-à-vis the studios. Luckily, he was already heading for a divorce. Also, the press could be relied upon to protect a motion picture star.

New York Assistant District Attorney Peter J. Donohue began to delay prosecution. He said he was waiting to see letters proving espionage that had gone through British censorship in Bermuda under Sir William Stephenson. It seems unbelievable that the letters had not been yielded up before. Why were they not?

After many skillful obstructions, the trial at last began, in December 1943. Milton S. Gould knew that condemnation for treason or espionage of a resident alien could result in his client's death in the electric chair; by skill and plea bargaining, he had the charge changed to improper declarations upon entry to the United States. Vejarano went to the luxurious minimum-security prison farm at Danbury, Connecticut, for a trifling two years.

Just after starting to serve his sentence, on January 28, 1944, Vejarano contacted the FBI and gave its agent E. E. Conroy in New York a most interesting series of facts. He described a visit to Berlin in May and June of 1937, when he had been treated at a hospital for his spinal problems. He visited the Franco embassy to pay his respects to a friend of his family, a member of the Spanish diplomatic corps named Antonio Vargas. Vargas introduced him to a German military agent, Errol Flynn's Nazi associate, Dr. Hermann Erben.

Vargas explained that Erben had just returned from the Spanish front in the company of Flynn and had taken numerous pictures of gun establishments and military objectives behind the Loyalist lines. Dr. Erben had a number of photographs with him. Vargas stepped out of the room. Erben told Vejarano that he and Flynn had tried to join the Franco forces but instead had obtained visas to go behind the Loyalist lines. Erben was revealed as "a member of the Military Secret Service of Germany"; he had already taken one set of pictures to the Abwehr headquarters in Berlin. Vejarano examined the pictures, and in several of them he noted that

Erben was "in company with Errol Flynn and the various military objectives which the German had photographed." E. E. Conroy, of the New York staff of the FBI, forwarded this information to Hollywood, where it was promptly and predictably buried. Subsequently, the Austrian journalist Rudolph Stoiber, who is completing a major book on Erben and Flynn's Nazi association, discovered from the internal evidence of Erben's diaries and letters that Flynn himself took thirteen reels of film of the Loyalist installations and handed them over to the Fascist spy Bradish Johnson in Paris.

Released from prison and divorced from his wife, who, to her credit, abandoned him when she found out who he was, Vejarano, with extraordinary nerve, again applied for a job with Sterling Products, in Latin America. That he still had great and powerful friends may be illustrated by the fact that he lived in a comfortable apartment at 156 East Seventy-third Street in Manhattan, a very good address. Finally, this grew too much for the FBI and he was deported to Lisbon on March 24, 1945, while the war was still going on, on the Portuguese vessel SS *Quanza*, on which Dr. Erben had once served as ship's physician. All of Vejarano's information was, by now, securely in German hands.

16

The Schellenberg Conspiracy

The SS, of which the SD was so crucial a part, always carried with it an atmosphere of the elite, and the respect of people in high places. That the respect extended to the Church of Rome is illustrated by the fact that in 1946 the Catholic archbishop of Freiburg told an American military interrogator that his archdiocese "considered the SS to be the most respectable of the Nazi Party organizations." SS men, Schellenberg included, enjoyed the sexiest and the most glamorous uniform available in the German hierarchy: a black cap decorated with a silver death's head, a black tunic worn over a handsome brown shirt and black tie, a heavy black belt, and black breeches and boots. Various silver insignia indicated rank. The SD and the SS officers came from the right-wing elite, those with money and commercial interests that lay outside the German borders. Thus, the fact that it was the SD which specialized in every kind of subversion, intrigue, and ruination appealed directly to Allied connections more than any other service. Its leaders belonged to the community of world money; their allegiance was not to the upstart, working-class Hitler, but to the memory of SS leader Heinrich Himmler's idol, King Henry I of Saxony, and to the Stein bank of Cologne, which financed Himmler's inner circle under the aegis of the international banker Kurt von Schroeder.

Not only Max von Hohenlohe and his second cousin Stefanie served Himmler's cause. Other figures of the SS or SD inner circle were the Grand Duke of Mecklenburg, Prince Wilhelm of Hesse, and the Prince von Hohenzollern. Most of the Prussian elite, few of whom approved of

Hitler, gravitated happily to Himmler. They were prepared to overlook Himmler's depressing origins and undistinguished occupation as a chicken farmer, because of the unique power he wielded, his lip service to Catholicism, and his international connections: he had substantial investments in the United States. Only his personal loyalty to Hitler, as much a petit-bourgeois loyalty as anything else, prevented this cluster of right-wing Nazis from securing his support in their various attempts to remove Hitler and to set up an international front against Russia. However, they could rely on such upper-middle-class figures as Franz Six of SD AMT VII, who was later aided and abetted by U.S. Intelligence, and above all Walter Schellenberg, who combined a solid upper-middle-class background with a reliably lower-middle-brow intelligence.

Walter Schellenberg was born on January 16, 1910, in Saarbrücken; he enjoyed a university education in jurisprudence. He joined the SS and became a member of the Nazi Party in 1933; between that year and 1935 he was trained in all aspects of security-police work, graduating to the SD, a secret army of one hundred thousand informers who investigated Jewish cells, reported vigorously on Communists, and threaded through universities and businesses looking for the slightest indication of disloyalty to the Third Reich. The purpose of the SD was, first and foremost, to repel Communist infiltration; Schellenberg was obsessed with communism as a force of pure evil, an attitude that such celebrated Catholic dignitaries as the Prince von Hohenlohe naturally supported. The Bavarians in particular were pronounced in their anticommunism, and Schellenberg's teams, when he took over official positions in the SD one after the other, would make sure that any fugitive Soviet-inspired cells were flushed out and liquidated.

Sickly, very thin, his skin stretched tight over high cheekbones, with a pallid complexion, Schellenberg looked the perfect picture of a superspy. He even had a hollow tooth containing a deadly poison that could be released into his system in an instant. He fell under the influence of Reinhard Heydrich, the arrogant and dangerous SD leader who correctly saw Schellenberg's potential as legalist and espionage leader; and he headed up AMT VI after 1939. The two men worked closely together through a network of German foreign embassies and legations, including several in the United States and Great Britain, until war broke out in each country. But soon Schellenberg proved to be extremely dangerous to Ribbentrop, scheming against him and using the various consular and embassy channels to bring about negotiations with foreign powers. Matters reached a head in Romania, as we shall see in the chapter on Nicolae Malaxa, when the SD deliberately entered into arrangements with the British and the Soviets.

Why did Schellenberg and AMT VI want to form special relationships with the extreme right wing of the Allied governments? Why did they scheme, along with their State Department counterparts, to secure the downfall of Hitler and the rise to power of Himmler? The reasons were various: in the imagined new scheme of things, Schellenberg would at the very least supplant Ribbentrop in a Himmler government; he would have the opportunity to engineer the downfall of Stalin; he would secure permanent ties with Rome, and he would fulfill a dream of being fully accepted in Washington and Whitehall by the people he liked best. Furthermore, he had the foresight, after the collapse of peace negotiations with Britain, to realize that Hitler's policy of radical confrontation, and his failure to understand America, had already doomed the Third Reich. A Fourth Reich must now be planned on the predestined ashes of the old, and it must be secured by a transatlantic hegemony of money and power.

Shortly before Pearl Harbor, Frederico Stallforth, an American banker from Boston with feet in the usual number of camps,* arrived in Berlin and conveyed that Roosevelt would make peace moves between Germany and Britain if Hitler were removed. Schellenberg was interested and noted the fact that Mussolini was considered a go-between; indeed, Schellenberg's special team talked to Stallforth along the same lines that Halifax was recommending in London. Soon after Pearl Harbor, Max von Hohenlohe had a meeting with Schellenberg, followed soon after by a similar discussion in Madrid.

In 1942, following the assassination of Heydrich in Czechoslovakia, Schellenberg obtained considerably more power. He decided to bring a full-scale peace proposal to Sir Samuel Hoare, of the Halifax faction, who was now British ambassador to Spain. He also established contacts with Karl Lindemann, head of Standard Oil's German subsidiary and a key figure in the central finance group of the Himmler circle. A further contact was Fritz Klein, close friend of Generalissimo Chiang Kai-shek and friend also of John Foster and Allen Dulles, both of whom had connec-

---

* In *A Man Called Intrepid,* Sir William Stephenson claimed that he used this man's name as an alias—an absurd assertion, like most in his book.

tions to the Nazi-affiliated Chase and Schroeder banks. Indeed, Allen Dulles would soon conveniently become OSS leader in Switzerland under General William Donovan.

Schellenberg brought Hohenlohe and Lindemann together to discuss negotiated peace with the Allies. Finally, Hohenlohe was delegated to talk to Sir Samuel Hoare. Despite the fact that Germany was at war with Great Britain, Hohenlohe and Hoare were great friends.

Later that summer, in the month of August, Schellenberg discussed with Himmler his proposal to bring about peace, basing his plea on the theory that there was no chance of Germany's winning the war. He was preaching to the converted. Himmler approved his getting in touch with British consul general Eric Cable in Switzerland, via a Stuttgart manufacturer, a Swiss hotelier, and a German honorary Swedish consul in Stuttgart. Similar negotiations took place with Carl Burckhardt, of the German-Swiss Red Cross, and Count Ciano, Mussolini's son-in-law and Italian Foreign Minister. Once again, Hitler must be removed and Himmler would take over. Himmler was swayed by medical reports showing that Hitler was suffering from the effects of syphilis and should be in a sanatorium. Himmler formed a special relationship with Fritz Kersten, former "physician" to Queen Wilhelmina of the Netherlands, who was now masseur to Himmler. Finnish by birth, Kersten used a massage technique that seemingly gave him a Rasputin-like hold over both Himmler and Schellenberg. He supposedly aided Schellenberg's harrowing liver and gallbladder conditions; as early as 1942, Kersten, who spoke good English, was marked down to enter into special arrangements with the Americans.

In November of that year, the question of the ubiquitous Max von Hohenlohe's meeting with Sir Samuel Hoare was once more raised. Hohenlohe, who was general agent for Germany's Skoda works in Western Europe, had his private secretary, Herr Spitzi, released from military service and brought to Schellenberg's house for close discussions on initiating peace contacts. Hohenlohe and Spitzi left for Spain with specific instructions. They met with Hoare—a detail omitted from Sir Samuel's memoirs —and with the British military attaché in Madrid, General Torr. Further discussions were held with Swiss representatives in the matter of using Vatican channels, and Spitzi separately talked with the U.S. military attachés in Lisbon, Colonel Rousseau and his assistant, Colonel Demarest. However, whatever happened, Roosevelt's adamant position, and Churchill's, left the talks in the air.

Another contact still was Alexander Kreuter, partner of the Windsors' friend Charles Bedaux. Kreuter was an American Nazi collaborator in the French Worms Bank, which had Aryanized its entire board of Jewish executives when the Germans walked into Paris. Kreuter was connected to Dillon, Read, the Jewish banking firm (Dillon had aryanized his name) that had helped finance Hitler until 1934 and with whom Allen W. Dulles was involved. He was also close to the paranoid anti-Communist Under Secretary of the Navy James V. Forrestal. In order to secure Kreuter's support, Schellenberg helped him to transfer a very large sum of money to an unblocked account in Free French francs in France. Kreuter's activities with the Americans are obscure; he belonged to a joint American-French-British business group in Vichy and ran so close to the wind with Hitler that he was arrested on suspicion of espionage for America, and only Schellenberg's personal guarantee of his bona fides secured his release.

In December 1942, Schellenberg spent much of the time in Switzerland, negotiating with a special local emissary, Roger Masson, in meetings with British consular officials. In January 1943, he authorized Hohenlohe to meet with Allen W. Dulles in person at a point of contact in Geneva.

Allen Dulles was ideally chosen in the matter. Both he and his brother John Foster had extensive German connections. John Foster had been American representative at the conference for the regulation of Germany's foreign indebtedness which had resulted in 1933 in the reduction under the Hitler regime of such indebtedness overseas. He had acted as an attorney for General Franco and as a director of the International Nickel Company, which was charged with trading with the enemy in World War II. He was a single-minded and impassioned opponent of the Soviet Union who was to play a crucial role in the postwar confrontations that provoked the Cold War.

Allen Dulles was legal advisor to, and a director of, the Anglo-German Schroeder banking empire; the New York branch, which he represented, was a subsidiary of the London, Cologne, and Hamburg Schroeders. The Stein Bank, of Cologne, under Chairman Kurt von Schroeder, was a chief financier of Himmler, and of the hard-core SS inner circle.

Even when he went to Switzerland in 1942, given carte blanche by the Vichy government, one of his law partners, De Lano Andrews, took his place, thus securing the continued connection.

The Swiss offshoot of the Schroeder Bank was one of Dulles's men, a director of the New York branch, Lada Mocarski, who conveniently was also U.S. vice consul in Zürich. The American minister in Berne was Leland Harrison, who authorized shipments of oil of enemy origin through Switzerland in World War II, as well as allowing American oil companies to fuel the German and Hungarian embassies and consulates and the Germans to retain Standard Oil barges on the Rhine, rentals of which were paid to New York for the duration.

Dulles, when he arrived in Switzerland, made contact with the so-called opposition movement in Germany, including Schellenberg, Kaltenbrunner, Hjalmar Schacht, and others. Realizing that Hitler was losing the war, they sought to save their own necks and their financial alliances by making a separate peace. Since they opposed Hitler, who, as a nationalist and patriot, was determined to act against such internationalism, they would be able to resecure the Fascist alliance for the indefinite future. And they could also join with Dulles in whitewashing this activity in the eyes of the public, which was bamboozled into thinking that they were idealists and potential forgers of a new Germany.

That Dulles chose to be an ally of these self-serving individuals and their plans was indicative of his own brand of cosmopolitanism and certainly, despite claims to the contrary, had no support whatever in the White House. Indeed, he dealt with representatives of the Abwehr working on every side of the war, and allowed his own wires and telephone calls to Washington to be tapped, since Schellenberg's men broke the American diplomatic code.

Another figure in Dulles's chain of appeasement was Gerhardt Westrick, joint partner in the German law firm affiliated with the Dulleses. Westrick arranged to secure many American companies throughout World War II from nationalization and confiscation by the German Government. He was given power of attorney by these companies while in New York in 1940 to assure such protection. His partner in the Dulles association was Heinrich Albert, head of the Ford operation in Germany, who protected Ford interests in Nazi-occupied France, with the result that, on direct authorization from Edsel Ford, in Dearborn, Michigan, after Pearl Harbor, the branch of Ford at Poissy built trucks for the German Army which were used against U.S. troops on and after D day.

The series of connections could be extended indefinitely. The go-between in Switzerland was one of Dulles's right-hand men, described in the German documents as "Roberts,"† who met with Hohenlohe, code name Pauls, in mid-February. Hohenlohe first checked with the Spanish ambassador to the Vatican to make sure that Dulles was reliable. The ambassador replied that Dulles was "very influential and extremely popular with our allies . . . Hungary, Bulgaria, and Romania constantly tried to establish contact with him."

Others to whom Hohenlohe spoke to were Theodore Kordt, counselor-minister of the German embassy in Switzerland, who met throughout the war with British and American consuls; Otto Kocher, German ambassador to Switzerland; and Hans Sigmond von Bibra, counselor of the German embassy and leader of the German Nazis in Switzerland. Their collective opinion was uniformly in Dulles's favor. Anyone who is surprised at this in time of war has not followed the narrative so far.

Finally, after checking every lead, Hohenlohe decided to take "Mr. Bull"—Dulles's code name—by the horns. He also established a pleasant relationship with Leland Harrison.

The meeting with Hohenlohe was as pleasant for Dulles as it was for the prince. Records of the encounter show that there were three conversations in all in Berne and Geneva, the last of them taking place on April 3. The SS records are clearly authentic.‡ Fortunately, I have obtained the documents from the files of a reliable source in England via Professor Klaus von Klemperer, professor of history at Smith College. There is in my mind no doubt of their authenticity.

Dulles greeted Hohenlohe in a most friendly manner. The two men realized that they had met in Vienna in 1916 and again in New York in the 1920s. Dulles said he was happy to see Hohenlohe again after such a long time, in order to exchange ideas, for Hohenlohe had such an astute mind as far as European affairs were concerned. Dulles said he was "sick and tired of listening to stories of ruined politicians, emigrants, and prejudiced Jews." In his opinion, a peace should be achieved that all parties would be interested in maintaining.

He said that the German state had to remain in existence to maintain order and begin reconstruction, that the Czech question was of small importance, but it was necessary to form a *cordon sanitaire* against bolshe-

† Gero von Gaevernitz.

‡ Because they were translated and published in Communist periodicals such as *New Times*, every effort was made to discredit them.

vism and Pan-Slavism by "enlarging Poland toward the East and maintaining Romania and a strong Hungary." He believed that planned industrial production after the war, led by Germany's industries, would be desirable. Under no circumstances were the Russians to be admitted to Romania or Asia Minor. The British might enter into negotiations with the Russians over spheres of interest, but the United States would like to maintain "a modern and well-organized Europe as a high-income zone, market, and as a geopolitical factor."

Dulles pressed ahead. He said that it would be unbearable for any decent European to think that the Jews might return someday, and that there must be no toleration of a return of the Jewish power positions. He reiterated his desire for a greater European political federation—and foresaw the federal Germany that in fact took place. He said that Hitler would not be accepted as the leader of a restored Germany. He made the curious assertion that the Americans were only continuing the war to get rid of the Jews and that there were people in America who were intending to send the Jews to Africa. This was Hitler's dream of course: that the Jews would go to Madagascar and stay there. Dulles seems to have confused the clubland view of blacks and Jews.

Dulles now proceeded to supply Hohenlohe with dollops of secret intelligence, announcing that the U.S. Army would not land in Spain but, after conquering Tunisia, would advance from Africa toward the Ploesti oil fields to cut off the German oil supplies. He said that it was likely the Allies would land in Sicily to cut off Rommel and control Italy from there, and thus secure the advance in the Balkans.

Having given virtually the entire battle plan for Europe, top secret at the time, to one of Germany's agents, Allen Dulles proceeded to the almost unnecessary rider that he had very good relations with the Vatican. He said American Catholics had a decisive voice in such matters.

Dulles referred to the meetings between Hohenlohe and Sir Samuel Hoare and Fritz Spitzi (code name Alfonso) with the Americans in Spain and Lisbon. Dulles said he would be glad to meet Spitzi anytime and was prepared to give all guarantees; he recommended a code word for a telephone call. If for any reason Spitzi could not make the meeting, Dulles would look forward to meeting Karl Lindemann, of Standard Oil. At the end of the discussion, Dulles advised the American embassy in Madrid "to be of assistance to Hohenlohe at any time." Next day, Hohenlohe met with "Roberts," who said that Roosevelt had authorized the meeting. This was a total lie, of course.

In other meetings, Dulles spoke of "Papal action in the area of negotiations" and of his personally having arranged for Spellman to see the Pope to further these discussions, and he predicted that "the next world war would be between the U.S.A. and the Soviet Union." In meetings with other German representatives, which were backed by the former Chancellor of Germany Dr. Christian Wirth, who attended certain of them, Dulles obtained a great deal of information relating to Germany and plans for its reconstruction after the war. He talked of giving preference to Bavaria, a not surprising decision, and described a recent speech by Dr. Goebbels as "a work of genius; I have rarely read a speech with such rational pleasure."

There were much further discussion and further false assertions that he had "the complete support of Roosevelt." He talked at length about the intricacies of the southern European invasion plans and said, representing himself and the extreme right wing, rather than Roosevelt, "The British-American relationship has not improved. Downing Street's attempts at blackmail by playing the Russian card were not looked upon kindly by Washington." He was referring to the fact that Britain was, already in this period, beginning to make deals with the Russians in the Balkans—a clear slap at Churchill, who would soon intervene directly when Donovan's men started contacting such ambivalent figures as the Chetnik leader Draža Mihajlović.

Whether Dulles actually tried to bring proposals to Washington is unknown. Whatever happened, the scheme didn't work and clearly fell on deaf ears at the White House. In March 1943, Schellenberg began discussions toward Hitler's downfall with Erna Hanfstaengl, sister of Putzi Hanfstaengl, the close friend of Hitler and former propaganda specialist. Putzi was now enjoying a comfortable house arrest in Washington and would soon be supplying such useless intelligence as an account of Hitler's "homosexual circle," clearly supplied for the benefit of his interrogatory officer, who, due to some inexplicable hiatus in judgment by the War Department, was none other than Somerset Maugham's dissolute and drunken gay secretary-companion, Gerald Haxton.

Fräulein Hanfstaengl promised to confer with Randolph Churchill on a special mission to England. She was very close to Himmler's wife and promised to arrange with Himmler to have Hitler at Berchtesgaden, where he would be held under SS detention and "a de facto government of twelve under Hermann Schmitz of I.G. Farben." When Fräulein Hanfstaengl had fulfilled her momentous mission, she would proceed to open an art shop in Paris as a cover. Her ridiculous venture of course came to nothing, and finally Schellenberg, who was dubious about it, withdrew support.

Why did Schellenberg lend his name to such a scheme? Clearly because he was ready to snatch at any straw in order to see Hitler deposed and a government ready for peace with the West installed. In May, Schellenberg authorized Spitzi and his associates to recommence meetings with the American military attaché in Lisbon. In July, Donovan and the OSS began to take matters into their own hands. No doubt inspired by the invigorating meeting in Switzerland, Donovan embarked on the so-called "M" project. Theodore A. Morde, a former explorer and journalist and Middle East correspondent for *Reader's Digest*, arrived in Cairo on Donovan's orders to meet with local OSS chief Colonel Guenther. He was on his way to meet with Franz von Papen, German minister in Turkey, lying to Guenther that Von Papen had nothing to do with Hitler's becoming Chancellor in 1933. Morde traveled to Turkey by train in October, where he was met in Ankara by another OSS representative. Several connections were made to allow Morde to contact Alexander Rustow, a professor friend of Von Papen's, and the manager of the Orient Bank, Herr Posth. These informants advised that Von Papen was near the city at the German summer embassy and would be prepared to receive Morde.

Meanwhile, Posth called Von Papen to say that everything was ready and that "the American citizen with a Portuguese passport who wanted to speak with him urgently on behalf of President Roosevelt" was waiting for an audience. Von Papen was nervous in case Morde might be an agent provocateur. But the German ambassador had already been in touch with Roosevelt's personal representative in Turkey, George H. Earle, to try to arrange peace—with the peripatetic politician Adam von Trott zu Solz as go-between. Von Papen felt that Morde came from Earle and agreed to see him. In fact, Earle was not connected to the Morde mission.

Morde walked into the embassy reception room, showed his Portuguese passport, and a microfilm of his peace plan, and quickly revealed to Von Papen's careful questioning that he knew nothing of the Earle contact. Nevertheless, he claimed that Roosevelt had authorized him, had read with interest a speech Von Papen had given in March recommending negotiations, and wanted to know the names of people in Germany with whom it might be possible to negotiate.

A major prerequisite was that Hitler be arrested: kidnapped by landing his aircraft in Allied territory on one of his flights to the front. Next day, Von Papen arranged for Morde to go to Posth's lakeside country home, while Von Papen himself made his way there by motor launch. By now, the German had read the details of the peace proposal on microfilm and learned that it was more or less on the same lines as the Dulles proposals. Germany would be set up as the dominating force in industry and agriculture in continental Europe, at the heart of a continental state run by Germany, the U.S.A., and Great Britain as a focus of trade; all Lend-Lease and aid to the Soviet Union would cease, and Russia would never invade one inch of German territory. The document obtained by the author via the daughter of Archibald Coleman, one of Donovan's key contacts in Turkey, is almost identical with Dulles's terms of proposal, thus casting further doubt on charges that the Soviets forged Hohenlohe's reports on Dulles.

When Morde returned to Washington, he went to see the playwright Robert Sherwood, Roosevelt's trusted adviser and speechwriter. Sherwood became suspicious when Morde claimed he had been authorized by General Hurley. Sherwood, in a memorandum to the President dated October 26, 1943, stated that General Hurley in fact denied any responsibility for the Morde mission and denounced Morde.

He charged Morde with merely using the mission to promote *Reader's Digest.* ("It is my suggestion that, in view of Morde's dangerous activities, there might be some way to prevent the issuance of any more passports to men who are going overseas in wartime solely for the purpose of increasing the circulation of the Reader's Digest, particularly among our American troops.")

By contrast, Donovan, in a memorandum to the President dated October 29, 1943, begged Roosevelt to give the plan most serious consideration, claiming that if the scheme worked it would "strengthen your position morally at the peace table." It would, of course, have done nothing of the sort; it was on a level with most of Donovan's wartime suggestions. Donovan compounded this folly with the lie that the Morde mission had been authorized by General Pat Hurley. Roosevelt canceled the plans.

A similar plan was afoot that summer in Spain. George H. Earle was involved in this one too. Some further background is necessary on Earle.

He was a well-to-do ex-governor of Pennsylvania and an old confidant of Roosevelt's; in 1938, he had been a diplomatic agent with full powers in Bulgaria; in 1941, he had served in the Navy; and in 1943, Roosevelt had appointed him assistant naval attaché to the American embassy in Turkey. There, in the first weeks of his new post, he received a visit from Admiral Canaris, Chief of the Abwehr, with whom he conversed on the subject of joining the German underground to shorten the war and unite all forces against the Communist threat. Earle, who was violently anti-Communist and a wealthy adversary of Russian imperialism, promised to inform the President of the results of the meeting, but when he did so, Roosevelt did not reply and all future negotiations were suspended.

Soon after, Baron Kurt von Lersner, close friend of Von Papen, came to Earle with a proposal that superseded the Morde suggestion. Lersner told Earle that Von Papen approved of the discussion. Behind him and Von Papen there were a group of officers who would be prepared to carry off a sensational operation. With the collaboration of the officer commanding Hitler's cavalry division in East Prussia, they would enter General Headquarters, kidnap Hitler, and make the only peace condition: that the Russians be precluded from entering Germany.

Earle conveyed this idea to Roosevelt and again had no answer. At further meetings, the Germans invited Earle to fly to Germany, where they would work out the details of the operation. Negotiations continued later in Spain toward Hitler's kidnapping, and there was some discussion of his being abducted via the Roman Catholic Church. Indeed, Father Conrado Simonsen, Vatican liaison official, was authorized to cooperate with Catholic police attaché in Madrid Paul Winzer to bring off this feat with couriers, money, and help from Spain, South America, and Portugal. The plan backfired only when Winzer's courier stole the papers and sold them to MI6, which had never approved of such plans in the first place.

Simultaneously, Schellenberg authorized Kersten, his own and Himmler's masseur, to make negotiations in Stockholm with the Allies in October 1943. Hans Thomsen, released from White Sulphur Springs, Georgia, where he had been interned after Pearl Harbor following his major role in Washington, was now the German minister in Stockholm. Another useful contact was the prominent New York Attorney Abram Stevens Hewitt, a special emissary of Donovan and Donovan's associate Calvin Hoover in Scandinavia. Like Morde and Dulles, Hewitt stated incorrectly that he was a Roosevelt representative. He opened peace discussions with Kersten without authorization from anyone except the OSS leaders.

The discussions were more or less along the same lines as the others. Kersten wrote to Himmler on October 24 in a very sympathetic mood, urging Himmler to accept the conditions, which were identical to those laid down to Hohenlohe and Von Papen: removal of Hitler, restitution of the old German frontiers before the Treaty of Versailles, and control of the German armament industry. Once again, Russia would be removed from the European hegemony. Kersten kept pressing Himmler without much success, so Schellenberg went to see Hewitt himself at his hotel. Hewitt reiterated his desire to shift the German troops to the East to stem the Russians at the conclusion of the compromise peace.

A second meeting took place three days later. Hewitt said that, if his plan was unacceptable to Roosevelt, he would insert in the local papers for eight consecutive days between February 1 and 15, 1944: "For sale, valuable goldfish aquarium for 1,524 kroner." If the announcement did not appear, this should be taken as an indication that Hewitt's plan had not materialized. Hewitt would need that much time to make the arrangements in Washington. If the plan was acceptable, and the announcement inserted, Hewitt would communicate secretly under the cover name Siegel through the German embassy in Lisbon, and Schellenberg would respond under the name of Brown. Then Schellenberg would go to Himmler and inform Hewitt via Stockholm. Unfortunately, when Schellenberg went to Himmler in Munich in November, Himmler was preoccupied with the annual Nazi Party celebrations and could not be bothered. He discussed the matter with Ernst Kaltenbrunner, the Austrian thug who ran the SD and who had just been talking to Allen Dulles. Kaltenbrunner did not like the idea, and Himmler warned Schellenberg his act was tantamount to high treason and informed him there was a grave danger that the matter might leak to the press. Schellenberg dropped the negotiations and Hewitt was called to the White House and reprimanded by the President.

Early in 1944, a suggestion came to Schellenberg from a very celebrated source. Gabrielle (Coco) Chanel, the couturiere and perfume manufacturer, was brought to his attention by the right-hand man of Albert Speer, SS *Staatsrat* Walter Schiebe. Schiebe, who was Armaments Ministry department head, told Schellenberg that Madame Chanel was a close friend of Winston Churchill and a bitter enemy of Russia who knew the British Premier sufficiently well to undertake political negotiations with him toward peace. She also desired to help France and Germany, whose destinies she believed were inextricably linked. Schellenberg said to Schiebe that Chanel must be brought to Berlin at once. He was well aware of her international fame and her high-level contacts. He believed that she might be influential in London, now that Germany was clearly losing the war.

Chanel arrived in Berlin in April 1944. She found Schellenberg in an atmosphere resembling that to be found on a Hollywood spy-picture set. He showed her his hidden microphones in the lamp, under the desk, and in the walls; he showed her two automatic guns built into the desk itself, which fired off with machine-gun rapidity at the press of a button.

Schellenberg treated Chanel courteously, smiling charmingly as he displayed the hollow poison-filled tooth and a cabochon sapphire in which was also a hidden deadly poison. At the meeting, Chanel suggested that a friend of hers, Vera Lombardi, who was said to have a morganatic relationship to the British royal family, should be released from prison in Italy and sent to Madrid to hand over a letter of appeasement, written by Chanel to Churchill, to Sir Samuel Hoare, in Madrid. Her associate, Herr von Dincklage, of the Abwehr, who was with her in Berlin, would act as a link between herself, Schellenberg, and Vera Lombardi in the matter.

Schellenberg agreed at once. He was eager to ingratiate himself with Churchill—flawed by a streak of naïveté, he never understood that Churchill was unwavering in his opposition to any dealings with the Nazis.

Lombardi arrived in Madrid. But she was a loyal Englishwoman and went straight to the embassy and denounced Chanel as a German agent. She also named Spitzi, Max von Hohenlohe's assistant, who had brought her Chanel's letter of introduction to Hoare. Though no doubt Sir Samuel would in normal conditions have considered the proposition, he in fact was compelled to deactivate it in view of this disclosure. Schellenberg immediately cut off all contact with Chanel as well as with Lombardi; at the end of World War II, Chanel was arrested in Paris but released by the U.S. High Command within a few hours. Apparently, she named several names of people in high places who would be inconvenienced were she to stand trial.

Further negotiations were made with Erna Hanfstaengl, but she was considered unreliable and finally was dropped. Following the unsuccessful attempt on Hitler's life in 1944, Schellenberg waited a discreet interval and then made further contact with Dulles in Switzerland via an emissary named Eggen and Dulles's right-hand man Gero von Gaevernitz. However, Germany's position had deteriorated to such a point that only a surrender discussion was possible at this stage. Dulles would not have dared suggest anything else, and the meetings collapsed. Trying to protect his own skin, Schellenberg negotiated with Himmler to release numbers of Jews as a propaganda stunt. Meanwhile, Dulles began separate negotiations with Waffen SS general Karl Wolff, a former lieutenant in the grand duke of Hesse's regiment of Life Guards who had risen rapidly through the ranks. He was now high in the Himmler hierarchy as leader of the Military SS in Italy. Significantly, he drew checks for Himmler on the special SS account R, using the fund established by subsidiaries of American General Electric and Standard Oil. Wolff was thus a suitable contact for Dulles. He had an additional advantage: he had had an audience with Pope Pius XII in April 1944 via his close friend the historian and SS liaison officer Dr. Eugen Dollmann. Not in the least fazed by the nature of his guest and go-between, the Pope was delighted with Wolff and said to him, "How much misery might have been avoided if God had led you to me earlier. Allow me to send you on your dangerous road with my blessing on you and your family." The "dangerous road" to which the Pontiff referred was Wolff's plan to set up a special and separate peace with Dulles.

Ernst Kaltenbrunner, SS leader, was on the committee of discussion regarding these arrangements and indeed alleged at his trial at Nuremberg that he met Dulles in person. Wolff carried to Berlin a full account of his conversations with Dulles, conferring with Kaltenbrunner at his evacuation center, a farmhouse on the Autobahn near Berlin. Describing the contents of three separate conversations, Wolff said that he wanted "to build a bridge to the West" and that by handing over northern Italy with the condition that the German troops remain in power and retain their weapons, there would be set up "part of the proposed police force of the Western powers against Russia."

Dulles's real purpose in these meetings was to eliminate the Communist second front in Italy; Stalin got wind of this and was appalled to discover that in fact as a result of the early negotiations the Germans had been permitted to dispatch three divisions from Italy to the Eastern Front to attack Russia. He was driven to wire Roosevelt directly, frankly accusing the Allies of tricking the Soviet Union; Roosevelt, as usual, had not been briefed by Donovan on these underhand arrangements and cabled Stalin on April 5, 1945, expressing resentment towards Soviet Intelligence for such "vile misrepresentation of my actions or those of my trusted subordinates." Stalin correctly stated in his response that he had never doubted Roosevelt's own integrity or trustworthiness; his agent clearly had informed him of those who truly were backing this Italian conspiracy. He very much admired Roosevelt for playing a clean game and indeed was saddened by Roosevelt's death a few days later. Nevertheless, his knowledge of this grievous manipulation in Italy added fuel to the fire that had been kindled by Dulles's previous manipulations toward negotiated peace.

By now, Dulles could dissemble no longer. Eisenhower was quite opposed to such finagling, and with the President dying, there was no chance of bamboozling the Supreme Commander on the pretext that Roosevelt authorized these arrangements. Wolff agreed to a German capitulation in Italy; at the same time, Dulles was able to suppress the Communists. Himmler got wind of this, and Wolff flew to Berlin on April 16 wondering if Hitler would arrest him. He had in fact betrayed the Third Reich. But Himmler had a problem: since he had connived in all the previous arrangements via Schellenberg, it would be very risky for him to turn on Wolff, who might easily inform on him. Instead, he listened blandly to Wolff's specious explanations at the Hotel Adlon.

Kaltenbrunner walked into the hotel suite at the end of the meeting. He said that he had been advised that Wolff had negotiated with Cardinal Schuster of Milan for the surrender of the German Army; Wolff denied it. Wolff was very shrewd: he said he would be delighted to accompany Himmler and Kaltenbrunner to Hitler to have them repeat any charges of treason they might make. He played his card correctly: Himmler backed off, knowing that Wolff would give his game away and destroy him. As a result, Kaltenbrunner agreed to accompany Wolff to the Berlin bunker; neither would disclose the truth about the other.

At 4 A.M. on April 18, 1945, Kaltenbrunner and Wolff entered the bunker, where they met a shambling and disheveled Führer. Wolff reminded the Führer that he had told Wolff that if the new rocket weapons were not available, there must be some attempt made to achieve an armistice without dishonor. This was so totally against Hitler's entire psychology and personal policy that it can only be explained by his increasing mental disintegration, combined with the influence upon him of a particular clique that included Kaltenbrunner and Hitler's mistress, Eva Braun.

Wolff said to the Führer, incorrectly, "I am happy to be able to report to you, my Führer, that I have succeeded in opening doors through Mr. Allen Dulles to the President, Prime Minister Churchill, and Field Marshal Alexander. I request instructions for the future." Hitler's demented condition was so extreme that he actually accepted this absurdity and asked Wolff to return later that day. At a second meeting, he pointed a trembling finger at the SS leader and said, all in a rush, "Go back to Italy. Keep up your relationship with the Americans but see that you get better terms. Stall a bit. Give my best wishes to my friend the Duce. To you my thanks and my appreciation."* Wolff flew to Italy to sign the capitulation order, and Dollmann, the go-between, appropriately lit a candle to the Madonna del Rosario.

---

* For a detailed account of these arrangements, see Heinz Höhne's definitive *The Order of the Death's Head: The History of the S.S.*

17

Into the Cold War

Along with the desire to enlist all possible former members of the German secret services in the American cause, the United States Government, in the immediate postwar period, began looking for scientists to assist in the development of atomic weapons. Background and political orientation were considered insignificant beside the possible usefulness of those who had been outstanding in the field of secret weapons, particularly flying bombs. To anyone who lived through World War II, the memory of the bombs, with their sinister loud buzz, sudden moment of silence, and then deadly explosion would never be forgotten.

Various task forces under the command of Supreme Headquarters, Allied Expeditionary Forces (SHAEF), spread through Germany in the postwar period minutely examining rocket labs and factories, and sophisticated radar and communication systems centers. Many of these had been operated by International Standard Electric, a subsidiary of ITT, of which Walter Schellenberg was a director and shareholder by arrangement with ITT's American chairman, Colonel Sosthenes Behn.

Colonel Behn clearly realized that with Walter Schellenberg receiving a director's salary he would protect Behn's operation in Germany. So completely was Behn on both sides of the war that he encouraged Standard Electric to develop shells operated by remote control, at the same time that he sold the U.S. forces the so-called Huff-Duff warning system, which announced the arrival of those shells and made it possible to demolish them. Later, Standard Electric developed a method of avoiding detection for these missiles.

The Department of the Navy was especially interested in Dr. Herbert Wagner, chief design engineer of the H.S.-293—the first German guided missile used in combat. On May 4, 1945, Wagner took navy men to a cache in the Harz Mountains where he had hidden cases full of blueprints and models. At an underground plant outside Nordhausen, he showed the design of his latest antiaircraft rocket, Butterfly. He was brought to Washington, where he prepared for a possible rocket attack on Japan that was preempted by Truman's decision to drop the atom bomb on Hiroshima and Nagasaki.

Other experts were assembled. The list was long. Among them were authorities on low-pressure chambers in airplanes, authorities on the Fritz X, an air-to-surface missile, the BV-246 glide bomb, and the use of infrared cells to control missiles.

Leaders of Göring's Air Ministry notable in the prosecution of war were put up at hotels, wined, and dined while their boss was left to take poison at Nuremberg. Apparently, the elimination of Reichsmarschall Göring by public trial and his own hand was sufficient to clear the air completely of the so-called black Luftwaffe's illegal construction in defiance of the conditions of the Versailles Treaty and that air force's all-out use in pulverizing Great Britain. After all, the British and American air forces had achieved revenge by firebombing Dresden and Cologne—with the notable exception of the Ford Motor Works, in the latter city, which boasted pictures of Hitler and Henry Ford side by side behind the executive desks for the duration of World War II.

The Jewish David Sarnoff, chairman of the Radio Corporation of America, who had been a wartime partner in the Nazi-controlled Transradio Corporation, made the announcement in June 1945 that the acquisition of German scientists in the communications field was "desirable" because "Security for any nation henceforth depends . . . to a very large extent upon its place in the scientific sun."

Sarnoff was in a position to know. As I explored in great detail in *Trading with the Enemy,* Sarnoff and RCA shared Transradio with the equal shareholders Telefunken, Italradio, Nippon Radio, and British Cable and Wireless. In the middle of the war, Transradio opened a telephoto circuit between Buenos Aires and Tokyo, which resulted in crucial intelligence passing into enemy hands. This proved too much even for the ubiquitous Breckinridge Long, head of the Visa Division of the State Department and precluder of Jewish immigration, who complained in various memoranda that American ships were going down because of the leakages. No doubt German and Japanese ships were going down for the same reason; it was a question of who got more in the intelligence trade-offs.

I.G. Farben scientists involved in the building of rubber factories for use at Auschwitz were instantly brought back to power. The poison-gas expert Otto Ambros was brought into the United States by the ubiquitous Peter Grace, of the Grace Line, whose apotheosis was achieved by his membership in Ronald Reagan's kitchen cabinet.

There was an unseemly struggle for German scientists between Britain, the U.S.S.R., and America. The United States obtained the lion's share of the rocket experts. After a great deal of squabbling, the important General Walter Dornberger, whom the British considered a "menace of the first order," was given the position of director of research and development at the Bell Aircraft Factory—the report of Counter-Intelligence Corps bugging of Dornberger's cell later alleged that he was "untrustworthy . . . in seeking to turn ally against ally."

The business of bringing in scientists was known at first as Project Overcast. A leading figure of the project was the celebrated Dr. Wernher von Braun, who emerged as a popular American star of the scientific world and the space program, his fame far exceeding that of his fellows. When the various scientists arrived at the United States and were put up at the so-called Camp Overcast, at Wright Field, they proved to be a collection of prima donnas. They complained about the fact that they were not treated as leading Americans would be: that their mail and packages were restricted, that their conditions were not lavish, that they were confined to base. They were of course allowed to go to movies and the theater, shop, and attend chapel. A priest held regular services for the Catholics, a minister for the Protestants.

Some scientists were more fortunate. At Port Washington, they lived in comfortable conditions at a castle that had been built by the multimillionaire Jay Gould. They soaked in marble bathtubs and ate in an imposing dining room. Wernher von Braun was quite comfortable at Fort Bliss. The scientists were deliberately placed all over the map, partly because they were not completely trusted—there was always the danger of possible Soviet penetration—and partly because the armed forces were uneasy about the public getting on to Project Overcast and asking too many questions. Which inevitably it would and did.

It was in 1946 that George F. Kennan, counselor to the U.S. embassy in Moscow, sent his celebrated telegram to the State Department announcing the Soviet Union's detailed and aggressive plans against the United States. Warning the American Government to expect the Russians to seek to penetrate, undermine, dominate, and destroy the Free World, he drew attention to plans to develop Russian armed forces to the limit. Kennan's wire helped to start the Cold War, reaping the whirlwind of mutual suspicion and hatred that with tragic irony he deplored himself in his volume of lectures *The Nuclear Delusion*, published in 1982. There was already talk of World War III by 1946, and hysteria began to seize the extreme American Right, which had waited for the inconvenient Nazi High Command to step aside or die so that a more reliable clique could take over and create a powerful Western bloc centered in Berlin.

By 1946, the Soviet armies were, as Kennan today admits, exhausted. Even in the unlikely event that plans were afoot for the Soviet occupation of Western Europe, it would have been a physical impossibility, because the railroad gauges failed to match and transportation of troops and weapons by any other means would have been unthinkable. The Russians had not developed at that early stage the sophisticated nuclear weaponry that could effectively demolish the Western capitals. Moreover, and more important, not even the Dulles brothers could come up with a shred of documentary evidence that the Soviets had even the beginnings of an idea of invading and destroying Paris, London, and New York, whatever their plans may have been for the Slavic territories.

In this atmosphere of fantasy and paranoia, the German scientists were naturally in their element. As the Cold War deepened, they were able to secure more satisfactory conditions and were given access to incomes, houses, and all the benefits of American citizenship. Their families, rather crudely treated at first, were softly handled and imported; some of the scientists married American women and started American families.

Inevitably, the embattled American intellectual Left, already feeling the icy breeze of the approaching McCarthy Era, which was to emasculate them, got together in university common rooms, cold-water flats, and cramped mid-Manhattan apartments and began tearing their hair in annoyance and frustration over Operation Overcast, which was now becoming known with equal alliterativeness as Operation (or Project) Paper Clip.

The Society for the Prevention of World War III, which included among its membership Clifton Fadiman, Louis Mumford, Louis Nizer, William Shirer, and Darryl Zanuck correctly denounced the employment of these Germans. But very few were listening. In March 1946, the National Conference on the German Problem met at the Waldorf-Astoria Hotel, in New York City, at the invitation of Eleanor Roosevelt and Edgar Ansel Mowrer. Among those there were Henry Morgenthau, Jr., Sumner Welles, whose career had been destroyed by J. Edgar Hoover and former ambassador William Bullitt, Albert Einstein, and Helen Gahagan Douglas.

The conference called for the suspension of all immigration of Nazis and for punishment of the middle-level Nazi leaders. The members particularly took after Project Paper Clip. But again, the public was largely indifferent.

Such meetings provided cannon fodder for the likes of J. Parnell Thomas, chairman of the House UnAmerican Activities Committee, who was destined to wind up in the same prison as Ring Lardner, Jr., one of the so-called Hollywood Ten, for padding the committee accounts. Joe McCarthy was sharpening his teeth on such gatherings. As the American weather vane turned more and more sharply to the right, even the words of Rabbi Stephen S. Wise, unexceptionable president of the American Jewish Congress, caused little stir when he announced that the wife of one of the Wright Field rocket team had been a Nazi Party official and therefore a war criminal by definition. Rabbi Wise said in May 1946, "This operation [Paper Clip] is all the more deplorable at a time when officials of our government find every possible reason for failing to fulfill the declared policy of President Truman to rescue as many victims of the Nazi terror as our immigration laws permit. . . . As long as we reward the former servants of Hitler while leaving his victims in DP camps, we cannot even pretend that we are making any real effort to achieve the aims we fought for."

But these noble words fell on deaf ears. A few cranks peppered the scientists at Wright Field and El Paso and their other locations with rude letters; a half dozen newspapers ran sniping comments in small print in the turnover pages of the correspondence columns. A kind of invisible cloud of censorship descended on the country when any criticism of Nazi collaboration arose. Meanwhile, the War Department was enlisting thousands of hard-core Nazi thugs as intelligence agents.

On March 12, 1947, the President made his famous Truman Doctrine speech, outright declaring the Soviet Union the "enemy." By 1948, the Air Force had decided to go all out and whitewash Paper Clip in public. Senator Harry F. Byrd published a detailed account of Paper Clip as a useful arm of the American defense system in *The American Magazine*. He admitted that most of the scientists were Nazis but stated with some ingenuity that their "very arrogance and vanity" had led them to give us their secrets and that they had been trained out of the contemptuousness toward "American democracy, culture, institutions, even housing . . ." but "the question is not whether we like or hate the Germans . . . in my opinion, we are entitled to exploit these talents to our best possible advantage." This was presumably intended to overrule complaints that Hitler's minions had been awarded the boon of American citizenship.

There was a fierce attack on Project Paper Clip in two articles in *The Nation* in 1949. Morton Hunt wrote about the entire scandal, quoting remarks by one of the Nazi scientists at a grand reception in a university: "The FBI didn't care about my being in the Nazi Party. I think they understood about that. What they wanted to know was whether perhaps I was a Communist." Nothing further needed to be said.

✳✳✳✳✳✳✳ 18

The Romanian Connection: Richard Nixon's Partner

Perhaps the most celebrated instance of a Nazi supporter entering the United States after World War II was that of Nicolae Malaxa, one of the wealthiest industrialists in Romania. He was a remarkable man. Short, lean, with a thin, sharp, inquisitive nose, a jutting chin, piercing, intense dark eyes, and thick dark hair, he was acute, witty, and incisive. A bon vivant, his gourmet appetite was restricted only by a chronic ulcer condition. He spoke in aphorisms: When arranging an early-morning meeting, he would say, "The fox that doesn't get up early in the morning doesn't catch any chickens." And when he wanted to discourage his American attorney from having a meal before a meeting, he would say, "In Romania, we don't feed the horses until after the race."

This humorous and devious multimillionaire tycoon became the chief financier (along with his Jewish rival, Max Ausnit) of the Romanian Legion of the Order of the Archangel Michael, a terrorist anti-Jewish organization numbering its membership in the hundreds of thousands. The Legion, sometimes known as the Iron Guard, a loose term largely discontinued by the late 1930s, received the support of the dreaded SD, the foreign-intelligence branch of the Nazi SS. That support was personally ensured by the all-important Reinhard Heydrich. Hitler greatly disapproved of the SD's support of the Legion; Ribbentrop, the German Foreign Minister, favored General Ion Antonescu, the Legion's most committed enemy, and backed him financially.

Malaxa began his career before World War I as a chemical engineer employed by the Romanian State Railways, inspecting materials for the Purchasing Department. He used his personal charm to ingratiate himself with the Railways' general manager to allow him to open a small repair shop for railway cars at the provisional capital of Iași. After the war, he left the Railways, started a small shop of his own, and went bankrupt; in Bucharest, he used his great enterprise and influence with his former patron and general manager, Alexander Perieteanu, to secure contracts to repair cars. He organized Malaxa & Co. with his patron as a silent partner. When Perieteanu became head of the Technical Council of the Railways, Malaxa made substantial profits and formed the basis of his fortune.

Malaxa insinuated himself with German locomotive enterprises; he launched the German company Borsig in Romania. Later, he bought out Borsig's interests. He moved into a mansion in Bucharest and became a prominent society figure, pleasing everyone with his wit, style, and charm. He was very close to Madame Magda Lupescu, the mistress of King Carol, somehow evading criticism despite the fact she was Jewish. Because of his influence over Magda Lupescu, he in turn achieved influence over the King, who virtually placed the entire state treasury at Malaxa's disposal. Financed by the government, he snapped up almost a third of the methane gas interests in Romania, the second-largest in the world. He also absorbed iron works, railroad and steel yards, and locomotive production. He used taxpayers' money to feather his own nest, at one time clashing with army chief of staff Ion Antonescu when he made armaments deals with the French. When Antonescu tried to block the deal, Malaxa went to see King Carol and had Antonescu dismissed. Antonescu never forgave him. He became Malaxa's enemy from that moment on.

No doubt inspired by his rivalry, Malaxa was pleased to join his rival, Max Ausnit, in financing the Legion of the Order of the Archangel Michael. By 1931, he was the sole owner of a Romanian stock corporation whose plants produced diesel engines, self-propelled railroad cars, tractors, and oil drilling and refinery equipment. He owned a rolling mill that produced steel tubes, developed the richest deposits of natural gas in Europe, and (together with Standard Oil of New Jersey) dominated the oil producing and refining business in the country.

He was the leading builder of oil pipes in Romania, and for that reason was crucial to the Germans, who would depend upon Romania and its neighbor Hungary for oil and gas supplies in a future war.

The Legion sprang, like most Fascistic organizations, from the terrors of 1919, when millions of Europeans feared that bolshevism, which had overthrown the czars, would sweep like a scourge across Europe. The flames of anticommunism were fanned by those theorists and speech-makers who declared that the cause of communism was the Jewish world conspiracy. The first to rise and create the Legion and enlist its cohorts was the inflammatory and handsome student leader Corneliu Codreanu, who stood on platforms denouncing Communist demonstrations and charging that the starved people of Romania were threatened by the "Ju-daic criminal hand from Moscow." Inciting large numbers of peasants to his flag, Codreanu became a kind of Hitler, demolishing Jewish homes, overthrowing alleged Communist cells, and agitating against the capital-ists who ran the country. Beginning in 1929, his legionnaires marched through valleys and rode over mountain paths in green shirts and with turkey feathers in their fur caps, assembling meetings by torchlight in ancient graveyards where peasant audiences were dazzled by the youth's denunciation of the Jewish bankers. Soon the legionnaires dramatically assumed white crosses on their shirts—like Crusaders—and in 1930 set fire to a Jewish settlement and burned its citizens to death. That same year, Codreanu formed the Iron Guard as a militant youth organization designed to combat communism. When a Guard member shot at a Bu-charest journalist who had criticized Codreanu, the government tried to dissolve the Legion, and open warfare broke out between the Legion and the government. Splinter groups with a distinctive Nazi element, one of them called Swastika of Fire, sprang up. Magda Lupescu became the object of Codreanu's hate and the incarnation of his nightmare of a Jew-ish conspiracy. It is therefore ironical that Malaxa, as her closest friend, supported her most violent enemies.

In the mid 1930s, the King did everything possible to suppress the Legion short of civil war. The country erupted in violent clashes of legion-naire and soldier. It was at this stage that the SD became involved, greatly infuriating Ribbentrop. The legionnaires were blamed, rightly or wrongly, for the assassination of the Romanian Prime Minister, Ion Ducà, in 1933.

Although it was often claimed that money came from the SS, Malaxa and Max Ausnit were the chief supporters of the Legion financially, per-haps because they hoped to obtain power in a new government following a Codreanu coup d'état. Also, it is probable that the Jewish Ausnit wanted to protect himself from being liquidated by the Legion.

By 1938, King Carol was fighting the Legion, which had obtained even more support from the Nazis. So extreme was the Legion's power that King Carol tried to appease it by mirroring its policies in depriving Jews of citizenship (despite his Jewish mistress), closing their businesses, and eliminating their licenses. At the same time, he even used Antonescu to propose a coalition government to Codreanu to try to overcome the danger of full-scale revolution. He also wanted to appease the peasantry in this. But Codreanu was uncompromising and refused to accept the arrangement. As a result, King Carol had several thousand legionnaires arrested. On November 30, 1938, he had Codreanu and thirteen other legionnaires packed into a truck, tied hand and foot, and taken to a remote country location, where they were strangled to death by garrote and finished with shots to the head. They were thrown into a common grave.

Hitler undoubtedly approved of this action and indeed had met with King Carol just two days earlier at Berchtesgaden. A critic of Codreanu's murder without trial was the twenty-four-year-old student leader Viorel Trifa—one of the recipients of Malaxa's and Ausnit's bounty—of whom more in another chapter.

Malaxa clearly realized that the next stage of the story presented great danger to him. Horia Sima, who succeeded Codreanu as head of the Legion, was scarcely in the same class; indeed, he altogether lacked the charisma of his predecessor, and Malaxa feared that he would be outwitted by Antonescu. Sima's attempted coup d'état of January 1941 is discussed in the Trifa chapter (see page 221).

Malaxa, who was bound up with the Legion and had long since crossed Antonescu, was in a serious position in 1941. He had foreseen disaster and in 1939 had deposited $1,400,000 in the Chase Bank in New York City; his daughter Irene had obtained a $300,000 trust fund to secure her future in the United States. Simultaneously, Max Ausnit's brother Edgar assured the Ausnit future in the United States by obtaining support in New York; Edgar Ausnit's British-Jewish wife worked for Bundles for Britain, and Edgar invested in the Transatlantic Export Corporation, transferring Romanian funds to Manhattan via South America and Mexico. Edgar also arranged a forge capable of producing fifty thousand bombs per annum, ordered for Romania from Bethlehem Steel, which lay useless on the New York wharves for years because of export restrictions. Like Malaxa, Ausnit had substantial holdings in the Chase Bank, and he manipulated currency with his close friend and associate the ubiquitous Serge Rubinstein.

Further to hedge his bets, Edgar Ausnit arranged an escape route to Canada for his brother Max when the heat was on from Hitler. Meantime, Malaxa made a deal with Albert Göring, brother of Hermann Göring and a proponent of his expansionist policies in Europe. Albert Göring and Malaxa met in Bucharest on June 20, 1940, signing an agreement allying the Malaxa interests with Göring's own Brunner-Waffenwerke. Albert Göring wrote in a subsequent summary of the meeting in the form of a letter to Malaxa (June 21, 1940), "In this connection your interests, my dear Mr. Malaxa, are the same as ours." Shares in both companies would be issued on a passe-partout basis, and joint boards would be formed under a Göring-Malaxa presidency.

As well as securing this alliance with the Göring family, which was of course intended as insurance against Antonescu and the Hitler faction, Malaxa further established a foothold in the United States by forming the Metalax Manufacturing Corporation, in Manhattan. However, every effort to save himself failed. Following the January revolution, Antonescu had him arrested, on February 1, 1941, and charged with backing the revolt and harboring legionnaires in his house. He expertly defended his case, disingenuously using the fact that the legionnaires he had allegedly harbored had in fact wrecked his house. During his brief imprisonment, Romania and Nazi Germany jointly combined forces to run his enterprises. It became clear to him that Albert Göring had double-crossed him. Albert, who was part of the Hitler-Ribbentrop faction against Himmler and Heydrich, had made a secret partnership with Antonescu.

The furious Malaxa was asked to sign the papers necessary in Romanian law to effect the alliance with German and Romanian interests running his company. At a series of meetings at the Council of Ministers, in the presence of Vice President Mihail Antonescu and German trade delegate Guido Schmidt, Malaxa pointed out in vain that he had a legal contract with Albert Göring. This plea was, of course, useless, and since he refused to sign the necessary documents, his properties were expropriated and passed over to the protectorate of the Romanian state under Antonescu. It was Antonescu's triumph.

On September 11, 1941, the Romanian-German Company for Industry and Trade was formed to run the Malaxa enterprises, with Albert Göring and Antonescu as partners. In 1943, when the Germans withdrew from Romania following their defeat at Stalingrad, Albert Göring surrendered his share of the properties. The Romanian Government lost colossal sums through running the business incompetently, and within eight months of the German withdrawal, Malaxa was back in charge and beginning to turn a profit.

When the Russians took over Romania, in 1945, they approved Malaxa's resumption of power over his own properties, though they did remove one steel rolling mill piece by piece to the Soviet Union. The Soviets even authorized the payment of $2,400,000 in American currency to Malaxa for the mills, despite the fact that both this transaction and his being permitted to run an operation on capitalist principles and with independent funding was in direct contradiction of Communist principles.

Later in 1945, Malaxa, accompanied by Romanian premier Groza and Vice President Tatarescu, traveled to Moscow to seek official permission to resume trade with the United States. Not only did Stalin's government make no objection to such an arrangement, it asked to be included, and indeed it was felt to be in Russia's best interests for America, Romania, and Russia to combine in an economic union presided over by Malaxa.

Thus, Nicolae Malaxa moved from being a supporter of the Legion and a partner of Reichsmarschall Göring's brother to becoming a key figure in the Soviet economy.

At the end of 1945, Malaxa hired the distinguished Bernard R. Lauren, of Engel, Judge & Miller, New York lawyers, to represent him in the United States. He also set up a liaison with Grady C. McGlasson, formerly of the OSS, whom he had dealt with in Romania, an agent for the automobile manufacturer Harry Dodge. Malaxa arranged to meet with Lauren in Istanbul in January 1946, to discuss the production, assembly, and distribution of Kaiser-Frazer automobiles and tractors in Romania and the rest of Soviet-occupied Europe. At a meeting between Lauren, McGlasson, and representatives of the State Department in Washington headed by Robert Wright, Lauren said that he felt Malaxa had "collaborated with the Germans only under pressure, and that in spite of his affiliation with the Iron Guard, the Nazis, etc., he was not an enemy of the democracies." (Asked about this in July 1983, at his home in Manhattan, Mr. Lauren said that he still was not sure whether Malaxa had been a Nazi sympathizer or not.) Robert Wright pointed out that "there was evidence that Malaxa had been on all sides of the fence at various times and had a reputation of an opportunist." That stated the facts exactly.

Wright added that Malaxa was "unquestionably on good terms with the present Romanian government."

Before Lauren left for Istanbul, he discussed with various American firms a joint American-Romanian stock company to develop steel tubes without solder, natural-gas supplies, and tractors, as well as automobiles. Lauren's travel arrangements to Turkey were authorized by the State Department; he traveled by Army Air Transport plane, because the matter was "in the national interest." Among the plans developed when Lauren arrived in Istanbul for numerous lunches and dinners with Malaxa, were plans for American penicillin factories to be built in Romania, with Russia and the United States enjoying equal shares. Lauren guaranteed to unblock Malaxa's $1,400,000 in the Chase Bank and to support Malaxa at the State Department level, establishing the First Allied Company, with 45 percent American and 55 percent Malaxan capital.

Malaxa reached still farther up: on February 21, he had a meeting with Emil Kekich, commercial attaché to the official United States Mission to Bucharest. He informed Kekich of his desire for Romanian-Russian-American economic collaboration. Discussing his negotiations with the various U.S. business interests, he said, looking into the future, "When the American and British armies move out of Europe, isn't it logical to expect that the physical, moral, and spiritual force represented by these armies will be supplanted by economic work? I would emphasize Romania's importance, because it is in a peculiar position in relation to Russia in comparison even with other countries in which the Russians are interested, such as Poland, Czechoslovakia, Yugoslavia, Bulgaria, and Hungary . . . we must accept things as they are."

Kekich visited Malaxa's plant, which had close to nine thousand employees. Four fifths of the locomotives, diesel motors, tractors, and railroad cars Malaxa produced were sold directly to the Soviet Union. The plant was plastered with pictures of Stalin, Lenin, Marx, and Engels, and Soviet and Romanian flags fluttered from the roof. There was only one Stars and Stripes, hanging in an obscure office; the plant superintendent told Kekich he was sorry there were not more.

U.S. Secretary of State Dean Acheson cabled his embassy in Bucharest on March 14, 1946, confirming that Russia had approved the U.S. participation with Malaxa on "a tripartite basis." He added, inter alia, "Alleged Soviet willingness may indicate realization inadequacy of U.S.S.R. economic policy in Romania and need for U.S. assistance." On

February 26, Lauren reported in detail to the State Department on his meetings with Malaxa and urged the Department to assist him in freeing several hundred thousand dollars of Malaxa's frozen Chase assets. Despite considerable elements of doubt, he achieved this purpose. In a memorandum to the Department on March 26, he echoed Malaxa's exhortations to achieve economic collaboration with the Soviets and to develop "associations of friendship with the Russians in business that can materially assist in paving the way for dealings directly between American and Russian business."

Lauren asked for Malaxa's funds in order to supply him with American staff for technical advice and legal assistance, pointing out that Americans would now be able to share in the vast resources of natural gas, tubing, railroad stocks, and locomotive factories in which Malaxa was dominant. Simultaneously, the Romanian Minister of Finance conveniently concurred with Malaxa in stating that the funds deposited at the Chase were not the property of the government (in fact, by Romanian Communist law, they were) but, rather, of Malaxa himself. Indeed, in a document made out by the Romanian Ministry of Industry and Commerce dated April 13, 1945, Romania had given Malaxa a charter to set up a joint government and a Malaxan judicial board to smooth over any legal difficulties in his capitalist enterprises in a Communist economy. By early 1946, the Romanian Government was supplying Malaxa with twenty-one thousand tons of steel a year, a working capital of four billion lei, five billion lei in industrial construction contracts, and three billion two hundred million lei in locomotive orders. Moreover, the government paid Malaxa billions in reparations for the suspension of his activities during the war.

In May 1946, the OSS's Grady McGlasson, by now president of Graham-Paige International Corporation, called at the State Department to discuss a sudden change of policy. Kaiser-Frazer, part of the Graham-Paige empire, had decided they dared not release their patents to Malaxa for fabrication in Romania, because the Russians might annex them. They would only offer Malaxa a distributorship. The matter would be discussed when Malaxa arrived with a Romanian trade mission that summer. It was hoped that a satisfactory arrangement would be reached at that time.

Simultaneously, Malaxa was involved in further establishing penicillin production in Romania. McGlasson offered to bring Malaxa in to talk with members of the Department when he came to Washington.

Malaxa arrived in the United States on schedule in September and had meetings with State Department representatives. All of these were most cordial. While in New York, he had a splendid time with Bernard Lauren, staying in a large suite at the old Ambassador Hotel. He lived it up as much as his ulcers would allow, expansively luxuriating while Lauren fixed him up with the necessary visas. It seems clear that Malaxa's chief motive in the United States was to unblock his American assets and to obtain American support for the safety of his Romanian properties. It seems that his previous financing of the Legion made no difference to Immigration officials, who may or may not have been aware of the Legion's SD connections. Certainly, any suggestion that Malaxa was a "Nazi," made in later years, was unfounded; he would have supported anyone who could assist his commercial cause, and he was committed to communism only so long as it suited his purposes.

Malaxa also involved the distinguished firm of Lehmann Brothers in his plans, assuring their interest in substantial deals with 50 percent Soviet interest. Already, he was beginning to shift his ground as the political situation in Europe deteriorated and the Iron Curtain started to descend. He began talking, late in 1946 and into 1947, of no longer forming an overt Russian alliance but, rather, of driving a wedge into the Communist bloc by making the Romanian people conscious of the value of American investment capital. In early 1947, he drew up an elaborate plan to ally himself with International Harvester, seeking to have that company ship a huge quantity of heavy machinery to Romania. When the company proved unable to meet this colossal order, it agreed to supply blueprints and specifications for joint production.

Malaxa convinced Harvester's executive vice president, G. C. Hoyt, that Romania was short of tractors and that supplying them to the agrarian populace would cause a division against Russia. However, it is clear that Malaxa could supply no guarantees that the American products built from American blueprints would not find their way to the Soviet Union. In a series of memoranda, the diplomat Burton Y. Berry, representative of the United States in Romania, made it clear that the fact that because the Soviet Union had authorized Malaxa's visit to Washington, his activities were extremely open to question in the matter. Berry also noted that Max Ausnit, Malaxa's former enemy, was again involved with him in this matter. Berry wrote to Washington on July 2, 1946, "It is the Mission's considered opinion that Messrs. Malaxa and Ausnit are truly between the devil and the sea. They feel instinctively, perhaps, that they are Soviet captives as much as are all businessmen in Romania. They may be playing the Soviet game more under duress than in enthusiasm, hoping that in the course of time international developments will bail them out of Soviet control. They have a very solid argument in believing that to preserve any degree of political and economic independence they must have foreign, particularly American, help."

One personage who clearly held suspicions of Malaxa was President Truman, who refused to receive him, despite—or because of—the fact that Malaxa was carrying a letter from the duplicitous King Michael of Romania.

By 1947, Malaxa was no longer represented by Bernard R. Lauren, but by John Pehle, the former Treasury foreign-funds-control representative who had been responsible for freezing his funds at the Chase Bank in 1941. He had shrewdly hired Pehle to unblock the funds that Pehle himself had made unavailable. Malaxa, Pehle, and Randolph Paul (former Treasury counsel and anti-Nazi) met with the Texas millionaire politician Will Clayton, who had formerly given assistance to Nazi interests at the State Department, to discuss the need for Romanian corn imports. Thus, former enemies sat together around a conference table to assist a former Fascist backer and present Communist collaborator in enhancing his business interests and reputation in Romania. Challenged directly on the matter, Pehle, who had played a crucial part in fighting for Jewish immigration in World War II, says today (1983) that he had simply regarded Malaxa as a client who had hired a lawyer and that he had no idea whether Malaxa was a Fascist or Communist supporter.

As the Cold War progressed, all of Malaxa's plans collapsed. Romania became more deeply Communist and confiscated both Malaxa's and Ausnit's holdings. However, Malaxa, forming and re-forming like an amoeba, was indestructible. He obtained his citizenship via the Immigration and Naturalization Service and moved forward to a future partnership with none other than Richard Milhous Nixon.

It is certainly a peculiar irony that Nixon was in partnership with a personage whose financial and political fortunes were intricately entwined with the Soviet Union.

The Nixon connection had begun in 1951. Malaxa had continued to apply for permanent residence under the Displaced Persons Act now that his presence in the United States was no longer authorized by Russia or

Romania. On September 26, 1951, the Immigration and Naturalization Service, choosing to overlook the testimony of witnesses (including Max Ausnit) attesting to Malaxa's Nazi and Communist affiliations, for reasons best known to itself found in his favor and recommended that he be admitted permanently. Asked to explain this curious fact, Mr. Bernard Lauren says, "The people in Washington were as sophisticated as you or I. They knew perfectly well that Malaxa played every side of the political game. Didn't every business leader everywhere?"

Malaxa was pleased to find the matter was pressed by INS in Congress, but the INS's recommendation did not receive congressional approval. Malaxa's name was added to a joint Senate resolution which, if passed (it was not), would have adjusted Malaxa's status.

Mr. Nixon, senator from California, then stepped in with striking determination to have Malaxa's name appended to legislation that would permit the Romanian's entry. Indeed, Nixon pressed for the introduction of a private bill to permit Malaxa to remain permanently in the country, a bill introduced by the chairman of the Judiciary Committee of the Senate; a number of other senators presented names to the chairman for inclusion in an omnibus resolution. Congressmen Francis Walter, chairman of the Immigration Subcommittee, and Emmanuel Celler of New York, chairman of the Judiciary Committee, deleted Malaxa's name by special order from the resolution itself, a fact which has not been publicized. Undaunted, Nixon continued in his association with Malaxa.

The channel for the association was the Western Tube Corporation, registered in California and Delaware, a company which had a sort of phantom existence, since it is not listed in Poore's Register for 1951–53. Western Tube's alleged purpose was to manufacture seamless tubing for oil drilling at a time when sheet tubing of this nature was unavailable in California. Malaxa, be it noted, had specialized in this type of tubing in Romania; there is no question that such a company would have had to operate under the Truman administration, since this was in the midst of the Korean War. Thus, the products of Western Tube were to be shipped under government aegis against a Communist enemy. It was clear that Malaxa now no longer felt any "loyalty" to the Communist empire; and in fact, Romania had recently, and appropriately, attached his properties.

Perhaps coincidentally, perhaps not, Western Tube was set up in Whittier, Nixon's home town, in March 1951—an unlikely location for a steel production corporation, since Whittier was in the midst of a farming district. Western Tube's address was identical with that of Bewley, Knoop and Nixon, law offices in which Nixon was a partner: 607 Bank of America Building. Thomas Bewley, the senior partner, was agent, director, and secretary of Western Tube. It must be pointed out that Nixon by now was not involved with the firm directly, but his name was on the door nonetheless, and it cannot be overlooked that his best friend in the area, Herman L. Perry, was Western Tube's vice president.

On May 17, 1951, Western Tube, which was still just a pie in the sky, filed an application for first preference quota for Malaxa on the ground that he was indispensable in the building of a war production plant that would be useful in the war against communism and that his presence in Whittier was required to be permanent, since the plant was to be erected there.

Even the most simple-minded individual on Capitol Hill must by now have grasped the fact that Western Tube was simply a device for ensuring the permanent residence of an undesirable alien and that Malaxa would be entirely useless in a battle against a political bloc that until recently had chosen to give him sustenance. However, on September 14, 1951, William F. Knowland (the senior senator from California) and Richard M. Nixon, writing under the banner of the U.S. Senate Committee on Labor and Public Welfare, sent a letter to Manly Fleischmann, Administrator, Defense Production Administration, GAO Building, Washington, D.C. The letter read as follows:

> We understand that Western Tube Corp. filed an application with your Administration on May 17, 1951, for a certificate of necessity in connection with the plant it proposes to build in California to manufacture seamless tubing for oil wells. File #TA 9660 was assigned to the application. California, as you may know, is the second largest state in both oil reserves and oil production. . . . It is our understanding that at the present time there is no plant in California for the manufacture of seamless tubing for oil wells. . . . It is important, strategically and economically, both for Calif. and the entire United States, that a plant for the manufacture of seamless tubing for oil wells be erected near the California oil fields. We therefore urge that every consideration that it may merit be given to the pending application.

Impressed by the urgency of the appeal, the DPA unwisely gave permission; and once the Eisenhower administration took over, with Nixon as Vice President, it was inevitable that Malaxa would achieve his purpose. He turned up as, of all things, a Canadian, and acquired his green card as a permanent American resident on September 26, 1953. It was repeated in congressional debate that Western Tube was a dummy corporation and a front, because it did not build a single plant or issue a single instrument of war and was dissolved as soon as it had achieved its purpose and obtained its tax deductions.

In fact, it has been stated on the Hill by no less an authority than former California congressman John F. Shelley that Mr. Nixon obtained for Malaxa a Certificate of Tax Necessity which brought about a tax write-off of several million dollars on a factory that did not exist. And it should be pointed out that Malaxa's former nemesis Burton Y. Berry, acting assistant secretary of state for Near Eastern affairs in 1952 and U.S. representative in Romania from 1944 until 1947 now exposed Malaxa to the Justice Department as an opportunist with feet in both the Nazi and Communist camps. This fact was scarcely unknown to Richard Nixon.

Characteristically, Malaxa, armed with his permanent American residency, turned up in Argentina to set up business arrangements with the Perón regime. When he returned to the United States in December 1955, a rare bird in the Immigration and Naturalization Service took exception to his background and excluded him from reentry. He had failed to answer questions on his past affiliations, and he challenged the decision against him on the ground that the special inquiry officer should have questioned him personally and had "improperly drawn adverse inferences" from his resolute silences. In the subsequent argument, Malaxa still declined to disclose the appropriate facts. No doubt he was more uneasy about discussing his Communist affiliations than his Nazi connections.

He applied to the Board of Immigration Appeals, which took the view, interestingly enough, that Malaxa was right: the special inquiry officer should have questioned Malaxa himself and should not have drawn adverse inferences from his silences. The appeals board swept aside the slightest suggestion of a rehearing to obtain answers to the questions. Not only did the board reach the curious conclusion that Malaxa had nothing whatever to do with Nazis, Communists, or any other affiliation contrary to the interests of the United States, but it readmitted him as a permanent resident.

The case went up for review by Vice President Nixon's friend and Attorney General William Rogers, who properly determined that questions concerning Malaxa's Nazi and Communist connections should have been answered and that, indeed, adverse inferences could be drawn from his silences, but nevertheless affirmed the appeals board's decision and allowed Malaxa to stay in the United States for good. Malaxa moved into a handsome apartment at 1158 Fifth Avenue, where he remained in comfort until his death, in 1965.

Three years before his demise, Representatives Frank Kowalski of Connecticut and John Shelley of California presented all of the appropriate facts to Congress and demanded that Malaxa be deported. However, the Kennedy administration did nothing about the matter. This active collaborator with both the Legion and its splinter Communist-backed group, with Albert Göring and the Stalinist economic administrators, with the postwar Romanian Government and the Peronista regime, passed away comfortably in his bed.

The Romanian Connection:
The Bishop of Hell

If Malaxa represented the secular arm of Romanian collaboration with the Axis then Viorel Trifa represented the religious arm. A fiery member of the student movement and an impassioned figure of the Romanian Orthodox Church, Trifa progressed from obscurity in the backwoods of his native country to the imposing position of addressing the U.S. Senate in an act of prayer at the alleged invitation of Vice President Nixon in May 1955.

Viorel Trifa was born in 1914 near Câmpeni, Romania, then part of the Austro-Hungarian Empire; he was raised as a royalist; pictures of the kings of Romania decorated his home. His parents were smallholders, eking out a modest living on their property, raising cows in a stark, fir-dotted landscape of rocky outcrops and savage, windswept hills. The oldest of seven children, he helped his father cut and sell lumber and studied privately with his father, who doubled as a teacher. The family was intensely nationalistic and was consumed with a hatred of Jews.

In 1927, Trifa won a scholarship to a lyceum. He fell under the religious and political influence of his uncle Iosif, a stern and inflexible Romanian Orthodox priest who found his reflection in the humorless and severe young boy. Trifa wrote at a very early age for his uncle's newspapers, which were subsidized within the Orthodoxy.

Trifa proved to be a gifted student at theological college, graduating with distinction at the age of twenty-one in 1935. He was a student activist from the beginning. He railed against Jewish culture, charging the

Jews with financing the Russian revolution. He also attacked King Carol, who was descended from Queen Victoria, for acquiring a Jewish mistress, Malaxa's friend Magda Lupescu. By 1936, as president of the University Students' Center of the University of Bucharest, he was the most powerful figure in the city's student movement, preaching to the converted as he allied himself with Codreanu, with whom he had much in common. His meeting with Codreanu that year inspired him to deprive Jews of their meager foothold in the university, and he also bought Jewish support from Jewish merchants in the markets of Bucharest in exchange for protection when the revolution came.

At the 1936 Student Congress, Trifa addressed the crowd with fiery rhetoric, denouncing the monarch and calling for a pogrom. He was arrested for creating a disturbance but released for lack of evidence. When his colleague in the service of fascism Bucharest University student Ion Mota was killed fighting for Franco in Spain, Mota's funeral and that of his friend and colleague Vasile Marin became a circus in Bucharest. Trifa met the funeral train in person at the border. He stood by the coffins as the locomotive chugged its way past long rows of sobbing peasants to Bucharest. At the funeral itself, Trifa proudly joined German, Spanish, Italian, and Japanese diplomatic representatives in the cortege. Already, the student fighters had achieved legendary status in Fascist circles in Europe.

In 1938, when Carol finally closed in on the student movement and had Codreanu strangled, Trifa fled to Transylvania, hiding in the homes of various anti-Semitic farmers. He proceeded to Poland and thence to Berlin, where Codreanu's wife, Elena, and the new, self-inflated Legion leader Horia Sima, had understandably found refuge.

When war broke out in Europe, in September 1939, Trifa was at the University of Berlin, paying for his studies by tutoring. He linked up with the fanatical Ukrainian undercover squads being trained by the Nazis for the future conquest of Russia. He was greatly influenced by Alfred Rosenberg, who wrote of a restoration of the ancient German Empire. When the hated King Carol abdicated and Sima returned to Bucharest, to ally with Codreanu's father, the coast seemed clear for Trifa to make his way back himself. With theatrical emphasis, he returned by train with Elena Codreanu; they were greeted by an enthusiastic crowd of supporters at the train station.

At the urgent request of the martyr Ion Mota's widow, Trifa edited her late husband's inflammatory Fascist newspaper *Libertatia*, urging a direct alliance with Nazi Germany. He addressed crowds to the same effect. His years in Berlin had convinced him that Hitler was the only solution to Judaism and communism. In September 1940, soon after his return, he was elected president of the Supreme Council of the National Union of Romanian Christian Students. He gave his express approval of King Carol's son, King Michael, who was making his own accommodations with Hitler and had cleansed the nest of his father's Jewish mistress.

In speeches delivered to the Student Union, Trifa encouraged the advent of the New Order, predicted that Romania and Germany would together be victorious over Great Britain, and tacitly supported an uneasy political marriage of convenience in the form of a Sima-Antonescu coalition government with Michael as its figurehead. At the same time, Trifa was scheming along with Malaxa to overthrow Antonescu and put the Legion's extremist wing into power, thus splintering that wing away from the more loyal central faction.

According to German Foreign Office documents, it was believed that the Communists and MI6 encouraged Malaxa and the other splinter-group backers in order to drive a wedge into the Axis. Hitler, it will be recalled, officially backed Antonescu, along with Ribbentrop; both the Führer and his Foreign Minister correctly mistrusted Malaxa, Sima, Trifa, and the other extremists and believed that chaos would result if the Legion leftists ran the country.

A major incident took place on November 27, 1940. Inspired by Trifa, Sima ordered the bodies of Codreanu and thirteen other legionnaires dug up by torchlight from the Jilava prison to be reinterred in consecrated grounds. Hundreds of fanatics gathered as members of the Legion prised open the tombs with iron staves. When the decomposed corpses with the copper garrote wires twined around their necks were dragged from the ground, the crowd went mad. The motley collection of Communists, Fascists, Liberals, priests, peasants, and heterodox rebels slaughtered the prisoners in the cells and roamed about the city, murdering at random. Half a million men rallied to the green flag of the Legion and were issued the Legion's green regulation shirts.

Malaxa and Trifa seized the occasion. Malaxa saw profits in supplying the Legion with machine guns, rifles, and even two tanks. At the same time, it goes without saying, he was supplying the government. Hedging all bets, he allowed the leading shop steward in his factory to head up a

Communist-inspired splinter group which would need all the arms it could get. At the same time, Trifa used his influence with the students, unhesitatingly allowing the very Communists he ideologically deplored to dominate his various meetings. He was prepared to use anyone to achieve his and Sima's purpose: to spearhead a rebellion via the student body.

Antonescu was desperate. Foreseeing disaster, and allied to a weak and vacillating king, he was alarmed when Sima, himself not noted for strength of character, was emboldened by Trifa and the other fanatics to demand total power for the legionnaires. Wilhelm Fabricius, German minister in Romania, and his colleague Hermann Neubacher, in those pre-Mihajlovich days economic attaché to the Nazi legation, tried to smooth over the troubled waters by arranging discussions with Sima and Antonescu. They were afraid that if the government collapsed, there would be no guarantees that the Nazis would retain their foothold in the crucial Romanian oil fields, which supplied more than one third of Germany's entire petroleum imports and without which she would be handicapped in the present war with Britain and the future war with the Soviet Union.

Supported by Fabricius and Neubacher, Antonescu traveled to see Hitler and was reassured of his support in any future alliance. Antonescu returned to Romania in the wake of the Jilava incident, happily anticipating that Hitler would strengthen his arm. Large numbers of German troops supplemented the existing protective forces in the country. Trifa publicly welcomed their arrival, and Malaxa found yet another outlet for his armaments.

On January 16, 1941, Antonescu was back with Hitler at Berchtesgaden. He reminded Hitler of Soviet penetration into the Legion and the centralist Legion's desire to remain loyal to the government. He emphasized the necessity to bring the centralist group into an alliance with the Nazi government. Hitler urged him to become the leader of the Iron Guard and to work closely with Hitler's new representative in Bucharest, Manfred von Killinger.

Back in Bucharest, Antonescu had meetings with Killinger. It will be recalled that Killinger had played a crucial role in California as San Francisco consul general in 1937, and was very close to Hitler personally as well as a fanatical Nazi of the SA school of thought and an impassioned anti-Communist. He recommended to Antonescu that any insurrection within the Legion be brutally punished, since it would come from Marxist sources and British Intelligence.

On January 18, 1941, the chief of the Railway Transport of the German Army in Romania, Major Doehring, was murdered by a Greek boxer who was alleged to be in the pay of the British. Antonescu immediately fired the legionnaire Minister of the Interior and the police chief, who was also suspected of being a British agent. The left elements of the Legion, led by Trifa, prepared to strike back.

In this, they were greatly encouraged by the SD and its sabotage and espionage squad headed up in Romania by the key contact Otto von Bolschwing, who, as we shall see, wound up in a comfortable sinecure in Silicon Valley, California. What was the reason for this support? The SD, under the devious Walter Schellenberg, was fighting a political battle with Ribbentrop and was aggravated by his influence over Hitler. Schellenberg apparently believed that by bringing about a coup d'état he personally could ingratiate himself with the Führer. This folly provoked the events that followed in the next few days.

On Sunday, January 19, 1941, Trifa gave a public speech in favor of the Nazis. On Monday, Horia Sima summoned him and instructed him to address a student demonstration in front of the university. At seven o'clock that evening, in the icy winter darkness, a chilly wind whirling snowflakes around his head, the twenty-six-year-old man stood at the foot of the statue of the legendary Michael the Brave, delivering a manifesto aimed directly at the Jews. He regurgitated charges that the Greek assassin of Doehring was in British pay and that the killer's defendants were a figure in Antonescu's Secret Service, and two others, who were involved with Jews and Greeks. He called upon Antonescu to replace all Jews and Masons in the government and to have a government dominated by the Legion. This was peculiarly ironical in view of the British involvement.

According to numerous eyewitnesses and records, Trifa thus, intentionally or not, sparked the revolt that followed, involving an extensive pogrom armed by Malaxa.

On January 22, street fighting broke out in Bucharest, accompanied by outbreaks in many other cities, as all save the diehard supporters of Antonescu in the Guard splintered off to join the Communist faction led by Codreanu's father. By seven o'clock at night, the capital resembled a morgue. All automobiles were kept off the streets, along with buses and trolley cars. Antonescu, locked up in his palace with an armed guard, forbade the Bucharestians to leave their homes on a strict, pain-of-death curfew.

Meanwhile, the Greek community was mopped up by police because of the killing of Doehring. All communication with Bucharest was severed and every telephone was disconnected. Leaflets were circulated by the Communists charging the centrists of the Guard of selling the Legion out.

There was a riot before the Bucharest prefecture when iron guards refused to submit to police orders. They marched through the prefecture square singing legionnaire songs until a royalist crowd attacked them with tanks armed with scratch crews. The legionnaires made an onslaught on the tanks with pickaxes, disabling the caterpillar-tread wheels with horse blankets thrown into the machinery. Royal guards fired on them and killed two of them.

The legionnaires were, as usual, completely out of control. They used the excuse to kill at random; soon more than two thousand dead lay in the Bucharest streets. The newly appointed Romanian Minister of the Interior, General Dimitru Popescu, issued an edict that any civilian found with firearms after twenty-four hours would be killed instantly. The fighting spread to eleven major cities, as far as the borders of Hungary; the legionnaires seized the government radio station and printshops, led again by Trifa and Dimitru Grozea of the Legionnaire Workers' Corps. They tried to seize the National Theater, driving a mob of women volunteers in front of them. The Antonescu army drenched them with fire hoses; the water froze on them in the icy temperature of the night. Inevitably, the Jews were victimized. The Iron Guard leftist extremists, virtually a rabble, rather than an organized political party, burst into Jewish houses, dragged out the occupants, and made an onslaught on the Sephardic Temple, throwing out prayer books, tapestries, and holy relics and setting them on fire, forcing Jewish citizens to dance about the bonfire until they were worn out. When they fell to the ground, the legionnaires burned them alive.

Soon the entire Jewish ghetto was destroyed. Two hundred Jews were packed into trucks and taken to the city slaughterhouse, where they were hung on meat hooks, their throats cut, and the blood allowed to run out in an obscene parody of kosher butchery; some were beheaded with meat cleavers while they knelt at chopping blocks. Eyewitnesses testified that Trifa was involved in these onslaughts. One witness to both Trifa's speech and the pogrom was a young, non-Jewish art student, Konstantin Antonovich, who recalled in his New York home in July 1983:

> Along with many other young people, I was tossed into a cell in total darkness. I called out into the black night, to people I could not see, "Who are you?" And a cry came back, "We are Jews!" Luckily, I knew the chief warden. I managed to scribble a note in the dark and send it up via a jailer. I was summoned to the warden's office. As I was halfway up the stairs, I heard a terrible groaning behind me and the sound of beatings and gunshots. The people behind me were being murdered.

Within a day, Bucharest was devastated by bloodshed and explosions. The troops were all looking for Sima and for Trifa and their cohorts. There were rumors flying constantly; but it was certain that hundreds of Jews had died, and in one apartment building alone, eighty-nine men, women, and children were slaughtered and lay in heaps. Hitler was furious and ordered Von Killinger and Neubacher to flush out the rebels immediately. At the same time, he raged at Himmler and Schellenberg for having defied his official policy in the Balkans by playing along with Communist-Soviet elements and the British. Malaxa was held responsible, which led to his immediate trial as the rebellion was quelled. It was determined that he had supplied much of the 32,635 machine guns, rifles, revolvers, and hand grenades and nearly 400,000 rounds of ammunition. Many of the machine guns additionally supplied were believed to come from American sources. It may have been a coincidence that the ubiquitous General William Donovan was in Sofia, Bulgaria, that week. At the same time, Malaxa's associate the Romanian banker Oscar Kaufmann fled to London with close to a hundred thousand dollars in American money and was tried in absentia for acting in collusion with British and American interests. Antonescu announced a full-scale National Socialist state, exactly what Hitler wanted from the beginning. He had hoped that the wobbly Antonescu would firm up in the crisis, and he was greatly pleased.

In the immediate wake of the rebellion, it emerged that Otto von Bolschwing, chief liaison between the SD and the legionnaires, was sheltering Trifa and some of the other leaders in the special annex of the SD near the German legation itself. Neubacher wrote to Carl Clodius, of Ribbentrop's economic staff, on January 25 that the intention must in future be to secure the solidarity of the Legion and not to attempt to eliminate it; he was sure that the Legion would accept all the arrangements for the future. At a meeting with Sima, Neubacher persuaded the Legion to stop all street fighting and join forces with all extremist groups under the Führer. By January 27, Killinger was able to cable Ribbentrop: "Tranquillity reigns throughout the country." He stated categorically that the uprising was exploited "by English agents, and particularly by Russian agents, who prepared the revolution by propaganda and provocation. . . . Besides other weapons, eighty-five of the most modern submachine guns of American origin were confiscated."

Killinger, acting under Hitler's orders, would not drastically punish the legionnaires for their activities. It was far more important not to provoke the solid, loyal body of the Legion by executing their rebellious colleagues. Indeed, once it was determined that the SD was hiding Trifa and the other leaders of the Legion, it was decided to treat them reasonably.

When the legionnaires were arrested, Von Bolschwing came to see Killinger and protested strongly. Von Bolschwing assured Schellenberg of his loyalty and that the legionnaires were in fact strongly pro-German. Immediately, eight of the legionnaire leaders were transferred to Germany, followed by Trifa himself. Although it was sometimes claimed that the SD protected the legionnaires by giving them special conditions of imprisonment, the truth of the matter is that, as German Foreign Office records show, Hitler personally made sure that Antonescu treated the legionnaires with care and consideration; indeed, this special treatment would not have been possible without Hitler's specific approval. Even Malaxa escaped severe punishment, due to the necessity of appeasing the Legion. Only a handful were sentenced to forced labor and none were executed. The one insurrectionist laborer who was killed by a firing squad was not a legionnaire.

The legionnaires were put in "protective custody." Trifa managed to flee by train to the Yugoslav border but was seized in German uniform and joined several of his compatriots in an outdoor SS camp at Berkenbrueck, Germany. The conditions were more or less the same as those experienced by SS guards. Still in his twenties, and in robust health, Trifa stood up to the modest discomforts of what amounted to a house arrest. On Christmas Day 1942, he was transferred to Buchenwald and then to Dachau. While Jews were slaughtered not far away, he enjoyed the privileges of exercise, rough but acceptable food, his own clothing, access to a laundry, and conversation with his fellows. However, it is clear that the Germans didn't trust him, and he was forbidden any mail or telephone calls.

Still vigorous and showing few signs of his imprisonment, he was released on August 30, 1944. By now, Malaxa was showing his powers of survival in a Russian-dominated Romania. Trifa became secretary to Visarian Pujù, patriarch of the Romanian Orthodox Church in Vienna. According to various sources, Trifa joined Sima's exiled government in Vienna.

On May 8, 1945, after the collapse of Germany and Austria, Trifa was arrested by the Soviet Army and handed over to the NKVD.

Later, he taught at the Italian missionary college of San Giuseppe in Ronzano, in the subjects of history, geography, and languages. He became part of the "Forul Legionaire," a group, led by Constantin Papanace and headquartered in Rome, that was financed by the Vatican. Since he had led the students in a rebellion backed in part by British Intelligence and the Americans, he certainly had no fear of problems from British or American elements in Italy. Moreover, he confidently embarked upon plans to come to the United States, where he was offered a valuable position as editor of the Romanian-American episcopate magazine *Solia*. By a special irony, the magazine concerned was violently anti-Communist, a fact which scarcely rippled the surface of Trifa's multinational mind.

Trifa accepted the position with the magazine. He was, after all, not inexperienced: in a 1940 copy of his personally edited *Libertatia*, there was an article headlined "The Country Shakes Off the Kike Plague."

Trifa arrived in New York on July 17, 1950, signing an affidavit that he had never advocated the persecution of anybody because of race, religion, or national origin (Form I-144.) He was admitted as a stateless person under the convenient provisions of the Displaced Persons Act despite the existence of a January 16, 1950 army report listing his activities. Apparently, the investigation into him was not thorough, as it had been with Malaxa. It has been claimed that Trifa was brought in under the protection of U.S. Intelligence. Certainly, soon after his arrival, on December 18, 1951, an army intelligence report reached all government departments, giving a list of Trifa's activities with the Iron Guard and suggesting that he was being financed by clandestine legionnaires abroad. The report was specific and damning. Mentions were made of his anti-Semitic remarks. Other documents that have turned up are a CIC report stating that Trifa "may have misrepresented the facts" in obtaining his visa from the U.S. officials in Italy. The files also include a history of the Iron Guard, originating from Army Intelligence. Interestingly, it has been a consistent theme of Trifa's own attorneys that the government officials admitted him with full knowledge of his background.

Trifa became far more prominent in the United States than he had been in Europe. From an obscure teaching post he was elevated without Holy Orders to a bishopric with startling rapidity. On April 27, 1952, with the aforementioned documents in the hands of the authorities, he was made Bishop Valerian D. Trifa in a special ceremony held at Bala-Cynwyd, Pennsylvania. He was now a prominent figure of the Romanian Orthodox Church. He was also anointed bishop of the Autocephalous Orthodox Church of America, centered in Syossett, Long Island. This was entirely in contravention of church laws, since he had never taken Holy Orders, nor had he been a deacon or any other official of that or any other religion.

Indeed, he was even anointed by a noncanonical metropolitan, since the only way he could have been officially and properly anointed was to go to Romania. And there, with the rise of the Communist regime, the nationalization of Malaxa's businesses and the total discrediting of the Legion, he would have been persona non grata or worse.

Trifa rapidly rose to be the most important person in the Romanian Orthodox Church in America and proceeded toward obtaining his citizenship with the same calm resolution as Malaxa. Unfortunately for him, there was at least one person in the United States who took the gravest exception to Trifa's position. Dr. Charles Kremer, a New York City dentist, had been aware of Trifa's activities from the time of the Legion rebellion. Kremer was appalled to learn that Trifa had not only arrived in the country but had improperly assumed an ecclesiastical position.

Kremer, a Jewish Romanian, was several years Trifa's senior. He had left his native country at the age of twenty-two, stowing away on a freighter bound for Port Said. Through contacts in Egypt, he had obtained passage to Britain and thence had made his way to New York, where he was admitted on November 12, 1919.

He worked his way through the University of Pennsylvania dental school as a waiter on eighteen-hour shifts and set up practice in Manhattan, where he often gave free treatments to needy patients. His life from the beginning was caught up in righteousness.

Shortly after leading the Senate in prayer at the alleged invitation of Richard Nixon, Trifa filed an application for naturalization to the Immigration and Naturalization Service at Detroit on August 3, 1955. Oddly, he was asked to what organizations he had belonged and the answer that he had merely belonged to student and religious organizations was accepted. It might well be asked whether the Immigration officials did or did not acquaint themselves with the contents of files in which details of his former activities were made clear. In either case, he apparently had no more problem than Malaxa in moving forward rapidly to his citizenship, which was granted, over the protests of Dr. Kremer and numerous others, on May 13, 1957. Kremer had already gone to Romania and unearthed substantial records from newspapers showing that Trifa was publicly visible as a prominent figure in the 1941 revolt, but this seemed to weigh not at all with the authorities.

Perhaps the involvement of British Intelligence in the rebellion was still viewed as an embarrassment by the government. Perhaps the Trifa matter was lost—or treated as inconsequential—by a slow-moving bureaucracy.

Kremer became an increasingly lone wolf. For twenty years, he badgered attorneys general and Immigration officials. In 1973, he wrote to Ralph B. Guy, Jr., of the Department of Justice, demanding Trifa be denaturalized. Mr. Guy sent the letter to the Immigration and Naturalization Service in Detroit. A. J. Salturelli, of INS, replied that all charges against Trifa had been investigated exhaustively and there was no ground upon which he might be removed. This simply confirmed previous INS letters to Trifa which stated there was no evidence to pursue him with at all. In November 1973, Kremer put together eighty-eight pieces of evidence without success. No one was prepared to act. Even the constant motions of Rabbi Rosen of Romania, the World Jewish Congress, and other bodies made no headway. Columns by Drew Pearson and Walter Winchell and long articles by Charles R. Allen, the foremost authority on Nazis in America, bore no fruit. No administration seemed interested in pursuing the matter, and indeed Kremer met with constant obstructionism in the Jewish community itself. Day after day, night after night, Kremer kept hammering away, and at last he had a break. Hilley Ward, of the Detroit *Free Press,* in a 1972 interview with Trifa, got him to admit membership in the Legion. Kremer was jubilant. Based on this public admission, Kremer was able, after some twenty years, to interest Charles

Gordon, counsel of the Immigration and Naturalization Service. And there was a deeper reason.

By a paradox, Richard Nixon himself was the cause of this change. With his concern (later expressed in his establishing of a special relationship with China) to drive a wedge into the Communist bloc, he had exchanged visits with Romanian premier Nicolae Ceausescu in 1969 and 1970 and had encouraged expanding trade relations with Romania very much along the lines Malaxa had initiated in 1946. Indeed, he took a leaf out of Malaxa's book, since Malaxa had managed to claim, as the Cold War emerged, that he, too, wanted to drive a wedge by providing commercial sanctions via the U.S. State Department. In view of the anticipated most-favored-nation arrangements and the improvement of American-Romanian relations, it was no longer necessary to protect Trifa. His usefulness as a possible anti-Romanian cleric or wild card in the Cold War had ceased to exist.

Kremer properly took credit for what followed, but there was more to it than an act of biblical vengeance. Trifa's slow but sure downfall was sealed by mere convenience. Trifa blamed the Communists for backing Kremer, a sign that even he did not entirely understand the situation. Nevertheless, Kremer proceeded to accumulate documents, and Trifa continued to prepare an elaborate defense.

American support for Israel in the early 1970s still further hammered nails into Trifa's coffin. Official policy ensured the rise to prominence of Congresswoman Elizabeth Holtzman, who set up the Nazi War Crime Litigation Unit, which, under INS, pursued Nazis in America on a modest budget raised to five million dollars by 1979. At last, Kremer could operate within an officially recognized situation. Denaturalization proceedings began against Trifa on May 16, 1975.

Trifa went to Europe trying to accumulate a powerful defense, while Kremer, though still struggling with inadequate funding, traveled everywhere and appeared on television and radio, defying death threats from legionnaires in exile and their supporters, to pursue Trifa through thick and thin. The crusade took every last cent of Kremer's money. At last, the good dentist obtained the justice he sought, and in 1982 Trifa was forced to consent to an entry of Order of Deportation and to depart the country within sixty days after permission and necessary travel documents to enter any other country were received. It was a voluntary decision taken on advice of counsel, allegedly to avoid years of protracted struggle. But

Kremer's revenge was not complete. No country would accept Archbishop (as he was now known) Trifa. Kremer hoped Romania would accept him, but it would have been greatly embarrassing for the Romanian Government to have to try somebody so useful to the Communist cause in the past. Switzerland was among the first to reject him; too many inconvenient questions might be raised about Swiss multinationalism in time of war. At the outset of July, 1983, Kremer left for Israel to try to persuade Prime Minister Begin to bring Trifa in and try him on genocide charges. The chief prosecutor of Adolf Eichmann, Gideon Hausner, promised to help. Later, in 1984, Trifa was at last deported—to Portugal, where he was greeted by a delegation of his Orthodox peers, and was settled into a comfortable residence in Lisbon.

✸✸✸✸✸✸✸ 20

The Romanian Connection: The Baron of Silicon Valley

Otto von Bolschwing, who sheltered the rebellious figures of the Legion in his special annex of the SD in Bucharest and was the chief contact between Schellenberg, the AO, and the Legion, also found his way to the United States. Von Bolschwing was aided, as we shall see, by U.S. Army connections. Indeed, Von Bolschwing formed the third part of the Romanian triumvirate, as dedicated in his anti-Semitism and his concern for the international hegemony of the German right wing as his sometime confreres.

Otto Albrecht Alfred von Bolschwing was born on October 15, 1909, in Schönbruch, East Prussia, so firmly placed on the demarcation line between Poland and the Soviet Union today that the line runs through the house in which he lived. His father, Richard Otto Wilhelm Ferdinand, Baron von Bolschwing, was killed in action in the First World War on the Eastern Front; his mother was also of aristocratic origin. Otto, his three sisters, and his brother were as devoted as their parents to royalism, the cause of the extreme Right: he dreamed of the restoration of the Hapsburgs. He was educated at the University of London, where he studied languages and international law, connecting to right-wing organizations at that place of learning; and he became an apprentice with MacAndrews & Company, a division of the Royal Mail Steamship Company, in London. Thus, he obtained a strong sense of internationalism and a command of English at an early age—a background that stood him in good stead when he later emigrated to the United States.

He went through law school at the University of Breslau, simultaneously acting as general manager of a factory in Upper Silesia and owner of a coal mine in Poland. In 1932, he became sales representative for the British and Foreign Investment Corporation and Billiter Trust, headed by Lord Haldon, of Fleet Street, London. He joined the Nazi Party on April 1 of that year, without any objections from his employers. Because of his foothold in Silesia and Poland, he was concerned that communism would absorb his properties and that only by fastening upon himself the symbol of the swastika could he ensure protection when the chips were down.

Also in that period, Von Bolschwing achieved his apotheosis while still in his twenties: he formed an alliance with Adolf Eichmann, who, while fanatically anti-Jewish, met with Feivel Polkes, of the Haganah, via Von Bolschwing, and thus became a so-called authority on Jewish affairs. While playing along with the Haganah, Von Bolschwing and Eichmann together worked out a future policy of eliminating Jewish financial holdings and personal properties, recommending without reserve a reign of terror that would drive the Jews from Germany.

Back in Berlin in 1936, Von Bolschwing ran an import-export company called Impehag and married his first wife. He became a practicing lawyer in 1937 and general manager of, in succession, R. M. Maassen, textiles, and Pharmachemie, a pharmaceutical manufacturing company in Hamburg.

In September 1939, when war broke out in Europe, Von Bolschwing was drafted into the SS. Schellenberg appointed him to Amt (Office) VI of the SD, the foreign, political and intelligence service of the SS. He contacted three close associates of Amt VI, friends of his of several years' standing, and told them he was determined not to be merely "an auxiliary policeman." A high-level figure of AEG, German subsidiary of General Electric, which retained its connections with the parent company even during World War II and which was a chief financier of Himmler, demanded the bribe of ten thousand dollars in Swiss francs, to be paid to a bank in Sweden, which would ensure him a position with Intelligence. Schellenberg paid the money, and in November 1939 Von Bolschwing was affirmed in a staff position in economic intelligence.

This information may be found in the Von Bolschwing army files obtained by the California journalist Peter Carey. It was typical of the arrangements that I explored more fully in *Trading with the Enemy*. AEG was represented in the group known as the Circle of Friends of Economy, which also had a representative from a subsidiary of Standard Oil of New Jersey. Throughout the war, the Circle met with Himmler and other leaders of the SS and supplied very substantial sums, along with I.G. Farben, for the special account of Himmler. This account was sponsored and maintained by the Stein Bank, of Cologne, whose chairman, Kurt von Schroeder, was associated with Allen Dulles in the Schroeder Bank of New York and was connected to the Schroeder Bank in London, which also had Nazi connections.

Along with two of his old friends of Amt VI, Von Bolschwing was appointed to Bucharest, where the crucial issue arose of securing the country's vast oil supplies for the Third Reich. At the same time, an alliance was established with Malaxa as the leading industrialist in the area; it seems clear that from the beginning it was felt desirable to secure power over the oil fields for the SS, rather than for the Ribbentrop faction. Von Bolschwing was at the same time conniving with Carl Clodius, deputy director of Ribbentrop's economic policy department, and he was running the mineral branch of the German ministry in Bucharest. Under instructions to support the SS at every turn against the AO and the Berlin Foreign Ministry, he intrigued constantly behind the scenes to find out what the embassy was up to in Romania.

He thus became an outright espionage agent, using the sophisticated talents developed in Palestine when he was scheming both with the Haganah and with the Third Reich, with Eichmann and the Jews. Schellenberg assigned him to the Malaxa/left-wing branch of the Legion, which led Von Bolschwing to scheme with British Intelligence and with the Soviets. Indeed, German reports show that some meetings of the Legion were held in the American embassy.

His main contact was Trifa's friend Constantin Papanace, the Roman Catholic leader and chief economic figure of the Iron Guard's so-called left wing, who, as Minister of Economics in the coalition government of Antonescu and Horia Simà was responsible for the Romanian oil industry. As we know, some six years later, Papanace was to turn up as the Roman Catholic umbrella for Trifa in Italy.

Von Bolschwing's assignment was to ensure that Papanace allowed the Germans to take over the oil industry. But Von Bolschwing actually supported the Legion position that the oil fields should remain Romanian —a position with which the Soviets naturally concurred, since full German control would provide a major threat to Russia. Schellenberg apparently gave Von Bolschwing authorization to continue this scheming, chiefly to infuriate and frustrate Göring and Ribbentrop, who would benefit financially from the oil fields' annexation.

When, in January of 1941, Manfred von Killinger was appointed minister in Bucharest, it was clear that Von Bolschwing would have to act rapidly. Scheming with Hermann Neubacher, who was playing both ends against the middle, he suddenly became chief of the SD in Romania. We already know his personal involvement in the attempted January coup d'état, although the butchery of the Jews was not quite on the cards. In fact, the brutal lack of discipline on the part of the left wing of the Legion worked against Von Bolschwing's policies and helped to wreck his plan for a takeover.

According to a statement he made to U.S. intelligence at the end of World War II, Von Bolschwing personally carried Horia Sima in the trunk of his car to the home of Andreas Schmidt, the German minority leader at Kronstadt, and arranged for the transportation of Constantin Papanace and twelve other Legion leaders by military hospital transport to Germany. He also tried to have Neubacher and Antonescu bring about a special armistice in the very midst of the massacre. Antonescu accepted the arrangement, then revoked it an hour later.

As we know, Von Bolschwing protested to Killinger against the arrests of the legionnaires and his hiding of them in his house; he went from the meeting to report to Schellenberg.

During the period between December 1941 and August 1942, Von Bolschwing existed in limbo. Hitler remained exasperated by the failed revolt, but as we know, by agreement with Antonescu and in order not to infuriate the Legion centrist group which was now with Antonescu, authorized the modest house imprisonment of Trifa and did not seek Malaxa's liquidation. However, Von Bolschwing hung in the balance, since he was not essential to either side and had badly flubbed his mission. In August 1942, a thorough investigation into his political reliability must have shown his collaboration with the Soviets, the British, and the Americans. He was arrested by the Gestapo and taken to Vienna to be kept incommunicado; later, he was transferred to the Gestapo headquarters in Berlin, where he was placed in solitary confinement. It is clear that the reason for this was to protect him from Hitler's wrath. Hitler was also infuriated by the escape of Horia Sima from prison, and was looking for every scapegoat. Unlike the SS and the SD leaders, Hitler detested the idea of multinational intrigue and trade-offs, believing in nationalist solidarity and single-minded Germanism.

In 1943, Von Bolschwing returned to Vienna, where he recommenced his industrial activities. He was under constant surveillance, because clearly not even his own SD could trust him. His mail came late, and traces of glue appeared over the edges, indicating the letters had probably been opened. According to his own interrogatory reports, his phone line was marked by clicks and he was shadowed by plainclothesmen in the streets. He also operated in Amsterdam, where he set up a real estate business, known as the Bankvorronroerende Zaken, under the SD umbrella. This bank was formed to liquidate Jewish properties and enrich Von Bolschwing personally.

Back in Vienna, he allied himself with Captain Jonetz, head of the Abwehr's Naval Intelligence Liaison Division in Vienna. After the attempt on Hitler's life in July 1944, and the discrediting of Canaris, head of the Abwehr, Jonetz fell under Schellenberg and worked very closely with Von Bolschwing, who employed Jonetz's French girlfriend in his company.

In January 1945, Jonetz warned Von Bolschwing that he was suspected of collaborating across the line with the Allies; to escape arrest by Hitler, he fled to the Tyrol and hid in a mountain hut in the Ötz Valley until the U.S. forces arrived.

While in the Tyrol, he was contacted by the U.S. Army Counter-Intelligence Corps, which also was contacting Klaus Barbie, Reinhard Gehlen, and Otto Skorzeny for identical reasons at the same time. In return for his immunity from arrest and imprisonment, he agreed to turn double agent under the Donovan banner. Since he already had American and British connections through the 1941 attempted coup d'état and the Schellenberg operation, with its constant wartime negotiations with the Allies, he was considered indispensable. He supplied valuable intelligence on movements and strengths of German military in those last months of the war, and on rocket research at Camp Schlatt, Ötz Valley. Like Barbie, he advanced rapidly; and by 1947 he was involved with the reconstituted Gehlen organization, of which more in a later chapter. He obtained security clearances and passport privileges under Donovan's OSS in order to penetrate the Iron Curtain and bring home crucial anti-Soviet information. So advanced did he become that he was given an elaborate estate in Salzburg, a high salary, and a position with the Austrian League for the

United Nations. He was cleared in the process of de-Nazification and became an Austrian citizen in 1948, despite the fact that German Foreign Ministry files showing his involvement with Malaxa, Trifa, the SD, and the Soviets were in full possession of Donovan's internal offices.

Von Bolschwing became nervous about the Gehlen organization in its offensive intelligence against the Eastern bloc. He was increasingly—and correctly—certain that the Russians were penetrating the organization and obtaining secret intelligence from Moscow. Indeed, he became increasingly aware that he was under close Soviet surveillance, which is scarcely surprising, since large black limousines were constantly drawing up at his front door, disgorging Catholic, and particularly Jesuit, leaders and U.S. Army officers for meetings.

He continued as a CIC officer until 1954, when he was allowed to emigrate to the United States. The application for the Immigrant Visa and Alien Registration was signed by Lieutenant Colonel Roy F. Goggin in 1953.* Naturalized on April 6, 1959, Bolschwing was employed by Alfred E. Driscoll, former governor of New Jersey and president of Warner-Lambert, the big pharmaceutical company, who paid him from his personal funds to travel to Europe in August 1957 as his personal emissary.

In 1963, the fast-moving executive joined the Cabot Corporation. Linked to certain right-wing activists in various countries, the Cabots of Boston were extremely powerful—as evinced in the famous rhyme which ends with "Where the Lowells talk to the Cabots/And the Cabots talk only to God!"—and intricately tied to the forefront of the Republican establishment. The Cabot Corporation was one of America's richest, developing chemical-production and natural-gas supplies. Thomas Dudley Cabot, the distinguished chairman of the board, was director of international security affairs at the State Department in 1951, at a time when so many key figures of the Nazi intelligence were admitted and when, it is generally agreed, the CIA was dealing in State Department-laundered funds. Von Bolschwing maneuvered throughout Europe in 1963, 1964, and until 1967 for Cabot in Britain, the Netherlands, France, Italy, and Germany. In fact, for almost two years, he represented Cabot in Frankfurt.

Later, he joined Transinternational Computer Investment Corpora-

* See following page.

Form FS-256a
(Revised August 1962)

Approved Bureau Budget
No. 47 - R106.1

FOREIGN SERVICE OF THE UNITED STATES OF AMERICA

APPLICATION FOR IMMIGRANT VISA
OR AND ALIEN REGISTRATION

I- 259338

8610051

I, the undersigned, being duly sworn, state the following facts regarding myself and hereby make application for an IMMIGRANT VISA and ALIEN REGISTRATION under the Immigration and Nationality Act to the American .... Consulate General..............

at .... Munich, Germany ....

1. Family name	Given name	Initial	2. Place and date of birth	Age
von BOLSCHWING	Otto	A.S.	Oct 15, 1909, Schoenbruck/Ostpreussen Germany	44

3. Other names by which I have been known

xxx

4. Last permanent residence

Muenchen, Geiselgasteigstrasse 77

5. Address in the United States

Washington 25, D.C.

6. Name and address of person to whom destined, if any

Roy F. COGGIN, 1436 Mass Ave. Lexington, Mass.

7. Name and address of nearest relative in home country

brother: Karl L. von BOLSCHWING, Burg Flammerheim near Koeln

8. Travel documents presented

Travel Document

9. Hair	10. Eyes	11. Height	12. Weight	13. Nationality	15. Race	17. Sex	18. Marital status
blond	gray	6 1	182	stateless	German	M ☒ F ☐	Married ☒ Single ☐ Widowed ☐ Divorced ☐

14. Complexion	16. Ethnic Classification
fair	German

20. Distinguishing marks

21. Languages spoken, read, or written

German, English, French, Italian, Arabien

19. Occupation

financial advisor

22. Intended United States port of entry

New York

23. Final destination

Washington, D.C.

24. I have (a) X (no) through ticket to destination

25. Purpose of going to the United States

to reside

26. Places of previous residence   Koenigsberg Germany, London England, Hamburg Germany, Beuthen O/S Germany, Berlin Germany, Jerusalem Israel, Bucharest Rumania, Rome Italy, Wien Austria, Salzburg Austria, and Muenchen, Germany

27. Names and places of residence of spouse and minor children

wife: Ruth von BOLSCHWING, nee von PFAUNDLER, see No 4

child: Gisbert von BOLSCHWING, see No 4

tion (TCI), in Silicon Valley, registered in Sacramento, and became a crucial figure as consultant in Germany and Switzerland, rising to vice president in April 1970. A complete sheaf of his business references and contacts is included in his secret intelligence files, among them directors of the Berliner Handels Gesellschaft, a major German bank, the president of the Deutsche Bank, and officials of the First National Bank of Boston and the Chase Manhattan Bank. Thus, he was allied with Rockefellers and Serge Semenenko: sure signs of his advanced status among the multinationals.

Unfortunately for all concerned, TCI was not loyal to its CIA-government protectorate, and in 1972 Von Bolschwing stood accused of complicity in perpetrating the biggest securities fraud in California history.

TCI collapsed in a welter of lawsuits and bankruptcy proceedings; Von Bolschwing suddenly became dispensable by everyone: he had broken the Eleventh Commandment and was no longer a profitable asset for his banker backers or the CIA. It is possible also that he was involved in the frequent leakages of strategic chips to the Soviets. He was back in the situation he had been in when he flopped in the attempted coup in Romania, playing along with American, British, Soviet, and SD gamesters. Aided by his son, today a prominent San Francisco attorney, he tried to bolster his sagging fortunes, but, like Trifa, he was a victim of renewed U.S. Government encouragement of Romania and splinterist activity in the Balkans.

In 1979, the newly formed U.S. Justice Department Office of Special Investigations, initiated by Congresswoman Elizabeth Holtzman, closed in on him and he was brought in for a hearing, with the inevitable results. He protested his usefulness to U.S. Intelligence and the immunity promises made to him, but he should have known better than to rely upon the security of any intelligence service or any government in the face of political expediency and a rising wave of public opinion. His wife committed suicide and his health went to pieces. Even as he lay in the hospital, a brutal photograph in the local San Jose paper announced his indictment for lying about his past when he obtained his citizenship; the question was, Had he lied about it? The actual documents are under lock and key at present. But an educated guess would confirm that the facts were scarcely unknown to the Immigration and Naturalization Service. Von Bolschwing died in 1982, following a prolonged illness, but at least he had one satisfaction: though required to surrender his American citizenship, he was, like Malaxa, allowed to remain in the country for the rest of his natural life.

✶✶✶✶✶✶✶ 21

The Skorzeny Plot

Official representatives of the United States Government wasted little time after World War II in getting into touch with one of the most dangerous of Walter Schellenberg's special team, the indispensable SD agent Otto Skorzeny. Skorzeny was a war criminal of great importance who should certainly have walked to the scaffold at Nuremberg along with his superiors of Hitler's Cabinet. But he was to stand first in line with Otto von Bolschwing and Reinhard Gehlen to offer his useful services to the Allies. As a result, and not for the first or the last time, General Donovan found use for a Nazi.

Skorzeny was born on June 12, 1908, in Vienna. An able student, he graduated from the University of Vienna on December 11, 1931, with a first-class engineering degree. Fierce, intense, and fearless, he loved to fight duels and boasted fifteen scars, including a vivid slash on his right cheek. He was physically strong and forceful, with a lean, muscular physique. He had little or no intellect as such: his life was rooted in the physical, and like most young bucks of his generation his first thought was to go into the Army. His parents were keen Nazis, and he joined the Party himself in 1933, proving to be a successful adherent of the cause as well as a Gold Medal winner in the Nazi auto races, near Vienna.

He joined the SS and the Gestapo and was very active during the Anschluss. He was a close friend of Ernst Kaltenbrunner, who was to be his boss, and he joined the Waffen SS (the branch of the SS under arms) in 1939. He became an officer in January 1941, attached to an artillery regiment first and then progressing to service in the Soviet Union with the so-called SS Division Reich. He tended to be unruly and drunken; he was hard to discipline, but he was dedicated to the Third Reich and passionately committed to destroy every Russian who crossed his path. Due to illness, followed by wounds, he was withdrawn from the front, and in April 1943 was instructed to join Amt VI of the SD, to which Otto von Bolschwing belonged. Schellenberg saw in him an impassioned, loyal, and dedicated servant, who, nevertheless, would have to be controlled. He presented a picture of physical power, with his massive shoulders, barking voice, and melodramatic sword slash across his face. Schellenberg instructed him to build up a school for special agents in sabotage, espionage, and commando work. He trained some one hundred and fifty students, fit young men, many of them drawn from civilian ranks; he commanded Fighting Battalion 502, delegated to special assignments that involved great daring and expertise. Kaltenbrunner was in charge of the operation, with more intimate control exercised by his subordinate Schellenberg. Ultimately, all decisions emerged from Hitler and Himmler, both of whom had a special fondness for Skorzeny and relied upon him heavily.

He taught his agents to master the talents of penetration, interception, and subversion. Moreover, each of his students was put through a grueling course of killer exercises, obstacle courses, and harsh boot-camp training. They had to learn how to master automobiles, locomotives, boats of every description, grenades, machine guns, rifles, and all sizes of aircraft. They had to master several foreign languages and know the intricate structure of bombs, shells, and tanks. The results were spectacular: an expert intelligence squad in terms of physical fitness, technical competence, and ruthless daring.

In July 1943, Skorzeny experienced the ultimate: he was summoned to Hitler's quarters in the Wolf's Lair, at Rastenburg, East Prussia. When Hitler discovered that Skorzeny was an Austrian, he was delighted: the formative years of his manhood had been spent in Vienna and he knew he could trust Austrians more than anybody else. Hitler told Skorzeny that he had a special job for him in Italy: he wanted him to rescue Mussolini and bring him to Germany for a top-level meeting; Mussolini had disappeared following the collapse of the Italian Government in the face of the Allies. King Victor Emmanuel was now in charge, along with Marshal Pietro Badoglio, and Hitler was afraid the monarch would bring about a total disintegration of the Italian segment of the Axis. Hitler was determined that the new government not hand Mussolini over to the Allies. Skorzeny flew to Italy with General Kurt Student, commander of XI Parachute Corps. He began research together with fifty men of his battalion. He determined that Mussolini was imprisoned on an island in the Gulf of Naples. No sooner had he determined this, than he found that the Italian dictator had been transferred via a destroyer to a hotel on a mountain in the Appennines.

It was difficult to achieve the rescue by parachute, because the hotel was very high in the mountains. The plan was to land some men by glider and bring others from the valley to go up by cable car, but experts said it was impossible to land at such a height. Skorzeny was determined to go ahead and flew with nine planes to his destination. He had to guide the entire operation from his own glider.

He flew over his troops in the valley, and then, having signaled them, made a daring crash landing, since the chosen landing area was too steep for a conventional touchdown. The plane was almost completely destroyed, but Skorzeny and a crack team of nine men got out almost unscathed. Skorzeny led his small troop to the terrace in front of the hotel, where he saw Mussolini standing at a window. He simply walked into the hotel while two of his men climbed up a lightning conductor and got into Mussolini's room. They quickly overpowered the Italian officers in charge and made off in a scout plane with their celebrated captive. From there, they flew to Vienna, where they moved into the Hotel Imperial. Himmler was delighted, and Hitler called Skorzeny to say that he had carried out a mission that would go down in history.

The next plan was to kidnap Marshal Tito of Yugoslavia. Unlike the duplicitous Chetnik leader Mihajlović, Tito was unequivocally in the service of the British and the Americans. Significantly, Hitler considered him, not Mihajlovitch, who always protested that he was against the Nazis, a prime target. But the plan proved impossible to carry out.

Skorzeny parachuted agents into France during the fall and winter of 1944, and he was involved in the setting up of the complex intelligence operation known as Werewolf, which was run directly by Himmler and in which Skorzeny worked very closely with Kaltenbrunner. Schellenberg was greatly irritated by Werewolf, because his subtle and devious nature was offended by the brutal bluntness of Werewolf's espionage and sabotage activities. Indeed, Kaltenbrunner's violent nature irritated Schellenberg more and more, and no doubt Schellenberg, the quintessential internationalist, who continued to scheme with representatives of the Allies behind the scenes, feared that the loudmouthed Werewolf members might discover and leak his plots. Fortunately for all concerned, Skorzeny had no idea what they were up to; he stayed fiercely loyal to Hitler.

His next assignment was as dangerous and spectacular as his Mussolini mission. He had orders to kidnap Admiral Miklós Horthy, Regent of Hungary and alleged secret backer of Draža Mihajlovíc, who was with the SD. Horthy, though as indispensable as Antonescu in Romania, and also a special choice of the German extreme right wing led by the von Hohenlohes, was also a problem to Hitler. He intensely disliked Mussolini and, once it was obvious Hitler was losing the war, began to fool around with the Soviets, the Americans, and the British. Hitler was very nervous that Horthy would withdraw Hungary from the Axis. At a meeting at Klessheim Castle, near Salzburg, Horthy and Hitler engaged in a violent quarrel; when Horthy boarded his special train to leave for Budapest, Hitler ordered a fake air-raid warning and had his troops throw a smoke screen around the castle; the train was forbidden to leave and Horthy became a prisoner. As a result, he promised loyalty to the Third Reich; but the instant he was back in Budapest, he began making peace negotiations with Moscow.

This was the last straw. On September 13, 1944, Hitler summoned Skorzeny, along with Generals Keitel and Yodl, Himmler, and Ribbentrop to the Wolf's Lair and ordered Skorzeny to occupy Horthy's Budapest headquarters and kidnap the Nazi-turned-Soviet Horthy at once.

Operating under the pseudonym of Dr. Solar Wolff, derived from his Werewolf assignment, Skorzeny flew to Budapest and began making inquiries so that he could determine details of the defenses of Horthy's citadel on Castle Hill. The hill bristled with armaments and was completely surrounded by troops; posing as a tourist, Skorzeny went everywhere, looking to see whether there was any spot where his aerial force could land. There was not. It was a very difficult situation. And a frontal assault was out of the question with so small a troop. Even when General Bach-Zelewski, of Hitler's anti-Partisan military operation, arrived in a private plane with a massive mortar gun, Skorzeny was uncertain.

Some other form of penetration was necessary. He discovered that Admiral Horthy's handsome son, Miki, was meeting with emissaries of Marshal Tito to discuss the Soviet alliance. Perhaps it would be possible to kidnap Miki, who was the admiral's only surviving boy and the apple of his eye, and hold him hostage in order to secure the Admiral's dubious loyalty.

Through his undercover team, Skorzeny found that Tito's men and Miki were to meet on October 15. He cased the building; two of his men took an apartment on the third floor. Some commandos hid in the apartment and others in the adjoining park, while others still were dressed up in German Army uniforms and patrolled the street. The raid was head on and violent. Skorzeny's men engaged the Hungarians in a blaze of gunfire. Although injured, Skorzeny threw a hand grenade into the lobby, causing marble slabs to crash onto the troops and block them off from the raiders. Skorzeny and his men grabbed Miki Horthy and rolled him into a rug, carried him down the stairs, and hurled him unceremoniously into a van. From there, he was tossed like so much luggage into a plane and flown to Vienna.

Next day, Edmund Veesenmayer, German emissary in Budapest, met with Horthy, who broke down in tears and promised to stop dealing with Russia. But it was too late. A radio announcement declared that peace had been made with the Soviets. Skorzeny asked for Horthy's abdication or the alternative of a full-scale attack on the castle. Horthy fled and placed himself under the "protection" of a Waffen SS general. In effect, this meant that Horthy was already in a surrender position.

Hitler was again delighted. Back at the Wolf's Lair, Skorzeny was asked to take a leading role in a major counteroffensive against the Allies, in which he would dress up with his men in American uniforms as a major act of deception during the Ardennes offensive. This activity was a triumph: many Americans died as a result, and soon Skorzeny was first on the Americans' most-wanted list. Back at Hitler's headquarters in late 1944, Skorzeny realized the war was already over, but his loyalty to the Führer was unwavering. He would do anything required of him. He undertook a series of secret missions, many of them in collaboration with Reinhard Gehlen, in charge of anti-Soviet espionage operations as chief of the Army High Command in the East.

Skorzeny entered a new and remarkable phase of his career. Martin Bormann and Himmler put him in charge of transferring the treasure of the Führer and his aides in gold, jewelry, and silver to safety where it could be used for the future. In Red Cross ambulances, he sent the treasure to burial places, along with two million American dollars, two million Swiss francs, and a five-million-gold-mark stamp collection. Some of it was hidden in mountains; more was sent through normal channels to Swiss banks or to South America by neutral vessel.

The role of the Red Cross in operating on both sides of the war as a neutral organization is certainly worthy of examination. General Robert C. Davis, head of the New York chapter of the Red Cross, was chairman of the aforementioned Transradio, which had throughout World War II leading American (Colonel Sarnoff), British, German, Italian, and Japanese members, who would be represented by proxy at board meetings in each other's nation for the duration. Also, the Red Cross played a special role after World War II in aiding and abetting the transfer of Nazis out of Europe, as is evidenced in a Department of State, Office of American Republic Affairs, report by Vincent La Vista in Rome to Herbert J. Cummings, of State, on July 14, 1947. Schellenberg's sworn statements to British Intelligence show that such figures as Carl Burckhardt and Count Bernadotte of the Red Cross played a crucial role in negotiated peace arrangements during the war. Skorzeny played a crucial role in transferring vast sums of major German companies, including Krupp, I.G. Farben, and Volkswagen, to safe holdings in Turkish, Spanish, and Portuguese banks. He dreamed of preparing an escape route for Hitler and envisaged flying him to safety in Buenos Aires.

Right to the end of the war, Skorzeny never stopped planning ways of protecting and aiding the Führer. Losing the war was a torture to him, and another frustration was that he never succeeded in carrying out his promise to capture or murder General Eisenhower. He was like a cornered wolf, struggling on almost to the last day of the conflict. But he knew the future meant nothing but trial and execution unless he could strike a deal with the hated Americans, whose uniforms he and his men had worn in France in 1944.

He advised the Americans of his whereabouts by note from a hiding place in the Austrian Tyrol. He climbed into an American jeep with a captain who barely understood him when he explained who he was but was very impressed when he finally found out. At Salzburg, Skorzeny surrendered himself officially and was subjected to search and interrogation. The 307th Battalion of the Counter-Intelligence Corps was in charge of him, as it was in charge of Klaus Barbie, Reinhard Gehlen, and Otto von Bolschwing. Like Barbie, Gehlen, and other high-ranking figures of the Third Reich, Skorzeny offered his services to fight communism. He knew that this offer was one that would be readily accepted in American circles. He wanted to join the American plan for the anti-Soviet bloc in Western Europe.

He was sent to Nuremberg, where he went through interrogations. Of all people, Avery Brundage, who had addressed America First meetings and had been responsible for United States participation in the Olympic Games of 1936, in Germany, was selected to interrogate him, a particular service that Brundage also performed for the U.S. Government in the instances of Fritz Wiedemann, Gehlen, and other treacherous figures. Apart from the fact that he actually said he had "never heard" of Ernst Kaltenbrunner, Brundage was poorly briefed. He utterly failed to bring out Skorzeny's responsibility for the mass liquidation of Americans or anything else inconvenient that might fall into the hands of the liberals or the Soviets.

One issue that was raised was Skorzeny's role in the Malmédy Massacre, in which one of his officers murdered one hundred Americans, but even this was swept under the carpet, and later, it is interesting to note, Senator Joe McCarthy defended the killers. General Donovan traveled to Nuremberg to talk to Skorzeny, a fact which, among others, was omitted from Anthony Cave Brown's biography of Donovan. Skorzeny was transferred to Dachau, where he was charged with aiding and abetting the murder of American prisoners and told he would stand trial. Investigations into his various contacts and correspondence established that he had a network of special commandos and SS men all over Europe, most of them members of his original operation.

The trial, which took place in August of 1946, was something of a farce. It was claimed that insufficient evidence was available and the prosecution was muddled; Skorzeny was acquitted despite his role as a war criminal. Released, Skorzeny found that the Danish and Czech governments were demanding him for trial themselves, but the United States refused to extradite him to Czechoslovakia, and Denmark suddenly dropped its charges. Again, Skorzeny offered his services against communism. At the same time, he was making contacts with SS men who promised him employment with Soviet Intelligence. Wanted for denazification hearings, he was imprisoned temporarily in Darmstadt, but his network closed in and, inevitably, a rescue plan was organized. On July 27, 1947, three of his SS specialists traveling by car with American military license plates and military-police uniforms provided by sympathetic Americans, arrived at the Darmstadt Internment Camp. The leader presented official orders, forged through those same American contacts, to the guard, with instructions to take Skorzeny to Nuremberg. Very smoothly, Skorzeny was conducted to the gate, and vanished.

Like Gehlen, Skorzeny now became a most crucial figure in the secret war against the Soviet Union. According to several sources, Skorzeny was taken to Georgia, U.S.A., to demonstrate an experimental flying apparatus used in instant rescues. He was seen in Madrid, and in Bavaria, conferring with CIC officers; finally, he joined up directly with Gehlen, who became the chief spy master against the Soviets in Europe. Skorzeny's movements were mysterious and complex until, in 1950, he was photographed unexpectedly by a hotshot cameraman for the magazine *Ce Soir*. Jews, and other French and Russian victims of the Nazis attacked the fact that he was alive and well and living in Paris with an attractive brunette, and when *Le Figaro* published parts of his reminiscences, a Communist demonstration swept through the newspaper building and threw the staff into the street.

When the head of the Sûreté was approached by a citizens committee to ask what Skorzeny was doing in France, the answer was that he was cleared by the Americans. This was satisfactory to nobody and kicked up violent anti-American feeling in Paris. Skorzeny returned to Germany, to find that the Korean War was on and anti-Communists were considered very valuable. He was now firmly under the protection of the CIA and Konrad Adenauer, who was busy restoring many major Nazis to high office. Whitewashed by the American press, Adenauer was more responsible than anyone else for restoring the second-level hierarchy of the Nazi Party to postwar political positions in Germany.

Skorzeny moved to Spain, where he enjoyed a warm welcome from the Spanish Government. There he met with the indispensable, American-educated Hjalmar Horace Greeley Schacht, a crucial figure in the formation of the international spiderweb of Nazi economic power, who had made mincemeat of prosecutor Robert Jackson at the Nuremberg trials and had been acquitted. Schacht and Skorzeny entered work together to reconstruct the industrial alliances with Spain which had been partly undermined due to wartime communication problems. He also worked with the leading Belgian nationalist Léon Degrelle, who had escaped execution for high treason in Belgium and was now assisting Klaus Barbie. Others who joined the group in Madrid were many Nazi figures amnestied by the U.S. high command in Europe. Skorzeny used these high-level contacts to aid and abet his comrades of the SD and SS in exile. Huge, cheerful, untouched by his experiences, Skorzeny was the toast of the Nazi faction in Spain, and entertained lavishly with exile funds.

He fell in love with and married Schacht's niece Ilse and moved into a magnificent villa in a fashionable section of the Spanish capital. Ilsa Skorzeny was believed to be representing Skorzeny and Schacht in arms transhipments to Egypt, while Skorzeny himself schemed against the British and made deals with the Americans for arms shipments. Skorzeny made special deals with Voest (also known as United Austrian Iron and Steel works), representing Voest in Latin American countries; the chief clerk of Voest was Göring's brother-in-law. Skorzeny was still under CIA cover. He never stopped arranging with Schacht for the distribution of funds to the Nazi old guard.

He organized Die Spinne, the Spider organization, which financed escaped Nazi war criminals via Switzerland, Austria, and Italy, often with Nazi buried treasure or sales of art that had been taken from Jews in occupied territories. Several of the team of the Spider operated by driving army newspaper *Stars and Stripes* trucks; in Italy, Adolf Eichmann made use of a Skorzeny contact via Roman Catholic channels that also aided Trifa and Von Bolschwing. The powerful Odessa organization, for Nazis in exile, centered on Skorzeny, and many industrialists helped. Skorzeny set up special cells in Hungary under the Hungarian Nazi Dr. Karoly Ney. Skorzeny also, predictably, found a useful headquarters in Ireland, via IRA connections. In 1951, the distinguished French director of motion pictures Barbet Schroeder, who was living in Ibiza, in the Balearics, recalled that the talk of the island was Skorzeny's residence aboard the yacht *Zaca*, owned by Errol Flynn. He himself saw a man answering Skorzeny's description boarding and leaving the yacht. Flynn had been a contact between the IRA and German Intelligence in the 1930s, according to MI5 files at the Ministry of Defence, in London.

Skorzeny moved to the Middle East in 1953. It was a haven for Nazism: Schellenberg's special agent the Grand Mufti of Jerusalem had operated extensively in the region during World War II. Egypt was especially fertile ground. King Farouk had been intricately involved with the Nazis, and when the CIA under Allen Dulles encouraged Gamal Abdel Nasser to become the essential dictator of the country, there was an even more favorable atmosphere for Nazis. Gehlen, Schacht, and Dulles were mutually involved in the selection of Skorzeny as chief military adviser to

General Mohammed Naguib. The intrinsic anti-Semitism of this cabal was helpful in an Arab country; Gehlen and Skorzeny injected new life into the Egyptian Secret Service by supplying it with former SS officers under Dulles's authorization.

Skorzeny laced Egypt with Nazis including Adolf Eichmann, General Oskar Dirlewanger, known as the "Butcher of Warsaw" for his mass murder of the Jews, and Leopold Gleim, Himmler's chief in Poland. Skorzeny's medical staff for his new recruits was Buchenwald medical officer Dr. Hans Eisele, assisted by Dachau Medical Officer Heinrich Willermann. In many conferences with Lieutenant Colonel Nasser, Skorzeny more and more successfully built up the Egyptian Gestapo. He was at every level authorized not only by the CIA but by the Adenauer government. Skorzeny even trained a four-hundred-unit SS veteran battalion that trained Palestine terrorists to attack Israel through the Gaza Strip. At the same time, Egypt directly consolidated connections to American Nazism. Such violently anti-Semitic American publications as Gerald L. K. Smith's *The Cross and the Flag,* Gerald B. Winrod's *The Defender,* and Frank Britton's *The American Nationalist* were widely distributed by the Arab League, and Egypt's ambassador to the United Nations personally bought a hundred subscriptions to *The Cross and the Flag.* Allen Zoll, of the fascistic National Council for American Education, was received by Naguib in Cairo, followed by the equally dangerous Merwin K. Hart of the National Economic Council. In conference with Egypt's leaders, these men confirmed Skorzeny's full-scale attack on the Jews, thus endearing themselves to their hosts. Concentration camps were set up under Skorzeny to liquidate the Egyptian Jews. The remnants of Rommel's Afrika Korps were enlisted by him for desert warfare, and his security police were almost all from the SS and handed over to Nasser intact.

Assassinations were commonplace. When Nasser took over as Prime Minister and Head of State in 1954, Skorzeny joined him in his pan-Arabism and laid the groundwork for his mass despoliation of Jews. They were imprisoned, stripped of their property, or driven into exile. Their shops, factories, firms and bank accounts were confiscated. A total of $122,000,000 worth of property was confiscated. Mass murder followed mass murder; when Skorzeny moved out, he left under Dulles' protection the equivalent of a Nazi government. It is worth noting that, during his reign, John Foster Dulles, Allen's brother, paid a visit as Secretary of State for Eisenhower and gave to Naguib a pearl-handled pistol inscribed with the words: "To General Mohammed Naguib from his friend, Eisen-hower." A few days later, Dulles received a Bible from Prime Minister David Ben-Gurion in Tel Aviv.

In 1957, Skorzeny traveled to Ireland and bought Martinstown House, Kilcullen, County Kildare, ironically from a British colonel who had fought against Skorzeny in the war. He trained the IRA in terrorist tactics.* He immediately spread out and bought, with the incomparable Nazi treasure, no less than seventy estates, the money carried via Alexander von Dornberg, formerly of the SD. Many high-ranking figures of the SD occupied the estates free of charge, and even their property taxes were paid for by the Nazis. From the Irish base, this massive SD operation functioned until severe criticism from the British aristocratic community that was being threatened by the IRA resulted in the group's departure.

Skorzeny returned to Germany once more and held an elaborate meeting of Odessa on January 25, 1957, at Kronenstrasse, in Stuttgart. Among those present were Eugen Gerstenmayer, of the German Government, who had arranged for former SS leaders to retain their ranks in German Intelligence (a measure passed into law); Paul Wegener, SD leader; Paul Hausser, Waffen SS general; and Goebbels' right-hand man, Werner Naumann.

Soon after, largely through Gerstenmayer's efforts, Adenauer authorized a measure allowing former SD and SS members who had served Himmler for a minimum of ten years a state pension. Unquestionably, Skorzeny used his influence. According to Simon Wiesenthal, there are ninety thousand SS war criminals alive today (1984); Wiesenthal discovered that Skorzeny was tied to many of them. He discovered that he was very much behind Franz Stangl, former commander of Treblinka, who had murdered four hundred thousand Jews at the camp. After years of working with Skorzeny and Gehlen in Egypt, Stangl went to Brazil, where Skorzeny found him a job with Volkswagen. Wiesenthal traced Skorzeny to his home in São Paulo, but at every level Skorzeny bribed the Brazilian civil service and police to protect Stangl. Wiesenthal struggled on through the mid-1960s. Then, at last, the Nazi hunter got a break: There was a new governor, Roberto Sodre. Sodre agreed to read the dossier, and Stangl was arrested on February 28, 1967. Skorzeny managed to arrange for one of his contacts to steal the records in Germany. But fortunately there were

* See Chapter 9.

duplicates at the Berlin Document Center, which were enough for Wiesenthal.

After a great many struggles and complexities, with Skorzeny fighting desperately to avoid Stangl's trial, Stangl finally was transferred to Germany, but he died in prison. Again and again, Skorzeny used his influence to protect Nazi after Nazi, most notably Josef Mengele, the notorious doctor at Auschwitz.

Skorzeny got Mengele out of Germany to Argentina along with Eichmann and with the protection of Evita Perón. Eventually, Skorzeny conducted Mengele to Paraguay, where he became security adviser to Paraguay's President, General Alfredo Stroessner. Skorzeny's headquarters was a hideout on a farm near Asunción. It was surrounded by armed guards and savage dogs.

Skorzeny's biggest defeat came with the kidnapping of Eichmann under Wiesenthal's guidance by the Israeli Secret Police. Skorzeny had never ceased to protect Eichmann but felt that he must announce publicly that he had not. He placed an advertisement in *Volunteer*, a Bonn, Germany, newspaper, saying that he had not helped Eichmann in his flight, but soon after the announcement appeared, he flew to Beirut, Lebanon, to hold a meeting at which large funds were raised for Eichmann's defense. Meanwhile, he continued to shelter Mengele.

Wiesenthal was still determined to catch Mengele. In 1964, SS leader Hubert Cukurs, called the Monster of Riga, who murdered thirty-two thousand Latvian Jews, worked with Skorzeny running a seaplane concession near Rio. He knew Mengele's whereabouts in Paraguay and offered to lead Israeli Intelligence to the spot where Mengele was hidden for $150,000. Unfortunately, Cukurs failed to secure an armed guard. Skorzeny got onto Cukurs and sent two agents from Düsseldorf to the informer. In February 1965, Cukurs's body was found in a trunk in Montevideo, horribly torn apart, with the skull smashed in.

In 1970, Skorzeny became ill. He suffered from constant back pain from Russian shrapnel and the crash landing in his glider during the Mussolini mission. Also, he no longer had the support of U.S. Intelligence and had to move constantly to avoid Israeli agents. At a clinic in Madrid, he learned that he had cancer of the spine. The operation was successful but it took weeks of agonizing therapy for him to walk again, and then the tumors spread through his system. He rallied sufficiently to support Juan Perón when he returned to power in Argentina in 1973, and he made all the arrangements for Evita's body to be brought from Italy to Buenos Aires as a symbolic support to her husband. When Perón died, in July 1974, Skorzeny saw to it that her embalmed body lay perfectly preserved in state beside the corpse.

Later that year, Skorzeny attended a Mass for the souls of Hitler and Mussolini along with his old Belgian collaborator Léon Degrelle. Skorzeny did not long survive that important occasion. He died on July 7, 1975, and was cremated. His ashes were interred with ceremony in Vienna.

✠✠✠✠✠✠ 22

A Nazi in the Pentagon

The involvement of Reinhard Gehlen, the great German spy master, in the efforts of American counterintelligence was an adventure in international intrigue for which it would be hard to find a parallel. Heinz Höhne, the German journalist and popular historian, wrote of Gehlen, "Nothing less than magical power was ascribed to this spy of the century; he allegedly knew everything; no steel safe or secret file seemed secure when he was around. Stories were woven around him whenever he appeared, noiseless on rubber-soled shoes, [his eyes] invariably concealed behind dark glasses. . . ." Gehlen's face, in a photograph that appeared on the cover of the German magazine *Der Spiegel* in September 1954, makes a strong impression: the eyes stare out directly, like the eyes of a ventriloquist's dummy; the forehead is immensely high, concealing a multitude of secrets; the nose is patrician and the ears too large for the face: the ears of a watchdog. The skin has a corpse-like whiteness, unlined and blank as the plastic skin of a doll. Like Schellenberg, Gehlen was as perfect a picture of a spy as any played by a German émigré actor in a Hollywood motion picture made during World War II.

Gehlen was born in 1902, the son of a lieutenant in an artillery regiment, at Erfurt, Germany. His father was obsessed with controlling and Germanizing the Slavic elements in the district, which was very close to Poland, and indeed when the family moved to Breslau, the obsession deepened. Moreover, Gehlen's father talked constantly of the problem of *Lebensraum*, the theme of living space which propelled Hitler and had existed since the days of Himmler's idol, Henry I of Saxony. He talked constantly of the *Drang nach Osten*, the drive toward the East, and he even wrote a book about this, calling for the incorporation of Slavic Europe into the German hegemony.

Gehlen was cool, expert, good at mathematics, and a skilled debater in high school; when he graduated, he served in the 6th Light Artillery Regiment in 1921. Like most of his fellow soldiers, he was painfully aware of the crippling terms of the Versailles Treaty, which restricted the Army to a mere hundred thousand men and cut its budgets and pay brutally to a minimum. Along with his hatred of the Slavs, this feeling of betrayal by the West rankled in him as fiercely as it did in Hitler.

Gehlen joined the Hanover Cavalry School and the commander's assistants training course in Berlin in 1933. He rose rapidly through the ranks during Hitler's remilitarization in breach of the Versailles Treaty, and by 1935 he was actually attached to the general staff and involved in planning and chart making. He was so successful that in 1936 he joined the Operations Section, and at the age of thirty-three he rose to be major, joining the 213th Infantry Division, under General Franz Halder, army chief of staff. Halder was a major choice of the German royalist clique to take over with Himmler in World War II.

Thus, Gehlen became associated with the extreme right wing that was opposed to Hitler. Halder deeply admired Gehlen and engaged him specifically for operations against the Soviet Union; significantly, Gehlen became, in 1940, head of the Eastern Group of Colonel Adolf Heusinger's Operations Section.

Heusinger shared Halder's opinion of Gehlen, who became consumed with the Russian issue. In April 1942, Gehlen headed the special organization of intelligence on the Eastern Front, setting up his own general mechanism to incorporate SD and Abwehr in use against the Soviets. He reorganized the existing intelligence unit known as Foreign Armies East, and began interrogating Russian prisoners of war in order to turn them around against Stalin. He managed to infiltrate the Baltic itself, parachuting in members of his unit to whip up partisan organizations, provide warnings of Russian counterattacks and movements, and supply information on the determination of Stalin to hold fast to Stalingrad. Unfortunately, Hitler took little note of many of his reports and seemed incapable of grasping the reality of the fact that Russia was destroying the German war machine. However, Gehlen achieved his purpose vis-à-vis

Himmler and Schellenberg by surpassing all other Western intelligence services in supplying a complete inside look at Russia's activities. Unlike Allen Dulles's reports from Switzerland, which were not only erroneous in many cases but delivered via a diplomatic code long since broken by the SD, Gehlen was usually faultless, and Schellenberg had the deepest appreciation of him. He said in his secret interrogatory report declassified in 1982, "He was an excellent General Staff officer who enjoyed all around esteem." Gehlen was Schellenberg's strongest supporter in the Army. However, Kaltenbrunner was jealous of Gehlen and hated his extraordinary hold over Hitler and Himmler.

Finally, Gehlen stumbled. In February 1945, he made the serious mistake of failing to predict an attack on the German Infantry by the Eleventh Ukrainian Army from the direction of Posen. Hitler flew into a rage at this failure, and Kaltenbrunner told Schellenberg at a Berlin lunch party, "This little sausage of Von [sic] Gehlen now has got to go west too —he probably relied too much on your poor intelligence service." Gehlen met with Schellenberg privately in March and told him that he estimated that military resistance would last another two months. Then the end had to be expected. Preparations would have to be made. Gehlen told Schellenberg that the only man with the necessary imagination to undertake the task he had in mind was Himmler. Himmler should be commander of the Home Army and build up with Gehlen and Schellenberg a special force built on the lines of the Polish resistance movement. Gehlen offered to put his army contacts directly under Schellenberg. He said he would pretend to take four weeks' leave and would set up the arrangements in private. He would do a comprehensive survey of the Polish Resistance Force in order to determine the correct approach. The evening ended with Schellenberg assuring him he would take the matter up with Himmler. Of course, it was essential that Kaltenbrunner not know about these arrangements. The purpose was identical with that pursued by Schellenberg with Dulles and Donovan: the rise to power of Himmler as Führer of the Fourth Reich.

Ten days later, Schellenberg had prepared with Gehlen a thorough survey of the structure of the Polish Resistance Force. Armed with this, Schellenberg went to Himmler, who dismissed the whole thing with a wave of the hand. Himmler said, "This is complete nonsense. If I should discuss this plan I would be the first defeatist of the Third Reich. This fact would be served boiling hot to the Führer. You need not tell this to

Gehlen. You need only explain to him that I strictly refused to accept the plan."

It is clear that Himmler was once more terrified that Hitler might find out what he had done with the Allies and liquidate him. When war ended and Hitler blew his brains out in the bunker, Gehlen inevitably gravitated toward the Americans. He knew how indispensable he would be against the Soviet Union; no doubt Schellenberg had already conveyed to him the gist of the Hohenlohe meetings with Dulles. As early as April 1945, Dulles had been advised by Fritz Kolbe, of the German Foreign Office, that Gehlen was a most useful contact—as useful as Schellenberg. Indeed, Gehlen had a complete set of microfilms of his massive intelligence operation with him in the Alps. Dulles learned that Gehlen had been trying to secure cooperation from U.S. high-level military counterintelligence circles in handing over his complete files and substantial organization to the United States. Many of these operatives were still in place in Russia and the Balkans. It is interesting that the CIC was quite prepared to deal with Skorzeny, Von Bolschwing, and others of that ilk, but the Corps was nervous about Gehlen; they did not fully understand his importance, because they did not have enough experts on Eastern Front matters to check him out.

Finally, William R. Phillip, a G2 colonel, decided to move on Gehlen and reported Gehlen's whereabouts, at the POW camp at Oberursel, to his commanding officer, Brigadier General Edwin L. Sibert. Sibert was chief of intelligence of the Twelfth U.S. Army Group and had already, under Dulles and Gero von Gaevernitz, employed Nazi officers for U.S. intelligence purposes.

Therefore, he was ideally placed to deal with Gehlen. Gehlen was anxious to save his neck and to join the U.S.A. in destroying the Soviet Union, at a time when Eisenhower was specifically encouraging a postwar U.S.-Soviet grand alliance. Gehlen gave Sibert a complete picture of his Foreign Armies East operation and warned Sibert that the Russians would immediately secure their Eastern European and Balkans hegemony into a Communist empire that "would result in all-out war against the Allies." Despite the fact that this statement was not supported by a single captured document and that Russia lay in exhausted ruins, as George F. Kennan has definitively told us, Sibert absorbed this information with gratitude. In defiance of Eisenhower's expressed policies, which were to secure the destruction of Nazism as well as support Russia as an ally,

Sibert instantly took this important package to Dulles. Dulles and General Donovan authorized a special kind of VIP to take charge of the Gehlen matter: a personage who, interestingly, fails to appear in the existing biographies of Gehlen.

This personage was Frank Wisner. He was a distinguished New York lawyer, a colleague of the appeaser Abram Stevens Hewitt. He was born in Laurel, Mississippi, in 1909 and received his B.A. from the University of Virginia, followed by a law degree from the same institution. From 1935 to 1941 he was a power in the Manhattan legal hierarchy, serving with the distinguished firm of Carter, Ledyard & Milburn.

Wisner joined the U.S. Naval Reserve in the fall of 1941; in 1943, Donovan enlisted Wisner in the OSS and sent him to the Balkans. At the end of the war, he was deeply concerned with anti-Soviet activities and was ideally experienced for the Gehlen connection. Via Sibert, Donovan, Dulles, and Wisner, it was decided that Gehlen should go to the United States to confer with the War Department on plans for infiltrating the Soviets. Again, it has to be said that this was entirely in contravention of official U.S. policy under President Harry Truman and supreme commander General Dwight D. Eisenhower.

In August 1945, General Walter Bedell Smith's private plane was used to fly Gehlen and five of his general staff to the American capital. They traveled in plain clothes, one of their members using a violin case for a suitcase. It is interesting to note that Bedell Smith was Eisenhower's chief of staff. Much honored, he was now embarking on an act for which he easily could have been court-martialed, but sufficient contacts existed in the State Department Visa Division and the INS to allow this Nazi group in.

Significantly, Allen Dulles made no mention of this matter, or even of Gehlen, in his books on the OSS.

The meetings were held in great secrecy at the War Department under Donovan. According to Heinz Höhne, among those in the group were Donovan's General George V. Strong, strategic analyst for the OSS; Brigadier General John R. Magruder, also of Intelligence; Professor Sherman Kent; New York lawyer Loftus Becker; and the well-known Wall Street figure Walter Reid Wolf. Almost all were wealthy Republicans obsessed with the Soviet threat; they were delighted with the opportunity to meet Gehlen and his group. For years afterward, efforts were made to have those present at the meetings disclose the facts, without success. Gehlen and his men stayed for almost a year, until July 1946. In June of that year, General Sibert inquired directly whether Gehlen could be used specifically for American purposes in Europe. The answer was in the affirmative.

The conditions were as follows: the OSS would finance the Gehlen organization outright, and the condition would be that nothing would harm West German interests. There was certainly no problem with that. Furthermore, the organization would not merely be an auxiliary of the OSS, but would obtain the same independence that it had had under Himmler. It would be strictly under Gehlen's control, answerable only to the U.S. authorities by Gehlen specifically via liaison. It would be required to gather intelligence only within the Eastern bloc, and when a sovereign German government was established it would be solely responsible to that government while at the same time, of course, maintaining its American connection.

The War Department—again acting contrary to Eisenhower's directives—set up a special board to back the operation. Loftus Becker and Sherman Kent, who later became crucial figures of the CIA, and Walter Reid Wolf were the civilian leaders. The budget for the first year was no less than $3.4 million of the unsuspecting American taxpayer's money. A crucial figure in these arrangements was Eric Waldmann, political scientist and intellectual.

Back in Germany, Gehlen set up his headquarters in the Taunus region between Falkenstein and Kronberg, at Kransberg Castle and a hunting lodge owned by Georg von Opel. Under Gehlen, his right-hand man, Hermann Baun, set up the organization in two parts, one involved in acquiring intelligence material and the other responsible for analyses. In the autumn of 1946, Gehlen began gathering Abwehr and SD officials; the CIC was jealous of the Sibert-Dulles conspiracy and tried unsuccessfully to secure former SD and Abwehr officers before Gehlen could get to them; they were simply returning to their jobs.

The organization spread from being a mere penetration behind the Iron Curtain to offering nonmilitary investigations in the Western Zone. Gehlen men traveled with false documents and false names. Often, they investigated political figures of whom Gehlen was suspicious. They in fact became the SD-Abwehr reincarnated.

They examined political parties and mass organizations, as well as alleged Communist cells. There was no question of any financial problem. The U.S. taxpayer coughed up well over a hundred million dollars between 1946 and 1950 to finance this American Gestapo, this conduit for SS men on the run. In the very early stages, commodities were surrendered in payment, beginning with nylon hose, soap, CARE packages, millions of cigarettes, and canned food. Each man was given fifteen hundred dollars per mission along with two or three cartons of cigarettes and a CARE package. Each operative was insured for one hundred thousand Reichsmarks. Counterfeiting stations were set up to supply false documents, Communist Party membership books, travel permits, and necessary bureaucratic rubber stamps.

In 1948, Gehlen was awarded the Gran Croce al Merito con Placca, one of the highest awards of the Sovereign Military Order of Malta, which has numbered among its members Colonel (later General) William Donovan, John McCone of the CIA, and James Jesus Angleton.

As the Cold War emerged, and rhetoric in Washington led by Secretary of State James F. Byrnes became more inflammatory, Gehlen's operation flourished. Walter Schellenberg, who had virtually created the whole approach that his former aide was developing, could gain little comfort from the fruition of his postwar dream, since he was apparently considered dispensable once British Intelligence had milked him, in London. He was in prison for a short period before his always poor health gave way, and he died in 1952.

Gehlen's operation prospered at the same time that John Foster Dulles and Allen Dulles and Brigadier General William Draper among others helped to spearhead the reconstruction of Nazi Germany. Under Chancellor Adenauer, a substantial number of outright Nazi ideologues emerged in positions of power. Thus, Gehlen was not merely running a surreptitious operation. He became a glamorous figure, meeting journalists under melodramatic circumstances in parks late at night in a black Mercedes, with blue-tinted glasses and an SS greatcoat slung around his shoulders, whispering, "I am Gehlen," with calculatedly feverish intensity.

German magazines fell over each other to write about this latter-day Dr. Mabuse or to offer inordinate sums for his memoirs. He had triumphed where such comparatively harmless figures as the befuddled Joachim von Ribbentrop had not.

Gehlen's main condition was that he be given a free selection of his fellow workers, who would be released at once from prisoner-of-war and internment camps; and his whole operation would be strictly German, all its top positions filled exclusively with German experts.

In the summer of 1946, Gehlen contacted EUCOM (U.S. Military Command in Europe), which subsequently endeavored to meet Gehlen's wishes to the fullest extent. He contacted Generals Blumentritt, and von Glasenapp, Lieutenant Colonel Baron von Wertheim (former commander of Hitler's escort battalion), and Lieutenant Colonel Maecker. In addition, he hired General Adolf Heusinger, whose task was to set up recruiting offices in cities of the U.S. Zone, beginning with four such offices in Munich in the winter of 1946, all of which were under the control of the U.S. Army Counter-Intelligence Corps. After a period, CIC became a rear cover for the Gehlen organization.

Word of Gehlen's organization soon reached leading SS figures living in hiding. They rushed to place themselves at Gehlen's disposal. And, more important, they needed jobs.

The Gehlen organization grew at great speed, with the takeover of double agents, the infiltration of the French Secret Service (see the chapter on Klaus Barbie), and the addition of the Abwehr—a phantasmal resurrection of Admiral Canaris' organization. Wolfgang Hoeher joined Gehlen in running the Abwehr section from the beginning of 1951. He was instructed to find former members of the Abwehr, the SD, and the Gestapo toward this end, despite (or because of) the fact (and this is typical of the operation) that, as his statements on record in Berlin clearly show, he was an outright Communist sympathizer and violently anti-American.

He helped to plant agents in the political and economic key positions of the Bonn Republic. His Abwehr agents sat in ministries, *Land* governments, the police, customs, political parties, and unions. Most of this investigative work was pointless, since the Adenauer government was so riddled with Nazis already that the chances of a stray Communist emerging were rare. In fact, in the whole of Hoeher's reports he points to no supercolossal exposé of a Stalinist in Bonn. One might add that the only Stalinist perceivable in his reports is their author.

Adenauer allegedly depended on the Gehlen service more than his own, and it was inevitable he would take it over. He seemed unaware of the fact that he was paying substantial salaries to individuals who were singularly ill-equipped to conduct high office, had never passed a civil-service exam, and whose experience of politics was largely restricted to rounding up Jews. The Economic Miracle thus had its comic and sinister underside. It was achieved more through the hardworking German people than through their corrupt and meaningless administration threaded through with spies who were mostly exchanging drinks with creatures of their own kind.

Many leaders of the Gehlen operation functioned in businesses, led by the Ernst Meissner Company, of Karlsruhe, which acted as fronts while supplying extensive employment. These companies engaged large numbers of Gestapo men, financial backers of small anti-Jewish cells, and overworked, hysterical Nazi activist women looking for Communists under every bed, including their own.

Aside from feeding hundreds of once out of work S.S. veterans, the Gehlen organization served one irrefutable function. It fed the paranoia of both the American and West German governments, while simultaneously supplying the Russians with intelligence and unlimited propaganda material to use against the West. The Russian secret service was equally ruthless and had many bureaucratic flaws, but it had the signal merit of not being highly advertised. It worked with intense secrecy, though gathering equally little of consequence, since, again, the merest examination of a magazine or newspaper provided almost all strategic information. Even the atomic secrets leak for which the Rosenbergs went to the electric chair had its origins in Lend-Lease and the shipment of crucial information to Russia on atomic science.

The West German police force covered for Gehlen at every turn. So vast was the flow of forged documents that it was very difficult to analyze, to distinguish, to discern one traveler from another. When so many secret agents were traveling about, it was a lucky man who was not brought in and questioned on his documents.

So extravagant was this operation that U.S. military airplanes were commandeered for Gehlen's chiefs of staff, flying incessantly between Berlin and Frankfurt free of charge. American military planes also carried couriers and secret mail. High-level conferences were held on financing; meetings took place at which American weapons were handed out; jobs were scattered like grain to fowl. The organization worked very closely with Allen Dulles's CIA. It ran a kind of friendly competition for agents and information with a maze of U.S. services including CIC and MID (the Military Intelligence Detachment).

Despite competition, Gehlen, through his contacts in displaced persons camps, tenement buildings, underground clubs, and bars, recruited the most substantial network of all. Offered amnesty from imprisonment, decent food, women, liquor, and a future brighter than years of abject poverty, imprisonment, or death, few could resist the snake charmer's flute. They flocked to the Swastika under the unique protection of the Stars and Stripes.

When a new recruit arrived at his castle headquarters, Gehlen greeted him with a handshake and a special speech followed by the recruit's solemn declaration of secrecy, loyalty, and a promise to honor the strict codes of the secret brotherhood. The most scrupulous conditions were laid down, identical with those required by the SS: the recruit must train to the point of athletic excellence, strength, and agility and must master the use of every conceivable camera and instrument of destruction.

Many members of the organization were Russians brought out of prisoner-of-war camps and returned to them fully trained. They would then proceed back to Russia, where they would supply bits and pieces of information on oil fields, grain supplies, arms entrepots, submarine yards, coal deliveries, tank construction. One agent was specifically assigned as a garbage-truck driver to pick up rubbish from the chemical works at great risk to his health and forward them to Gehlen. No doubt they carried much information to Russia as well.

It is known that even at this early stage the Soviets had penetrated the Gehlen organization. Also, he was carrying far too many former SS men just in order to give them a stipend, board, and lodging. He was a clear illustration of the corrupt nature of most secret intelligence organizations, which exist very often as old-boy networks without scruple, at the expense of the taxpayer and, far too often, of national security. His operation grew so massively that in 1948 he shifted it to a new headquarters in Pullach, south of Munich. He now operated from a compound completely encircled by a mile-long wall and containing close to two-score buildings, including twenty houses fully furnished, bunkers, huts, a mess hall, a dormitory, and shower rooms and toilets. It had once been the headquarters of Hess and Kesselring; the U.S. taxpayer was still paying.

Gehlen called this barracks Camp Nicholas, naming it after the patron saint of Christmas. Gehlen moved in with his wife, son, and three daughters; his house boasted the German Eagle straddling the front door. Soon, wives and children of his agents also moved in. Schools were set up on the spot. It was a city with laws unto itself; and Gehlen by now had a power far surpassing that which he had enjoyed in World War II.

He clashed with his liaison, Colonel Leabert of U.S. Military Intelligence and decided to remove himself from G2 in 1948, joining the newly formed CIA. He signed a contract with the CIA in June 1949 and entered into the field of economic and political espionage against the Eastern bloc. He worked constantly on the supposition that war between the United States and Russia was inevitable.

Under CIA protection, his organization flourished mightily. He fostered the delusion that Russia would advance beyond the frontiers allowed to it by the border lines of conquest in international law. Until very recent history, no such coercion or annexation took place, since the policy of Moscow was always infiltration and subversion in what are now called Third World countries and suppression of its new Eastern European colonies, rather than a direct onslaught on Western Europe. But it was in Gehlen's interest, and that of his employers, to foster this fantasy. And the delusion was also sustained by the Soviet propaganda machine, which Gehlen deliberately chose to take at face value for his own reasons.

By 1953, the Communist-riddled Neo-Nazi network was fully operative in Czechoslovakia, Hungary, Poland, and Romania. Poland was first priority. One piece of information "leaked" to the West came from Prague, involving a brand-new shell developed in Kharkov which had a simple but safe detonator; if the missile was used as a bomb, the detonator, without further setting, enabled it to explode either at some precisely precalculated height, giving a shrapnel effect, or on impact. When the CIA liaison asked for the actual detonator, Gehlen supplied it: he even produced a complete technical and ballistic report on it. This information was of course a useful propaganda weapon for the Russians. He trained Estonians, Lithuanians, and Latvians, paying them the sum of one hundred dollars a day for every day they spent in Russia. They had free medical care and life insurance, and during their training under the CIA in Bavaria they were given an income and free board and lodging. They were trained further at Fort Bragg, in North Carolina, in night swimming, skin and scuba diving, camouflage, and forest reconnoitering. They were also taught parachuting; once fully trained, they were returned to Gehlen for their missions.

Given Russian clothing, passports, coupons, work permits, and union membership cards, they were equipped with expensive watches and rubles sewn into their clothes for information barter. Since going across land would have been far too dangerous, they were used in converted E boats from World War II for shipment to the Baltic. Their commander was

CIA employee Nazi Rear Admiral Hans-Helmut Klose. The E boats were refitted in Portsmouth, England, and made their way to the Baltic salmon fisheries. They crept close to shore with muffled engines, and the spies came in on rubber dinghies. Then Polish Counter-Intelligence caught one of the E-boat squads. Further missions had to be canceled. Gehlen had to return to his use of émigrés as double agents.

On July 12, 1954, *Newsweek* published a story about Gehlen, pointing out that there was talk of transferring the whole organization to the West German Government on the basis of the terms originally agreed to in its initial charter. Chancellor Adenauer, who had already engaged Adolf Heusinger and other World War II Germans in high office, was very pleased to hear the news. Heusinger told Gehlen he should definitely make the move; obviously, he could not assume control of all U.S. Intelligence as he would have liked to do, since even the American public might have gotten on to this. Under the Adenauer government, he might achieve absolute power. And that, of course, was his final purpose.

In the early 1950s, the ORG was a German-American agency without any absolutely official position in Western Europe. Adenauer offered more. He met with Gehlen and they liked each other. Adenauer, whose skilled public-relations outfit, fostered by U.S. publicity, presented him as a decent enemy of Nazis, very much wanted to engage this most diabolical of Nazis.

Adenauer agreed that war between West and East was likely and that the Communists were a threat to West Germany. Gehlen promised to use his informants to pick up intelligence on Communist agitation in the Rhine and the Ruhr.

Further discussions took place. Already, before any official appointment, Gehlen had a position without portfolio in the German Government. Adenauer agreed to set up a special fund under chancellery provisions to support Gehlen's operation.

Still, Gehlen was reluctant to leave his American umbrella. He felt safe and comfortable under it. Then, in 1954, a change took place: Adenauer went to Washington, where he dined with Major General Arthur Trudeau, head of U.S. Army Intelligence. Trudeau said that he had become uneasy about the CIA-ORG connection and that he felt that there might be problems of moles. Gehlen was furious when Adenauer told him about this. He wrote to Allen Dulles as head of the CIA, and Dulles was equally inflamed. Dulles demanded that Eisenhower reprimand

Trudeau, and Eisenhower did. Trudeau was dismissed on the spot and sent off to Asia.

Eisenhower's action in this matter is a total reversal of his earlier stance, but by now he had grown into a hardened realist. Nevertheless, Gehlen did have a problem. He was in fact in constant danger of his operation being publicly exposed. Soon after, the press revealed that a double agent had in fact penetrated the organization—he was one of many, of course. His name was Hans Joachim Geyer, who wrote detective novels under the pen name Henry Troll. He began work as an investigator in East Germany; then he was bought by Soviet Counterespionage and turned around. He photographed all the documents in his safe, and the material was smuggled into East Berlin. He made a slip. When he applied for a new secretary, he met the applicants in cafes instead of in offices, making rather surreptitious inquiries about their background. One girl was irritated by his sinister manner and thought he might be in the white-slave traffic. She reported him to the West Berlin police, who arrived in his absence on the night of October 29, 1953. When he came back, he saw that they had been there and fled with his documents to East Berlin. This act of panic disclosed the whole mole operation. The disclosure wrought havoc in the organization, and the headlines did not help. Gehlen then handed his operation over to the German Government—and thus passes out of the pages of this chronicle; meanwhile, Gehlen's boss also benefited from assistance by the Allies, even acquiring the support of President John F. Kennedy and his brother Bobby.

General Adolf Ernst Heusinger was a career military officer from the beginning.* He rose from the rank of ensign in the German Imperial Army to the powerful position of chief of operations and plans for the High Command of the German Army in World War II.

Born in 1897 in Holzminden, Germany, Heusinger was descended from a distinguished family of churchmen and jurists. Enlisted in the armed forces in 1914, at the age of seventeen, he became a platoon leader and was wounded at Verdun and held as a prisoner of war in 1918 after winning two Iron Crosses for bravery.

By 1932, he was a captain and was brevetted major to the Army High Command. A colonel in 1938, he was appointed by Hitler chief of the Army High Command Operations Division in 1940.

---

* I am indebted to Charles Allen Jr. for the substance of this material.

He classically represented that group which sought the continuing power of Germany as a world force and who retained a vision of the hegemony of the Third Reich on the international scene. He fostered the mythology of independence of Hitler and the Nazi Party, thus protecting himself if the Third Reich collapsed, while at the same time serving Hitler well, and indeed being directly under his control. He was placed in charge of Operation Sea Lion, the proposed invasion-of-England plan, which called for a landing of a quarter of a million German troops in southeastern England and the rapid seizure of London. Heusinger was to be responsible to Colonel General Halder, chief of the German General Staff, who was the choice of the Princess Stefanie Hohenlohe to bring about a negotiated peace in 1940.

By World War II, Heusinger was at the highest level of the German General Staff. By 1944, he was very much in unofficial charge of the extraordinary Gehlen operation. At the end of the war, he skillfully turned coat and emerged unscathed from the early interrogatory stages of the Nuremberg war crimes trials. He provoked the contempt of Göring, among others, when he provided the statements needed to add a weight of evidence against the accused. He was cleared as a war criminal and went around calling himself "an American consultant," a term later echoed by the State Department in importing him to the United States.

Although he was frequently listed as one of those who planned the abortive assassination of Hitler in 1944, he was in fact one of the few who stood by the Führer in his hour of need. He knew of Hitler's lust for power, and it is estimated that he was responsible for liquidating some eight hundred thousand Jews on the Eastern Front under Hitler's personal instruction. Colonel General Jodl, his immediate superior, was hanged for those crimes on October 16, 1946, and Heusinger went free. He was lucky that, like Schellenberg, he was on the second rung of power and virtually unknown.

When Heusinger was released, in 1948, he was part of the Bureau Gehlen; his old subordinate had given him a job even when he was still in prison. During a mere two years in jail, he was able to be a useful Nazi contact, like Skorzeny in Dachau. Gehlen, following thirteen months of briefing at the War Department, was the first to give Heusinger a real taste of what power in the United States hierarchy might mean. And because Heusinger had a special knowledge of the Russian region, liaising with Schellenberg and using Schellenberg's ITT operation, he would undoubtedly be useful to the Americans.

Heusinger spent three years with Bureau Gehlen. He helped Gehlen reconstitute the Gestapo under American cover. He also helped create a new German General Staff and encouraged Gehlen in setting up the special bureau when Germany became a republic under Adenauer in 1955.

Heusinger accepted Adenauer's invitation to plan the new West German Army at the same time that Gehlen set up his own network.

Heusinger reached his apotheosis on April Fool's Day 1961, when he appeared, resplendent in uniform, as the central figure of a gala occasion. He became the chairman of the Permanent Military Committee of the North Atlantic Treaty Organization at an elaborate ceremony in Washington's State Department Building. President John F. Kennedy, accompanied by General L. L. Lemnitzer, chairman of the Joint Chiefs of Staff, and Admiral of the Fleet Earl Mountbatten, opened the meeting. It was the first convocation of NATO's Permanent Military Committee. The President warmly welcomed the Nazi chairman and announced that NATO would now be allowed contributions of nuclear arms as a fourth power.

Thus was achieved the fulfillment of the dreams of those middle-level German Gestapo, SS, SD, and military commanders who were perfectly happy to see their inconveniently famous leaders perish from cyanide capsule or hangman's noose. For those the public did not know, and therefore could not identify, the future was unassailably bright.

✳✳✳✳✳✳✳ 23

Postwar Activism

Immediately after World War II, Nazi activism in America continued apace. Such Fascists as Merwin K. Hart, of the Constitutional Educational League, and Gerald L. K. Smith proceeded without interruption in their various activities. In May 1951, Smith's *The Cross and the Flag*, which had not been interrupted by the inconvenient advent of World War II, reproduced an article from an early (1915) issue of the United States Military Academy *Howitzer Year Book*, which gave a description of Dwight D. Eisenhower as a Jew. The article stated that Eisenhower was a "Swedish kike" and otherwise vilified him in the most scabrous manner. Harry S Truman was also branded a Jew; his middle name became Solomon.

The Reverend Gerald B. Winrod, of Wichita, Kansas, also emerged with "irrefutable proof" that Eisenhower was the candidate of Jewish plotters. His magazine *The Defender*, filled with statements of this kind, achieved a remarkable circulation of one hundred thousand in 1952. Leon de Aryan, of San Diego, California, made identical statements in the pages of *The Broom*, and so did Stephen Menoff in *American Commentator*. Eisenhower was known as the kikes' Ike, and leaflets were printed under the name *Ike Eisenhower, the Swedish Jew*.

Senator Joe McCarthy's proselytizer Joseph P. Kamp also maintained attacks on Eisenhower in his magazine *Headlines*, which contained equally virulent onslaughts on Norman Thomas, Sidney Hillman, and Anna Rosenberg. On the other hand, Gerald L. K. Smith and several other Fascists were keenly in support of General Douglas MacArthur and fought for his nomination for President in 1952. Students of history may recall that MacArthur was mentioned by the 1934 conspirators who sought to overthrow the government as a possible alternative to General Smedley D. Butler of the Marines as President.* MacArthur did not consent to any such nomination for a so-called third party, but his name was still used on the tickets. Vivien Kellems, who, it will be recalled, had corresponded through World War II with the Nazi agent Count von Zeidlitz in Buenos Aires and had fought personal income tax, was named as Vice President by the so-called Constitution Party; another nominee was California State Senator Jack Tenney.

After Eisenhower's inauguration, the Constitution Party kept up its attack. Senator McCarthy had its full endorsement during the Fort Monmouth scandal, when he used "evidence" of a Communist spy ring at the fort "in order to flush it free of Jews." Again and again, anybody Jewish in federal or state politics was crucified by the various organizations, including Operation America Inc. and For America, resurrected versions of America First, with national and foreign policies, boards, and substantial financing. In May 1954, Colonel Robert McCormick of the Chicago *Tribune*, General Robert E. Wood, and Dr. George Stuart Benson were featured at a luncheon of For America in Chicago. The organizing committee was made up of Burton K. Wheeler, Hamilton Fish, and John T. Flynn, among others. The policy was no longer isolationist, in view of the "Russian menace." Father Coughlin bestowed his dubious blessings upon the occasion.

The organizations proliferated in the 1950s to a degree almost inconceivable even in the careless rapture of the early 1940s. There was the Congress of Freedom, not to be confused with the more intellectually respectable CIA-connected Congress for Cultural Freedom, and the aggressive group headed by Dan Smoot, of Dallas, a self-styled authority on every aspect of communism, whose favorite targets were Ed Murrow, Jack Kennedy and, needless to say, Eleanor Roosevelt. There was H. L. Hunt, worth approximately three billion dollars, with an income of fifty million dollars a year, whose Life Line Foundation received a postal subsidy and a tax exemption as a religious organization.

Life Line had three hundred radio stations and fifty-five television

* See my book *Trading with the Enemy* (1983).

stations, emitting a constant stream of Nazified propaganda in collaboration with Dan Smoot, Merwin K. Hart, and Gerald Smith. The John Birch Society climbed on the bandwagon.

There was the Liberty Amendment Committee of the U.S.A., headed by Willis E. Stone, who should have known better, since he was in the direct line of Thomas Stone, a signer of the Declaration of Independence.

Another figure of this group was Benjamin H. Freedman, of New York, backer of the publication *Common Sense*—a misnomer if ever there was one.

As we now know, Nazis were being restored to high levels under the Adenauer regime in Germany with the approval of the Truman and Eisenhower administrations. In February 1950, the House passed a bill to admit persons who had been members of Nazi, Fascist, or other non-Communist organizations abroad (the bill stated that such membership had to be shown to be "involuntary," whatever that might mean).

Meanwhile, there were sporadic outbursts of neo-Nazi violence in the United States itself. On November 10, 1952, police smashed a Nazi storm troopers' club in New Orleans, held nine, and confiscated swastikas, arms caches, and torture instruments. A similar outbreak was discovered in Pennsylvania when teenage boys wearing Nazi armbands were caught in a violent raid on a synagogue.

In 1957, 1958, and 1959, other small cells of student insurrectionists were discovered. But it was not until the full-scale activity of George Lincoln Rockwell that the worst demonstrations took place.

The Sixties Führer

Few people noticed the dark, muscular man in a white shirt as he backed his automobile out of a shopping center in Arlington, Virginia, on the afternoon of August 26, 1967. He looked like a vacuum-cleaner salesman or store clerk; he had just been to the laundromat, where he had chatted informally with two of the customers. As he left the parking lot, two shots rang out, fired in rapid succession from the roof of the shopping center. The laundromat's owner, J. W. Hancock, saw the man in the white shirt open the car door and fall on his back, covered with soap flakes. Hancock ran over to him and saw that the man's head and chest were bleeding. Customers from the laundromat and neighboring shops noticed a small, stocky man in a rumpled black suit racing across the roof.

Mrs. Louis M. Burgess, whose house was on a corner of the street, glanced up from her kitchen sink to see the same man trying to make his way down a drainpipe into her yard. Her boxer dog bit at the youth's feet and he shouted furiously; he fell down the wall and hit the yard painfully. Recovering, he vaulted the wall and ran along the street to a bus stop. A police officer cruising in his squad car noticed him, badly shaking and limping from the fall, and recognized him instantly as a close associate of the dead man. He arrested him when he began running down the street.

The murdered man was the remarkable George Lincoln Rockwell, who single-handedly revived nazism in the United States in the 1960s. While many Nazis, imported from Europe to be trained in scientific or counterespionage activities, were still in the country and had been granted their citizenship, Rockwell was too publicly visible to be protected by the anti-Communist forces. He made the mistake of being flagrant from the beginning, of attracting the same kind of publicity that had been sought by Kuhn and Kunze, Schwinn and Klaprott in the 1930s.

Rockwell was born in 1919, the son of a vaudeville comedian, Doc Rockwell. Born in a trunk, George Lincoln early acquired a theatrical flair that was to prove his undoing in later years. Despite anti-Semitism, which was part of his nature from the first, he often boasted of having been petted by Groucho Marx at the age of three. He was a poor student, and his early schooling at Hebron Academy, in Maine, was less than impressive. However, his sturdy physique earned him respect on the football field. He graduated with poor grades from Brown University, having become known for the violence and brutality of his artwork in painting class: his drawings and paintings were saturated with images of death and destruction. Eager for action, impatient, nervous, high-strung, and edgy, Rockwell enlisted in the Naval Air Corps in World War II. Later, he expressed regret at having sunk two U-boats; although he enjoyed the physical pleasure of flying, he detested the fact that he had to punish Hitler's servants. His guilt over his war experiences thrust him into his career of nazism later on.

He seemed headed for a career similar to that of his famous namesake Norman Rockwell when he won a thousand-dollar poster contest sponsored by the National Society of Illustrators in 1948. He was entirely at home in the world of artists, but his sudden calling up for the Korean War damaged his career, and he developed his intense hatred of communism while on service in the Orient. He attended a speech in San Diego given by the Reverend Gerald L. K. Smith, who urged his audience to read the holy pages of *Mein Kampf*. On duty in Iceland, Rockwell was mesmerized by Hitler's memoirs and took his second wife, Thora, to Berchtesgaden for their honeymoon. They wandered, deeply fascinated, through Hitler's Eagle's Nest.

In Washington in the 1950s, Rockwell devoted himself to stirring up anticommunism through an organization which became known as The Die Hards. Later, he formed the AFCO, or American Federation of Conservative Organizations, with a headquarters in Arlington. In an article in *The American Mercury* for January 1957, he charged that the American Government had "socialized Iceland," and he expressed his support for Senator McCarthy's policy of exposing Communist sympathizers. In

1957, Rockwell worked for another right-wing, fanatical organization known as The United White Party; a year later, he was a member of the National Committee to Free America from Jewish Domination.

He was financed by the extremely reactionary, wealthy Harold Noel Arrowsmith, of Baltimore. He duped Arrowsmith into investing heavily in him; Arrowsmith gave him a fee of a thousand dollars to lead a picketing line of Fascists at the gates of the White House. Rockwell carried a sign which read, "Save Ike [President Eisenhower] from the Kikes." When Arrowsmith decided he had had enough of Rockwell's hysterical tantrums, the anti-Semitic but middle-of-the-road financier dropped him. Rockwell invaded Arrowsmith's home during the businessman's absence. He defied eviction notices and displayed Nazi flags all over the place. Angry Jews threw bombs at the house, but Rockwell was uninjured. It took a whole year for Arrowsmith to get Rockwell out of his home.

Rockwell set up his headquarters in Arlington and sought members. He began distributing leaflets headed "American Nazi Party." One of his chief theses was that blacks should be shipped back to Africa with money raised from Jews who had been dispossessed. He and his cohorts began to hold public meetings in Washington; at last, as Rockwell had hoped, the press began to take notice. Like his predecessors of the 1930s and 1940s, Rockwell was fortunate that he was protected by the First Amendment. When he sought permission to give a lecture in Union Square, New York City, on July 4, 1960, the liberal-minded Public Awareness Society tried to have him stopped. There was a hearing on the matter following Rockwell's First Amendment appeal on June 22, 1960, in the Supreme Court of the State of New York. Judge Vincent A. Lupiano presided. A large number of Jewish protesters were present, angrily shouting at Rockwell and his storm troopers; some of the Jews had survived Auschwitz and Belsen and were dressed in their striped prison pajamas. Much to Rockwell's delight, there was a full contingent of radio and television interviewers present. Asked if he would have 80 percent of all Jews murdered on his acquisition of national power, Rockwell said that he would indeed take care of the matter. Several people screamed, "Kill him!" and the police had to throw a cordon around Rockwell in order to get him into the courtroom.

Mayor Wagner took over the case as special magistrate and told Parks Commissioner Newbold Morris that Rockwell must be forbidden to give a public address. Wagner's rationale was that there would be a riot and

Rockwell would be thrown out of town. He said that Rockwell would preach racial hatred and cause a public exhibition of violence that would be unacceptable. However, in an editorial the next day, the New York *Times* was adamant that Rockwell should be given a chance to speak—that to deny him the opportunity was a total abrogation of the First Amendment.

Attorney Lester Fahn of the Jewish War Veterans swore out a warrant for Rockwell's arrest. Although the warrant was not acted upon, it proved effective in keeping him out of New York for several years. However, Rockwell returned to Washington and kept up rallies in public parks that were greeted with mingled boos and cheers.

On January 14, 1961, Rockwell was in Boston, where he and his gang picketed the movie *Exodus*, a story of Jewish immigrants to Israel following World War II. No sooner had he arrived than the crowd of fifteen hundred people standing in line attacked him with stones and eggs. Several police managed to seize him and rush him through the back of the theater into a patrol car; three others of his group were similarly "rescued" and taken to the precinct for protective custody. Others of the troopers were wandering about, having lost their way to the theater; they were rounded up and run out of town.

Rockwell and his men moved to New Orleans, where they began a tour of the southern states in a bus with "We Hate Jew Communism" written on the side. They picketed *Exodus* whenever possible, carrying banners that read, "America for Whites and Gas Chamber for Traitors." Jailed in New Orleans, Rockwell went on a hunger strike for five days. When he was released on bail, he cabled his fellow troopers, who had scattered to surrounding towns: START EATING AND GOD BLESS YOU. SIEG HEIL.

At the end of January 1961, Rockwell was invited to speak at a rally of a right-wing Australian group on May 1 in Sydney. Australian Minister of Immigration Alexander Downer flatly refused to grant him a visa. Prime Minister Robert Menzies concurred. Rockwell, who was delighted by Australia's all-white immigration policy, was severely disappointed.

In July 1961, two of Rockwell's Gauleiters were arrested for handcuffing and third-degreeing a Jewish high school student. In 1965, he was involved in several grotesque incidents: He made a public announcement that he would not pay income tax. In the meantime, a related group bombed a synagogue in Bridgeport, Connecticut, painted the word "Jew" on the front doors, and issued inflammatory leaflets. When there was a sitdown of white and negro youths at the White House, protesting their conditions, two Rockwell men aggressively picketed and tried to disrupt the group.

In 1962, Rockwell was planning a massive rally as early as January to celebrate Hitler's birthday, in April.

In March, three of his party members were arrested for illegally wearing army uniforms while picketing a Communist rally. Other members picketed a Young Americans for Freedom rally in New York City; while Rockwell was visiting the San Diego State College campus, a student struck him violently in the face. The FBI was alerted to a bomb threat against Rockwell on an American Airlines flight two days later.

A Senate committee on un-American activities heard various Nazi Party officials testify that they had been muzzled for refusing to remove lapel swastikas. Rockwell made so violent an appearance at the hearing that he was ejected; meanwhile, his proposed Hitler-birthday rally had to be canceled when Boston officials refused to rent him the Boston Arena.

He tried to go to Great Britain to join London Nazi Colin Jordan at a rally in Gloucestershire. The British Government forbade him entry, but he arrived anyway via Ireland. He was ordered deported at once. He was seized in London following a violent incident at the Gloucestershire rally in which the villagers of Guiting Woods raided the meeting, wrecked the tents, and tore down the swastika flag, one member being injured by a storm trooper's bullet.

Back in Washington, Rockwell had seven of his men picket the White House in protest; another member vigorously assaulted Dr. Martin Luther King, Jr. Rockwell appeared on a New York radio station, in a staged address to party members who impersonated "cursing, howling Jews" who artificially heckled him. Whenever any attempt was made to stop Rockwell's flagrant savagery, the ACLU stepped in and outright forbade any further interference. Few people could vie with Rockwell in terms of headline grabbing; one of these was "Captain" Robert A. Lloyd, who ran into the House of Representatives in blackface and a stovepipe hat screaming, "Long live Rockwell," and asking to be seated as a Mississippi congressman in a hideous parody of a "coon" accent.

On February 9, 1966, Rockwell was at last arrested on a disorderly conduct charge for rioting that month in New York, and by a stroke of fate he was hauled before a black judge and defended by a Jewish lawyer.

He was told to stand trial in New York City. The arrest was attacked by the Ku Klux Klan. The Jewish defender, Martin Berger, got Rockwell out on one hundred dollars bail posted by a storm trooper. A preliminary hearing was scheduled for April 11 before Criminal Court Judge Neal P. Bottiglieri. Berger moved to dismiss the complaint on the ground that Rockwell's statements were protected by the First Amendment. Moreover, he said, six years had elapsed since the first offense—overlooking the later ones.

The trial was constantly delayed while Rockwell fretted over his inactivity in his so-called barracks in Arlington, Virginia. It was just a rundown white house feebly surrounded by barbed wire. He would sit at night with his party leaders, grumbling about the niggers and the kikes despite the fact that he had a Jewish lawyer—and he had chosen that lawyer himself.

The trial at last took place in New York City in June. Jerome Cohen, counsel to the Jewish War Veterans, initiated the prosecution. He charged that Rockwell had inflamed the crowd to Nazi activism. The defense called for a dismissal of the charge on the basis of free speech and cited Justice William O. Douglas's "clear and present danger" stricture. The bench produced its own precedents and citations. Rockwell had cause to smile. He sat calmly in the courtroom while the judge and the prosecutors upheld the right to free speech which he himself had done everything to remove. However, he became increasingly bored before the trial reached its foregone conclusion in his acquittal. He was free to proceed as he chose, to influence American opinion.

He did not live long to enjoy his freedom. On August 25, 1967, his Goebbels, John Patler, whom Rockwell had dismissed that March for fomenting dissent between fair-skinned and dark-skinned members, slew him in the parking lot. Permission was given by the Department of Defense for him to be buried in Nazi uniform at Culpeper Cemetery, in Virginia, but the Party members at the funeral were not allowed to wear swastikas. Rockwell was buried with military honors following a sixty-five-mile procession.

Patler went through three psychiatric tests and finally was allowed to stand trial for homicide. He was found guilty on December 15, 1967, and condemned to twenty years in prison.

George Lincoln Rockwell left a legacy. Nazi outbreaks of violence occurred for many years after his death. The National Socialist Party of America, led by Frank Collin, headquartered in Chicago, was protected by the First Amendment at one court hearing on its legality after another. It demonstrated constantly in the streets of Skokie, Illinois, in the late 1970s. The ACLU challenged all ordinances that called for fines or imprisonment for displays of militant power with swastika flags and SS-like uniforms. Forty thousand of Skokie's seventy thousand residents were Jewish, and seven thousand of those had suffered in the concentration camps of Hitler's Germany.

When a July 4 march was announced in 1977, Rabbi Meir Kahane announced there would certainly be violence. It was alleged that one neo-Nazi had actually killed a Jew, Sidney Cohen, by forcing him to ingest hydrogen cyanide, a poison used at Auschwitz.

The July 4 march was canceled when threats from Jewish activists terrified Collin and his storm troopers. Finally, an appellate court forbade marching with swastikas despite widespread ACLU protests. Late in July, some of Collin's men were charged with being involved in a violent antiblack demonstration; rocks and bottles were found on the roof of the Nazi headquarters. Then eight members of the group were indicted in December for beating Ralph Locker, a Jewish Defense League member, in a fight outside the Chicago Palmer House Hotel. The sporadic outbreaks of violence and savagery continued until the 1980s; Rockwell's spirit rode again.

The Road to Barbie

For fifteen years after World War II was over, there was a prolonged silence on the matter of the whereabouts of some 280 Nazi war criminals imported into the United States. The public was ignorant of the matter of the Department of Justice's and the State Department's complicity in bringing enemy nationals in under the Displaced Persons Act.

A rare instance occurred in April 1953, when an argument broke loose at the monthly meeting on April 27 of that year, of the New York County Medical Society.

A Vienna speech specialist, Dr. Godfrey E. Arnold, applied for membership; he had been recommended by the Executive Committee. Six prominent doctors reported that the committee had acted on the recommendation despite the fact that they had uniformly been advised by the office of John J. McCloy, High Commissioner for Germany, that Dr. Arnold had been allegedly with the SS following his Nazi Party inauguration, on July 1, 1940.

The hospital's commissioner, Marcus D. Kogel, stated that he had in fact barred Arnold from hospital work when he learned of his alleged Nazi associations. Interestingly, the committee members tried to discredit the documentation and insist that Arnold had not been charged with war crimes. Arnold was felt to be innocent because he had worked for the U.S. Army in Germany and had been allowed to take out citizenship papers.

One of Dr. Arnold's few critics was his predecessor as chief of the Speech Department of the University of Vienna Clinic. Speaking in concert with Sigmund Freud's daughter-in-law, Dr. Emil Froeschels asserted that when the Nazis entered Vienna, on March 14, 1938, Dr. Arnold took over the clinic under Gestapo supervision. The end result was that Arnold was barred.

In 1973, it was announced that Sol Marks, of the Department of Immigration and Naturalization, would be starting a nationwide effort to deal with former war criminals. One of these was Archbishop Trifa, particulars of whose career have been dealt with here already. Another was Mrs. Hermine Braunsteiner Ryan, a former concentration-camp guard. Marks was designated in charge in New York, running thirty district-office investigations. Jewish organizations compiled a list of sixty-five suspects of whom nine had died and seventeen could not be traced; of the remaining figures, twenty-five were naturalized Americans.

One case that was reopened was that of Boleslavs Maikovskis, a Latvian who had allegedly been sentenced to death in absentia by the Soviet Union for alleged killings as a camp guard. It was believed that Maikovskis had worked for American intelligence agencies. Maikovskis lived in Mineola, Long Island.

Officials led by Immigration investigator Sam Zutty stated that there were major difficulties both in obtaining evidence from the Soviet Union and fighting their way through complicated denaturalization red tape. In fact, even if an individual citizenship should be successfully revoked, an individual who was married or had children who were citizens was not subject to deportation.

Two determined men, Vincent A. Schiano, chief Immigration and Naturalization Service trial attorney, and Anthony J. DeVito, INS investigator, had both resigned, DeVito in particular because he claimed obstruction in the investigation of Maikovskis, allegedly because of Maikovskis' former role as a U.S. intelligence agent. Further hamperings occurred when the new team ran into public criticism for even dealing with the Russians on any level to obtain information. The publication of Aleksandr Solzhenitsyn's famous book *The Gulag Archipelago* had provoked very strong anti-Soviet feelings even among some liberals at the time.

On November 23, 1974, Ralph Blumenthal, whose articles in the New York *Times* spearheaded a drive to expose Nazis, revealed that there were constant delays in the first year following the announcement of the drive. Representative Elizabeth Holtzman, of Brooklyn, had found, she told Blumenthal, very little evidence of progress as a result of her hammering away from her seat on the House Immigration Subcommittee. She was disturbed about the fact that Dr. Hubertus Strughold, a space scientist, had been excused from further investigation into alleged Nazi activities; it was charged that his protection came from the CIA.

She joined Representative Joshua Eilberg (D., Pennsylvania) in scoring the State Department for failing to cooperate with Immigration in the matter. Henry Wagner, INS officer in charge of parts of the investigation, said in comment on Ms. Holtzman's charges, "If we take someone and hang them from the lamppost, is that progress?" Nevertheless, Wagner could not answer satisfactorily the several resignations of decent men because they were thwarted by the protection of Nazis, nor could he overcome such documentary evidence as that produced by Charles R. Allen, Jr., former senior editor of *The Nation* and pioneer author of books on nazism, who had presented to the authorities a U.S. Army document translated from the German and placing Dr. Strughold at a 1942 Nazi conference discussing medical experiments in concentration camps. The document was published in the December 1974 issue of the monthly magazine *Jewish Currents*. Blumenthal frankly asserted that Strughold had been used by American intelligence services; as part of Project (or operation) Paper Clip, he had come from Heidelberg to Randolph Field and Brooks Air Force Base to work for the U.S. Air Force.

Meanwhile, Mrs. Ryan, the Nazi concentration-camp guard who became a housewife in Queens, had left for Germany, thus achieving the distinction of being the only individual (at time of writing, in 1984) to be deported for Nazi activities.

In August 1975, Elizabeth Holtzman was still in a state of frustration. She besieged Secretary of State Henry Kissinger (who interestingly enough had been with CIC in Germany in 1946), asking him to take more action, and demanding that more action be taken to get in touch with the Iron Curtain countries for information. She was convinced that the Nazis in America had friends in high places.

That December, Holtzman introduced a bill authorizing the government to deport or exclude aliens proved to have been involved in Nazi war crimes. By September of 1976, Leonard P. Chapman, INS commissioner, announced that seven alleged collaborators were marked for deportation for concealing war crimes when they entered the country.

The obstructionism continued. As an example, the State Department consistently fought against the extradition to Yugoslavia of Andrija Artukovic, of Surfside, California, who had been Croatian Minister of the Interior and had entered the United States at a time when he was alleged in State Department documents and British-embassy reports to be a Nazi collaborator. Exactly why the State Department constantly obstructed the Department of Justice remains obscure.

Representative Holtzman uncompromisingly pursued her target. She was extremely angry with the Administration and refused to forbear when she was crossed again and again. The case of Artukovic especially annoyed her, since, she asserted, he had been charged in absentia in 1948 with responsibility for the mass murder of Jews and Gypsies under Nazi control.

A serious case was that of Edgars Laipenieks, of San Diego, who stated publicly that he had worked for the CIA. A former Olympic sports coach, he was alleged to have been a Latvian secret agent during World War II. Laipenieks showed reporters Robert Dorn and Martin Gerchen, of the San Diego *Evening Tribune*, a letter from the CIA dated July 20, 1976, revealing concern and interest and thanks for "your past assistance to the agency."

CIA officials admitted that they had had some association with Laipenieks, and Laipenieks stated that he had been approached in 1960 at the Rome Olympic Games; he had transferred to Chile as a skiing instructor, had immigrated to the United States in 1960, and had coached track and field in Denver and San Diego. He had apparently been briefed in Washington in the summer of 1963 and had traveled as a secret agent in 1968 to obtain information on satellite weaponry of the Soviet Union.

Meanwhile, action against Archbishop Trifa continued. Other cases collapsed for lack of evidence—often at the appellate level. In August 1977 and again in July 1978, the Subcommittee on Immigration, Citizenship and International Law of the Committee on the Judiciary of the House of Representatives of the Ninety-fifth Congress held a series of sessions on the question of alleged Nazi war criminals in America.

The Honorable Joshua Eilberg expressed his concern at the failure of the U.S. Government to prevent the entry of war criminals into the United States, to investigate those who applied for naturalization, and to proceed properly to deport war criminals.

Victor L. Lowe, of the General Accounting Office, stated that he had been denied access to critically important records despite the existence of the Budget and Accounting Act of 1921 and the Legislative

Reorganization Act of 1970, which authorized release of all information to the GAO. Lowe, in answer to a direct question by Eilberg ("Has there been a plot?"), asserted unequivocally, "Yes."

The committee, calling on various witnesses, obtained an account of possible cover-up, and obstructionism, and certainly of inefficiency at every level and in every branch of the bureaucracy.

The slowness with which these cases and others were handled provoked widespread Jewish criticism. Indeed, in June 1978, the House approved a substantial appropriation for a Nazi War Crime Litigation Unit. Simultaneously, the House Judiciary Committee sought to have the CIA, the FBI, and the Department of Defense disclose their files, their connections to Nazis. That effort was foredoomed.

Ms. Holtzman still fought to introduce her bill. She was still frustrated but felt sustained by the appointment of the lawyer Martin Mendelsohn, hired by David W. Crosland, INS counsel, to be the official Nazi hunter for the United States. Meanwhile, the General Accounting Office of the State Department had issued a report asserting that the CIA had used twenty-one Nazi war criminals as sources of information and had paid seven of them in cash for their efforts.

On July 11, the House Judiciary Committee voted twenty-one to five to release a bill closing a loophole in the immigration laws which did not allow the deporting of anyone guilty of persecuting others because of race, religion, national origin, or political opinion. The New York *Times* editors on July 30 attacked the release of the bill, savaging Elizabeth Holtzman, "whose deceptively simple words create a dangerous minefield." The *Times* pointed out that the bill would bar almost "any white South African, even a private citizen" or an Englishman in the British Army in Northern Ireland or an Israeli who participated in the invasion of Lebanon or the occupation of a town on the West Bank.

On August 5, 1978, somebody took a potshot at Maikovskis, who, wounded by a bullet in the right knee, was admitted to Nassau Hospital, Mineola, but recovered quickly. The Jewish Defense League denied any involvement, adding the comment, "The tragedy is he was just shot in the leg. A man like that deserves to die." The New York *Times* remarked, "That sounds uncomfortably like incitement to murder." The American–Jewish Congress said, "Those who want to really see war criminals punished must join in condemning this cruel, pointless and stupid act."

In November, a worldwide postcard campaign was announced, by

Austrian Nazi hunter Simon Wiesenthal, designed to convince the West German Government to extend its statute of limitations indefinitely on the prosecution of Nazi war criminals. This campaign was ultimately successful. Shortly before, President Jimmy Carter had at last signed the bill on the persecution issue to which the New York *Times* had so strenuously objected. At a meeting in New York City's Doral Hotel on November 10, Elizabeth Holtzman and Martin Mendelsohn supported the change in the statute of limitations.

In March 1979, government inquiry into the 175 Nazi war criminals in America became entangled in problems. Elizabeth Holtzman accused INS of failing to release over half of the two-million-dollar appropriation authorized for the special litigation unit in 1978. She wanted Congress to place the unit under the Attorney General directly. She said there were only two investigators trying to look into the many cases. She charged that not a single attorney had been hired since May of the preceding year to head up the task force.

In January 1980, Martin Mendelsohn resigned. When the Office of Special Investigations, under the Department of Justice Criminal Division, took up the work, Mendelsohn disagreed with Assistant Attorney General Philip B. Heyman and then went into private practice. Another who left the Department was John Loftus, taking with him a storehouse of information* on improper importation of Byelorussian pro-Nazi activists, which he used in a controversial book, *The Belarus Secret.* Mendelsohn charged that obstructionism was still the order of the day in the various government departments and that the wheels ground very slowly in almost every case; Loftus was even more critical, implying wholesale cover-up and deliberate jamming of the works at every level.

Attorney Allan A. Ryan joined the Office of Special Investigations. A cautious and conservative addition to the bureaucracy, he told the present writer that John Loftus's *The Belarus Secret* was "filled with inaccuracies." He had little better to say about Mendelsohn, whose professional and personal character was to earn him the position of legal counsel of the Simon Wiesenthal Center of Holocaust Studies.

Walter J. Rockler, head of the Office of Special Investigations under Philip B. Heyman's general direction, was much criticized by Mendelsohn

---

* The veracity of much of it is questioned by Charles R. Allen, Jr., Allan A. Ryan, and other experts.

and Loftus but admittedly had a difficult job. When he resigned to return to private practice and Ryan took over, the matter of getting to the bottom of cases proved increasingly vexing.

Immigration judges reversed on the appellate level the judgments against alleged Latvian war criminal Karlis Detlavs and the aforementioned Maikovskis. The government is seeking a new hearing to contest the appellate judgment.

The Klaus Barbie case erupted. And it was the Barbie case that was to focus, more than any other, on the problems of dealing with American collaboration with the Nazis.

******** **26**

Barbie

The Barbie case is, of course, the best-known example of collusion with the Nazis in the history of the U.S. intelligence services. His famous case history has tended to obscure the larger issue of collusion in the Pentagon and in the European high command with Gehlen and the SS—a collusion of which the Barbie affair was a minor if disturbing part.

In his book *The Belarus Secret*, John Loftus recalls his work as a special investigator for the Department of Justice, when he unearthed documents revealing that the order to hide Barbie came directly from the office of John J. McCloy, High Commissioner for Germany in the period immediately after the end of World War II. It has been confirmed by one of Barbie's controls, Erhard Dabringhaus, of the 970th CIC Battalion in Germany, that Barbie had a special relationship with General Julius Klein, a former figure of the OSS who acted as an adviser to McCloy on military questions. It is alleged by Scott Thompson in the magazine *Executive Intelligence Review* (March 1, 1983), that Barbie was debriefed by none other than Henry Kissinger, who was at that time serving with a CIC unit himself. It has been stated by Seymour Hersh in a recent book on Kissinger that the later Secretary of State was part of a CIC unit that specialized in turning Nazis around for use in the Cold War. John Loftus has charged that Kissinger played a similar role in the "conversion" of Skorzeny.

Barbie was born on October 25, 1913, in Bad Godesberg, near Bonn, Germany; he was an early member of the Hitler Youth movement and later joined the SD, the SS secret security service, under Walter Schellenberg.

His SS file, which still exists, states that he had "an extremely strong, positive attitude" toward Nazism. The only drawback was that his wife had gynecological problems which prevented him from having more than two children, a daughter and a son; fecundity was considered mandatory in SS men.

He joined the SS section which was specifically devoted to the solution of "the Jewish problem" and in 1942 was posted to Amsterdam, where he ordered the deportation of hundreds of Jews. He was transferred to Lyon in 1942, to quell the Resistance, which flourished despite the Vichy regime. According to several sources, he personally kicked his victims in the stomach, the genitals, and the kidneys and beat them with a blackjack. He stands charged with having caused the injuries that brought about the death of the celebrated Resistance leader Jean Moulin. He even executed some people with an ax, according to his accusers.

The report prepared by Allan A. Ryan of the Department of Justice Criminal Division in August 1983 is a most disturbing document. In its conclusions and recommendations, the report states that Barbie's employment was in the best interests of the United States, that he was "available and effective and loyal and reliable." Mr. Ryan continues with the statement, "Whatever his crimes, he [Barbie] has never been in the same category as Adolf Eichmann, Heinrich Himmler, Reinhardt Heydrich or other SS leaders." One might ask whether the fact that he caused the deaths of only some four thousand people renders him less guilty than those who killed millions. Such speciousness is typical, as I pointed out along with the rabbis of the Wiesenthal Center at a nationally televised press conference in December 1982, of the report as a whole. Mr. Ryan continued, "I cannot conclude that those who made the decision to employ and rely on Klaus Barbie ought now to be vilified for the decision." He is virtually alone in that opinion.

Moreover, the report fails to point out that there is not a single document obtained in the massive document file supplied as an appendix to the report or in ancillary documents that Mr. Ryan did not release and which I obtained from the Department of the Army at Fort Meade, to support the report's very contention. In close to a million words of cramped and well-nigh unreadable material, there is no detail given of crucial information obtained by Barbie that could not have been obtained from reading a newspaper or magazine or listening to the radio. Instead, one again gets the impression of a gigantic confidence trick like his superior Gehlen's in which Barbie simply secured a job for himself and his friends at the expense of a duped and benighted CIC command.

The Barbie case cannot be understood unless it is seen in a wider context of betrayal. The United States Government arguably had to sustain an uneasy relationship with Vichy until the invasion of North Africa under General Eisenhower in November 1942. Unfortunately, the support of Admiral Darlan, the devious collaborationist who met death from an assassin's bullet soon after his purpose had been served, also had to be secured for political purposes. Meanwhile the Resistance was left floundering without weapons.

Once the invasion had taken place, even the slightest pragmatic excuse for cooperation with Vichy automatically disappeared. However, it was not until August of 1943, nine months from the moment of the invasion, that the French Liberation Council was officially recognized by the United States Government and at last some help, albeit too little and too late, was grudgingly given. The reasons for the delay connect directly to Barbie. Jean Moulin, the Resistance leader whom Barbie murdered, was the official representative of Charles De Gaulle, and De Gaulle had, unlike Vichy, from the outset of the war been utterly deprived of American support. Thus, the United States Government surrendered the opportunity to find a place forever in French hearts by giving intense support in money and arms to that great leader whom Roosevelt deeply mistrusted and whom Cordell Hull utterly disliked. The reason is clear: not only was De Gaulle inconvenient vis-à-vis the Vichy policy and the presence in France of the right-wing extremists Admiral William D. Leahy and career diplomat Robert D. Murphy, but he also represented a direct threat to America's vision of postwar imperial power in Europe. Potential dictatorships, even benign ones, threatened to throw a monkey wrench into belligerent American diplomacy.

And there was more to it even than that. Jean Moulin was a moderate, but he drew together all elements of the Resistance and, inconvenient fact of facts, a high proportion of the Resistance figures were Communists. Like it or not, it had to be faced that the French Communists* were the most single-minded of the enemies of fascism in France. It was bad

---

* Many of them anti-Soviet; some later embraced Maoism.

enough to face the fact that we were in wartime alliance with the Soviet Union; harder to accept was that we were soon going to be compelled to claim credit for help to a Resistance movement inspired by communism, albeit not Moscow-authorized.

And thus, when the Barbie case broke, in 1983, the American press displayed much hypocrisy, talking of "French guilt" over Vichy while totally concealing from a forgetful public the fact that the American Government had recognized Vichy and shafted De Gaulle, and later had failed to support the Resistance until almost a year after it should have done so. The death of Jean Moulin stands as much on the American conscience as the French—or should. No wonder the official response by Mitterrand to the hollow apology of Allan Ryan and the State Department was terse and unforgiving.

Barbie first swam into the American view in 1945, when he arrived, from Switzerland via the French Zone, in the American Zone of occupied Germany. He immediately began working à la Gehlen with other former SS men to set up a complicated network that would actually or theoretically serve any power—British, American, or (especially) Russian—but emphatically not French. One main purpose of this group was to supply forged documents, passes, and money to allow former Nazi leaders to get away into Spain. There are numerous hints in the documents of spidery contacts to Léon Degrelle, celebrated dandy and millionaire Belgian leader of the Fascist Rex movement, who was living under the convenient protection of Generalissimo Franco in Madrid. Indeed, one of Barbie's two top aides was Karl Schaeffer, Degrelle's Belgian chief adjutant, who helped finance Barbie's operation through the sale of a priceless carpet that Degrelle had owned in Belgium.† Barbie's other aide-de-camp was a leader of the Hitler Youth movement named Rolf Wolkening, also a Degrelle follower.

Barbie worked closely with a prominent SS leader, Wolfgang Otto, former adjutant to General "Sepp" Dietrich. Figures of his entourage

---

† Léon Degrelle is still at it. He appears on the pages of *The Journal for Historical Review*, published in Torrance, California, which states among other things that the Holocaust was an invention of the Jews. The *Journal*'s editors recently (1982) arranged a conference at which Degrelle appeared to praise the Waffen SS.

were disguised as a gardener in an insane asylum, the director of a blind men's home, and the Turkish consul in Munich. All were wanted for war crimes.

Barbie's job was to weld the various organizations into a unity. Barbie and Otto were knitted into an illegal right-wing movement which was to attract fugitives from automatic arrest, dissatisfied Nazis, and the like, by appealing to nationalistic feelings, pride in the power and pomp of the old paramilitary organizations of the Nazi Party, and dissatisfaction with the present low estate into which the former elite of the nation had fallen during the occupation.

Once the nets were formed, Barbie and his fellows of the SS believed the organization could be used as a powerful bargaining lever with the Western Allies or the Russians in the event of another war or the threat of such a war. Neither Barbie nor Otto was certain how they might use the power they were building, only that the day would come when a *Putsch* would make them the ruling element in Germany.

Barbie and his friends moved from one seedy lodging house to another, existing on minimal amounts of money but still far better off than the millions of Germans who were starving and homeless in the wake of the nation's defeat. Their wives and children were tucked away in small villages in the country, because they could not possibly be subjected to the rigors of this ferretlike existence in the ruins caused by the bombing raids; and also they might be security risks. It was an underground existence, lived on the edge of desperation, with information sold to the highest bidder, and no possible hope of family life.

The Barbie network used secret radio stations, couriers, coded messages, and mail drops, hid arms in caches, infiltrated the police, made connections to Denmark, Spain, Switzerland, and Italy as escape routes, and liquidated all persons who constituted a security threat. Barbie was in touch with Franz Six, chief of Amt VII of the SD, and the SS leaders Erik Mueller and Klaus von Kielpinski. The latter was a crucial contact in the Russian Zone.

Even before Barbie had set up his nets, he was recognized by a French Resistance man named Michel Thomas, who had been brutally treated by Barbie in person, and was now an agent at CIC in Munich. Thomas says he presented a report based upon interrogations of captured SS officers, giving a full account of Barbie's activities in Lyon. This report appears to have been shredded.

In the summer of 1946, Barbie was using—by coincidence or not—the cover name Josef Mertens; interestingly, the Gehlen net in the same area used the overall cover name Heinz Mertens. Gehlen had returned from Washington that year to set up his organization under CIC control.

In June 1946, CIC Region IV swooped and arrested Barbie, Schaeffer, and Wolkening, putting them in prison incommunicado in Memmingen. A memorandum from the special agent in charge of them at the time, dated August 2, states that "top secret information" would be endangered if they were allowed to communicate with their families. That proviso would not have applied had they not been privy to internal CIC information.

Barbie and his friends were released after only fifteen days. Why? Clearly, because they were to be followed. However, they slipped out of contact, thereby double-crossing their controls, and CIC in Marburg started to look for them. On September 4, 1946, a woman named Erika Loss called CIC headquarters and said she could tip off the Americans to one of Barbie's main contacts. This was a farmer, formerly an SS man, named Heinrich Welle, living on a farm near Ellringhausen. On September 6, two CIC agents, two German policemen, and a driver went up to the farmhouse in a forest.

The two CIC men, both of them German, pretended to be Gestapo and talked to the owner, who was extremely suspicious at first but gradually was convinced and gave them some leads. The leads ran out, however, and Barbie, Schaeffer, and Wolkening (now alias Graf) moved to Hamburg, in the British Zone, on November 10, 1946. There, a British agent, Dr. Emil Hoffman, contacted them. Hoffman had known Schaeffer and Graf for some time and had first met Barbie in July. Hoffman had originally been in the SA, the Storm Troopers, and later had worked under Von Killinger in Bucharest at the time of the Legion revolt. He may have been working for the British that early, which would explain Von Killinger's knowledge of British SIS infiltration in the Legion situation and his immediate dismissal of Hoffman at the time.

In Hamburg, Barbie contacted a woman he had known in Paris, secretary of a Gestapo leader, who was nervous and refused to house him. He called on a British agent named Cloede, a former Nazi leader, and stayed with him that night; Schaeffer and Wolkening stayed with Wolkening's former secretary in Brussels. On the evening of November 10, Cloede told Barbie that he had just met a former Waffen SS cadet and SD member by the name of Acker, who "wanted to meet" Barbie. Cloede stated that he would advise Acker when Barbie arrived in Hamburg. Barbie told Cloede he objected to having his whereabouts made known to a stranger, and to meeting Acker. But Cloede sent the telegram to Acker anyway and invited him to come to Hamburg.

Cloede told Barbie that he and his group had three hundred pistols; he offered Barbie one, but Barbie refused it. Cloede also said that his group had a radio transmitter which he had bought with funds supplied by Barbie through the various networks. The transmitter had been stolen from a British unit, and the men, former SS comrades, had been paid with the marks. The weapons and the radio transmitter were preparations against a possible Russian attack.

Barbie and Schaeffer arranged for the sale of stolen jewelry to aid their activities. Barbie decided to move on to Hannover on November 12 on the 11:55 P.M. train. But Cloede talked him into meeting Acker at the Café Larrange, in the Hamburg Gänsemarkt, at five o'clock. Cloede made the introduction and then Barbie, Schaeffer, Wolkening, and Acker went to a restaurant named the Fawn. Acker was nervous, talked excessively about his SD membership, and mentioned the names and whereabouts of several SS leaders Barbie knew. Acker spoke of blowing up a French headquarters near Stuttgart. Acker said he, too, was going to Hannover.

Late that night, Barbie, Schaeffer, and Wolkening went to the Altona railway station to board the train for Hannover. Barbie noticed a British police sedan following the streetcar but thought little of it. Just before the train departed, four British agents came into their compartment and arrested the three men. There had been no sign of Acker.

At first, Barbie thought there had been a mistake. But the British captain said to them, obviously knowing who they were, "Well, my dear friends, *we* are not Americans. You are not going to run away from us." Barbie realized at once that Cloede must be a British agent. He was one of only two people who knew about Barbie's arrest in Marburg and the escape.

Barbie and his companions were taken to British Field Secret Service Headquarters (MI6) in Hamburg. They were stripped and searched, and their belts, suspenders, shoelaces, personal papers, and membership lists were taken from them.

They were locked in the basement in cells. Each cell was secured with an ordinary padlock.

During the night, Barbie heard Schaeffer and Wolkening, who were in the same cell, down the corridor; they began to converse through the bars. They decided that only Cloede or Acker could have caused their arrest. On the first night, British soldiers checked on them every half hour. But at noon on November 14, Schaeffer and Wolkening found a small iron bar and a flashlight in their cell. They discovered that their padlock could be broken with the iron bar and so could Barbie's.

On the night of November 14, there was only one guard. They decided to make a break at midnight. They could hear the guard playing the flute upstairs. The music covered their escape. They broke the padlocks and walked to a glass door, but it was locked from the outside. The boiler room and basement windows were blocked. They took the bold step of sneaking behind the guard, crawling through a window onto a roof, and jumping into a park. They hid in a friendly nightwatchman's house; other friends gave them money.

To cover for Acker, MI6 engineered a fake search from door to door that was widely discussed, but Barbie was not deceived, and Acker, code name Mouse, had to be terminated.‡

As a result of this experience, Barbie was extremely nervous about the British. Hoffman, whom he did not suspect, for some reason, of leading him into the trap, kept nudging him to join British intelligence, but he held back. However, MI6 kept pushing so hard through Hoffman that Barbie began to weaken.

Meanwhile, CIC was still pursuing Barbie. There was a raid on one of his new nets by the CIC operation known as Selection Board. On February 22, Barbie slipped into a bathroom, out of a window, and into a waste dump to escape. After the raid, he daringly sneaked back into his room and slept the rest of the night. He used the name Becker so as to confuse the raiders, since there was another Becker in the group, who was arrested.

CIC agents kept pursuing Barbie. He moved between various towns, always restless, always finding new contacts. One of his main connections was a man named Naumann, former SD chief of Leipzig. By April, Barbie was number three on the CIC target list of Operation Selection Board.

Barbie was contacted by a man named Kurt Josef Merk, who had been a colleague of his in France and had worked for both the SD and the

‡ The Mouse material is missing from the Ryan report.

Abwehr. Merk was taken in under automatic-arrest category, cleared of subversive charges, and enlisted into the U.S. cause as an exceptionally useful agent. Merk persuaded his control, Colonel Robert S. Taylor, of 66th CIC, that Barbie should be enlisted. Taylor was interested. Meanwhile, one of Barbie's contacts, a Major Schenk of the SS, was enlisted with the British in Hamburg and urged them to redouble efforts to get Barbie. But Barbie agreed to go with Merk.

With Barbie under the name Becker, and Merk under the name Petersen, the two men had a meeting with Taylor in April. Taylor liked Barbie and wrote in a report that he was "an idealistic Nazi." The report, dated April 18, stated, "Barbie impressed this agent as an honest man, both intellectually and personally, absolutely without nerves or fear. He is strongly anti-Communist—he believes that he and his beliefs were betrayed by the Nazis in power." Taylor recommended to his superiors Barbie's enlistment, and there was no argument from headquarters in Munich despite the fact that Barbie's history was available there both in Michel Thomas's report on the Lyon atrocities and in Wanted War Criminals lists, circulated to army headquarters, in which Barbie was posted as a murderer.

Taylor arranged a room for Barbie at the Bahnhof Hotel in Marburg. Barbie set up a net called Bureau Petersen, later changed to Bureau Larsen. The net was supposed to uncover Soviet networks, but essentially Barbie and Merk were after the French. Whatever else they did, the French came first. Barbie would never forgive De Gaulle for his anti-Nazism and wanted to "prove" that French intelligence in Germany was Communist-controlled, when in fact, in 1947, it was a clean nest.

Taylor and Barbie became intimate friends. Taylor also deeply admired and liked Merk. A team of sixty-five were hired as a net. But the bulk of the group were unreliable, involved in fencing jewels, stealing, and buying and selling drugs. Much of the information supplied was nonsense. None of the agents could be relied upon, although Taylor and others were obliged to aggrandize the group to justify its employment.

Taylor married, and returned to the United States in August 1947. Camille S. Hajdu was one of the officers who took over from Taylor. Reporting on Barbie, he disclosed on November 21, 1947, when somebody higher up felt that Barbie was unreliable and should be arrested, one of his reasons for keeping him on: "It is . . . felt that his arrest and possibly his delivery to British authorities would damage considerably the trust and faith which informants place in this organization."

He was constantly a security threat to the United States at the end of 1947. Theoretically, he was supposed to be reorganizing the secret police, exposing Soviet penetration, and shafting the French. But he had connections to the Soviets and to black-market activities (particularly in soap and in jewels), counterfeiting money, obtaining false ration cards, and even planning murders.

A later report, dated July 28, 1948, following yet another order for his arrest for malfeasance, read, "It is not deemed advisable to intern [him] . . . his knowledge as to the mission of CIC, its agents, subagents, funds etc., is too great. If Barbie were interned . . . upon his release or escape . . . he would contact either the French or the British Intelligence and work for them."

Barbie and Merk were each paid sixteen hundred dollars a month for their services. But by August 1948 Bureau Larsen had been compromised and had to be shifted to Augsburg. The network came under the direction of Erhard Dabringhaus, who today is professor of German at Wayne State University. The operation was more or less the same as before. Yet a careful reading of the documents and an interview with Dabringhaus shows that the operation, compromised or not, was largely useless. According to Michel Thomas, it consisted largely of clipping articles out of Iron Curtain magazines. Apart from details of the location of a uranium mine in Yugoslavia, found in one such magazine, it seems to have done almost nothing.

Bureau Larsen simply supplied useless reports on the possible weaknesses of other SS and Abwehr personnel. Generally, they seemed to have simply been finding a sinecure for their former colleagues in SD and duping the Americans.

By October 1948 the membership of Bureau Petersen, or Larsen, declined to a pitiful twelve members. Some of the members dropped were involved in robberies, smuggling, possible Soviet agenting, and an organization similar to that which Killinger had belonged to in the 1930s. This hit squad would liquidate Germans who had worked against former SS men. "A centralized net is difficult to control," understandably wrote CIC officer Earl S. Browning, Jr., on October 25, 1948.

On May 14, 1949, *Paris Presse* published an item describing Barbie's brutal activities in Lyon. Twice, French officials had questioned Barbie in connection with the trial of author René Hardy, who was alleged to have collaborated with Barbie when supposedly in charge of Resistance operations (he was acquitted). However, the French had not succeeded in extraditing Barbie; according to CIC reports, they had never really tried, since Barbie would make unfortunate disclosures about the appeasement policies of such leading French politicians as André François-Poncet, French High Commissioner in Germany and former ambassador to Hitler. According to the article, French authorities had appealed officially to U.S. High Commissioner John J. McCloy for the extradition of Barbie from Germany, but had gotten nowhere.

Due to the embarrassment of Barbie's possible public exposure, he had to be officially dumped. However, CIC dared not let him completely off the hook, in case he exposed CIC's involvement with the Nazis. The matter went all the way up to EUCOM, which tried to wash its hands of the whole matter. On November 7, 1949, François-Poncet backed the French ambassador in Washington in seeking the extradition of Barbie. But nothing happened.

On May 3, 1950, a CIC report stated: "Since this headquarters has not notified the British . . . it was deemed inadvisable that the reason they had not been so informed stemmed from the fact that Barbie was used by CIC as an informant." In other words, Barbie's location, uncertain for a short period, was now known, but the British must not know it. The British were still trying to get him, even at this stage, through Hoffman. By May 11, 1950, Barbie was still working for CIC as a secret informant in spite of everything. And he was still being hidden from the French and the British. His file cards were destroyed, so that there was no record on him that anyone could find, and he was paid under the table. When newspaper reporters came looking for him, they were told that nothing was known about him other than what had appeared in the paper. He was needed for the second trial of the alleged French collaborationist and author René Hardy, in 1950, but again he was hidden, and soon after, Hardy was again acquitted; the French Government had no conclusive evidence on Hardy. Notes and telegrams, some of them in code, flew between various EUCOM headquarters, as the frantic efforts to hide Barbie became more and more extreme. The Communists had a field day. In a May 1950 issue, the French Communist magazine L'Humanité, furious over the acquittal of Hardy, said angrily, "Barbie has been drafted by American Secret Service . . . why don't these phony defenders of perse-

cuted innocents . . . publicly insist on Barbie's surrender to French justice . . . because after his acquittal, they want to use Hardy's Gestapo
training for their own dirty ends."

There was widespread agitation for Barbie's release throughout Europe. George B. Riggin, of 66th CIC, on May 11, 1950, wrote, "It is
desired to record for possible future reference the actions taken by this
region regarding the employment and carding of Klaus Barbie as a source;
the subsequent dropping of source, and the maintenance of contact so as
to enable easy location and apprehension should French authorities demand his extradition."

In a lengthy undated memorandum of early 1951, the CIC discussed
the matter of "informant disposal" and "emigration methods" referring to
the so-called rat-line or Nazi evacuation to Central and South America,
that had been in existence since 1948 and took its cue from Barbie's
operations. At a cost of a thousand dollars each adult, CIC was transferring inconvenient Nazis via Austria to Italy, where they were provided
with legal documentation "[t]hrough devious means there" at the Vatican.
The whole operation was run by CIC in Salzburg. The documentation—
passports, visas, and so forth—was illegally prepared on secret printing
presses by special CIC units in Italy. Some figures of the SS were marked
down for Australia, others for South America. They were sent on to further CIC bodies, and then in a kind of human chain to Rome, where the
Vatican experts were waiting to take care of them, led by a Monsignor
Hudal, an Austrian national.

On arrival in Italy, the immigrant was placed in a hotel and given an
income in dollars. He must be treated with great consideration, but the
moment he boarded ship he must forget everything. The Department of
State must mandatorily be advised of the immigrant's real name, aliases,
date and place of birth, physical description, and date and place of departure. Through the Department of State, the U.S. diplomatic or consular
representative in the receiving country was informed that the immigrant
was formerly of interest to American Intelligence.

Children went at half price. People over thirty might cost a little
more. Some received VIP treatment, which cost the U.S. taxpayer fourteen hundred dollars per head for the first-class fare. On the budget would
be food and clothing during the stay in Austria and Italy. Each was given
pocket money at time of embarkation.

Transfer of funds must not go through normal command channels but by receipt between representatives of 430th CIC and 66th CIC. Money going across the Austrian border was transferred by courier as a secret document properly sealed and stamped.

Representatives of 430th CIC and G2 were most cordial with each other—and openhanded—in discussing the evacuation plans. The 430th took complete responsibility. There was no limit to the number of people that could be processed.

On December 5, 1951, there was a direct reference to plans to move Barbie under the name Klaus Altman. His family would accompany him. Top security must be preserved at all times. He must travel through Austrian and Italian consulates. Essentially, this was an Austrian operation under local CIC.

The utmost care must be taken not to disclose CIC's involvement. The potential embarrassment was unlimited; so the memoranda grew more and more tense, complex, and intricate.

Barbie was transferred via the Vatican; a Ukrainian priest was specifically engaged to make the necessary arrangements. Bolivia was chosen as Barbie's new home. Six years later, while operating a carpenter shop in La Paz, he became a Bolivian citizen.

In the summer of 1966, an NBC television program in the United States showed Barbie. A Mrs. Sandra S. Zanik of New York, wrote to Senator Jacob Javits and asked how such a person could be at large when many of his victims had died. In a document dated July 21, 1966, entitled Disposition Form, Army Intelligence sent an interoffice memorandum to branches referring to Mrs. Zanik's letter. There is an interesting blackout in the appropriate document. Referring to the fact that the NBC program dealt with Barbie, "an informant of 66th CIC from 1948 [sic] to 1951," the document said, "It was then determined that Army Intelligence had no contact with subject since early 1951. Further checking also revealed that although no contact was had with Barbie . . ." and then the blackout occurs. Does this not mean that his whereabouts must have been known to another agency? Until the passage is declassified, it is impossible to be sure.

At all events, from 1966 until 1983, a period of seventeen years, not only the Army but State remained silent on Barbie. Later, State was officially absolved by Allan Ryan, probably under pressure.

It is interesting that many later documents relating to Barbie are missing from the Ryan appendix volume, along with earlier ones. A document dated February 13, 1967, signed R.R.P. and emanating from the office of the assistant chief of staff for intelligence, Department of the Army, refers to Barbie and blacks out another passage which surely must refer to the CIA. In Section Four, it says, "It is requested that ———— be queried for any available information on subject." Photographs are enclosed of Barbie in 1951. In another document, with no date but emanating clearly from April 1967, Alfred W. Bagot, colonel, general staff chief of the Resources Division of the Army, requested data from headquarters. The report dealt with Barbie's residing in La Paz and operating a carpenter shop. He traveled frequently for lumber purchases. Bagot asked for confirmation that Altman was Barbie.

It has been alleged that Barbie was controlled by the CIA in South America, but the CIA has strenuously denied this.

In 1981 and 1982, Serge and Beate Klarsfeld, French Nazi hunters, risked their lives to uncover the truth about Barbie. When there was a change of government in Bolivia, and when he was brought in on fraud charges, Barbie was shipped to Lyon and handed over for trial. He had already been convicted twice and sentenced to death in absentia for torturing and executing four thousand Jews and French Resistance fighters. Those military penalties were now invalid, due to the statute of limitations, so Barbie could be tried only for crimes against humanity. Among these were stripping an orphanage of forty-one Jewish children and their teachers and shipping them to Auchswitz, and beating French Resistance leader Jean Moulin to death.

As for the CIC officers who had protected Barbie, they could not be tried for aiding and abetting a war criminal, as statutes of limitation had run out on them also and they had merely been acting within the terms of U.S. foreign policy, whether directly authorized or not. Furthermore, their collusion scarcely caused a ripple when it was exposed. There was very little public outcry on the matter even in the Jewish sector. When Michel Thomas, Resistance hero, who had reported Barbie to the CIC in 1945, came to Los Angeles at my suggestion as the guest of the Simon Wiesenthal Center of Holocaust Studies, in August 1983, there was a press conference and some coverage, but few cries of outrage. It seemed that Nazi collaboration has its greatest protection not in Army Intelligence, not in high places, but in the short memories of the American public.

Epilogue

Since the writing of the introduction to this book, a number of new examples have come to my attention of whitewashes of Nazis and Nazi collaborators and attempts to aid and abet the neo-Nazi cause even at this stage, some forty years after the conclusion of World War II. Indeed, today the spotlight on the subject of Nazism has never been more intensely focused—another reason for writing this book.

In the 1982 biography of P. G. Wodehouse written by Lady Frances Donaldson, the noted British biographer and historian, Lady Donaldson claims that Wodehouse, creator of the immortal Jeeves, was so completely ignorant of world events that, when he was released from a prison camp and taken to Berlin to make broadcasts for the Germans when his native country, Great Britain, was at war with Germany, he had no idea that the war had any significance and acted with complete naïveté and ignorance. Lady Donaldson asks a series of rhetorical questions, challenging the reader to answer the question why Wodehouse should not have made the broadcasts, since not to have done so would have been suicide and, anyway, how was he to support himself at the very expensive Hotel Adlon, the most luxurious hostelry in Berlin, unless he had some form of income?

Lady Donaldson overlooks Wodehouse's political sophistication, anti-Semitism, and sympathy for the German cause, and she forgets that many people died, preferring death to dishonor, rather than work for the Germans in any capacity. Surely, the fact that Wodehouse's broadcasts, directed toward the United States and designed to give the impression that life in a German prisoner-of-war camp was by no means a journey through the vale of tears, served a most useful propaganda function for the Nazis. Wodehouse, whom I knew, so far from being the ignoramus portrayed in Lady Donaldson's prose, was a well-traveled man of the world who knew exactly what he was doing.

Indeed, recently declassified documents obtained under the Freedom of Information Act disclose a fact that has escaped the no doubt sincere Lady Donaldson's attention. Wodehouse, a naturalized American, resident on Long Island, was in the direct pay of the German Government, and in accepting that pay was guilty of treason. On page six of a report made by German Foreign Minister Joachim von Ribbentrop, and prepared under the auspices of the U.S. Forces' European Theater Military Intelligence Service Center, dated November 28, 1945, Ribbentrop stated under oath, "Towards the end [of the war] I was made responsible for paying [Wodehouse's] expenses whilst he was in Paris."*

It is worth noting that the Germans held Paris until the Americans walked in and that therefore Wodehouse was still living in German-occupied territory with checks signed on Ribbentrop's special account, which must have been authorized by Hitler directly as the Foreign Minister's only superior in the Nazi hierarchy other than Göring.

Another who was whitewashed until a recent biography, *The Roots of Treason*, by E. Fuller Torrey (New York: McGraw-Hill, 1984), was published, was Ezra Pound, the celebrated American poet who broadcast from Rome during World War II on behalf of the Axis. It was claimed that he was insane and that his incarceration in a psychiatric hospital in Washington, D.C., was sufficient punishment, since his madness was a totally acceptable defense for his behavior. Dr. Torrey, himself on the staff of St. Elizabeth's Hospital, where Pound remained for some years after the war, has documentarily established that when Pound short-waved statements about "the Jews in the White House" or the "Jew radios" and press of America, and spoke of the superiority of the Axis to the Allies, he knew exactly what he was doing. Dr. Torrey alleges evidence that psychiatrists and poets conspired jointly to falsify the truth and protect a Nazi sympathizer.

Yet another whitewash has recurred again and again in the matter of

---

* Document declassified by U.S. Army Intelligence Command, April 1983. (Unfortunately, Lady Donaldson did not have access to this appropriate documentation.)

Charles Howard Ellis, the right-hand man of Sir William Stephenson, who made him consul general for Great Britain in New York City from 1940 until the end of World War II, in charge of passports and visas for such U.S. immigrants as the Australian Errol Flynn. Sir William has tried to paper over the fact that he unwittingly appointed a Nazi agent who already had made links to the Soviets. Chapman Pincher, the distinguished British journalist, has exhaustively documented in his well-known book *Their Trade is Treachery* (New York: Bantam, 1982) the fact that Ellis was a self-confessed German agent, representing the Abwehr. When the book appeared, Ellis's daughter asked Margaret Thatcher, Prime Minister of Great Britain, whether her father could be cleared of such charges. Mrs. Thatcher, while expressing sorrow that the dead could be attacked with impunity, was unable to issue a denial.

Stephenson bombarded Pincher and other writers with telegrams, angrily denying that he had employed a Nazi in his office at British Security Coordination, thereby allowing his entire American operation to be leaked. He even denied that he had turned Ellis around from the German cause to the British. He then published, through his ghost and colleague, the similarly named Canadian author William Stevenson, a 1984 book entitled *Intrepid's Last Case.* In this book, Sir William and his amanuensis tried strenuously to clean up the act once and for all. They tried to deny, despite the record, the fact that Ellis had leaked crucial secrets to Igor Gouzenko, the notorious Communist agent in Canada, and then, retrospectively and without a scrap of original research in the files in Washington, denied that Ellis was a Nazi at any time, or a Communist. They used the old canard that the Soviets had planted disinformation that Ellis was working for the KGB in order to discredit him and render him useless to the British. No documentary evidence exists to support this contention, either in the pages of *Intrepid's Last Case* or elsewhere, as Edward Jay Epstein pointed out in the New York *Times Book Review.*

This is one in a long list of misleading actions taken by Sir William Stephenson with the assistance of his scribe. What are we to make of it? Obviously, it passes comprehension and imagination that Sir William deliberately nestled a German viper in his bosom during the war and then proceeded to protect a Communist after the war. One has to assume that Ellis was "turned around" in London before he went to the United States and that Sir William was deliberately kept ignorant of this fact. Such folly is unhappily typical of intelligence services the world over. Stephenson was in fact relying on Ellis, even to the point of having him contribute some passages to the earlier *A Man Called Intrepid*, when he should not have done so. It is now generally agreed by Pincher and other experts in the field that Ellis's presence resulted in crucial leakages in the entire structure of British Security Coordination in New York.

Another book has appeared dealing with Ellis. It is a memoir, *Secret Intelligence Agent*, by Stephenson's former associate the respected British biographer H. Montgomery Hyde. In a previous biography of Sir William, also authorized, entitled *The Quiet Canadian*, Hyde and Stephenson have misremembered the character and activities of Fritz Wiedemann, German consul general in San Francisco.

They stated that in return for important information supplied by Wiedemann, Sir William gave him a safe-conduct to the Orient, in order to avoid Hitler's wrath, and that he remained in obscurity in Tientsin, China, for the duration of the war as a harmless diplomatic official.

This is incorrect. Wiedemann was not given a safe-conduct by anybody, but left New York in July 1940 by Italian vessel with the authorization of the U.S. State Department and President Roosevelt along with other German consular personnel. Wiedemann proceeded to Berlin, where he met with the Führer and received orders to proceed to Brazil and Argentina, to protect the local ambassadors against anti-German demonstrators. Considered too dangerous even to land in pro-Nazi Chile, because of public disapproval, he proceeded by Japanese vessel to Yokohama, where he was officially appointed head of the Orientgruppe (the Nazi espionage ring in Asia), the most powerful figure of the Nazi regime in that region.

Documents on this matter are in public access and were at the time of Stephenson's life stories. A discussion occurs in the same book and in *A Man Called Intrepid* concerning Sir William Wiseman, another of Stephenson's special team and a former head of British Intelligence in the United States. Stephenson claims that Wiseman was authorized by the British Government and the FBI to conduct secret peace meetings with Wiedemann and the Princess Stefanie Hohenlohe. The FBI documents conclusively prove that he was not. In fact, the documents, available at the FBI headquarters in Washington, D.C., establish that Wiseman was directly working for the German cause right under Stephenson's nose and state that he was not authorized by any government.

We are left with no alternative but that of concluding that Stephenson's operation in the United States was riddled with subversion and therefore was compromised in terms of secret intelligence. The most charitable statement one can make about his self-defense in his extreme old age is that it is pitiful.

A similar defensiveness, unfortunately, perpetuates the myths that protect Nazis to this day. I have already remarked on *The Journal of Historical Review*. Published in Torrance, California, in a very handsome format, with expensive paper and alleged financing from extreme right-wing elements in the Middle West, this publication is perhaps the most striking embodiment of whitewashing of nazism in recent years. In the issue for Spring 1983, Professor Frank H. Hankins, sociologist, historian, and demographer, was resurrected from the graveyard; some years after his death, in 1970, his denial of the Holocaust appeared. In the same issue, one L. A. Rollins analyzes the death of the six million, dismissing it as folly, and attempting to demolish the entire story of genocide. In another issue, dated Winter 1982, there was a favorable account by the late Ranji Borra, of the Asian division of the Library of Congress, of the Indian nationalist Subhas Chandra Bose. Bose, a supporter of Hitler who had direct connections to the SD, is here described in glowing terms as a potential instrument of Indian liberation; not insignificantly, this senior reference librarian was a follower of Bose at a time when Bose was working against the interests of Great Britain and the United States.

Another resident of Washington is attorney Sterling Cole, for many years a congressman from New York State, who retired from the Hill to become a prominent lawyer specializing in immigration matters, in Washington, D.C. While in Vienna in the 1950s, as head of the Atomic Energy Commission, he became a patient and friend of Errol Flynn's Nazi associate Dr. Hermann Frederick Erben. Dr. Erben was born a Jew in Vienna and later abandoned his people to become a member of the SA, the most fanatical branch of the SS, and later the SD and the Abwehr. As an informant, he caused the deaths of many Americans in the prisoner-of-war camp Pootung Assembly Center, in Shanghai, during World War II. He blackmailed homosexual and drug-addicted employees of U.S. consulates just before Pearl Harbor in order to obtain official secrets, and he also turned around German-American soldiers and sailors to the Nazi cause. No doubt innocently, Mr. Cole made a series of attempts to reimport Dr. Erben to the United States on the ground that he was a friend of Errol Flynn and thus deserved the best of the American people. In 1982–83,

Rudolph Stoiber, former correspondent to the United Nations of Austrian ORF television, spent many months interviewing Dr. Erben for a proposed biography. He obtained new evidence in the form of Dr. Erben's letters and diaries of Erben's (and Errol Flynn's) Nazi connections. In January 1984, Stoiber forwarded the crucial documents to Mr. Cole, by certified mail, since he was disturbed to discover that Mr. Cole had written directly to President Ronald Reagan beseeching him to restore Dr. Erben's citizenship, which had been canceled for obvious reasons in April 1941. Mr. Stoiber retains a copy of that letter.

Mr. Cole chose not to respond or to indicate whether he had ceased and desisted from his attempts to reintroduce a Nazi into this country. He told Stoiber upon receipt of the documents that he disbelieved their contents. He would not desist in his efforts to aid Dr. Erben's reentry. I wrote to him, challenging him to answer why he was trying to reimport a Nazi. He did not reply, nor would he talk to me on the telephone.

The matter was then taken up by Rabbis Marvin Hier and Abraham Cooper of the Simon Wiesenthal Center of Holocaust Studies. They discussed the matter directly with presidential counsel, who informed them that no trace of the application to reintroduce Dr. Erben could be found. However, the matter was passed over to the Department of Justice.

Stoiber sent a copy of all correspondence in the matter, and some documents, to virtually every newspaper and television station in the nation. He also complained because CBS was whitewashing Dr. Erben in its miniseries based on Flynn's memoirs, *My Wicked, Wicked Ways,* as an eccentric tropical adventurer the Dutch Dr. Gerrit Koets, played by Darren McGavin. A deliberate cover-up was, Stoiber charged, part of a larger cover-up. Stoiber predictably ran up against a wall. Not a single publication ran this highly sensational story at all, and indeed no response was received from CBS, or any other medium, on this very important matter.

In view of the foregoing, it is impossible to escape the conclusion that, despite the fact that certain Nazis have been marked for deportation and that some qualified disapproval has been uttered in official quarters vis-à-vis U.S. military protection of such figures as Barbie and the late alleged mass murderer Kurt Rauff, an exile in Chile, who died in 1984, the same forces of camouflage, protection, and support for the anti-Semitic cause still exist in the United States. It is to draw attention to this fact that I have undertaken the writing of this book.

Selective Bibliography

Allen, Charles R., Jr. *Heusinger of the Fourth Reich*. New York: Marzani & Munsell, 1963.

Allen, Fred Lewis. *Only Yesterday. An Informal History of the Nineteen Twenties*. New York: Blue Ribbon Books, 1931.

Allen, Gary. *None Dare Call It Conspiracy*. Rossmoor, Calif.: Concord Press, 1971.

Alsop, John, and Robert Kintner. *American White Paper. The Story of American Diplomacy and the Second World War*. New York: Simon & Schuster, 1940.

Alsop, Stewart, and Thomas Braden. *Sub Rosa. The O.S.S. and American Espionage*. New York: Reynal & Hitchcock, 1946.

Aron, Robert. *The Vichy Regime, 1940–1944*, trans. Humphrey Hare. London: Putnam, 1958.

Anderson, Jack, and Roland May. *McCarthy: the Man, the Senator, the "Ism."* Boston: The Beacon Press, 1952.

Auty, Phyllis. *Tito: A Biography*. Harmondsworth: Penguin Books, 1974.

Bendiner, Robert. *The Riddle of the State Department*. New York: Farrar & Rinehart, 1942.

Boea, Angelo del, and Mario Giovana. *Fascism Today. A World Survey*, trans. R. H. Boothroyd. London: Heinemann, 1970.

Brinkley, George. *The Volunteer Army and Allied Intervention in South Russia, 1917–1921: A Study in the Politics and Diplomacy of the Russian Civil War*. Notre Dame, Ind.: University of Notre Dame Press, 1966.

310 SELECTIVE BIBLIOGRAPHY

Buckley, William F. *Rumbles Left and Right: A Book About Troublesome People and Ideas.* New York: G.P. Putnam's Sons, 1963.

"Cato." *Guilty Men.* New York: Frederick A. Stokes, 1940.

Cline, Ray S. *The United States Army in World War II. The War Department, Washington Command Post, the Operations Division.* Washington, D.C.: Office of the Chief of Military History, Department of the Army, 1951.

Cohn, Roy M. *McCarthy.* New York: The New American Library, 1968.

Cole, Wayne S. *America First. The Battle Against Intervention 1940–1941.* Madison: University of Wisconsin Press, 1953.

Connelly, Joseph. *P. G. Wodehouse: An Illustrated Biography.* London: Orbis Publishing, 1979.

Cook, Fred J. *The Nightmare Decade: The Life and Times of Senator Joe McCarthy.* New York: Random House, 1971.

Corson, William R. *The Armies of Ignorance. The Rise of The American Intelligence Empire.* New York: The Dial Press / James Wade, 1977.

Craven, Wesley Frank, and James Lea Cate, eds. *The Army Air Forces in World War II.* Chicago: University of Chicago Press, 1948.

Crosby, Donald F. *God, Church and Flag: Senator Joseph R. McCarthy and the Catholic Church 1950–1957.* Chapel Hill: University of North Carolina Press, 1978.

Cyprian, Tadeusz, and Jerzy Sawicki. *Nazi Rule in Poland 1939–1945.* Warsaw: Polonia Publishing House, n.d.

Dabringhaus, Erhard. *Klaus Barbie.* Washington, D.C.: Acropolis Books, 1984.

Dallas, Rita, and Jeanira Ratcliffe. *The Kennedy Case.* New York: G. P. Putnam's Sons, 1973.

Davidson, Houston. *Yellow Creek: The Story of Shanghai.* Philadelphia: Dufour Editions, 1964.

Deacon, Richard. *A History of the British Secret Service.* London: Frederick Muller, 1969.

Documents on German Foreign Policy 1918–1945. Washington, D.C.: U.S. Government Printing Office, 1967.

Dulles, Allen Welsh, and Hamilton Fish. *Can America Stay Neutral?* New York and London: Harper & Brothers Publishers, 1939.

Edwards, Jerome E. *The Foreign Policy of Colonel McCormick's Tribune, 1929–1941.* Reno: University of Nevada Press, 1971.

Evans, Medford. *The Assassination of Joe McCarthy.* Boston: Western Islands Publishers, 1970.

Feuerlicht, Roberta Strauss. *Joe McCarthy and McCarthyism: The Hate That Haunts America.* New York: McGraw-Hill Book Company, 1972.

Foley, Charles. *Commandos Extraordinaires,* trans. J. Fillion. Paris: Éditions France-Empire, 1955.

Ford, Corey. *Donovan of the O.S.S.* Boston: Little, Brown & Company, 1970.

Forster, Arnold, and Benjamin R. Epstein. *Danger on the Right.* New York: Random House, 1964.

Friedländer, Saul. *Pius XII and the Third Reich: A Documentation,* trans. Charles Fullman. New York: Alfred A. Knopf, 1966.

Frye, Alton. *Nazi Germany and the American Hemisphere 1933–1941.* New Haven and London: Yale University Press, 1967.

Germany, Auswärtiges Amt. *Britain's Designs on Norway: Documents Concerning the Anglo-French Policy of Extending the War.* Full Text of White Book No. 4, published by the German Foreign Office. New York: German Library of Information, 1940.

Gies, Joseph. *The Colonel of Chicago.* New York: E. P. Dutton, 1979.

Gilbert, Clinton Wallace. *You Takes Your Choice.* New York and London: G. P. Putnam's Sons, 1924.

Goldston, Robert Conroy. *The American Nightmare: Senator Joseph R. McCarthy and the Politics of Hate.* Indianapolis Ind.: Bobbs-Merrill Company, 1973.

Hanson, Arthur B. *Libel and Related Torts.* New York: The American Publishers Association Foundation, 1969.

Haswell, Jock. *British Military Intelligence.* London: Weidenfeld & Nicholson, 1973.

Höhne, Heinz. *The Order of the Death's Head: The Story of Hitler's S.S.,* trans. Richard Barry. New York: Coward, McCann, 1970.

——and Hermann Zolling. *The General Was a Spy: The Truth About General Gehlen and His Spy Ring,* trans. Richard Barry. New York: Coward, McCann, 1972.

Hoke, Henry. *It's a Secret.* New York: Reynal & Hitchcock, 1946.

Howard-Ellis, C. *The Origin, Structure and Working of the League of Nations.* Boston and New York: Houghton Mifflin, 1929.

Infield, Glenn B. *Skorzeny: Hitler's Commando.* New York: St. Martin's Press, 1981.

International Military Tribunal at Nuremberg. *The Trial of the Major War Criminals.* Washington, D.C.: U.S. Government Printing Office, 1953.

Investigation of Un-American Propaganda Activities in the United States. Hearings Before a Special Committee on Un-American Activities, House of Representatives. 75th Congress, 3rd Session, Acting Under House Resolution #282. Washington, D.C.: U.S. Government Printing Office, 1938.

Jasen, David Alan. *P. G. Wodehouse: A Portrait of a Master.* London: Garnstone Press, 1975.

Kacewicz, George V. *Great Britain, the Soviet Union, and the Polish Government in Exile (1939–1945).* The Hague: Martinus Nijhoff, 1979.

Kamenetsky, Ihor. *Secret Nazi Plans for Eastern Europe: A Study of Lebensraum Policies.* New York: Bookman Associates, 1961.

Killinger, Manfred von. *Das Waren Kerle.* Berlin: Wilhelm Limpert Verlag, 1937.

Kin, David George. *The Plot Against America: Senator Wheeler and the Forces Behind Him.* Missoula, Mont.: John E. Kennedy, 1946.

Kersten, Felix. *The Kersten Memoirs, 1940–1945,* trans. Constantine Fitzgibbon and James Oliver. London: Hitchinson, 1956.

Koeves, Tibor. *Satan in Top Hat: The Biography of Franz von Papen.* New York: Alliance Book Corporation, 1941.

Koskoff, David E. *Joseph P. Kennedy: A Life and Times.* Englewood Cliffs, N.J.: Prentice-Hall, 1974.

Langer, William L. *Our Vichy Gamble.* Hamden, Conn.: Archon Books, 1965.

Leverkühn, Paul. *German Military Intelligence,* trans. R. H. Stevens and Constantine Fitzgibbon. London: Weidenfeld & Nicholson, 1954.

Manhattan, Avro. *The Vatican in World Politics.* New York: Horizon Press, 1940.

Martin, David. *Ally Betrayed: The Uncensored Story of Tito and Mihailovich.* New York: Prentice-Hall, 1946.

———. *Patriot or Traitor: The Case of General Mihailovich. Proceedings and Report of the Commission of Inquiry of the Committee for a Fair Trial for Draja Mihailovich.* Stanford, Calif.: Hoover Institution Press, 1978.

Martin, Malachi. *Three Popes and the Cardinal.* New York: Farrar, Straus & Giroux, 1972.

Mayer, Arno. J. *Political Origins of the New Diplomacy 1917–1918*. New York: Howard Fertig, 1969.

Meynell, Francis. *My Lives*. London: The Bodley Head, 1971.

Mihailović, Draža. *General Mihailovich: The World's Verdict*. Eastgate, Gloucester, England: John Bellows, 1946.

Morgan, Ted. *Maugham*. New York: Simon & Schuster, 1980.

Murray, Robert K. *Red Scare: A Study in National Hysteria*. Minneapolis: University of Minnesota Press, 1955.

Norman, Charles. *Ezra Pound*. New York: The MacMillan Company, 1960.

Paine, Lauran. *Britain's Intelligence Service*. London: Robert Hale, 1979.

Papen, Franz von. *Memoirs*, trans. Brian Connell. London: André Deutsch, 1952.

Paris, Edmond. *The Vatican Against Europe*, trans. A. Robson. London and Geneva: P.R.M. Publishers, 1961.

A Partial Collection of Press Clippings Compiled by the National Committee of American Airmen to Aid General Draza Mihailovich and the Serbian People. Chicago, 1946.

Payne, Robert. *The Marshall Story. A Biography of General George C. Marshall*. New York: Prentice-Hall, 1951.

Pincher, Chapman. *Their Trade Is Treachery*. New York: Bantam, 1982.

Ransom, Harry Howe. *The Intelligence Establishment*. Cambridge, Mass.: Harvard University Press, 1970.

Reeves, Thomas C. *The Life and Times of Joe McCarthy: A Biography*. New York: Stein & Day, 1982.

Roberts, Walter R. *Tito, Mihailovic and the Allies, 1941–1945*. New Brunswick, N.J.: Rutgers University Press, 1973.

Rogge, O. John. *The Official German Report*, 3 vols. New York: Thomas Yoseloff, 1951.

Root, Waverley. *The Secret History of the War*. New York: Charles Scribner's Sons, 1945.

Rovere, Richard H. *Senator Joe McCarthy*. New York: Harcourt, Brace & World, 1959.

Rudel, Hans Ulrich. *Stuka Pilot*. Maidstone, Kent, England: George Mann, 1973.

Searls, Henry. *The Lost Prince, Young Joe, the Forgotten Kennedy: The Story of the Oldest Brother*. New York: The World Publishing Company, 1969.

Sillitoe, Percy. *Cloak Without Dagger*. New York: Abelard-Schuman, 1955.

Stenehjem, Michele Flynn. *An American First: John T. Flynn and the America First Committee*. New Rochelle, N.Y.: Arlington House, 1976.

Stephen, John J. *The Russian Fascists: Tragedy and Farce in Exile 1925–1945*. New York: Harper & Row, 1978.

Stock, Noel. *The Life of Ezra Pound*. London: Routledge & Kegan Paul, 1970.

Strong, Kenneth. *Intelligence at the Top: The Recollections of an Intelligence Officer*. Garden City, N.Y.: Doubleday, 1969.

Study and Investigation of the Federal Communications Commission: Hearings Before the Select Committee to Investigate the Federal Communications Commission, House of Representatives, 78th Congress, 1st Session, Acting Under House Resolution #21. Washington, D.C.: U.S. Government Printing Office, 1943.

Study of International Communications: Hearings Before a Subcommittee of the Committee on Interstate Commerce, United States Senate, 79th Congress, 1st Session, pursuant to Senate Resolution #187. Washington, D.C.: U.S. Government Printing Office, 1945.

Swanberg, W. A. *Luce and His Empire*. New York: Charles Scribner's Sons, 1972.

Szoszkies, Henryk J. *No Traveler Returns: The Story of Hitler's Greatest Crime*. Garden City, N.Y.: Doubleday, Doran & Company, 1945.

Tauber, Kurt P. *Beyond Eagle and Swastika: German Nationalism Since 1945*, 2 vols. Middletown, Conn.: Wesleyan University Press, 1967.

Thomas, Lately. *When Even Angels Weep: The Senator Joseph McCarthy Affair —a Story Without a Hero*. New York: William Morrow, 1973.

Tomasevich, Jozo. *The Chetniks: War and Revolution in Yugoslavia, 1941–1945*. Stanford, Calif.: Stanford University Press, 1975.

Tompkins, Peter. *The Murder of Admiral Darlan: A Study in Conspiracy*. New York: Simon & Schuster, 1965.

Trefousse, H. L. *German and American Neutrality 1939–1941*. New York: Bookman Associates, 1951.

The Trial of Dragoljub-Draža Mihailović: Stenographic Record and Documents from the Trial of Dragoljub-Draža Mihailović. Belgrade: Union of the Journalists Associations of the Federative People's Republic of Yugoslavia, 1946.

Trivanovitch, Vaso. *The Case of Drazha Mihailovich: Highlights of the Evidence Against the Chetnik Leader*. New York: United Committee of South-Slavic Americans, n.d.

Waldrop, Frank C. *McCormick of Chicago: An Unconventional Portrait of a Controversial Figure.* Englewood Cliffs, N.J.: Prentice-Hall, 1966.

Wedemeyer, Albert Coady. *Wedemeyer Reports!* New York: Henry Holt, 1958.

Wendt, Lloyd. *Chicago Tribune: The Rise of a Great American Newspaper.* New York: Rand McNally, 1979.

Whalen, Richard. *The Founding Father: The Story of Joseph P. Kennedy.* New York: The New American Library, 1964.

Wheeler, Burton K., and Paul F. Healy. *Yankee from the West: The Candid Turbulent Life Story of the Yankee-born U.S. Senator from Montana.* New York: Doubleday, 1962.

Wheeler, Mark C. *Britain and the War for Yugoslavia 1940–1943.* New York: Columbia University Press, 1980.

White, Leigh. *The Long Balkan Night.* New York: Charles Scribner's Sons, 1944.

Winterbotham, F. W. *Secret and Personal.* London: William Kimber, 1983.

Yergin, Daniel. *Shattered Peace: The Origins of the Cold War and the National Security State.* Boston: Houghton Mifflin, 1977.

Author's Note

The bulk of the documentary sources in this book have been obtained
from the Diplomatic Records Branch of the National Archives and
Records Service, in Washington D.C.; the FBI; and the Department of
the Army, Intelligence and Security Command, at Fort Meade, Maryland.
Some twenty-eight thousand pages of documents are on file in the author's collection at the University of Southern California's Doheny Library Special Collections Division and may be consulted by arrangement.
To list all documents would be tedious for the general reader, to whom
this book is addressed. Scholars are urged to examine the documents; a
guide to sources is given below.

1. Origins: The Bund

The material on Hans Thomsen is gleaned from *Documents on German Foreign
Policy 1918–1945* (U.S. Government Printing Office, 1967) and from the interrogation of Thomsen prepared by Dr. Robert M. W. Kempner on April 25, 1947,
available in the Charles Higham collection at the University of Southern California. Henceforth this collection will be referred to as CHUSC.

The material on the Bund is drawn from the files of the New York *Times* and
the Washington *Post*. Those who wish to consult the matter further can find the
exhaustive Bund files in the keeping of George Wagner, at the National Archives
and Records Service, in Washington, D.C. (Modern Military Branch).

2. The Nazis and America First

The main source here is the report prepared by J. Edgar Hoover and Percy Foxworth dated February 13, 1942, and sent to President Franklin D. Roosevelt for his special attention. The document is available from Mr. Robert Parks, at the Roosevelt Memorial Library, at Hyde Park, New York. Further documents are available from the U.S. Army Security and Intelligence Command, Fort Meade, Maryland.

3. The White Book

The White Books I, II, and III are available at most major public libraries. For congressional debates on the matter, the *Congressional Record* for the appropriate dates should be consulted.

4. The Kennedy Connection

The exhaustive file on Tyler Kent, including his trial in London, surrounding evidence, and subsequent attempts to free him, may be found at the Library of the University of Yale. The Roosevelt-Churchill correspondence is available from the Public Record Office in London. A useful summary is to be found in the London *Times* for December 4, 1982, page six, features section. Nigel West, in the same publication for December 10, 1983, page four, explores Kent's alleged Soviet connections. (CHUSC).

The details of the Wohlthat-Mooney meetings are in the James D. Mooney collection at the University of Georgetown, D.C., Special Collections Division, and at CHUSC.

5. and 6. The Capitol Hill Conspiracy and Close-up on Sedition

The best source here is the unhappily forgotten book *The Official German Report,* by O. John Rogge. The New York *Times* covered the matter carefully; the *Documents on German Foreign Policy 1918–1945* are a further source. Those who wish to explore further are referred to the seized Abwehr files, care of George Wagner at the National Archive, in particular the files on Senator Burton K. Wheeler.

7. The Father of the Little Flower

The files on Father Charles E. Coughlin at the Diplomatic Records Room of the National Archives and Records Service are useful; full card indexes are supplied. Alfred E. Kahn's *The Hour* and George Seldes's *In Fact,* both available from the Greenwood Press, Connecticut, by special order in volume form, are prime sources, along with the FBI main files.

8. The Plot to Kill the President

The New York *Times* covered most carefully the Christian Front activities, but more detailed documentation is to be found in the Diplomatic Records Branch of the National Archives and Records Service, Room Six E (catalogued). The trial transcripts themselves have been destroyed. However, the *Times* covered the hearings fully day to day.

9. The Attempt to Kill the King and Queen of England

CHUSC has a complete set of documents on Sean Russell. The scholar is referred to the Scotland Yard letters in that collection, obtained for the author by Professor Carolle F. Carter, of San Jose State University, California. The declassified FBI file on Russell has been a major source.

10. The White Russian Nazis

Albert E. Kahn's collected *The Hour* (1940–41) (Greenwood Press) is a good source. For those who wish to explore the subject further, the FBI files on Pelypenko and Vonsiatsky, and those in the Diplomatic Records Branch, are accessible; also see *In Fact* for February 11, 1946, for the documentary evidence of Coughlin's actual payment by the German authorities. John J. Stephan's *The Russian Fascists: Tragedy and Farce in Exile, 1925–1945* (New York: Harper & Row, 1978) provides a different account.

11. The Theft of Rainbow Five

A letter (undated) from Brigadier General Carter W. Clarke (retired) to the author is a useful source (CHUSC). General Wedemeyer's *Wedemeyer Reports* gives a full account. A letter to the President from Henry L. Stimson (March 2, 1942) effectively clears Wedemeyer's name (CHUSC). Exhaustive files may be consulted at the National Archives, care of Marcus Cunliffe. The documents on General Newton Cavalcanti are at the Diplomatic Records Branch.

12. The Pearl Harbor Plans

The three main sources here are *Report of the Joint Fact Finding Committee of the Committee on Un-American Activities in California*, Volume 2 (1945), the Seventy-eighth Congress: House of Representatives Investigations of the National War Effort, Report No. 1638, June 14, 1944, and *Proceedings Before the Army Pearl Harbor Board*, Volume 28 of the Joint Committee hearings, September 4, 1944. The Library of Congress has a complete set.

13. The Windsor Plot

Documents on German Foreign Policy 1918–1945 is the best source. The Hoover memoranda to Roosevelt at Hyde Park (Robert Parks, archivist) comment accurately on the picture.

14. The Sphinx of Sweden

The FBI main file on Axel Wenner-Gren, much of which exists at the Diplomatic Records Branch and in CHUSC, is very detailed. The Oakes murder was covered by the New York *Times*, and a transcript of the trial may be found at the Nassau Court House, Bahamas.

15. The Man Who Used Cary Grant

The source here is the very large file on Count Vejarano y Cassina in the Diplomatic Records Branch, supplemented by the FBI main file. No biography of Cary Grant refers to this incident.

16. The Schellenberg Conspiracy

The massive Schellenberg documents are in the author's possession, including the British Intelligence reports. The documents on Ernst Kaltenbrunner are also in CHUSC and are useful as a supplement.

17. Into the Cold War

The New York *Times* and the Washington *Post* fully covered these developments.

18. The Romanian Connection: Richard Nixon's Partner

The Malaxa documents are available at the Diplomatic Records Branch of the National Archives and CHUSC. The *Documents on German Foreign Policy 1918–1945* fill in the picture.

19. The Romanian Connection: The Bishop of Hell

The Trifa documents are available from Dr. Charles Kremer who can be written to in care of the author and CHUSC. The *Documents on German Foreign Policy 1918–1945* fill in the picture.

20. The Romanian Connection: The Baron of Silicon Valley

A main source is the U.S. District Court for the Northern District of California: Trans-International Computer Investment Corporation, Debtor. Deposition of

Otto A. von Bolschwing. December 28, 1971. Surrounding subpoenaed documents give a history of his case. The *Documents on German Foreign Policy 1918–1945* fill in the picture.

21. The Skorzeny Plot

The massive file on Otto Skorzeny in the Army Intelligence and Security Command files at Fort Meade, Maryland, is the main source (CHUSC). Glenn B. Infield's *Skorzeny: Hitler's Commando* (New York: St. Martin's Press, 1981) is reliable.

22. A Nazi in the Pentagon

The documents of the Army Intelligence and Security Command, at Fort Meade, Maryland, are especially useful. For a more accessible study, Heinz Höhne and Hermann Zolling's *The General Was a Spy* is recommended. On Heusinger, Charles R. Allen, Jr.'s, *Heusinger of the Fourth Reich* is a good source.

23. Postwar Activism

The New York *Times* is a main source; exhaustive files on postwar activism are available at the Southern California Library in Los Angeles, a collection of special materials on aspects of nazism in the United States.

24. The Sixties Führer

Rockwell's story was amply covered by publications including *Esquire*, the New York *Times*, and the Washington *Post*. The FBI has a substantial file on the subject.

25. The Road to Barbie

A good source here is the file of the Anti-Defamation League of B'Nai B'Rith in New York. The New York *Times*, especially in articles by Ralph Blumenthal, made an admirable survey.

26. Barbie

The Barbie case is fully covered in files obtainable from the Department of the Army, Fort George G. Meade, Maryland (CHUSC). The Ryan Report is to be read with caution.

Index